Macroeconomic Essentials

Third Edition

Peter E. Kennedy

Macroeconomic Essentials
Understanding Economics in the News

Third Edition

The MIT Press
Cambridge, Massachusetts
London, England

For information about special quantity discounts, please email special_sales@mitpress.mit.edu

This book was set in Times by Toppan Best-set Premedia Limited.
Printed and bound in the United States of America.

Library of Congress Cataloging-in-Publication Data

Kennedy, Peter, 1943–
    Macroeconomic essentials : understanding economics in the news / Peter Kennedy.—3rd ed.
        p.   cm.
    Includes index.
    ISBN 978-0-262-01467-0 (hbk. : alk. paper)—ISBN 978-0-262-51480-4 (pbk. : alk. paper)
1. Macroeconomics. 2. Economic policy. I. Title.
    HB172.5.K457 2010
    339–dc22
                                                                            2009050748

10 9 8 7 6 5 4 3 2 1

Dedicated, with love, to N.C.

Contents

Preface

This book was written to provide instructors with an introductory text suitable for teaching students practical macroeconomics useful for interpreting macroeconomic commentary found in the business sections of newspapers. The earlier editions' success indicates that many instructors are unhappy with the encyclopedic approach of the traditional texts, with their emphasis on technical matters and lack of attention to real-world applications. Some instructors used earlier editions as a text for a regular principles-of-macroeconomics class, some used it for an applied course following a traditional macro-principles class, some used it as a supplementary text for a traditional macro-principles course, and some used it as a text for an MBA macroeconomics course. All used it to produce students capable of interpreting media commentary on the macroeconomy.

Still students find this book much more challenging than traditional macroeconomics textbooks. Although the body of the text is easy to read, answering the end-of-chapter questions requires a thorough understanding of related macroeconomic concepts, good problem-solving skills, and an ability to connect to the real world. In contrast, traditional texts typically have end-of-chapter questions that do not connect to the real world; they ask students to fish through the text to find an answer, or work through technical exercises involving shifting curves on diagrams. In my experience the top half of a typical principles class loves the way this book connects to the real world and challenges their thinking skills, but the bottom half of the class is very unhappy because their usual strategy of memorizing things at the last minute does not work.

This third edition maintains the three distinguishing features of the earlier editions: it is concise, nontechnical, and applied. It should continue to appeal to instructors and students swamped by the encyclopedic approach of traditional principles texts, to instructors teaching mainly business students interested in relevance, and to instructors teaching a policy- or applications-oriented macroeconomics course.

Why and how is this book concise? Educational psychologists have been telling instructors for years that it is better to teach students a small amount of important material well than to cover a large amount of material less thoroughly. Accordingly, this book concentrates on the important concepts of macroeconomics, forgoing pages of supplementary material that is interesting and useful but not essential. This book summarizes the essentials that students need to know, as well as providing numerous examples of applications.

Why and how is this book nontechnical? What do we want our students to be able to do upon completing their macroeconomics course, manipulate a 45-degree line diagram and derive the multiplier, or interpret and evaluate media commentary on the macroeconomy? I am not alone in believing that for many students the latter is preferable, and that in terms of meeting this latter goal there is a high opportunity cost associated with pressing students to learn algebraic and graphical derivations. Only graphs with exceptional pedagogical value, such as the aggregate-supply/aggregate-demand diagram and its alter ego, the Phillips curve, are employed in this book. This less-technical approach does not mean a loss of rigor, however. A different kind of rigor appears, involving critical thinking skills that most students find very challenging.

Why and how is this book applied? Although those seeking a degree in economics need to become conversant with the technical skills and theoretical nuances of professional economists, it is not necessary that these dominate introductory courses where many students are not committed economics majors and the opportunity cost is high. This is even more the case for business-oriented students. The application orientation of this text is accomplished by providing hundreds (over 700!) of two- or three-sentence news clips, all but a few based on actual news reports, as illustrations or student exercises. Much can be learned from working through these clippings—institutional facts, policy nuances, common misunderstandings, perspective on magnitudes, alternative viewpoints, and political realities, as well as how theoretical concepts are applied.

Chapter 1 describes what readers will find in this text, but several features should be emphasized.

1. Do not be fooled by the "nontechnical" flavor of the book. The material is intellectually demanding and is presented at a high conceptual level necessary for successful interpretation and evaluation of media commentary. Some challenging topics, such as real versus nominal interest rates and international phenomena, are given much more emphasis than in traditional texts because they play such a prominent role in media interpretation.

2. Some of the most common technical material has made its way into the text via optional end-of-chapter appendixes. Appendixes 5.3 and 6.1 explain the 45-degree line diagram and the graphical derivation of the *AD* curve, for example.

3. To smooth exposition, in each chapter I have set some material aside in boxed areas called curiosities. These are short expositions of important related topics. They should be considered integral parts of the chapter.

4. Each chapter ends with examples of news clippings and answers to related questions, followed by several exercises based on news clips. Many chapters also have a set of

numerical exercises asking students to test their understanding of concepts by calculating their implications in terms of numerical examples. To aid independent study, answers to all even-numbered questions are provided in appendix B. Available at my website (www.sfu.ca/~kennedy) is a set of additional media questions (with answers to even-numbered questions), extended from time to time to cover recent issues in the news.

5. Some end-of-chapter questions are easy, but many can be quite difficult, primarily because news clips seldom announce the macroeconomic concept relevant to their interpretation and journalists never spell things out as completely as do textbooks. When students complain about this I respond by saying "Welcome to the real world!" In this edition I have separated out the more challenging end-of-chapter questions to make it easier for instructors to tailor the book to their students. And as in earlier editions, I have given even numbers to questions that are such that having answers available (in appendix B) is pedagogically the right thing to do.

There are several major changes in the third edition.

- The exposition of microeconomic supply and demand has been moved from an appendix at the end of the book to a new chapter 2. Also in chapter 2 is an overview of the structure of macroeconomic modeling, referred to as a "big picture."

- The chapters on crowding out and on budget deficits and the national debt have been removed (reviewers claimed they were not being used). Their content, slimmed down, has been moved to chapter 5 on the role of aggregate demand—the Keynesian model.

- The contents of the chapter on the real cause of inflation have been consolidated and moved into an appendix to chapter 12 on stagflation.

- In the chapter introducing interest rates, chapter 10, the explanation of the interest rate associated with long-term bonds has been rewritten, exploiting an easy-to-understand approximation that in earlier editions appeared in an appendix.

- The essence of the subprime mortgage crisis is presented in section 5.4.

- The end-of-chapter questions have been divided into two groups, to identify those questions students are likely to find more challenging.

- At the end of each section within a chapter a sample exam question appears; answers to these questions are provided in appendix A. Students using this book need to re-orient their study skills from memorization to understanding. Working through sample questions is a crucial ingredient in this reorientation.

- Some of the earlier edition's "curiosities" have disappeared, and some new curiosities have been added, most notably 3.1: Do We Really Keep Track of Every Dollar of Spending Every Year?, 5.7: How Big Is the Deficit?, 7.2: Why Does the Standard of Living Vary So Much across Countries?, 10.2: Why Are Bond Prices Never Equal to

Their Face Values?, 10.3 What Is Quantitative Easing?, and 11.3: What Is the Taylor Rule?

Innumerable minor changes have been made to improve exposition, and news clips questions have been added to refer to recent events. As with the earlier editions, however, there is no pretense that the news clips are capable of covering current events—by the time this book is published, it will be out of date in this respect. But the macroeconomic concepts that the news clips in this book illustrate remain of import to students regardless of the vintage of the associated news reports; understanding these concepts, as opposed to being up on current events, remains the goal of the book.

Those adopting the book for classroom use can request from the publisher an Instructor's Manual providing answers to odd-numbered questions and suggestions for lecturing. Available to all at www.sfu.ca/~kennedy is a bank of multiple-choice questions (with answers) tailored to the unique character of the text. My students tell me that the single most important thing to do to achieve success with this book is to stay up-to-date with the bank of multiple-choice questions. Answers are provided, so it gives feedback on how well the course material is understood, and which topics are in need of review. Most of the multiple-choice questions are based on news clips, so they provide hints on how to answer the end-of-chapter news clips questions. And they are good preparation for any multiple-choice dimension of an exam.

My thanks to the anonymous reviewers whose suggestions played a big part in this revision. I did not always take their advice, however, so responsibility for any shortcomings lies entirely with me.

1 Introduction

There are three kinds of economics: curve-shifting, pop-art, and media. Formal theorizing favored by academic economists usually involves shifting curves on diagrams, so is called *curve-shifting economics*. Its technical character makes it suitable mainly to those seeking a university degree in economics. *Pop-art economics* is found in economics best-sellers. Although fun, it is too often harebrained. *Media economics* is the economics encountered on the business pages of newspapers and on television. This is what business people and interested laypersons need to know about economics and what undergraduate students should be learning about economics in addition to curve-shifting. It is the kind of economics a reader will learn from this book.

These types of economics each have two variants: microeconomics and macroeconomics. The former analyzes the behavior of individual firms and consumers, with attention focused on issues such as how consumers make choices, how firms determine prices, and the implications of government-imposed sales taxes or quotas. The latter, the subject of this book, looks at the big picture, analyzing economywide variables such as inflation, unemployment, interest rates, and exchange rates. Attention focuses on issues such as what determines business cycles, how interest rates are set, and the implications of the government's printing more money or fixing the exchange rate.

The purpose of this chapter is to introduce the reader to media economics and provide a summary of the major macroeconomic concepts expounded in this book.

Upon completion of this chapter you should

- know what kind of economics you will learn from reading this book and
- have an overview of the important macroeconomic ideas it contains.

1.1   Media Economics

Textbooks written for economics majors present economics using the language and perspective of professional economists. Students learn to analyze economic phenomena through economic models, formalized with graphs and, at advanced levels, algebra and calculus. Much time is devoted to learning how to manipulate various graphical or algebraic models that have come to serve as an intellectual framework for economists.

In one respect it is entirely appropriate that these textbooks have this flavor because it reflects accurately what academic economists do: they build, manipulate, and estimate economic models to aid in explanation, prediction, and policy formulation. Possession of a degree in economics means one is familiar with the terminology of these models and the technical means by which they are manipulated. At the undergraduate textbook level, the technical dimension is predominantly in the form of graphical analysis, so this type of economics is accordingly referred to as *curve-shifting economics*. At advanced levels, the technical dimension is dominated by algebraic formulas in which Greek letters play prominent roles. Hence this type of economics is sometimes called *Greek-letter economics*, a term introduced by Nobel laureate Paul Krugman in the preface of his book, *The Age of Diminished Expectations*.

At the other end of the spectrum from curve-shifting economics is the entirely nontechnical *pop-art economics* found in books sold to the general public, some of which actually become best-sellers. Krugman calls this *airport economics* because these books are most prominently displayed at airport bookstores where business travelers are likely to buy them. They usually have some ax to grind. Most tell tales of imminent disaster, and a few advocate specific panaceas. In general, these books do not teach their readers much about economics and, in any event, are not designed as textbooks.

In between these two extremes is the economics that appears in the media, most notably on the business pages of newspapers. This is *media economics*, which has two varieties: (1) what Krugman calls *up-and-down economics*—news reports preoccupied with latest ups or downs of economic numbers—and (2) *economic policy evaluation*—news commentary directed at explaining, praising, or condemning government macroeconomic policies. The main purpose of this book is to teach macroeconomic principles and how they can be used to interpret these two varieties of media economics.

1.2 Up-and-Down Economics

The following examples illustrate ways in which up-and-down economics appears in the media:

According to the latest statistics, housing starts are up, indicating unexpected strength in the economy. Bond prices fell on the news.

In his eyes the battle is between the rate-lowering effect of the U.S. recession and the high rate of inflation. That sums up the problem now facing the interest rate forecasters.

News that U.S. job creation in January was more robust than anticipated sent a signal to currency markets to expect a stepped-up fight against inflation, unleashing a bout of buying fervor for the U.S. dollar.

These examples are typical of commentary on business pages in the newspaper because they are relevant to money-making activity on bond or foreign exchange markets, or because they deal with variables such as interest rates that business people or mortgage renewers would be keen to forecast. Despite its practical value, however, most economists find up-and-down economics "stupefyingly boring" (to use Krugman's term) and are upset that most people think that up-and-down economics is what economists do.

Why do economists disclaim up-and-down economics? A major reason is that it is too simpleminded. The predictions of up-and-down economics result from applying macroeconomic principles in conjunction with simplifying assumptions that are not quite true. This practice allows quick and easy calculation of predictions that may be good first approximations, particularly for those forced to take immediate action. However, the process lacks the intellectual rigor so prized by academic economists. There is no recognition of how economic forces from a variety of sources interact to influence the variable in question, economic "laws" of questionable empirical validity are employed with unjustified confidence, long-run guides to economic behavior are used to predict results in the short run, and nuances of modern macroeconomic theorizing are ignored.

Despite this condemnation by academic economists, a major goal of this book is to teach readers up-and-down economics. There are several reasons for doing so.

1. Of most importance, by learning how to interpret news clips such as the preceding, students will genuinely learn, understand, and remember fundamental macroeconomic principles.

2. Although boring to academic economists, up-and-down economics is useful to those involved or just interested in the business world. For example, knowing that a rise in inflation will increase interest rates and thereby cause bond prices to fall can help one avoid capital losses on bond holdings. Because so many students studying economics these days are business students, such knowledge is of particular value.

3. By focusing on applications as they appear in the media, students will as a natural by-product learn much about the institutional structure of our economy.

4. It is necessary to understand up-and-down economics to be able to evaluate media commentary on policy issues, the second dimension of media economics.

1.3   Policy Evaluation

The second variety of media economics is economic policy evaluation. The following examples illustrate ways in which it appears in the media:

What cannot be done, various reformers in the U.S. notwithstanding, is to impose on any government the obligation to balance its budget annually. Consider the consequences. If it did work, it would introduce a major destabilizing element.

The monetarists will allow you to go ahead and ruin people and countries, but when eventually in good and common sense you say, "Enough is enough," the monetarists say, "Well, you spoiled the experiment."

This is the reason why the fixed exchange rate system was scrapped in 1971. The U.S. had been pursuing an inflationary monetary policy to help pay for the Vietnam war and new social programs, and its trading partners did not all want to participate in it.

In contrast to up-and-down economics, media commentary on economic policy is of considerable interest to academic economists, primarily because most feel strongly that policy analysis is one of the main reasons for studying macroeconomics. This book emphasizes this dimension of media economics by providing literally hundreds of short two- or three-sentence news clips such as the preceding, and by asking readers for interpretation and evaluation.

Students are not asked, however, to interpret or evaluate these news clips using the technical curve-shifting art of the professional economist. With one significant exception, our presentation of media economics avoids using graphs.

1.4   A Picture Can Be Worth a Thousand Words

The curve-shifting approach does have one advantage that we would be foolish to throw away: sometimes a graph can greatly facilitate exposition and understanding. The aggregate-supply/aggregate-demand diagram and its alter ego, the Phillips curve, are so valuable in this respect that they are shamelessly exploited. All other diagrams—most notably the supply/demand diagrams for money, labor, and the exchange rate—are bypassed. For those unfamiliar with supply and demand curves used in microeconomics, chapter 2 contains a brief exposition. Also in chapter 2, of value to everyone, is a "big picture" of the macroeconomy, providing a useful perspective on how macroeconomic thinking is structured.

In this big picture the macroeconomy is divided into four sectors—the goods and services sector, the labor sector, the monetary sector, and the international sector. Each of these sectors has supply and demand activity that creates forces for change. Macroeconomic analysis consists of exploiting these forces to create explanations for how variables such as unemployment, interest rates, and exchange rates are determined. The great value of the aggregate-supply/aggregate-demand diagram is that it captures this big picture in a simple fashion, facilitating understanding of macroeconomic activity.

This book is very short; attention is focused on the "really important" ideas of macroeconomics, with much of the encyclopedic and technical detail of traditional texts ignored. This approach should ensure that these really important ideas are properly learned and remembered. What are these really important ideas?

1.5 Really Important Macroeconomic Ideas

Listing the really important macroeconomic ideas is a challenging task because so many macroeconomic ideas are important that any one person's selection of a few as "really important" is bound to be controversial. The first step in creating such a list is to address the question "Really important for what?" The following list stems from the answer "Really important for understanding media commentary on the macroeconomy." It includes ideas important to those interested in how macroeconomics is relevant, ideas students should be sure to understand and take with them when they complete their course.

The list is included here to provide an overview of what can be expected throughout the rest of the book, though the reader may be unfamiliar with some of the terminology employed; a second reading, after completing the book, is advised. For convenience, one major idea has been drawn from each of the remaining chapters.

Chapter 2: Everything Depends on Everything Else.   When something changes in the macroeconomy, it affects everything else. If the interest rate increases, for example, it affects our exchange rate which affects our exports which affects our unemployment rate which affects the interest rate. Sorting all this out creates a major headache for students.

Chapter 3: Gross Deceptive Product.   Gross domestic product (GDP), the figurehead of our national economic accounts and the measure of our total annual output of goods and services, has many defects as a measure of our economic well-being or as a means of comparing standards of living across countries.

Chapter 4: Discouraged/Encouraged Workers.   Unemployed people who become discouraged by their unsuccessful search for work, and therefore stop searching, are suddenly no longer counted as unemployed. When the economy picks up, they can become encouraged and begin looking for work again, thus becoming counted as unemployed. This discouraged/encouraged worker phenomenon helps explain paradoxical movements in the measured rate of unemployment and is an example of the more general problem of difficulties in measuring economic variables.

Chapter 5: The Multiplier.   An increase in government spending can ultimately cause a greater increase in national income. This multiplied impact of fiscal policy is one basis for the Keynesian view that the government can and should intervene in the operation of the economy to maintain full employment, even if it implies creating a budget deficit.

Chapter 6: The Natural Rate of Unemployment.   The institutional structure of an economy gives rise to a "natural" rate of unemployment toward which the economy gravitates, consistent with a steady rate of inflation. Unfortunately, the natural rate is neither known nor constant over time. In the mid-1990s it was thought to be about 6 percent, but because in the late 1990s inflation did not appear as the unemployment rate fell, most economists have revised this figure to below 5 percent. An important implication is that efforts to lower unemployment below this natural rate can succeed only in the short run and only by accelerating inflation.

Chapter 7: Productivity.   In the long run, increases in our economic standard of living depend primarily on productivity increases. To achieve higher growth in productivity, we must increase national saving: present generations must sacrifice current consumption to improve productivity for future generations. Productivity increases often come about through "creative destruction," a process by which existing jobs are destroyed through the creation of new jobs embodying technological advances.

Chapter 8: Printing Money.   The U.S. central bank, the Federal Reserve (the Fed), "prints" money by buying bonds, enabling commercial banks to increase their loans and thereby expand the nation's money supply. Irregular relationships between economic activity and measures of the money supply create problems for monetary policy.

Chapter 9: Inflation and Money-Supply Growth.   In the long run, an economy's inflation is equal to the difference between the rate of growth of its money supply and its rate of growth of output. This statement reflects the monetarist belief that in the long run, inflation is always and everywhere a monetary phenomenon, which leads to their prescription that the Fed should be replaced by a robot programmed to increase the money supply at a low, steady rate, the genesis of the prominent "rules-versus-discretion" policy debate.

Chapter 10: Interest Rates and Bond Prices.   A genuine economic "law" is that there is an inverse relationship between the interest rate and the price of bonds. One implication of this law is that if the interest rate is forecast to rise, those holding bonds will try to sell them to avoid suffering a capital loss.

Chapter 11: Real-versus-Nominal Interest Rates.   The interest rate affecting aggregate demand is the real interest rate. The observed interest rate—the nominal interest rate—differs from the real interest rate in that it has a premium for expected inflation built into it. For practical purposes, the main determinant of change in the nominal interest rate is change in the expected rate of inflation. This difference between real and nominal interest rates helps explain many seeming anomalies, such as an increase in the money supply causing a rise rather than a fall in the interest rate.

Chapter 12: Inflation Asymmetry.   Inflation accelerates quickly, with only a small temporary reduction in unemployment below its natural rate, but lowering inflation requires an extended period of high unemployment, primarily because it takes so long for expectations of inflation to fall. It is this asymmetry that causes governments to fight inflation so tenaciously.

Chapter 13: Trade Deficit.   A continuing trade deficit is due not to a lack of competitiveness but rather to a sustained capital inflow, possibly caused by a high real interest rate created by a large government budget deficit.

Chapter 14: Monetary Policy Lost under Fixed Exchange Rates.   When a small economy fixes its exchange rate with a large economy, monetary policy must maintain the exchange rate and so cannot be used for other goals, such as controlling inflation. The small country must experience whatever monetary policy and inflation characterize the large country.

Chapter 15: Purchasing Power Parity.   Although changes in our real exchange rate occur because of phenomena such as natural resource discoveries, in the long run movements in our nominal exchange rate primarily reflect differences between our inflation rate and the inflation rates of our major trading partners. One implication is that a country with higher inflation than its trading partners should experience a steady depreciation of its nominal exchange rate.

Chapter 16: Interest Rate Parity.   Save for a risk premium, real interest rates tend to be approximately equal throughout the world, but nominal interest rates are not. The latter differ according to inflation rate differences or, equivalently, to expected exchange rate movements. One implication is that a country with an inflation rate markedly higher than its trading partners should be experiencing a higher nominal interest rate and a continual fall in its exchange rate.

Several of these and other macroeconomic principles give rise to formal equations that can be used as rules of thumb for predicting long-run macroeconomic behavior. Along with the aggregate-demand/aggregate-supply and Phillips-curve diagrams, as well as some definitions that can be written in equation form, these principles form the technical dimension of this book, providing sufficient background for students to move on to more advanced courses in macroeconomics.

Readers must be warned, however, that the nontechnical character of this book does not imply that its contents will be easy to learn or use, for the following reasons:

1. The media illustrations and questions based on them are challenging; they require problem-solving skills and demand that the student thoroughly understand the economic principles. Only rarely can questions be answered simply by looking up material in the book. Students who rely on memorization for academic success will not be happy in a course based on this text.

2. Many of the concepts on which this book concentrates are more advanced than those emphasized by traditional texts, reflecting the focus on media interpretation. For example, most traditional texts do little more than define the difference between real and nominal interest rates, but because this difference plays such a crucial role in interpreting media commentary related to interest rates, it is a key concept here.

3. Unfamiliar terminology pops up frequently. All readers can seek help in the glossary at the end of the book, and those for whom this book is a supplement to a traditional text can turn to it for help. Often, however, readers must employ "street smarts" to make sense of a journalist's metaphor or use of unfamiliar terminology. To aid student efforts to develop their street smarts, answers to all even-numbered questions appear in appendix B at the end of the book.

4. The concise nature of this book means that its pace is fast. New concepts arrive more quickly than in traditional texts, and easy concepts are given little elaboration. Readers accustomed to longer expositions may wish on occasion to refer to a traditional text for more detail.

Chapter Summary

■ Media economics consists of *up-and-down economics*, focusing on understanding what causes economic numbers such as interest rates, unemployment, or inflation to go up or down, and *economic policy evaluation*, focusing on adjudicating the merit of government policy. This book expounds macroeconomic principles important for media economics: some economic concepts prominent in traditional texts are dealt with very briefly, and other concepts, some not emphasized in traditional texts, are highlighted.

■ The book's conciseness implies that it must focus on "really important macroeconomic ideas," where "really important" refers to their role in media interpretation. A list of several such ideas was presented as a preview of this book's contents.

■ Traditional textbooks emphasize curve-shifting, an approach to economic analysis in which curves are shifted on diagrams to illustrate economic results. With the exception of the aggregate-supply/aggregate-demand diagram and the related Phillips-curve diagram (unfamiliar terms can be found in the glossary), both of which are truly worth a thousand words, this book avoids such technical material. Despite the book's non-technical nature, it is nevertheless intellectually demanding.

2   The Basics of Supply and Demand, and a Big Picture

It has been claimed that even a parrot can become an economist. Teach a parrot to say "supply and demand," and it can answer any question on economics! Throughout this book analyses of the forces of supply and demand are used to produce explanations of economic phenomena, but for the most part are not formalized via graphical representations. The purpose of this chapter is to ensure that all readers are conversant with the forces of supply and demand, to show how they are illustrated diagrammatically, and to provide some perspective on how supply and demand forces create a framework for analyzing the macroeconomy.

To this end, we begin by explaining the three fundamentals of microeconomic supply and demand analysis via a supply/demand diagram: the concept of an equilibrium, the forces of supply and demand that push a market to an equilibrium position, and the difference between a movement along a supply or demand curve and a shift in such a curve.

Following this we provide a "big picture" of how macroeconomists think about the macroeconomy. This big picture consists of four informal supply/demand diagrams, one representing each of the four major macroeconomic submarkets. These submarkets interact to determine the character of the overall macroeconomy; this interaction is very complex, which is why students have such difficulty with macroeconomic analysis—everything depends on everything else! The intention of this big picture is to provide readers with some perspective on how the macroeconomy operates and on how macroeconomists analyze it, to facilitate understanding the material throughout the rest of the book. Finally, we explain how the complicated interactive activity in the four markets is simplified for analysis. Later in the book this simplification gives rise to a single diagram (the aggregate-supply/aggregate-demand diagram) that summarizes and thereby avoids much curve-shifting associated with these markets' interaction.

Upon completion of this chapter you should

- ▪ understand the basics of supply and demand,
- ▪ have an overview of the structure of the macroeconomy, and
- ▪ realize why its analysis is so difficult.

2.1   Supply and Demand Diagram

Supply/demand diagrams list a quantity of some good or service on the horizontal axis and its price on the vertical axis. As price varies, the demand curve traces out the quantity of the good or service people want to buy in a particular market, other things remaining the same (*ceteris paribus*). The supply curve traces out the quantity of the good or service that people/firms want to supply to this market as the price changes, ceteris paribus.

To introduce the concept of supply and demand, let us look at the market for beef. Figure 2.1 is a supply and demand diagram for this market. On the vertical axis the price

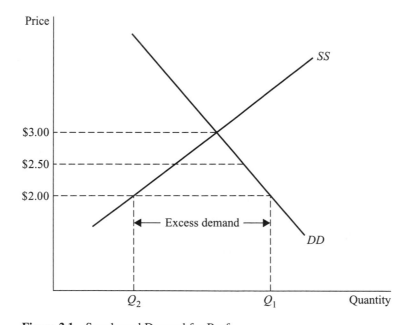

Figure 2.1   Supply and Demand for Beef
At price $2.00 there is an excess demand of $Q_1 - Q_2$; excess demand continues to push price up until equilibrium is attained at price $3.00.

of beef is measured, and on the horizontal axis quantity of beef is measured—either the quantity demanded, in the case of the demand curve, or the quantity supplied, in the case of the supply curve.

The demand curve *DD* in figure 2.1 portrays the amount of beef demanded for each price. With all other things remaining the same, especially the price of other meats, when the price of beef falls (as we move to a lower position on the vertical axis), people find it more attractive to buy beef instead of other goods, particularly other meats, so demand for beef increases. Therefore the demand curve for beef is downward-sloping.

The supply curve *SS* in this diagram portrays the quantity of beef that producers want to sell for each price. This quantity is determined by profit-maximizing on the part of beef producers. As the price rises, beef producers can cover the higher unit costs associated with increasing beef production and thus find it possible to make more profit by supplying more beef. In addition the higher price may entice new producers to enter this market. Therefore the supply curve for beef is upward-sloping.

2.2 Equilibrium

The intersection of supply and demand curves is of particular interest to economists. To see why, let us conduct the following thought experiment. If the price of beef in figure 2.1 is $2 per pound, a price below the intersection of the supply and demand curves, then the quantity of beef demanded, from the demand curve, would be Q_1, and the quantity of beef supplied, from the supply curve, would be a smaller quantity, Q_2. At the price $2, demand exceeds supply, represented by an *excess demand* of magnitude $Q_1 - Q_2$. At this price, beef producers will not be willing to satisfy the demand for beef. Two things will happen: (1) those unable to obtain beef will offer a higher price to beef producers to ensure that they, rather than someone else, get the available beef, and (2) beef producers will quickly deduce that profits can be increased by increasing price. Both of these phenomena reflect a fundamental law of supply and demand: *excess demand causes price to rise.*

If the price is increased to $2.50, as shown in figure 2.1, quantity demanded falls as we slide up the demand curve, and quantity supplied rises as we slide up the supply curve, shrinking the excess demand. Because excess demand remains, however, the price continues to rise. The excess demand pressure on price continues until the excess demand for beef disappears, which happens at a price of $3, given by the intersection of the supply and demand curves.

If we had begun our thought experiment at a price higher than $3, we would have found an *excess supply* of beef. Beef producers would not be able to sell all beef produced, and an unwanted beef inventory would accumulate. Recognizing this, customers might offer beef producers a lower price in the hope of getting a bargain. To get rid of the excess inventory, beef producers would accept such offers and might also initiate cuts in beef price. The consequence is that *excess supply causes price to fall.* This force lowering price continues so long as excess supply exists, so in this example price ultimately falls to $3.

The forces of supply and demand operate automatically to push the economy to the intersection of relevant supply and demand curves, a position in which there is no further pressure for change. Such a position is called an *equilibrium* position. Economists analyze a market by describing its equilibrium position, examining how quickly the automatic forces of supply and demand push the market to this equilibrium and noting how the equilibrium position changes whenever the market is subjected to a shock of some kind. A favorite shock to analyze is a government policy. For example, they may ask whether a government policy—such as increased government spending—can change the economy's equilibrium position and thus cause the economy to move in a particular direction.

What becomes of particular interest in the macroeconomic context is that the speed at which the economy reacts to disequilibrium forces varies markedly across different markets. In the beef market, for example, supply could be increased quickly in the short run, by slaughtering more cattle, but in the long run an increase in supply requires rearing more cattle, something that takes considerable time. Some macroeconomic markets, such as the market for foreign exchange, react very quickly to price changes, whereas other markets, such as the market for labor, do not. Sluggish reactions to disequilibria play an important role in explaining macroeconomic phenomena such as business cycles.

2.3   Shifts in Curves versus Movements along Curves

The supply and demand curves drawn in figure 2.1 reflect a ceteris paribus condition—namely that other conditions remained the same, but supply and demand are affected by more than just price. The level of income, for example, may also affect the amount demanded. Consequently diagrams requiring all other things to remain the same could be misleading. Some way must be found to include other variables in the supply/demand diagram. Let us return to our beef example to illustrate how this purpose is achieved.

Consider the market for beef illustrated in figure 2.2, where the economy is currently in equilibrium at point *A*, the intersection of its supply and demand curves at price $3 and quantity Q_e. Now suppose that income level rises, causing a 100-ton increase in our demand for beef. At each price level, the demand is 100 tons higher, so the entire demand curve must shift right by 100, portrayed in figure 2.2 as a rightward shift of *DD* to *DD′*. At the prevailing price of $3, the shift creates an excess demand in the market of $Q_s - Q_e = 100$. The excess demand causes upward pressure on price, moving the market to the new equilibrium at point *B,* the intersection of *DD′* and *SS.*

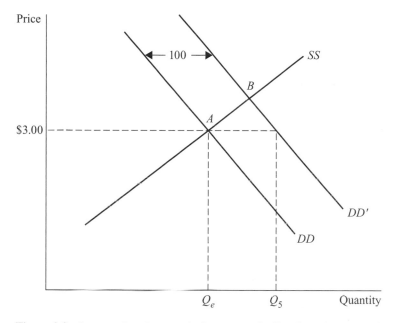

Figure 2.2   Impact of an Increase in Income on the Supply and Demand for Beef
The rise in income shifts *DD* to *DD'*, causing excess demand of $Q_5 - Q_e$; this pushes the market
from *A* to *B*.

This example has introduced a new principle in using supply and demand curves. Movements along the supply and demand curves reflect changes in price and quantity, the variables measured on the two axes of the supply/demand diagram. However, a change in a
variable not measured on these axes—in this example, a change in the income level—
causes a shift in one or both of the supply and demand curves. This shift in turn creates
a disequilibrium at the original price, which sets in motion automatic forces that push the
economy along the supply and demand curves to a new equilibrium. Understanding this
distinction between a *movement along* a curve and a *shift in* a curve should facilitate your
understanding of supply/demand diagrams.

The distinction allows a supply/demand diagram to reflect the influence of changes that
occur in other markets, thus permitting a more comprehensive analysis of the economy.
For example, a change in the market for chicken may lower the price of chicken, which
in turn should decrease the demand for beef, as people substitute the less-expensive
chicken for beef, shifting the demand curve for beef to the left and thereby affecting the
price of beef. Interaction between markets is particularly important in a macroeconomic
context because we are looking at the behavior of the economy as a whole rather than at
the behavior of a single market.

2.4   Media Examples

Let us complete this brief presentation of microeconomic supply and demand by looking at some examples of how supply and demand analysis can be used to interpret news clips.

Example 1

A freeze in southwestern U.S. and Mexican fields has resulted in damaged crops and inflated prices for produce such as lettuce, broccoli, and cauliflower.

How would this situation be interpreted on a supply/demand diagram?
At every price, supply of produce is now less, so the supply curve shifts to the left. This shift causes excess demand at current produce prices, thus pushing them up.

Example 2

Smith opined that higher prices may make it possible for some producers who closed during the last two years to reopen.

How would this possibility be interpreted on a supply/demand diagram?
The higher price slides us along the supply curve to a higher output. Some of that higher output comes from new producers.

Example 3

There are still 2,500 vacant units in the city and just so many tenants to go around. Landlords will have to take measures to get people in their buildings.

What is the current status of this market?
There is an excess supply of rental accommodation.

What measures will the landlords have to take?
They will be forced to lower rents.

Example 4

The economy is hot right now. People have higher incomes, so they want to borrow money to buy homes and big-ticket consumer durables. Imagine what this is doing to interest rates!

Use supply and demand analysis to explain what must be happening to interest rates.
Higher incomes have shifted the demand for loans to the right, creating an excess demand for loans at the current interest rate, the "price" of loans. This excess demand for loans pushes up this price, the interest rate.

Example 5

Higher American interest rates have caused foreigners to flock to the United States to buy our bonds. Surely this is the main reason why our exchange rate is so high.

Use supply and demand analysis to explain how the high interest rate could cause a high value of the U.S. dollar.

To buy our bonds, foreigners must first use their foreign currency to buy U.S. dollars. Thus the high U.S. interest rate has shifted the demand for U.S. dollars to the right. The excess demand for U.S. dollars bids up their price, the exchange rate.

Example 6

The expected price drop for cherries due to the bumper crop this year won't be as much as we thought, due to short supplies of pears and peaches.

Explain why the price of cherries is expected to drop.

A bumper crop means that the supply of cherries is much higher than expected, shifting the cherry supply curve to the right. This shift creates an excess supply at current cherry prices, pushing cherry prices down.

Why should short supplies of pears and peaches inhibit the fall in cherry prices?

Short supplies of pears and peaches should bid up their prices, causing people to demand more of alternative fruits such as cherries. This extra demand for cherries should inhibit their price fall.

Example 7

Bumper grain crops this year will further encourage meat production.

Explain the rationale behind this statement.

Bumper grain crops increase grain supply and push the price of grain down. The lower price of grain lowers the cost of producing meat, encouraging producers to increase meat production. The supply curve for meat shifts to the right.

2.5   Macroeconomic Markets

Economists analyze the macroeconomy by visualizing four broad markets: the goods and services market, the labor market, the money/bond market, and the foreign exchange market. Supply and demand forces in these markets determine the economy's important macroeconomic variables. The *goods and services market* determines the price level/ inflation rate and the amount of output/income produced annually by the economy. The *labor market* determines the wage rate and the employment/unemployment level. The *money market* determines the interest rate and the price of bonds. And the *foreign exchange market* determines the balance of payments and the exchange rate. Collectively these markets determine the values of the macroeconomic variables in which citizens and policy makers are most interested: inflation, unemployment, interest rates, and the exchange rate.

Market interaction makes macroeconomics challenging for students because analysis of one market cannot be undertaken in isolation from analysis of the other markets. The interest rate, for example, is determined in the money/bond market, but the interest rate affects demand in the goods and services market, which in turn affects the level of income, which in turn affects the demand for money/bonds in the money/bond market. Automatic forces of supply and demand serve to push each of these markets to equilibrium, with all four markets interacting. When all four markets are in equilibrium simultaneously, the economy as a whole is said to be in equilibrium.

Macroeconomics explains how the four markets interact—how and how quickly the automatic forces created by disequilibria serve to push the economy to an overall equilibrium, and how government intervention (by means of macroeconomic policy) can influence equilibrium or speed the process of adjustment to equilibrium.

Unemployment, for example, reflects disequilibrium in the labor market. Automatic adjustment forces pushing the economy back to full employment may operate too slowly, so one might ask what government policy would speed up this adjustment. Because of the interconnections between the four markets, it is not obvious what government policy would be best. To influence the labor market, for example, it is not necessary to intervene directly in this market. The government could intervene in one of the other markets, by using *fiscal policy* to affect demand in the goods and services market, or *monetary policy* to affect supply in the money/bond market, for example.

2.6   Picturing the Macroeconomic Markets

Ignoring a lot of technical details, we can visualize these markets in the four quadrants of figure 2.3. Each quadrant displays a supply/demand diagram similar to the supply/demand diagrams used to analyze a microeconomic market such as the market for beef, but there are some distinctive differences. The most prominent difference is that quantity in a macroeconomic market is an aggregate of quantities in different submarkets and price is an "average" or representative price of these submarkets.

The upper left quadrant represents the market for the total output of goods and services in the economy and so is in effect an aggregation of all the economy's microeconomic markets for goods and services. The price on the vertical axis measures an overall or average price level of all goods and services, rather than the price of a specific product, and the horizontal axis measures total output of the economy, rather than output of a specific product.

The upper right quadrant of figure 2.3 represents the money market. (As seen in a later chapter, the money market is also representing the bond market.) The "price" of money is the interest rate; the economy's many interest rates are represented by a single representative macroeconomic interest rate, which appears on the vertical axis. The horizontal axis measures the economy's supply of or demand for money, defined as the sum of cash in our pockets and balances in our bank accounts.

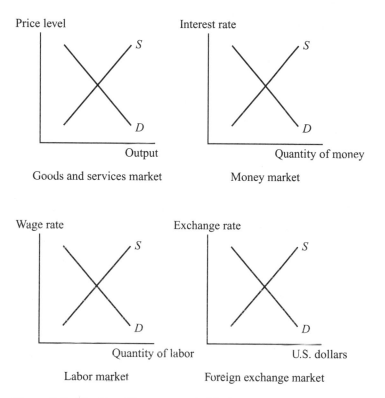

Figure 2.3 The Four Macroeconomic Markets

The lower left quadrant in figure 2.3 represents the labor market. Workers possess different skills, so in reality there is a large number of separate labor markets with different wage rates, each relating to specific skills and locations. Macroeconomists ignore all this, creating a conceptual overall market for labor in which there is a single, representative wage rate—measured on the vertical axis—and a generic quantity of labor—measured on the horizontal axis.

The bottom right quadrant of figure 2.3 represents the foreign exchange market where the forces of supply and demand determine the value of the U.S. dollar, the exchange rate, measured on the vertical axis as, for example, euros per dollar.

As with microeconomic supply and demand curves, changes in variables not measured on the axes cause shifts in these curves. Important shifts of these curves come from government policy. Through fiscal policy, the government changes its spending, thus shifting the demand curve for goods and services, and through monetary policy, the government shifts the supply curve in the money market. Other important shifts come from changes in the macroeconomic variables determined in other quadrants. Here are three prominent examples:

1. A change in the interest rate changes demand for goods and services (a lower interest rate means that it is cheaper to borrow to spend) as well as the demand for the U.S. dollar (a higher interest rate means that foreigners want more of our bonds and so demand more of our dollars to buy them).

2. A change in the price level affects the labor market. If prices rise, then for a given wage rate firms will find it profitable to increase output and will attempt to do so by increasing their demand for labor. The demand-for-labor curve will shift to the right. As the price level rises, however, workers will sooner or later discover that the purchasing power of their wage is lower and will accordingly be reluctant to work as much. The supply-of-labor curve will shift to the left.

3. A change in income (total output in the goods and services market) affects the demand for money (at a higher income we spend more and so keep more money in our pocket and in our bank account) and also affects the supply of the U.S. dollar on the foreign exchange market (a higher income means that we want to buy more imported goods and so supply more U.S. dollars to the foreign exchange market to get more foreign currency).

2.7   A "Big Picture" for Macroeconomics

The three examples listed above have an extremely important implication: a disequilibrium in any one of these four markets changes variables that in turn affect other markets, upsetting equilibrium in these markets that in turn changes other variables that in turn. . . . Any analysis of what is happening in one market immediately gets tangled up with repercussions from activity in the other three markets. It is this feature of macroeconomics that gives students headaches and makes macroeconomic analysis so frustrating. Two means of dealing with this problem are used in this book.

First, our analysis of the macroeconomy proceeds in stages. We begin by analyzing the goods and services market, ignoring the other three markets. When we have become comfortable with the fundamentals of the goods and services market, we splice the labor market into the stories we tell about how the goods and services market operates. Next we fade the labor market into the background (by assuming a recession, during which the labor market is not as active) and blend activity in the money market into the analysis of the goods and services market. And finally, we add in influences coming from the international sector. By proceeding in stages we build gradually to the problem of having to deal with everything happening at once. As will be seen later in the book, the money and the foreign exchange markets are very efficient, clearing to equilibrium very quickly. This means that whenever everything is happening at once, we can be quite confident that activity in these two markets is following expected supply/demand disequilibrium patterns, so that telling stories about how the economy is reacting to a shock can focus on the goods and services market and the labor market where the adjustment is sluggish.

Second, as will be seen in a later chapter, the fact that the money and foreign exchange markets equilibrate so quickly allows these markets to be put into the background, in the sense that they allow the four quadrant diagram to collapse into just two quadrants. And these two quadrants can each be represented by a single curve on a new diagram, so in effect the four quadrant diagram can be replaced by a single diagram, a diagram worth more than a thousand words. This single diagram, called the aggregate-supply/aggregate-demand diagram, will be used as an aid to telling stories about how the macroeconomy reacts to shocks such as policy action.

This short description of how we will overcome macroeconomic headaches paints a big picture of how economists think about the macroeconomy. The perspective it provides should be useful as we progress through this book.

3   Measuring GDP and Inflation

For at least five centuries systematic accounting systems have existed for private business, and data on individual behavior have always been available for collection. Microeconomics cannot complain of a lack of empirical data with which to verify its theories, quantify its conclusions, or suggest new directions for research. For macroeconomics, however, the situation is different: the financial, institutional, and legal resources of the government are necessary to collect aggregate data. Although governments have provided this data-collecting service for many years, until recently it was simply a convenient by-product of other government activities such as tax collecting. Until the beginning of the Second World War all these data consisted of indexes of price levels, production activity and employment, or trends in financial activity.

In the 1930s the Keynesian approach to macroeconomics (described in chapter 5) was introduced, offering an explanation and policy advice for the Great Depression. As the popularity of this new approach to macroeconomics grew, economists beseeched the government to collect data relevant to the testing and use of Keynesian theory. In response, the government developed the *National Income and Product Accounts* to measure economic activity, whose figurehead—GDP—appears frequently in the popular press.

The purpose of this chapter is to explain the basic structure of the national income accounts and offer some perspectives on the interpretation and use of the GDP measure. A source of confusion here is that the dollar value of GDP can increase because of price increases rather than increases in the amount of physical output produced in the economy. Sorting this out requires examining how price indexes are computed, a second purpose of this chapter. Annual percentage changes in a price index is the way we measure inflation, so a final purpose of this chapter is to discuss the measurement of inflation.

Upon completion of this chapter you should

- understand what GDP is and how it is measured,
- realize that using GDP to measure social welfare or to compare countries must be heavily qualified, and
- know what price indexes are and how they are used.

3.1   What Is GDP?

Gross domestic product (or GDP) is the total dollar value of all final goods and services produced in a country during a year. Several things about this definition should be noted:

1. Both goods, such as automobiles and top hats, and services, such as the help of lawyers and plumbers, are included.

2. Current market prices, reflecting the value society places on items, are used to aggregate different outputs to a dollar total. Government purchases, many of which do not occur on markets, are valued at their cost of production.

3. Only final goods and services are included. Intermediate goods, such as steel that has yet to be made into hammers and shovels, are not included. This practice avoids double-counting the steel.

4. This measure is an annual flow, a rate of production. A GDP of $6 trillion implies that the economy is producing $6 trillion worth of goods and services per year.

5. U.S. GDP measures production by U.S. citizens and foreigners alike inside the geographic borders of the United States and so unequivocally reflects economic activity in the United States. An alternative measure, Gross National Product (GNP), measures production by U.S. citizens, no matter where in the world they are located; in the United States typically GNP is 0.3 percent greater than GDP.

Economists and the media use many names besides GDP to refer to the nation's annual output of goods and services. Output, total output, national output, income, total income, national income, and aggregate supply are common. Algebraic representations use the capital letter Y. These names suggest that economists use the terminology *output* and *income* interchangeably; it is important to understand why.

The essence of why output and income are considered the same thing is that whatever is spent on a product (the value of that output) is divided up as income by those people producing it. Consider one element of GDP, a loaf of bread worth a dollar. With only a

Curiosity 3.1: Do We Really Keep Track of Every Dollar of Spending Every Year?

Yes and no. Some things, like spending on illegal activities, are deliberately not measured, and many other things, although they are measured, are measured through sophisticated guessing. One form of this guessing is imputation. Housing services, for example, are imputed by guessing what homeowners would have to pay to rent their own homes. Financial services are imputed by guessing what people would have to pay for these services were they not provided for free by the bank. About an eighth of consumer spending is measured via imputations. A second form of guessing is extrapolation. Every five years (e.g., in 2007) a full census measures almost all spending, but in between these years the national accounts statisticians exploit trends, information from surveys, and general measures of economic activity such as unemployment rates to guess at what is happening. A simple example is measuring purchases of electricity and natural gas by using a trend (for population growth) combined with weather information.

Extrapolation accounts for between 5 and 25 percent of the GDP measure, depending on the particular measure (quarterly versus annual, for example). This guessing is quite accurate—the every-five-years measure differs only by about 1 percent from guesses made for these years. The Bureau of Economic Analysis (BEA), responsible for producing the GDP measure, stresses that it is providing an accurate picture of economic activity, not a precise estimate. For a look at how the BEA deals with its innumerable estimation problems, see Landefeld, Seskin, and Fraumeni, "Taking the Pulse of the Economy: Measuring GDP," *Journal of Economic Perspectives* 22(2), Spring 2008, pp. 193–216. Its appendix lists many more sources of information on this topic.

few exceptions, every penny of this dollar's worth of bread can be traced back into somebody's pocket as income. Some of the dollar is profit/proprietor income to the grocer, baker, miller, and farmer (or dividend income to their stockholders); some is wage and salary income to their employees; some is interest income to the banker who has financed their loans (or interest income to those who purchased their corporate bonds); and some is rental income to their landlords. It is because of this equivalence that *total output*, GDP, is referred to as *total income*.

Laypersons' use of the word *income* is slightly different in that it reflects what we receive as income, regardless of whether it corresponds to output. There are three differences of note. First, of the dollar's worth of bread, some money will be set aside by the grocer, baker, miller, and farmer to cover depreciation—to pay for replacing their buildings and equipment when they have worn out—and thus will never make it into anyone's pocket as income. (The "gross" in gross domestic product means that the output measure does not account for depreciation; *net national product* measures output net of depreciation. Depreciation is about 12 percent of GDP.) Second, if the grocer, baker, miller, or farmer pays any indirect taxes, such as sales taxes, as the bread makes its way through the production process, then this money goes directly to the government and thus also does not make it into anyone's pocket as income. And third, transfer payments make up part of our income but do not correspond to output produced. Examples are government production subsidies, welfare and unemployment insurance payments, and gifts. Interest on government and consumer debt is also classified as transfer payments because, unlike interest paid by business, it does not reflect the cost of production activity. A subset of the national income accounts reports data on these kinds of measures.

As a nation, our annual income—what we have available to distribute to our citizens—is what we have produced during the year. Despite the fact that individual incomes do not quite match this concept of a nation's aggregate income, we will use the terminologies *aggregate output* and *aggregate income* interchangeably. This thinking suggests that GDP could be measured by adding up all incomes and making adjustments for the phenomena that we have noted. For those interested, appendix 3.1 at the end of this chapter shows how this process would be carried out. Some countries use this method to help in estimating GDP, but the United States uses a different method.

> **Sample Exam Question 3.1:**
> Which, if any, of the following directly increase GDP? (a) The government pays $500 to hire a useless paper-shuffler. (b) The government pays $500 to subsidize a firm recycling paper. (c) The government pays $500 to a lottery winner.

3.2   Estimating GDP

Suppose that all final output produced during the year was bought during the year. Then, by adding up all expenditure on final goods and services during the year, we have a measure of GDP, of what was produced during the year. This is the rationale behind the expenditure approach to measuring GDP, and with three major adjustments, it is the method by which U.S. GDP is estimated.

First, what if some of what was produced was not bought during the year? Suppose that a million dollars worth of furniture, manufactured during the year and so part of that year's GDP, was not purchased during the year. The national accounts statistician views this extra furniture as having been purchased by the manufacturers for the purpose of augmenting their inventory. This way, by imaginative accounting, items that were not bought become bought. This technique causes the adding-expenditures approach to measure what was actually produced, namely GDP. Similarly, of course, if during the year people bought more than was produced so that inventories fell, the national accounts statistician records this difference as a negative investment in inventories, lowering the adding-expenditures measure to measure accurately what was actually produced.

Second, what if some things bought during the year were used products, such as antiques, and so do not correspond to that year's production? Such items are not counted when adding all expenditures, but the fraction of such sales that reflects a purchase of the services provided by the antiques dealer is counted.

Third, what if some of the spending during the year was on imported goods and services, or on goods with imported components? Adding up all spending would then overestimate what was actually produced in the United States. This problem is solved by subtracting all imports.

Table 3.1 reports GDP measured via the expenditure approach. In 2007 GDP was about $14 billion, approximately $30,000 per person. Total expenditure on goods and services is broken into four general categories, corresponding to those formulated by Keynes: consumption expenditure (denoted C), investment expenditure (I), government expenditure (G), and foreign expenditure as exports (X). An extra category, imports (M), is subtracted from exports to produce net exports. This step removes the import component inherent in all categories so that we end up with total expenditure on domestically produced goods and services. It must be stressed that all spending here is on actual goods and services, so the investment is spending on such things as lathes, delivery trucks, factories, and shopping centers, not spending on financial investments such as stocks and

Table 3.1   U.S. Gross Domestic Product, 2007 ($ billions)

Consumption			**9,710**	70%
	Durable goods	1083		
	Nondurable goods	2,833		
	Services	5,794		
Investment			**2,130**	15%
	Nonresidential structures	480		
	Equipment and software	1,024		
	Residential	630		
	Change in inventories	−4		
Government			**2,675**	19%
	Federal defense	662		
	Federal nondefense	317		
	State and local	1,696		
Net exports			**−708**	−4%
	Exports	1,662		
	Imports	2,370		
Gross domestic product			**13,807**	100%

Source: www.bea.doc.gov.

bonds, and government spending is on things like highways and IRS accountants, not on transfer payments such as welfare payments that do not correspond to output. (Only about one-third of government spending is on final goods and services; the rest is mainly on transfer payments.)

Table 3.1 is a simplified version of a national accounts expenditure table; more detail can be found in the sources provided in curiosity 3.2. Notice that spending on inventory appears as "change in inventories"; it could be negative if inventories fell because more output was bought during the year than was produced during the year.

> **Sample Exam Question 3.2:**
> Suppose that inventories rise by $3 billion, consumption increases by $10 billion, welfare payments increase by $2 billion, and imports fall by $4 billion. By how much should measured GDP change?

3.3   GDP as Gross Deceptive Product

GDP is often used to measure an economy's level of well-being from one time period to another, and to compare one economy's welfare to another. A proper perspective must be brought to such uses of the GDP measure. Some examples follow:

1. Some things are produced but never sold and so are not included in GDP. A classic example is the work of homemakers, an omission from GDP that has angered women's rights activists. Another classic example is the case of a lawyer marrying her gardener. Suddenly she does not pay for gardening done on her property, and so this service is no longer counted in GDP. Comparisons between countries with different portions of their economy appearing on formal markets are suspect for this reason. National accounts statisticians impute to homeowners rent implicitly paid to themselves (and include this rent as expenditure on housing), impute to farmers income in the form of home consumption of crops, and impute a value for in-kind wages such as room and board, but clearly many nonmarket activities are missed. There are interesting implications for business-cycle measurement if people take advantage of unemployment to do more work around the home. A good source of information on this issue, with further references, is Katherine Abraham's 2008 testimony to a Senate subcommittee, found at http://commerce.senate.gov/public/_files/Abrahamtestimony3122008.pdf.

2. Some expenditures are hidden from data gatherers—illegal activities such as selling drugs and prostitution, and underground economic activity such as services provided for unrecorded (and so untaxable) cash transactions. An electrician wiring a plumber's home in return for which the plumber plumbs the electrician's home does not find its way into the GDP measure. Some people feel that illegal activities provide considerable

Curiosity 3.2: Where Can These Numbers Be Found?

Go to www.rfe.org to get to the "resources for economists" website where you can find anything you ever wanted to know about economics, including a plethora of economist jokes! Click on "data" to find a cornucopia of websites with economic data, both domestic and international.

The Economic Report of the President can be found here; its appendix B has conveniently gathered together data on all dimensions of the domestic economy. For more detailed information on specific measures the Bureau of Economic Analysis (BEA) publishes national accounts data in the Survey of Current Business, the Bureau of Labor Statistics (BLS) publishes price and unemployment data in the Monthly Labor Review, the Federal Reserve Board publishes interest rates and money supply data in the Federal Reserve Bulletin, and the International Monetary Fund (IMF) publishes international data in the International Financial Statistics and the World Economic Outlook. For most data, however, it is not necessary to find these publications in the library; searching the rfe website should enable you to find them on the Internet. For example, the contents of table 2.1 can be found at www.bea.gov, and the Organization for Economic Cooperation and Development (OECD) has international data on the main Western developed nations at www.oecd.org. The OECD annual publication Employment Outlook has a wealth of information on OECD labor markets. Did you know, for example, that in the United States the average annual hours actually worked per person employed in 2007 was 1,794 but in Germany was only 1,425? One reason is that Americans don't get as much vacation time as Europeans.

Help interpreting many of these and other numbers can be found in *Guide to Economic Indicators* by Norman Frumkin (Armonk, NY: M.E. Sharpe, 2006, fourth edition), *A Guide to Everyday Economic Statistics* by Gary Clayton and Martin Giesbrecht (New York: Irwin/McGraw-Hill, sixth edition, 2003), and in *The Data Game*, by Mark Maier (Armonk, NY: M.E. Sharpe, third edition, 1999). Actually a plethora of such books can be found by typing "economic indicators" into Amazon's website! The government statistical agency websites given above also have many information features such as answers to frequently asked questions.

benefit to society (as evidenced by the fact that so many people are so eager to participate in them), so their exclusion causes GDP to understate the benefit society derives from annual economic activity. The size of the U.S. underground economy is thought to be in the order of 10 percent of its GDP. For most other countries it is thought to be much larger, about 70 percent in Egypt, Thailand, and Bolivia; about 45 percent in Russia; about 30 percent in Greece and Italy; about 20 percent in Chile; and about 15 percent in Canada, Hong Kong, and Singapore. These numbers are not very accurate, but everyone agrees that over time the underground economy has grown dramatically in most countries, and will continue to do so.

3. Some items are included in GDP that do not reflect net benefits to society. The *Exxon Valdez* oil spill required over $2 billion of cleanup expenditure to bring us back to the pre-spill state. This expenditure is added into GDP, with no offsetting reduction of GDP

to reflect the pollution cost to society. A crime-ridden country spends a lot more on police protection, all added into GDP, to obtain the same state of security as that enjoyed by a more law-abiding country.

4. Government expenditure on goods and services is valued at cost, despite the fact that the benefit produced by this expenditure could be valued quite differently by the market forces used to value other components of GDP. On the one hand, if entry fees were charged to the Smithsonian museums, for example, the output thereby measured would probably exceed the museums' cost. On the other hand, everybody has a favorite example of what he or she considers to be wasteful government spending.

5. GDP does not account for nonrenewable natural resources used up in production processes. In Kuwait, for example, because so much of GDP takes the form of oil exports, the GDP measure is misleading as an indicator of the economy's sustainable output level.

6. Cross-country comparisons are rendered difficult by several factors: some countries spend a lot on housing to deal with a harsh climate, leisure-loving societies do not have their leisure valued, exchange rates used to express GDP figures in common currencies do not accurately reflect cost-of-living differences, and differences in income distributions are ignored.

Despite these problems in using GDP to measure an economy's welfare and to compare it to other economies, most economists are comfortable using GDP figures for comparisons over time, such as measuring an economy's growth rate. So long as the size of the underground economy is stable, there are no dramatic changes in crime and pollution, and the fraction of an economy's economic activity that appears on markets is relatively constant, growth measures should paint an adequate picture of economic progress.

But economic growth is not the only way of measuring progress, and many believe that the high profile of GDP has served to divert attention from other forms of human progress. One respected alternative measure is the *human development index*, developed in 1990 by the United Nations Development Programme. It is an index calculated as an equally weighted average of relative performances on measures of life expectancy, educational attainment, and income; it is highly correlated with the GDP measure, as might easily be guessed. Canada and the United States are the top countries by this measure. Another such measure is GPI, the *genuine progress indicator*, which adjusts GDP for income distribution, adds the value of household and volunteer work, and subtracts crime and pollution. (For more on these measures just google them!)

Just as a company would be unwise to chart its course by looking at its cash flow without looking at its balance sheet, so would a country be unwise to focus on GDP without looking at its its worth. The World Bank has ranked countries by per capita wealth, calculated by estimating the value of each country's natural resources, machinery, buildings, and other human-made capital and human resources. By this measure the wealthiest countries are those with few people and lots of oil, like the United Arab Emirates, and countries with few natural resources but substantial human ingenuity, such as Switzerland. Resource-rich Australia and Canada top this ranking; the United States is twelfth, just behind Norway.

One of the most prominent ways in which GDP changes can be misleading is if the effects of overall price changes on this measure are not taken into account. Doing so produces the important distinction between real and nominal GDP.

> **Sample Exam Question 3.3:**
> "It cost $2 billion to clean up the *Exxon Valdez* oil spill. Remarkably, this increased measured GDP."
>
> Did it increase GDP? If yes, should this amount have been subtracted instead of added, or what?

3.4   Real versus Nominal GDP

One way the GDP measure can increase is if the nation produces a larger physical quantity of goods and services, implying that more goods and services are available for distribution to participants in the economy. Such a change would be of importance to our standard of living. But GDP can also change simply because the prices of all goods and services rise, as they do during an inflation. In this case a larger GDP does not correspond to a larger physical quantity of goods and services. Typically each year GDP increases for both reasons, so some way of distinguishing changes in GDP due to physical changes in output from changes due to price level changes must be found.

This purpose is accomplished by distinguishing between *real* and *nominal* GDP. Nominal GDP is GDP valued at current prices, the number reported in the national accounts. Real GDP is GDP valued at prices prevailing during some base year, currently chosen by the national accounts statisticians to be 2000. For example, if we take the physical quantities of goods and services produced during 2007 and add them together by valuing them at year 2000 prices, we obtain 2007 GDP measured in 2000 prices, otherwise known as 2007 real GDP. If we do this for every year (i.e., measure every year's output in year 2000 prices), we get a series of GDP measures over time with prices held constant; changes in these real GDP measures reflect changes in physical quantities of goods and services produced.

To get real GDP for year t we have to change year t nominal output from year t prices to year 2000 prices. This is done by using year 2000 prices to value the year t output. Consider now the ratio of year t nominal GDP to year t real GDP:

$$\frac{\text{Nominal GDP}_t}{\text{Real GDP}_t}$$

The numerator and the denominator of this expression measure the same (year t) physical output but in different prices, so this ratio is a natural measure of the average price level in year t (the numerator prices) relative to the average price level in year 2000 (the denominator prices). If we calculate this ratio for all years, we get a series of numbers telling us the average price level in all years relative to the price level in year 2000. This is an example of a price index, usually denoted P_t, although the t subscript is seldom used; this particular price index is the *GDP deflator*.

For 2007 this GDP deflator number (P_{2007}) is 13,807.5/11,523.9 = 1.1982. What does this number mean? It is the ratio of the physical output of 2007 valued at 2007 prices (13,807.5 billions of 2007 dollars) to that same physical output valued at year 2000 prices (11,523.9 billions of 2000 dollars) and so is interpreted as expressing the degree to which the overall price level has risen from 2000 to 2007, in this case by 19.82 percent. When this calculation is done for each year, the resulting series of numbers is the GDP deflator. By tradition, the numbers in this series are multiplied by 100 so that, for example, the 1.1982 above becomes 119.82. To check your understanding here, you should see that the price index in the base year (in this case P_{2000}) is 100.0.

One of the main purposes of a price index is to quickly convert nominal variables (measured in current dollars) to their corresponding real variables (measured in base-period dollars). Conversion from any nominal value to its corresponding real value is done by dividing the nominal value by a suitable price index P so that, for example,

$$\text{Real GDP}_t = \frac{\text{Nominal GDP}_t}{P_t}$$

where P_t is the GDP deflator for time t. This is a general rule. For example, to convert nominal wage to real wage, one divides the nominal wage by a suitable price index.

In table 3.2 the GDP deflator has been calculated by dividing nominal GDP by real GDP (and multiplying by 100). Here are some things to notice. The base year price index is 100, as it should be. The overall price level rose steadily throughout this period, with years before the base year having price index values below 100. A slight recession occurred in 2000 to 2001; real GDP rose by a very small amount compared to other years, and per capita real GDP actually fell.

Percentage change in real GDP is the usual measure of an economy's real growth rate; percentage change in the GDP deflator is one way, but not the usual way, of measuring inflation.

Sample Exam Question 3.4:
Nominal GDP in 2003 was $11 trillion and the GDP deflator (2000 = 100) was 106.5.
  What is real 2003 GDP?

Table 3.2   Calculating the GDP Deflator

Year	Nominal GDP (billions of current $)	Real GDP (billions of 2000 $)	GDP deflator (2000 = 100)	Per capita real GDP
1998	$8,747.0	$9,066.9	96.48	$32,833
1999	$9,268.4	$9,470.3	97.87	$33,904
2000	$9,817.0	$9,817.0	100.00	$34,759
2001	$10,128.0	$9,890.7	102.40	$34,659
2002	$10,469.6	$10,048.8	104.19	$34,866
2003	$10,960.8	$10,301.0	106.41	$35,403
2004	$11,685.9	$10,675.8	109.46	$36,356
2005	$12,421.9	$10,989.5	113.03	$37,080
2006	$13,178.4	$11,294.8	116.68	$37,750
2007	$13,807.5	$11,523.9	119.82	$38,148

Source: www.measuringworth.org.

3.5   Measuring Inflation

Inflation is defined as a *persistent* rise in the general price level. This price level is usually measured by the *consumer price index* (or CPI), a price index designed to reflect growth in prices of consumer goods and services. If the prices of all consumer goods and services rise by 10 percent, the CPI rises by 10 percent to reflect these increases. The CPI is calculated by the Bureau of Labor Statistics (BLS) by observing changes in the cost of purchasing a typical bundle of consumer goods and services. As the cost of buying this bundle rises (falls), the CPI rises (falls). Thus the CPI is a weighted average of all consumer prices, with the weights given by the relative importance of different goods or services in the typical bundle of purchases. A survey of the prices of about 80,000 items is used in calculating the CPI each month. The typical bundle is updated every two years (in the even-numbered years) based on a national survey (the Consumer Expenditure Survey) involving 28,000 families, conducted during the previous two years. This bundle is divided into eight general categories; the following list gives their approximate weighting and examples of their components.

1. *Food and beverages* (16 percent): breakfast cereal, milk, coffee, chicken, wine, full service meals and snacks.

2. *Housing* (40 percent): rent of primary residence, owners' equivalent rent, fuel oil, bedroom furniture.

3. *Apparel* (5 percent): men's shirts and sweaters, women's dresses, jewelry.

Curiosity 3.3: How Do the GDP Deflator and the CPI Differ?

The GDP deflator and the CPI are both price indexes. The CPI is particularly well known because it measures changes in the cost of living and so is of more personal interest to individuals, and for that reason it is the price index normally used to calculate the rate of inflation. There are three major differences between these two indexes. First, the CPI reflects prices of only consumer goods and services, whereas the GDP deflator calculation includes prices of all output. Second, the CPI incorporates prices of imports, excluded from the GDP deflator calculation. And third, the GDP deflator allows the output basket to change each year, whereas for the CPI it changes only every two years and with a lag. Two minor differences are of note. First, once published the CPI is never revised, as are other statistics, because it is often used in contracts to measure cost-of-living wage adjustments. And second, these price indexes have different base years, currently 2000 for the GDP deflator, and 1982 to 1984 for the CPI. Despite these differences, both indexes produce very similar inflation measures.

Here is a technical detail for those really curious about price index calculations. The GDP deflator actually used is a chained index, calculated slightly differently than described in the text (but the resulting numbers are very similar). Real growth from one year to the next, say from 1992 to 1993, is calculated first by measuring and comparing the two years' physical outputs in 1992 prices and then by measuring and comparing the two years' physical outputs in 1993 prices. The geometric average of these two growth rates is used to measure real growth between these two years. This procedure is done for all adjacent years, and then the base-year value of GDP is augmented by these growth rates year by year (i.e., "chaining" the growth rates together) to produce the real GDP series. This series is then used to produce the corresponding "chained" price index by dividing nominal GDP by real GDP. This procedure reduces bias caused by changes in output bundles from year to year.

4. *Transportation* (18 percent): new vehicles, airline fares, gasoline, motor vehicle insurance.

5. *Medical care* (6 percent): prescription drugs and medical supplies, physicians' services, eyeglasses and eye care, hospital services.

6. *Recreation* (6 percent): televisions, cable television, pets and pet products, sports equipment, admissions.

7. *Education and communication* (5 percent): college tuition, postage, telephone services, computer software and accessories.

8. *Other goods and services* (4 percent): tobacco and smoking products, haircuts and other personal services, funeral expenses.

The CPI can be expressed as

$$\text{Consumer price index (CPI)} = \frac{\text{Current cost of typical bundle}}{\text{Base year cost of typical bundle}} \times 100$$

Although the typical bundle is updated regularly, the base year for the CPI has for continuity been kept as the 1982 to 1984 period. (The CPI numbers over this period average to 100.0.) Consequently the CPI is not actually calculated by using the preceding formula; it is calculated by using a "chaining" process where the current CPI is increased by the percentage increase in the cost of the current typical bundle during the current year. Speaking loosely, we could still think of the CPI as a price index that can be used to express nominal values in terms of 1983 dollars. Figure 3.1a graphs the CPI from 1960 to early 2009. Notice that there has been a steady increase in consumer prices over this period, but with a decrease in the last few months (as oil prices fell dramatically). Notice

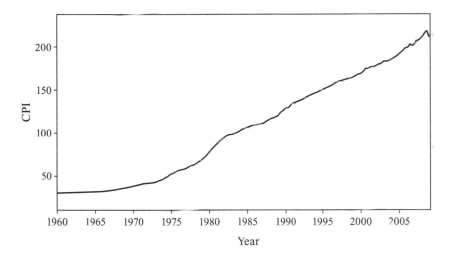

Figure 3.1a   Consumer Price Index

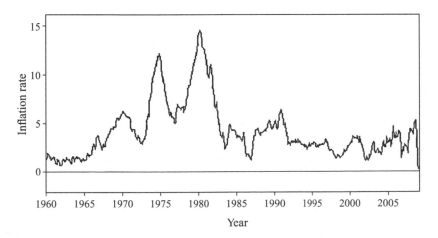

Figure 3.1b   Inflation

also that the later CPI values are in the order of 200, meaning that in these later years consumer prices were about twice what they were in 1983.

The CPI has a high profile, mainly because percentage change in the CPI is the main measure of inflation. Figure 3.1b graphs the annual inflation rate corresponding to the CPI shown in figure 3.1a, calculated monthly as the percentage change in the CPI over the preceding twelve months. Notice how much it has varied over the years, something not obvious from looking at figure 3.1a.

Although conceptually everyone "knows" what inflation is, from having to deal with it in everyday life, few recognize that measurement problems affect its interpretation. (Common misperceptions about the CPI are discussed by John Greenlees and Robert McClelland in the August 2008 *Monthly Labor Review*.) There are two main problems: what to do about changes in relative prices and what to do about quality changes.

A change in relative prices means that not all prices have changed by the same percentage amount. When relative prices change, consumers tend to buy fewer items that have become relatively more expensive and more items that are now relatively cheaper. The typical bundle changes in a way that causes the CPI calculation based on a fixed bundle to overestimate the change in the cost of living associated with the price changes. If inflation measures are used to measure changes in the cost of living, as they invariably are, it must be recognized that they are overestimates. This is the reason why the BLS has been updating the typical bundle every two years.

Changes in quality are difficult to incorporate into the price index. Their importance stems from the use of price indexes to reflect changes in the "purchasing power" of a dollar. If the quality of a good or service increases and its price rises to cover the higher cost of producing the higher quality product, this rise in price increases the price index, but the rise in the price index in this case does not reflect a fall in the value of what is purchased with a dollar. Similarly, if a computer becomes many times more powerful but its price doesn't change, the purchasing power of a dollar has increased because it can buy more computing, but the price index does not decrease to reflect this increase. Quality changes that take the form of introducing entirely new products present similar problems. The BLS deals with these by making imputations for quality changes in high-profile items such as automobiles, apparel, and computers, and by blending new products into the typical bundle, but clearly changes in quality remain a problem.

An interesting example is often used to clarify this point. Suppose that you were given $10,000 and told that you may spend it on 1999-quality goods and services at 1999 prices, or on 2009-quality goods and services at 2009 prices. If you choose the latter option you are implicitly saying that quality increases between 1999 and 2009 have offset the price increases and so "inflation" between 1999 and 2009 is zero or negative insofar as it affects the purchasing power of your dollar.

Another use of the CPI is as a benchmark to measure changes in relative prices. In 1980 the price of a large pepperoni pizza was about 8 dollars, and in 1997 was about 11 dollars, an increase of about 38 percent. Has the price of pepperoni pizza increased or decreased relative to other things? During this period the CPI increased by over 80 percent, so relative to other things pepperoni pizzas are now cheaper.

Most people, and governments, are unequivocally of the opinion that inflation is undesirable. These measurement problems indicate that measured inflation may not be a good guide to the extent to which inflation should be considered undesirable. Recent estimates suggest that current inflation measurement overestimates cost of living increases by about a percentage point:

- 0.3 percent because of consumer substitution,
- 0.2 percent because of inadequate reflection of improving quality,
- 0.3 percent because of delay in incorporating new products, and
- 0.2 percent because of improper measurement of a shift to discount retail outlets.

This is a politically sensitive issue—it is estimated that reducing social security indexing by 1 percent to account for the inflation measurement bias would save a trillion dollars over the next dozen years! Another issue is that the prices of some items can be very volatile, causing the CPI to misrepresent the level of longer run inflation. To deal with this, a measure of "core" inflation is produced that removes from the CPI the influence of the two most volatile prices, those of food and energy. In addition to these measurement problems, an examination of why inflation is undesirable suggests that, surprisingly, inflation is not nearly as severe a social ill as it is generally thought to be. (Google "Why do people dislike inflation?" to find a 1996 research paper by Robert Schiller providing interesting insight on this issue.)

> **Sample Exam Question 3.5:**
> In 2004 the CPI was 188.9, increasing to 195.3 in 2005.
>   What was the rate of inflation during this period?

3.6   The Costs of Inflation

Economists do not pay much heed to the usual complaints about inflation. For most people the impact of rising prices is offset by rising wages. Those living on fixed incomes, such as welfare recipients or old-age pensioners, can (although may not) be protected through appropriate policy action. Arbitrary redistribution of wealth, such as rises in real estate values, comes about mainly if an inflation is unanticipated, in which case economists would condemn it.

From their study of microeconomics economists know that our economic system works well because prices act as signals to induce producers to produce the things we value most

Curiosity 3.4: What Level of Inflation Should We Aim For?

In the early 1990s Governor John Crow of the Bank of Canada aimed for zero percent inflation. Most economists felt that this target was extreme; so did the Canadian government, which did not reappoint Crow. Alan Greenspan, chairman of the Board of Governors of the Federal Reserve System, the U.S. central bank, offered a more flexible target in a statement to the U.S. Committee on Banking, Housing and Urban Affairs in February 1989:

Maximum sustainable economic growth over time is the U.S. Federal Reserve's ultimate objective. The primary role of monetary policy in the pursuit of this goal is to foster price stability. For all practical purposes, price stability means that expected changes in the average price level are small enough and gradual enough that they do not materially enter business and household financial decisions.

Greenspan did not make the mistake of aiming for an unrealistic level that in any event is inappropriate, nor did he pin himself down to a specific level, the better to deal with criticism. An inflation rate of between 2 and 3 percent seems to be an acceptable target.

at the lowest cost—the right prices ensure that the economy maximizes the total welfare of its participants. This is what is meant when it is said that the price system is a very *efficient* way of allocating and distributing goods and services. To economists, the main cost of inflation is the resource misallocation it causes—the loss of efficiency that results because inflation distorts price signals. This happens in many different ways, some examples of which follow.

- During periods of inflation people are more interested in investing their savings in assets designed to protect them against inflation, such as real estate, rather than in productive investments that enhance the growth and efficiency of the economy. A classic example is people in Brazil holding wealth in the form of Volkswagens during high-inflation periods.

- During high inflation business finds it worthwhile to collect bills more promptly, using resources for this purpose that could otherwise have been used to produce goods or provide other services.

- Low inflations are steady and predictable; high inflations are volatile and unpredictable. This volatility creates uncertainty in the business community, reducing investment activity. Reduced investment in turn reduces economic growth. Some estimates suggest that reducing inflation from 10 to 5 percent will increase productivity by about 0.2 percent a year.

- Individuals reduce money holdings to cut wealth losses caused by rising prices, lowering the purchasing power of their cash and checking accounts. Getting along with fewer money holdings is inconvenient, misallocating the individual's personal resources of time, energy, and leisure. The cost of this inconvenience is estimated to be equivalent to about 0.05 percent of GDP per extra percentage point of inflation above normal.

- In the extreme case of hyperinflation, inflation of over 100 percent a year, the currency system breaks down, and the economy reverts to the far less efficient barter system. During the spectacular German hyperinflation of 1923 prices at times rose by over 200 percent *within a week*, severely affecting economic activity—people would work only if paid immediately, and spent every spare moment buying things to get rid of cash.

Offsetting these arguments, however, is the fact that many prices are inflexible or "sticky" in the downward direction. Many prices that should fall tend not to do so, instead just remaining constant. This implies that for the price system to operate efficiently, relative prices must change through selected price increases rather than by some prices rising and others falling. In reality the efficiencies of the price system can be gained only by allowing some inflation.

Most laypersons are amazed to discover that economists' measure of the harm done by inflation reflects phenomena of such seemingly little severity. It seems there are few substantive costs to modest inflation and even some benefits. Why then are we so paranoid about inflation?

For reasons explained at length later in this book, inflation is very quick to rise but very slow to fall. Although a low steady rate of inflation does not carry significant cost, a high cost must be paid in the form of a prolonged period of high unemployment to bring inflation down. We fear inflation because if it rises above the modest level we are willing to live with, we will have to pay a high unemployment cost to bring it back down.

Sample Exam Question 3.6:

"An inflation is OK if it is anticipated. An unanticipated inflation causes unfair redistributions of wealth, particularly from lenders to borrowers."

Explain why an unanticipated inflation redistributes from lenders to borrowers.

Media Illustrations

Example 1

The oil crisis caused U.S. oil companies' overseas profits to shoot up, producing a jump in GNP that could mislead policy makers.

GNP (gross national product) is output produced by Americans regardless of where that output is produced. How might this jump in GNP mislead policy makers?

One of the reasons the United States switched from GNP to GDP as its measure of output is that GNP movements can arise for reasons unconnected with domestic economic activity, as this example illustrates. In using GNP, policy makers may be misled into thinking that the U.S. economy is thriving and, as a consequence, may undertake inappropriate policy action.

Example 2

Suppose that a new computer costs one-quarter the price of existing computers and is proved to perform as well. Now when GDP is calculated, production of the same number of computers creates only one-quarter as much dollar output— GDP falls!

This example suggests that the great technology leaps in computing that we have been experiencing have served to decrease GDP, a conclusion that doesn't seem right. Is it right? If not, why not? If so, what would you suggest be done to deal with this problem? There is no problem here. Nominal GDP falls, but interest should center on real GDP. The fall in the price of computers is built into the GDP deflator, so real GDP should remain unchanged. Changes in the quantity of computers purchased because of the change in relative prices are ignored. To deal with such changes the typical bundle used by the national accounts statisticians would have to be changed.

Example 3

Society needs an index that incorporates the measures of economic welfare that GDP leaves out. If such an index came to replace GDP as the definitive measure of our general economic health, we could begin to look beyond the narrow definition of economic growth when formulating economic policy.

What measures of economic welfare does GDP leave out?
Economic welfare is affected by a lot of things that GDP does not capture adequately: quality changes in goods and services, leisure, income distribution, environmental quality, crime levels, work performed outside the marketplace, underground and illegal activities, climate, natural beauty, and personal freedoms, for example.

Example 4

Republicans are already eyeing changes to the inflation measure as a way to meet their goal of halving the budget deficit by 2002. The CPI is used to adjust social security and other benefits, as well as income-tax brackets, for inflation.

In what direction are these changes to the CPI? Why?
These changes are decreases in the CPI to remove the bias in the CPI due to quality changes, introduction of new products, movement toward discount retailers, and substitution of cheaper goods for more expensive items.

Explain how the changes to measuring the CPI would affect the budget deficit through social security benefits.
Each year social security payments are increased by the percentage increase in the cost of living as measured by the CPI. Consequently a smaller annual rise in the CPI measure

means a smaller annual increase in government outlays on social security benefits, reducing the budget deficit.

Explain how the changes to measuring the CPI would affect the budget deficit through income taxes.

A smaller increase in the CPI means a smaller adjustment upward in the income level above which people pay a higher marginal tax rate. Tax revenues would increase because more people would move into higher tax brackets.

Chapter Summary

- GDP, the amount of final goods and services produced by an economy during a year, is equal to the income generated in that economy during that year. It is measured by adding up all expenditures, correcting for inventory change, omitting expenditure on used items, and subtracting imports.

- Using GDP to measure social welfare or to compare countries is subject to many criticisms.

- Nominal GDP is GDP valued at current prices; real GDP is a measure of GDP that has the influence of the price level removed, calculated by dividing nominal GDP by a price index. Price indexes, such as the GDP deflator or the CPI, measure changes in the overall price level.

- To economists the main cost of a steady inflation is the resource misallocation it creates by distorting price signals. Increases in inflation are fought tenaciously because it is so costly in terms of unemployment to bring inflation back down to an acceptable level.

Formula Definitions

- GDP deflator $P = \dfrac{\text{GDP valued at current prices}}{\text{GDP valed at base year prices}} \times 100$

- Real GDP $= \dfrac{\text{Nominal GDP}}{P} \times 100$

- Consumer price index (CPI) $= \dfrac{\text{Current cost of typical bundle}}{\text{Base year cost of typical bundle}} \times 100$

- Inflation = Percentage change in CPI = $\% \, \Delta\text{CPI}$

Media Exercises

(Group B questions require more thought.)

A1. A government report traces the economy's stagnation in the last fifteen months to massive declines in spending on commercial construction, while residential construction grew at only half the pace of previous recoveries. Of recent note, however, is a fall in inventories.

a. In which category or categories of the national expenditure accounts, C, I, G, or X, would these spendings be recorded?

b. Does the fall in inventories appear in the accounts as a positive or a negative number? Why?

A2. Homemakers often feel their work is taken for granted, and advocates in the women's movement argue that the statistical invisibility of homemakers work has substantive policy implications.

What is meant by "statistical invisibility" here?

A3. For many people a rise in the consumer price index is not an accurate measure of how much their cost of living has increased. What about a nonsmoking vegetarian who walks to work, for example?

Why might the CPI not be applicable to this person?

A4. Note that the percent change in the GDP deflator is being used as the measure of inflation rather than the more familiar CPI. The GDP deflator is a price index that samples _____, not just those paid by _____.

a. What does CPI mean?

b. Fill in the blanks.

A5. Economists believe that one of the most important sources of bias in the CPI as a measure of the cost of living occurs when consumers shift their buying patterns in response to changing relative prices, substituting. . . .

Complete this clipping.

A6. Although GDP casts much light on the functioning of the economy, it has a blind spot for ecological concerns.

Explain the nature of this blind spot.

A7. And so the debate continues. Some feel that capital gains are undeserved and should be taxed at 100 percent, while others believe that doing so would

destroy entrepreneurial incentives. As for including them in GDP, that has already been decided by the national accounts statisticians.

Are capital gains included in GDP? Why or why not?

A8. The government insists that the CPI measures consumer prices, not the cost of living. But don't shoot the CPI—whether bringing good news or bad, it's the best messenger we've got.

a. What's the difference between the CPI and the cost of living?

b. Which rises by more during inflationary times? Explain your reasoning.

A9. The government must next explain why the relative weight of food was being reduced in the new price index despite recent rapid increases in food prices.

How would you explain this change?

A10. The economists who set up GDP also established a number of rather arbitrary conventions to distinguish between the investment and consumption components of GDP. Generally, goods and services purchased by households are treated as consumption expenditures. _____ purchases are the major exception to this rule and are included in the investment category of GDP.

Fill in the blank. What is the rationale behind this exception?

A11. As best we can tell, responded the central bank governor, the center of the 2 percent inflation target, namely 1 percent, appears to correspond to genuine price stability once the various sources of bias in the CPI are allowed for.

Give an example of bias in the CPI measure.

A12. A series of methodological improvements to the consumer price index that will continue into 1999 is expected to add about half a percentage point to measured productivity growth, raising the economy's sustainable rate of GDP growth from between 2 percent and 2.25 percent to between 2.5 percent and 2.75 percent.

How could changes to the CPI affect measured productivity growth?

B1. The Commerce department announced that it is shifting from 1987 to 1992 as the base year for calculating the nation's real GDP and price index. The new figures will account for changes in consumers' tastes, technological advances, and other phenomena.

a. In the new official figures, will the number for real GDP for 1987 become larger, smaller, or stay the same as it was before the base was changed to 1992?

b. In the new official figures, will the 1992 real GDP number be larger, smaller, or the same as the 1992 nominal GDP?

c. What will the new 1992 price index number be?

d. Will the new 1987 price index number be larger, smaller, or the same as it was before?

e. The clipping claims that consumer tastes and technological advances will be accounted for. How would this accounting be done?

B2. **Surprisingly, if the government hires a completely useless paper shuffler, GDP increases, but if General Motors hires this person, GDP remains unchanged, as it should.**

Is this correct? Explain your reasoning.

B3. **For the same price I can now buy a computer with four times as much power. Surely this must mean that our GDP has increased, but I don't see how—the same number of computers at the same price adds up to the same dollar output!**

Suppose that exactly the same number of computers is being produced and sold at the same price, but now they are more powerful. Should GDP increase? Does it increase?

B4. **Experts keen on the concept of green GDP have offered a variety of suggestions to make economic statistics more environmentally friendly.**

Give an example of such a suggestion.

B5. **Wilson claimed that a better measure of Turkish national income could be obtained by including money sent back to their families by Turks living and working in Germany, something that is currently ignored in the national accounts.**

Comment on this statement.

B6. **Although these seasonally adjusted GDP figures show nothing untoward, if we look at the seasonally unadjusted figures, a different story is told: real GDP dropped by 8 percent from the fourth to the first quarter!**

a. What does this information suggest is the normal behavior of unadjusted quarterly GDP when moving from the fourth to the first quarter? How can you tell?

b. What do you think is causing this effect?

B7. He argues that business spending on activities like research and development, management consulting, and employee training, health, and safety, now counted as intermediate business services and amounting to about $200 billion, should be added directly to the investment component of GDP, perhaps placed in a new subcategory called intangible capital or service capital. He also wants to shift consumer spending on education and on consumer durables from consumption to investment, and calculates that this shift would involve about $980 billion.

What do you think would happen to measured GDP if these proposals were adopted?

B8. The rapid development of computers makes it difficult to determine how much of the change in measured prices of computers is due to pure price change and how much to the change in quality of the product. It is clear that the cost of obtaining a given amount of computing capability has been falling.

What does this statement imply about how a change in computer prices should affect the CPI?

B9. The bank estimates that the annual inflation rate in January would have been only 3.5 percent rather than 4.1 percent had it not been for sales tax increases. And that estimate does not include any income tax increases.

How are sales tax increases incorporated in the price index? Why are they relevant? What about income taxes?

B10. CPI overstates increases in the cost of living by about 0.5 to 2 percent; eliminating this overestimation would increase tax revenue by about 9 billion and reduce social security payments by about 8 billion per year.

Explain why elimination of this overestimation would increase tax revenue and reduce social security benefits.

B11. The ionosphere is part of the economy too, that is, the real economy and not the artificial construct portrayed in the GDP. It does real work, as we would discover quickly if it were to collapse. Yet the GDP does not include this work. If we burn more gas, the expenditure gets added to the GDP. But there is no corresponding subtraction for the toll this burning takes on the thermostatic and buffering functions that the ionosphere provides. Nor is there a subtraction for the oil we take out of the ground.

What is the main point being made here?

Numerical Exercises

AN1.   **The Commerce Department revised its estimate of real GDP to $3.877 trillion, up from the earlier estimate of $3.835 trillion. Before adjusting for inflation, GDP was $4.603 trillion, up from $4.523 trillion.**

What were the GDP deflator values used for these two calculations?

AN2.   Which of the following raise measured GDP by $200?

   a. A steel company sells $200 of steel to an automobile manufacturer.

   b. You are hired by the government to shuffle paper uselessly for $200.

   c. You are hired by General Motors to shuffle paper uselessly for $200.

   d. An antiques dealer sells a $2,000 armoire, pocketing a 10 percent commission.

   e. You receive a $200 unemployment insurance check from the government.

   f. Your firm's inventories fall by $200 because of extra demand.

   g. You win $200 at the racetrack.

AN3.   Suppose that the sum of consumption, investment, and government spending is $620 billion, where investment includes involuntary inventory accumulation of $2 billion in addition to expenditure on plant and equipment, and government spending includes $5 billion interest payments on the national debt, $5 billion unemployment insurance payments, $10 billion social security payments, $2 billion in salaries to elected politicians, $14 billion in salaries to government employees, and $25 billion expenditure on goods and services produced by the private sector. If we imported $3 billion more than we exported, what is the measured GDP?

AN4.   If a typical market basket of goods and services cost $150 in 1992, the base year, and $180 in 1995, what is the price index in 1995?

AN5.   Suppose that inventories fall by $2 billion, consumption increases by $8 billion, unemployment insurance payments decline by $4 billion, and imports rise by $1 billion. By how much should measured GDP change?

AN6.   If in 1994 nominal GDP is 600 and real GDP is 500, then what is the GDP deflator for 1994?

AN7.   Suppose that the price index is 130 and a typical basket of goods and services costs $520. What would this typical basket have cost in the base year?

AN8.   If the CPI changes from 110 in 1993 to 120 in 1994, what is the rate of inflation?

AN9.   Suppose that the CPI is 100 in 1992, its base year. In 1993 and 1994 it is equal to 112 and 120, respectively. During 1995 the economy experienced an inflation of 10 percent.

    a. What rate of inflation characterized this economy during 1994?

    b. If consumption in 1994 was $300 billion in 1994 dollars, what is this consumption expressed in 1992 dollars?

    c. What is the 1995 value of the CPI?

AN10.   At my university tuition in 1972 was $15 per credit hour, and in 1999 it was $77 per credit hour. The CPI was 26.1 in 1972 and 110.9 in 1999 (1992 = 100). What was the 1972 tuition in 1999 dollars?

AN11.   Suppose that in 1995 the price index (base year 1992) was 120 and income was $760 billion. The corresponding numbers for 1996 are 125 and $820 billion. What is 1996 income expressed in 1995 dollars?

AN12.   **Historically there has been a 37 percent pass through from commodity price increases to core inflation. However, during the cycle lasting from 2002 to 2007, a 118 percent jump in commodity prices translated into only a 21 percent increase in the CPI, or _____ passthrough.**

    Fill in the blank.

BN1.   Suppose that a hamburger cost $1.50 last year and $1.65 this year, and the overall price index (the GDP deflator) rose from 125 last year to 150 this year.

    a. How much will 1,000 hamburgers contribute to this year's nominal GDP?

    b. How much will 1,000 hamburgers contribute to this year's real GDP?

    c. What was the rate of inflation (as measured by the GDP deflator) during the past year?

BN2.   Suppose that nominal GDP is $566 billion in 1992, $600 billion in 1993, and $642 billion in 1994. If 1992 is the base year, the price index is 105 in 1993, and real growth in 1994 is 3 percent, what is the price index in 1994?

BN3.   Suppose that in 1992 the price and quantity of energy were 1.00 and 50, respectively, and that in 1993 they were 1.04 and 60, respectively. In 1992 the price and quantity of all other consumer goods and services were 1.10 and 40, respectively, and in 1993 they were 1.20 and 30, respectively.

a. Using 1992 as a base year and the 1992 bundle as the typical bundle, what is the CPI in 1993?

b. What is the rate of inflation between 1992 and 1993?

c. Now suppose that these outputs comprise all of GDP. Keeping 1992 as the base year, what is the GDP deflator for 1993?

BN4. Suppose that the CPI is calculated assuming that one-quarter of expenses is for health, transportation, and entertainment and three-quarters are for all other items. When the prices of items in the first category double and the prices of all other items quadruple, does the CPI change overstate, understate, or measure accurately the change in the cost of living?

BN5. If GDP increases in nominal terms from $600 billion in 1994 to $663 billion in 1996 and the price index (1992 = 100) rises from 120 to 130, how much real growth (in 1992 dollars) in GDP occurred between 1994 and 1996?

BN6. Suppose that last year the price index (base year 1992) was 119 and income was $900 billion. The corresponding numbers for this year are 123 and $950 billion.

a. What is this year's income expressed in 1992 dollars?

b. What was inflation this year?

c. What was real growth this year?

Appendix 3.1   Measuring GDP by Adding up Incomes

Since with only a few exceptions every dollar of output produced makes its way into someone's pocket as income, it should be possible to measure GDP by adding up all incomes and making a few adjustments for the exceptions. This is the thinking that lies behind the adding-up-incomes approach to measuring GDP, an alternative to the adding-up-expenditures approach.

Incomes are placed into five categories: compensation of employees, proprietors' incomes, profits, interest incomes, and rental incomes. Only interest payments associated with productive activity are included; interest on government bonds and consumer loans is not included. These incomes are added and then the following four adjustments are made:

1. *Depreciation.* Firms set aside earnings to cover depreciation of their buildings and equipment; this part of output produced never makes it into anyone's pocket as income and so must be added on.

2. *Indirect taxes.* Firms may pay indirect taxes to the government such as sales taxes. This part of output produced does not make it into anyone's pocket as income and so must also be added on. (Why are indirect taxes counted as part of GDP? The tax-inclusive price measures what people are willing to pay for the good or service—they must value the good or service by at least this amount or they wouldn't buy it; since GDP purports to measure the value to society of output produced, the tax must be included in the GDP measure.)

3. *Subsidies.* Some firms may receive subsidies from the government, in which case the income they earn is overstated. Some of their income does not correspond to output produced, so subsidies must be subtracted.

4. *Foreign production.* Income received from foreign sources must be subtracted because it does not correspond to domestic production, and income paid to foreigners must be added.

Table 3.3 presents a greatly simplified example of how GDP is measured using this approach. The statistical discrepancy item is included to force this means of measuring GDP to produce the same number as the adding-up-expenditures measure shown in table 3.1. Some countries—Canada for example—believe that these means of measuring GDP are equally reliable and so produce their official GDP measure by averaging the two measures. This is accomplished by taking half of the difference between the two measures, calling it a statistical discrepancy, adding it to the smaller number, and subtracting it from the larger number. The United States feels that the adding-up-expenditures method is unequivocally superior and so uses it alone to produce its GDP measure. The income and

Table 3.3   GDP by Adding Income Payments, 2007 ($ billions)

Employee compensation	7,819
Proprietors' incomes	1,056
Corporate profits	1,492
Rental income	40
Net interest	900
plus: Indirect taxes	1,016
less: Subsidies	52
plus: Depreciation	1,721
plus: Income payments to foreigners	759
less: Income payments from foreigners	862
Gross domestic income	**13,889**
plus: Statistical discrepancy	−82
Gross domestic product (GDP)	**13,807**

Source: www.bea.gov.

expenditure approaches produce very similar measures of GDP in level, growth, and cyclical features, with the annual difference between the two averaging only about 0.2 percentage point.

There is a third way of measuring GDP, the *value-added* approach. Value added is the increase in the value of a commodity as it goes from one stage of the production process to another. If a baker buys flour for a dollar and then uses it to produce bread that is sold to the grocer for a dollar and twenty cents, the baker's value added is twenty cents. When the grocer sells the bread for a dollar and thirty cents, the value-added by the grocer is ten cents. These value addeds correspond to the income payments made to people during the production process with the baker and the grocer, respectively. By adding up all the value addeds, we are able to measure GDP.

4   Unemployment

During the 1970s and 1980s the American economy was remarkably successful in creating jobs for new entrants to the workforce, entrants whose numbers were exceptionally high—baby boomers were coming of age, females were leaving the home to work, and immigration had grown. This increase in U.S. employment is particularly impressive when contrasted with the minimal employment growth that characterized Europe during this period. This strong growth in employment was complemented by a good performance on the unemployment front: with the exception of the recessions of the early 1980s and early 1990s, unemployment in the United States, in sharp contrast to Europe, remained at reasonable levels, between 5 and 6 percent. But this relationship between employment growth and unemployment performance need not necessarily hold. On a per capita basis Canada during this period was even more successful than the United States in creating jobs but still experienced a growing unemployment rate. One purpose of this chapter is to explain why employment creation and the unemployment rate are not as closely related as might be expected.

Unemployment is implicitly if not explicitly a major topic of several later chapters, most notably chapter 5 explaining how government spending policy affects employment, and chapter 12 in which the infamous trade-off between inflation and unemployment is discussed. The contents of these later chapters will be enhanced by the perspective on unemployment provided by the current chapter.

4.1   Defining and Measuring Unemployment

The unemployment rate, graphed in figure 4.1 from 1960 to early 2009, is defined as the number of *unemployed,* people who want to have a job but do not have one, expressed as a percentage of the *labor force,* the total number of people aged 16 and over who want to have a job:

$$\text{Unemployment rate} = \frac{\text{Unemployed}}{\text{Labor force}}$$

Several qualifications, such as that the rate refers to the noninstitutionalized civilian population (i.e., excluding about 2.5 million prisoners, inmates of mental institutions, and about 1.5 million in the armed forces) aged sixteen and over, are incorporated in the official definition but do not affect its basic meaning. Figure 4.2 shows how these concepts are related.

Figure 4.1   Unemployment Rate

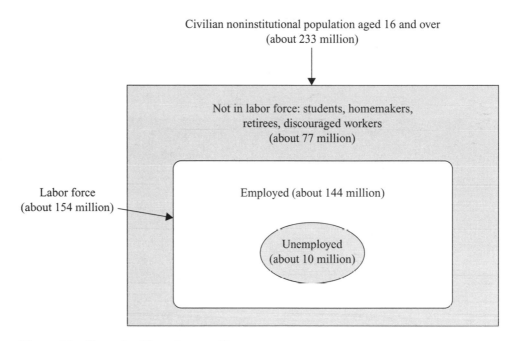

Civilian noninstitutional population aged 16 and over
(about 233 million)

Not in labor force: students, homemakers,
retirees, discouraged workers
(about 77 million)

Employed (about 144 million)

Unemployed
(about 10 million)

Labor force
(about 154 million)

Figure 4.2   Illustrating Unemployment Concepts
Source: www.bls.gov, November 2008 data.

The measured rate of unemployment can be an underestimate or an overestimate of this "true" unemployment rate. Underestimation occurs because part-time workers are counted as employed, even if they really want full-time work. Overestimation occurs when people not wanting work pretend to want work in order to collect unemployment benefits, when the unemployed are not willing to take a job unless it pays an unrealistically high wage rate, or when those measured as unemployed are actually "employed" in the underground economy. But the biggest problem with measuring unemployment is the discouraged/encouraged worker phenomenon.

The unemployed are people who want a job but don't have one. The main problem in measuring unemployment is finding some reliable way of determining who really wants a job. For lack of a better way, this is done by classifying as unemployed only those actively looking for work. Thus, to be counted officially as unemployed, someone must be without work and looking for work.

But what about people without work who have looked long and hard for a job and have become convinced that there is no job out there for them? They become discouraged in their search for a job and stop looking. Suddenly these *discouraged workers* are no longer counted as being in the labor force, and the measured unemployment rate falls. Many would claim that this results in an underestimate of the "true" rate of unemployment.

Curiosity 4.1: How Is Unemployment Measured?

Each month about 1,500 employees of the Bureau of the Census, on behalf of the Bureau of Labor Statistics (BLS), update the Current Population Survey (CPS) by interviewing about 60,000 households. (There are about 110 million households in the United States.) Each civilian household member 16 years of age or older is first asked if he or she did any work for pay during the last week, and if the answer is yes, even if it was just for an hour, that person is counted as employed. Those answering no are asked if they worked 15 hours or more without pay for a family business or farm, and if the answer is yes, they are counted as employed. Those answering no are asked if they are waiting to begin a confirmed job or to be called back to a job from which they have been laid off; if the answer is yes, they are counted as unemployed. Those answering no are asked if they have been doing anything to find work during the last four weeks, and if they answer yes, they are counted as unemployed. The others, those who have not been looking for work (e.g., because they are students or homemakers, or because they have given up hope of finding a job) are classified as not in the labor force. The official unemployment rate, sometimes referred to as U3, is calculated as the ratio of the unemployed to the sum of the employed and unemployed.

The BLS publishes other unemployment rate measures. For example, U1 is based on those who have been unemployed for 15 weeks or longer and is intended to reflect unemployment with a more substantive financial loss. In addition to those counted in U3, U4 includes discouraged workers, measured as those who want work, have searched for work during the preceding year, and claim they have stopped searching because of a lack of suitable jobs. Finally, U6, intended to reflect potential labor resources, includes those claiming to want work but not searching (for whatever reason) and part-time workers wanting full-time work. These alternative measures can be found on the BLS website in the unemployment rate latest numbers news release. In December 2008, U1 was 2.9 percent, U3 was 7.2 percent, U4 was 7.6 percent, and U6 was 13.5 percent. The gap between U3 and U4 is usually about two percentage points, but shrinks during booms and widens during recessions (as is the case for 2008).

In addition to these overall rates of unemployment, information on a variety of characteristics of the unemployed is reported. For example, in December 2008 the unemployment rate was 7.2 percent overall but 7.9 percent for males, 6.4 percent for females, 23.3 percent for males aged 16 to 19, 18.2 percent for females aged 16 to 19, 4.4 percent for married men (spouse present), 4.5 percent for married women (spouse present), 9.5 percent for women who maintain families. About 58 percent of the unemployed had lost their job, 25 percent were reentrants to the labor force, 9 percent were job leavers, and 8 percent were new entrants. About 29 percent had been unemployed for less than 5 weeks, 31 percent for 5 to 14 weeks, 17 percent for 15 to 26 weeks, and 23 percent for longer than 26 weeks.

Information from the CPS, as described above, is used to report the unemployment rate and the labor force participation rate. A different survey, the Current Employment Statistics survey, a monthly survey of 160,000 businesses and government agencies, is used to report jobs (referred to as nonfarm payroll employment) and hours worked.

This is not the only problem caused by the discouraged worker phenomenon. Whenever the economy recovers from a recession, these discouraged workers notice that times are better and that acquaintances have obtained jobs, encouraging them once again to look for work. These *encouraged workers* suddenly become counted as unemployed, causing a paradoxical rise in unemployment just when income and employment are increasing.

Sample Exam Question 4.1:
If the labor force is 100 million, the number of people with full-time jobs is 90 million, and the number of people with part-time jobs is 5 million, what is the unemployment rate?

4.2   The Employment/Unemployment Connection

One would think that an increase in employment must surely decrease unemployment. But we have just seen that movements of discouraged/encouraged workers out of and into the labor force can cause unemployment to change in a direction opposite to that in which employment is changing. This is a special case of a more general phenomenon. Every year thousands of new jobs are created, but also every year thousands of new members of the labor force appear, wanting those jobs. What happens to the unemployment rate depends on the relative magnitudes of the growth in jobs and the growth in the labor force. (The numbers involved here are big—in a typical nonrecession month about 300,000 jobs are created; in March of 2009, about 600,000 jobs were lost as the economy moved into recession.)

The creation of jobs is determined by the demand for the goods and services we produce, in turn affected by prices charged and government policies, among other things. This topic is discussed in later chapters. The growth of the labor force is affected by population growth and changes in the *participation rate*, the percentage of the civilian noninstitutional population aged 16 and over in the labor force, currently about 67 percent:

$$\text{Participation rate} = \frac{\text{Labor force}}{\text{Adult population}}$$

This dimension of unemployment is of particular interest because it is so often overlooked in discussions of unemployment.

The role of population growth is predictable. One can look ahead and see a wave of baby boomers leaving school and the number of immigrants as a known quantity. The role of changes in the participation rate is not so easy to predict. The women's liberation movement was one factor leading to annual increases in the female participation rate that were difficult to predict with any accuracy. During the last sixty years the female participation rate has increased from 32 to about 60 percent (due mainly to more paid work among mothers), and the male participation rate fell from 87 to about 75 percent (due mainly to earlier retirements), causing the overall participation rate to increase from about 60 to about 66 or 67 percent. Perhaps most difficult to predict in this regard are changes in the participation rate caused by the discouraged/encouraged worker phenomenon discussed earlier.

> **Sample Exam Question 4.2:**
> Suppose that the population over age 15 is 150 million, the number of discouraged workers is 5 million, the number of unemployed workers is 10 million, and there are 100 million employed.
>   What is the participation rate? ("Population" in these types of questions refers to the adult civilian, noninstitutionalized population.)

4.3   What Is Full Employment?

To an economist, full employment does not mean a position in which the unemployment rate is zero. Zero unemployment is not realistic, for several reasons. First, at any point in time some people are temporarily unemployed because they are in the midst of changing jobs or looking for an initial job. The unemployment corresponding to this ongoing process of improving the occupational and geographical match of workers and jobs is referred to as *frictional unemployment.*

Second, many people may be unemployed because technological progress has made their skills obsolete or because new trade agreements have changed the nature of what is produced domestically. They must retrain to obtain jobs. Both frictional unemployment and this *structural unemployment* are healthy because they mean that the economy is responding to the forces of change. Some workers are switching jobs to produce the goods and services that the changing tastes of society are demanding or to find jobs they will be happier doing. Other workers are retraining to keep up with technological innovations that improve productivity. Part of frictional and structural unemployment, however, reflects demographic factors such as the increased participation rate of females and the young. Many of the former need more training, having spent time as homemakers, and the latter are both unskilled and at a stage in life when switching jobs is more common.

The third reason that zero unemployment is unrealistic is that institutional phenomena may affect unemployment. For example, minimum wage laws may make it too costly to hire extra labor; generous unemployment benefits may make it easier to stay or become unemployed; government regulations, such as restrictions on how many hours per day a store can be open, may decrease job availability; and there may be racial or gender discrimination.

Curiosity 4.2: Why Is Unemployment So High in Europe?

Unemployment in Europe is markedly higher than that of the United States. The most persuasive explanations claim that this difference is due to a higher NRU in Europe caused by institutional differences such as higher minimum wages, more unionization, generous unemployment benefits, and various government regulations such as laws forcing Sunday closures and limitations on shop hours.

Layoff regulations and plant-closing laws, for example, make it very expensive for a firm to reduce its workforce, so they are reluctant to hire new workers, choosing instead to meet demand fluctuations by adjusting overtime. Reflecting this fact, in France the unemployed take five times as long to find a job as in the United States, but once employed are five times less likely to lose their job.

In Germany nonwage labor costs are 42 percent of gross wages, caused by a need to finance a very generous welfare system. Because of this, in the mid-1990s when the United States was experiencing an 11 percent increase in employment, Germany was experiencing a 7 percent decrease.

In short, it seems that the natural rate of unemployment is higher in Europe because of institutional phenomena. European countries are aware of this phenomenon and for several years have been undertaking significant labor market reforms, such as shrinking employment taxes, improving wage-bargaining procedures, lowering unemployment benefits, reducing employment protection, and increasing labor mobility. For information on this, the European Commission on Economic Affairs has a detailed database on European labor market reforms (google LABREF).

Google European unemployment for huge amounts of information on this general topic.

Unemployment arising from these three sources creates the NRU, the *natural rate of unemployment,* what economists mean by "full employment." This rate of unemployment was thought to be about 6 percent in the early 1990s, but it has fallen markedly since then (for a discussion of what may have caused this decrease, see curiosity 12.2 in chapter 12). The main point here is that the NRU is neither a fixed nor a known number, varying across countries and over time within a single country. It is affected by a wide range of institutional features: the current pace of technological change, the rate at which public tastes change, participation rate changes, the degree of labor geographic mobility, job vacancy information availability, union strength, the generosity of unemployment benefits, the proportion of long-term unemployed (who lose skills), the level of payroll taxes, the existence of coordinated national wage bargaining, employment protection legislation, and the availability and efficiency of labor-retraining programs. Many institutions pushing up the NRU, such as employment protection legislation, have been put in place by governments responding to political pressure from the employed (a majority) at the expense of the unemployed (a minority). The 2003 *OECD Employment Outlook* publication reports 2001 NRU measures for the OECD countries, based on a sophisticated averaging procedure. For the United States it was 5.1 percent, for France 9.3 percent, for Germany 7.3 percent, for Canada 6.9 percent, and for Japan 3.9 percent.

At any point in time an economy's unemployment rate can be below or above its natural rate of unemployment, as the economy cycles through booms and recessions. Such cycles are called business cycles, with the economy viewed as moving through four stages, an expansionary stage, a peak, a contractionary stage, and a trough. Loosely speaking, we could consider the economy to be in a recession whenever the unemployment rate is above the NRU, and in a boom whenever the unemployment rate is below the NRU. Much macroeconomic theorizing is concerned with generating an explanation for the business cycle phenomenon. Unemployment above the NRU is referred to as *cyclical* unemployment; it is often used to measure the cost to society of unemployment.

> **Sample Exam Question 4.3:**
> "In response to the initial increase in unemployment, governments reacted by taking the wrong measures. To alleviate the pain of unemployment, they increased the generosity and duration of benefits. To limit the increase in unemployment, they moved to prevent firms from laying off workers, through tougher employment protection laws."
> Why might these be viewed as the "wrong measures"?

4.4   The Cost of Unemployment

When operating at full employment, at the natural rate of unemployment, the economy is said to be producing its *potential* GDP. Figure 4.3 shows the difference between actual output and this potential level of output. (Potential output is not known, and there is considerable controversy associated with how it should be measured; in figure 4.3 it is measured using a simple long-run trend for GDP.) This difference, called the *output gap,* can be either positive or negative, depending on whether the economy is in a boom or a recession. During a recession, when unemployment exceeds the natural rate, this gap reflects output lost forever because of a failure to operate at full employment, and so is a popular way of measuring the cost of unemployment to society. Notice in figure 4.3 how large this loss was in 1982 and 1983 when unemployment was quite high. (Check back to figure 4.2 to see the high rate of unemployment in 1982–83.) Notice also how figure 4.3 shows clearly the cyclical behavior of the economy, something macroeconomists are keen to explain.

Some economists claim that this measure of the cost of unemployment is too facile, in that it does not account for the human suffering that unemployment also entails. Although true, this failure of the unemployment measure to capture human suffering is not easily remedied. In contrast to twenty years ago, a much greater fraction of the unemployed are members of the peripheral workforce, consisting of irregular or part-time participants in

Curiosity 4.3: What Is Okun's Law?

A rule of thumb, called Okun's law, is used to translate unemployment greater than the natural rate into an output gap and thereby to measure the cost to society of excessive unemployment. An extra percentage point of unemployment, above the natural rate, corresponds to an output gap of about two percentage points of potential GDP. This rule implies, for example, that if the NRU is 6 percent, an unemployment rate of 8 percent gives rise to an output gap of 4 percent of potential GDP, about 500 billion dollars!

It may seem odd that an extra 1 percent of unemployment is associated with more than a 1 percent change in GDP. This result occurs because firms find it more profitable to meet demand fluctuations by varying the workload of current workers rather than by varying the number of employees. Firms have a tendency to hoard labor as the economy moves into a recession, electing not to lay off as many workers as the drop in their sales would dictate. They make this choice because they do not want to risk losing workers whose skills and experience make them particularly valuable to their firm when the recession ends, and this policy allows firms to avoid the costs of hiring and training new workers.

Consequently output falls by more than unemployment rises when the economy moves into a recession, and during a recovery output can increase by making fuller use of the hoarded labor. Furthermore, when hoarded labor no longer exists, firms meet many fluctuations in demand by varying overtime, rather than by varying the number of employees. This response also reflects rational behavior on the part of the firm, since existing employees are more productive than new employees, hiring and training costs can be avoided, fringe benefit costs are unaffected, and layoff costs are not incurred.

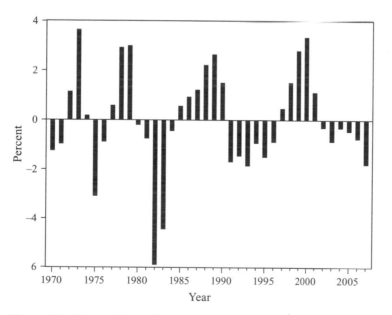

Figure 4.3   Percent Output Gap
Negative numbers mark a loss of actual output relative to actual output, measured as a percentage of actual output. Positive numbers mark periods of boom when the economy produced more than its "full-employment" output. Notice the pronounced cyclical behavior of the economy. Source: Author's calculations, undertaken by fitting a linear trend to the log of real GDP.

Curiosity 4.4: What Is Hysteresis?

The current level of unemployment may be a factor affecting the NRU. A high unemployment rate means a fall in overall worker experience and job skills, and may also change people's attitudes toward working, increasing both structural and frictional unemployment. Economists use the word hysteresis to refer to the phenomenon whereby the historical unemployment path taken by the economy affects its NRU and creates a vicious or a virtuous circle depending on whether current unemployment is high or low. Hysteresis is a possible explanation for a rising NRU during recessions, and it may be one ingredient in the remarkable performance of the U.S. economy in the late 1990s.

the job market rather than skilled adult workers who are the sole breadwinners of their family.

Sample Exam Question 4.4:
What is the connection between potential output and the NRU?

Media Illustrations

Example 1
The unemployment rate moved up to 7.8 percent (seasonally adjusted) in May from April's 7.7 percent, but not because of job losses. Indeed employment rose by a big 0.6 percent or 700,000 during the month. However, that wasn't as big as. . . .

Why would the unemployment rate be seasonally adjusted?
Seasonal adjustment removes changes that habitually occur during that month, so as to see if there is any novel change in the unemployment figure.

Complete the last sentence
. . . as big as the growth in the labor force—the number of people looking for a job.

Example 2
Employment is projected to revive at 3.5 percent per year. Since the trend rate of increase in the labor force is just less than 2 percent per year, that rate would seem to produce a healthy decline in the unemployment rate of 1.5 percentage points per year. Unfortunately, matters are not so simple because, as is by now well understood, the normal official unemployment rate does not include all the sources of slack in the labor market.

How has the 1.5 percentage point decrease in the unemployment rate been calculated?
The difference between the 3.5 percent growth in employment and the 2 percent growth in the labor force produces the 1.5 percentage point fall in the unemployment rate.

Give an example of a "source of slack" referred to in the clip, and explain what impact it would have on the 1.5 percentage point figure.
The discouraged/encouraged worker phenomenon is relevant here. The recovery may cause some discouraged workers to become encouraged to begin looking for work, causing the actual growth of the labor force to exceed its trend rate of 2 percent. This activity would decrease the 1.5 percentage point figure.

Example 3

A closer look at the numbers shows little to cheer about. The unemployment rate fell, but not because more jobs were created as implied by the press release that called it "good news" and a "good trend."

How could the unemployment rate fall if more jobs weren't created?
Job seekers could have become discouraged and stopped looking for work. This increase in the number of discouraged workers could have decreased the unemployment rate.

Why might the author of this clipping feel that there is "little to cheer about"?
It is difficult to view favorably a situation in which job prospects are so poor that people have given up even looking for a job.

Example 4

In a typical recession the unemployment rate moves up sharply, although it can take a few months for this to happen, since employers are loath to lay off people until they're sure sales are really down. Once the recession is over, the rate usually moves down again, although again there is a lag as employers don't start hiring until they're confident of the recovery.

Explain why it would be in employers' long-run interest to "hoard labor"—not to lay off as many workers as short-run considerations would suggest.
Firms are reluctant to lay off workers because they are afraid that these skilled and experienced workers may not be available after the recession. It is costly to hire and train new workers.

Use the concept of labor hoarding to offer an alternative explanation for why the unemployment rate is slow to move down after the recession ends.
When the recession ends and sales increase, the extra labor hoarded by the firm can meet the increased demand for the firm's output. There is no need for the firm to hire extra labor until demand for its output increases substantially.

Chapter Summary

- The unemployment measure is affected both by the number of new jobs created and by the number of people joining the labor force to seek jobs.

- Measured unemployment is for some reasons an underestimate and for other reasons an overestimate of the "true" rate of unemployment.

- The discouraged/encouraged worker phenomenon can explain paradoxical movements in measured unemployment.

- Full employment corresponds to the NRU or natural rate of unemployment, measured as the sum of frictional, structural, and institutionally induced unemployment.

- The output gap, often calculated by a rule of thumb called Okun's law, is used to measure the cost of unemployment to society.

Formula Definitions

- Unemployment rate $= \dfrac{\text{Unemployed}}{\text{Labor force}}$

- Participation rate $= \dfrac{\text{Labor force}}{\text{Adult population}}$

Media Exercises

(Group B questions require more thought.)

A1. **In any economic slowdown the unemployment rate rises, first and foremost, because employment growth slows or actually goes into negative territory. But how high the jobless rate goes can also depend very crucially on exactly how fast the labor force decides to grow.**

Explain how labor force growth plays a role here.

A2. **Labor force growth is the great unknown in forecasting unemployment rates because people's reactions are very difficult to gauge. For example, during recessions, will people not bother looking for a job because of the difficulty in finding one, or will they look even harder because of the need for additional family income when wage increases are coming in below the inflation rate?**

a. Explain how labor force growth influences the unemployment rate.

b. What impact will the two cited examples have on the measured unemployment rate?

A3. **This council, an advisory body with business and union representation, decided to rethink the concept of unemployment. It was intent on unraveling the paradox of substantial new job creation coupled with a high and largely unyielding jobless rate.**

How could this paradox come about?

A4. **Indeed, the council looks for pretty sluggish job growth during the rest of the year. That's likely to keep the unemployment rate stagnant, particularly as the recent increases in employment will probably encourage more people to join the labor force.**

a. Why would people be encouraged to join the labor force?

b. How will this development affect the unemployment rate?

c. What terminology do economists use to refer to this phenomenon?

A5. **The reduction in the unemployment rate that is projected to take place as a result of the budget proposals is expected to be moderated as participation rates continue to _____.**

Fill in the blank in this clip, and explain your rationale.

A6. **This is the critical assumption in the projection. If participation rates turn out to be _____, the unemployment rate will be higher, and vice versa for lower participation rates.**

Fill in the blank in this clip, and explain your rationale.

A7. **We consider it entirely possible that an encouraged worker effect will set in when employment picks up, which could lead to a paradoxical rise in the unemployment rate.**

Explain how this paradox could come about.

A8. **More job losses in the manufacturing sector helped pull employment down by 390,000 in November. Only the fact that this seasonally adjusted employment drop was matched by a _____ in the labor force kept the unemployment rate steady.**

Fill in the blank and explain your rationale.

A9. **Nationally the monthly survey of American households found 387,000 more people at work in February than in January, but many of the new jobs were only part-time, the Labor Department reported.**

    a. Does the creation of part-time jobs affect unemployment in the same way as the creation of full-time jobs?

    b. What can you say about the unemployment rate from this information?

A10. **The Bureau of Labor Statistics said Friday that the country lost 190,000 jobs in August and noted that the unemployment rate would be more than two percentage points higher than a year ago if there weren't so many. . . .**

Complete this clipping.

A11. **Job creation in October was much more robust than most forecasters had predicted, but the number of people either working or looking for work increased even more sharply.**

    a. What is happening to the unemployment rate?

    b. Should this news be viewed as positive or negative? Why?

A12. **And so we find ourselves in the strange situation in which employment is rising and at the same time unemployment is rising.**

Explain this phenomenon.

A13. **This is the critical assumption in the unemployment rate projection. If participation rates turn out to be higher, the unemployment rate will be _____, and if participation rates turn out to be lower, the unemployment rate will be _____.**

Fill in the blanks.

A14. **In the United States or Britain, economic recoveries put people back to work relatively quickly. But Germany is bogged down by high labor costs and other structural factors that discourage hiring. So the recent unemployment rate of 11.4 percent is not likely to fall by much in the near future.**

By what name would economists refer to this high German unemployment rate?

A15. **In the longer term, however, it is still more vital that Germany and the rest of Europe attack the high taxes, overgenerous welfare benefits, onerous labor-market restrictions, and red tape that are choking growth in _____.**

Fill in the blank.

A16. Even if employment continues to climb, the jobless rate will likely stay around its current level for the balance of this year, Cramer said. That's because. . . .

Complete this clipping.

A17. Although there was stellar job growth in 2002, it had little impact on the jobless rate because. . . ."

Complete this clipping.

A18. U.S. employers went on a hiring spree in October, adding 337,000 new jobs, many of them for hurricane cleanup. Despite this massive hiring the Labor Department reported a rise in the unemployment rate from 5.4 to 5.5 percent. The breakdown was as follows: the jobless rate for black people jumped to 10.7 from 10.3 percent; the rate for Hispanics fell to 6.7 from 7.1 percent, the rate for teenagers grew to 17.2 from 16.6 percent, and the rate for whites held at 4.7 percent.

How would you explain the rise in the unemployment rate in the face of so many new jobs.

B1. Labor force growth has, in the past, tended to reflect the economic situation. In almost all postwar recession years the participation rate fell slightly, with the result that. . . .

Complete this clipping by explaining how this phenomenon would affect the measured level of unemployment as the economy moved into recession.

B2. In fairness, the strong female job growth occurred partly because so many more women were available to work. The female participation rate rose to 55 percent from just 45 percent a decade earlier. That translated into an extra 17 million women in the labor force. In contrast, the male participation rate fell during the period, to 76 percent from 77 percent, which meant that there were only an extra ten million men in the labor force.

a. What is the definition of the female participation rate?

b. If the male participation rate fell, why are there more men in the labor force?

c. Can we conclude from this information that the female unemployment rate must have fallen relative to the male unemployment rate? Why or why not?

B3. Our jobless rate fell last month to its lowest level in three years. But if you think it's a sign that the economy is suddenly moving up, look again.

Why wouldn't a fall in the unemployment rate be a sign that the economy is moving up?

B4. **Unemployment insurance may increase the incidence and length of jobless-ness and has certain inflationary attributes, but these drawbacks are out-weighed by the positive social factors, according to a new study published by the Brookings Institution.**

a. How does unemployment insurance increase the incidence of joblessness?

b. How does it increase the length of joblessness?

B5. **There are some subsidy features to unemployment insurance, primarily for jobs that are unattractive or that offer seasonal or unstable employment. Without this subsidy, paid mainly by the government, many unskilled jobs would go begging.**

a. Explain how unemployment insurance subsidizes certain kinds of jobs.

b. What do you think would happen to wages paid for these jobs if unemployment insurance ceased to exist?

B6. **He is critical of the flat rate contribution schedule for unemployment insurance, which he says acts as a subsidy from companies with more stable employment levels to those which frequently lay off workers. This subsidy encourages firms to rely more heavily on layoffs of workers than other methods of adjusting to fluctuations in the demand for their output. He suggests that the excessive and inefficient bias toward layoffs in the system could be eliminated by adopting a system of experience rating, as is done in some states—a company's contribu-tions would be related to the amount of benefits drawn by its employees in the past.**

a. Does this subsidy mean that firms prone to laying off employees are paying lower wages than they would otherwise? Explain why or why not.

b. Would adoption of experience rating cause unemployment to become more or less sensitive to recessions? Explain.

B7. **Despite the changed composition of the jobless ranks, today's high unemploy-ment level is portrayed by some as a disaster of Great Depression proportions.**

Of what relevance here is the changed composition of the jobless?

B8. **Three percent real GDP growth is just about enough to keep the unemployment rate constant.**

Why wouldn't a zero growth rate keep unemployment constant?

B9. **Unfortunately, the workforce in the 1990s is projected to expand much more slowly in coming years both because the population is not increasing as rapidly and because it is unlikely that the participation of women will keep _____.**

   a. Why would a slower growth in the work force be regarded as unfortunate? Why might some view it as fortunate? Hint: Compare short- and long-run implications.

   b. Fill in the blank.

B10. **If the participation rate had remained steady instead of falling since the recession began, the unemployment rate would be 1.8 percent _____.**

   Fill in the blank.

B11. **The number of jobs created, rather than the unemployment rate, gives a more timely indication of the state of the economy.**

   Explain what thinking must lie behind this claim.

B12. **Low-paid, part-time jobs have long been exempt from tax and social security contributions. Many economists think that the government's plans to end this exemption will. . . .**

   Complete this clipping.

B13. **The chief problem is a sticky labor market, caused mainly by the hefty social security charges that employers have to pay for their workers, and by the high cost of laying them off. _____ may be as high as 10 percent.**

   Fill in the blank.

B14. **Though President Clinton has called for a global summit on unemployment, neither the president nor his critics have clearly formulated the most important economic question raised by his economic proposals. Should the United States, like the European Community, accept an ever higher _____ as the cost of expanding social programs.**

   Fill in the blank, and explain your rationale.

B15. **Federal government changes to the EI (employment insurance) program have caused the Atlantic region to suffer from two conflicting problems simultaneously—high unemployment and a labor shortage.**

   What EI changes could have caused this paradoxical situation?

B16. **One theory as to why productivity in Canada and Europe does not adjust to recessions as robustly as the United States is that the U.S. market is inherently more flexible. Its labor laws and work force practices allow. . . .**

Complete this statement to explain why productivity in the United States does not decline in recessions as rapidly as in Canada and Europe.

Numerical Exercises

(Group B questions require more thought.)

AN1. If the population 16 years of age and older is 160 million, the number of discouraged workers is 10 million, the labor force is 110 million, and total employment is 90 million, then what is the measured unemployment rate?

AN2. Suppose that the population over age 15 is 150 million, the number of discouraged workers is 5 million, the participation rate is 70 percent, and the unemployment rate is 10 percent. How many officially unemployed are there?

AN3. Suppose that the population over age 15 is 150 million, the participation rate is 60 percent, and the unemployment rate is 10 percent. If the number of encouraged workers increases by 2 million, what does the participation rate become?

AN4. Suppose that the population over age 15 is 150 million, the number of discouraged workers is 5 million, the unemployment rate is 10 percent, and there are 90 million employed. What is the participation rate?

AN5. Suppose that frictional unemployment is 1 percent, structural unemployment is 2 percent, cyclical unemployment is 3 percent, and unemployment due to unemployment insurance and minimum wage legislation is 4 percent. Then, based on this information, what is the NRU?

AN6. Suppose that the population over age 15 is 25 million, the participation rate is 80 percent, the number of discouraged workers is 1 million, the number of people with full-time jobs is 16 million, and the number of people with part-time jobs is 2 million. What is the measured unemployment rate?

AN7. Suppose that potential GDP is $900 billion and current unemployment is 10.5 percent. What would GDP have been if unemployment had been only 7.5 percent? Hint: Use Okun's law.

AN8. Suppose that the noninstitutionalized population 16 years of age and over is 20 million, 10 million of whom are female; the labor force is 16 million, 6 million of whom are female; and the number of people employed is 15 million, 5.5 million of whom are female. What is the female participation rate?

BN1. Suppose that the population over age 15 is 140 million, the participation rate is 60 percent, and the unemployment rate is 10 percent. If the number of discouraged workers increases by 2 million, what does the unemployment rate become?

BN2. Suppose that the population over age 15 is 150 million, the participation rate is 60 percent, and the unemployment rate is 10 percent. If the labor force grows by 3 percent and employment grows by 2 percent, what does the unemployment rate become?

5 The Role of Aggregate Demand

The purpose of this chapter is to examine the role played by aggregate demand for goods and services in determining the economy's level of national income, and thus explain the heart of the Keynesian approach to macroeconomics. Although this approach has been greatly modified over time, it remains the intellectual foundation of modern views of the macroeconomy. Its implication that government expenditure increases (or tax decreases) can pull the economy out of a recession offered policy activists a rationale for government intervention in the operation of the economy to achieve goals such as full employment.

With the publication of *The General Theory of Employment, Interest, and Money* in the midst of the Great Depression, John Maynard Keynes revolutionized macroeconomic thinking in many ways. He introduced a model he thought capable of explaining the existence of prolonged unemployment, something that previous macroeconomic models did not do. He stimulated research on fundamental economic relationships, such as the consumption function (how consumption demand responds to income changes), that had been overlooked. He argued persuasively for the need for government intervention in the operation of the economy, an issue that is still contentious, and he placed the level of aggregate demand for goods and services at center stage of macroeconomic analysis, a position it has maintained to this day, although now in tandem with other macroeconomic variables. Appendix 5.1 at the end of this chapter offers some perspective on Keynes's contribution by describing the classical approach to macroeconomics—the school of macroeconomic thought dominant prior to publication of Keynes's theory.

Milton Friedman, the leader of a school of thought opposing the Keynesian view of the world, in 1965 said, "We are all Keynesians now, and nobody is any longer a Keynesian." What he meant was that Keynes had so clearly described the working parts of the modern macroeconomy that whether you agreed with his assessment or not, you had to use his basic ideas and language even to disagree, which most economists were then—and still are—doing. The purpose of this chapter is to prepare for later macroeconomic analysis by learning these basic ideas, the foundation of macroeconomic thinking.

Upon completion of this chapter you should

- understand the central role played by aggregate demand in determining the level of national income,

- know the concept of the multiplier and so understand why a change in aggregate demand of x dollars changes national income by a multiple of x dollars,

- understand why changes in inventories can be used as a forecasting device,

- be familiar with the "crowding-out" phenomenon—the process whereby increasing government spending decreases ("crowds out") other types of aggregate demand, and

- be conversant with issues surrounding budget deficits and the national debt.

5.1   Aggregate Demand

The general idea behind the Keynesian approach is that natural forces cause our output of goods and services (i.e., aggregate supply, our national income) to match the level of aggregate demand for our goods and services. This match is called an *equilibrium* because at such a position there are no pressures for change. The automatic movement of income to match aggregate demand has two implications. First, to predict the level of national income, we should look at what is happening to the level of aggregate demand for our goods and services. Second, to influence the level of national income, we can change any component of domestic aggregate demand over which we have control—by changing government spending, for example, we can influence the economy and thereby achieve desired ends such as avoiding unemployment.

Keynes viewed aggregate demand for goods and services as comprising four major types of demand: demand by consumers for things such as toys and haircuts, referred to as C for consumption demand; demand by business firms for things such as factories, machinery, and delivery trucks, referred to as I for investment demand; demand by the government for things such as hospitals, accountants, and armies, referred to as G for government demand; and demand by foreigners for goods we send abroad, such as wheat and lumber, referred to as X for exports. Demand in each of these sectors includes demand for imported as well as domestic goods and services. To obtain what is important for the Keynesian view, aggregate demand for *domestically produced* goods and services, imports must be subtracted from the sum of C, I, G, and X. Textbooks often use a circular flow diagram to illustrate how these components of aggregate demand contribute to equilibrium. For those interested, this diagram (figure 5.5) is presented in appendix 5.2 at the end of this chapter.

Keynes split demand up into these different categories for a good reason. He believed that it would be easier for economists to analyze these categories of demand separately rather than as an aggregate. For example, the factors that determine the level of consumption demand are different from those determining investment demand; recognizing this difference should provide better insight into the operation of the economy and how it might respond to policy. Much of the historical development of the Keynesian approach has taken the form of investigating in detail the economic forces that determine demand in one of these sectors and then seeing the implications that this analysis has for the operation of the economy as a whole.

One of the simplest of Keynes's insights is that the level of consumption demand is affected by the level of income. As income increases, so does consumption, but not by as much because income earners (on average) save some income and set some aside to pay taxes. Economists usually capture this relationship by specifying that consumption is a function of after-tax (or *disposable*) income. As disposable income increases by, say, a thousand dollars, consumption demand increases by some fraction of the thousand dollars, say by $800. This fraction (0.8 in this example) is called the *marginal propensity to consume* (MPC). The MPC tells us what fraction of an *additional* dollar of disposable income will be spent on consumption. The fraction not spent on consumption is called the *marginal propensity to save*. This *consumption function*, as it is known, is a major ingredient in the Keynesian explanation of the determination of income. Much more complicated variants of the consumption function have been developed, involving additional explanatory variables, but this simple version suffices to illustrate the Keynesian approach. The other categories of aggregate demand also have functions explaining their levels, but for now we ignore these functions and assume the categories are fixed at constant levels.

Sample Exam Question 5.1:

In 2007 personal disposable income was $10,171 billion and consumption was $9,710 billion; in 2008 these figures were $10,646 and $10,057.

What is the MPC out of disposable income?

5.2 Determining National Income

Keynes believed that natural forces operating in the economy cause the level of aggregate supply of domestically produced goods and services (*AS*), also known as national income, to move in order to meet the level of aggregate demand for goods and services (*AD*). What are these forces?

Suppose that aggregate demand exceeds national income/output, a situation referred to as *excess aggregate demand*. In this case the output produced by the economy is not enough to satisfy all the aggregate demand, so firms producing and selling goods should experience a fall in inventories, a loss in sales from lack of inventories, or an increase in backlogged orders. Firms providing services should discover that some customers must be turned away or asked to schedule a much later appointment. Profit-maximizing firms could react to this situation in one of three main ways:

1. They could increase output to meet the higher level of aggregate demand by using existing employees and equipment more productively, by hiring additional workers, or by increasing workers' hours. Such firms are *quantity adjusters.*

2. They could increase prices to induce people to decrease aggregate demand to the level of output that is being produced. Such firms are *price adjusters.*

3. They could adopt some combination of the two preceding options, adjusting both price and quantity at the same time.

Let us look at each of these options in turn.

Quantity adjusting.   By increasing production, the firm addresses directly the problem of shrinking inventories or lost business. This is an especially appealing strategy if the firm is currently operating at less than full capacity, since increasing output can be accomplished at little additional cost.

Price adjusting.   This option is forced on a firm when it is operating at full capacity, since it is not possible to increase output.

Adjusting both price and quantity.   It could be that the firm is not at full capacity but is operating sufficiently close to full capacity that output increases incur a higher per-unit cost than the prevailing price. Workers may have to be paid overtime, or new, inexperienced (and therefore less productive) workers may need to be hired. Then a firm will increase output only if the price also increases, giving rise to a combination of price and quantity adjustments.

Curiosity 5.1: What about Unwanted Investment in Inventories?

Keynes specified each of the four demands—consumption demand, investment demand, government demand, and export demand—as that which a sector of the economy—consumers, business firms, the government, or foreigners—would *want* to purchase during any year. If a firm wanted to build up its inventories (e.g., because its business is growing), this wanted investment in inventories would be included in the Keynesian aggregate demand. But if inventory changes were not desired (e.g., because of an unexpected fall in sales), they would not be included in the Keynesian aggregate demand figure. Unwanted investment in inventories, discussed in chapter 3 as an accounting device enabling adding up demands to measure GDP, is not part of Keynesian aggregate demand.

As this discussion of quantity and price adjusting suggests, if firms are operating well below full capacity, and output can be increased without raising unit cost, then quantity adjustment is appropriate. If firms are operating at full capacity, and output cannot be increased, price adjustment is appropriate. If the firm is at an intermediate stage, at which output increases raise unit costs, both prices and output should be increased to maximize profit.

In the most simplified version of the Keynesian analysis, which we adopt in this chapter, the economy is specified to be operating well below full capacity so that quantity adjustment occurs and thus national income/output moves to equate itself to aggregate demand.

A similar result holds when national income exceeds aggregate demand. In this case not all of the output produced by the economy is bought. So firms producing and selling goods should experience a buildup of inventories, and firms providing services should discover that some employees are often idle. Profit-maximizing firms can react to this situation in one of three main ways:

1. Adjust quantity. Lay off workers or cut back workers' hours to stop producing the unwanted output.

2. Adjust price. Decrease prices to induce people to increase aggregate demand by enough to buy all of the output being produced.

3. Adopt some combination of the two preceding options. Adjust both price and quantity at the same time.

Quantity adjustment is the most natural reaction because it directly attacks the inventory buildup and the problem of idle employees. Cutting price is not likely to be a profit-maximizing move, even in tandem with output reduction, unless costs fall as well. The most likely scenario is that national income/output will adjust to match aggregate demand. As noted earlier, this is the heart of the Keynesian analysis: aggregate demand is the driving force that determines the level of national income.

> **Sample Exam Question 5.2:**
> "President Obama's first major policy decision is to call for a massive increase in government spending. This increase in aggregate demand should not flame inflation because. . . ."
> Complete this clipping.

5.3   The Multiplier

The policy conclusion of this Keynesian analysis is that by increasing aggregate demand the government can increase national income. An obvious way of doing so is by increasing government spending *G*. By this is meant a permanent increase in the level of government spending, say from $700 billion a year to $708 billion per year. (A one-time increase in government spending would increase income only temporarily.)

Suppose that *G* is increased by $8 billion, creating an excess demand of $8 billion. Inventories fall and business is turned away, signaling to producers that there is excess demand, so they react by increasing output/income. Suppose that national output/income increases by $8 billion. Will this result stop the forces pushing up output/income?

Although the initial excess demand of $8 billion has now been met by $8 billion of extra output, and it would seem that the forces pushing up income/output would be eliminated, this assumption is not so. This $8 billion increase in income itself creates extra demand. Consumers will want to increase consumption demand now that their income is higher, reopening the excess demand gap. This reaction renews the forces that stimulate the economy, causing this process to repeat itself and thus leading to an ever larger income level.

This repetitive process is outlined in figure 5.1, where the notation should be obvious (e.g., ↑ agg *D* for g&s stands for an increase in aggregate demand for goods and services).

General process	Numerical example
↑G ⇒ ↑ agg D for g & s	$8b ↑G ⇒ $8b ↑ agg D for g & s
⇒ excess D for g & s	⇒ $8b excess D for g & s
⇒ ↓ inventories, lost business	⇒ $8b ↓ inventories, lost business
⇒ signal to firms	⇒ signal to firms
⇒ ↑ output ⇒ ↓ excess D	⇒ $8b ↑ output ⇒ $8b ↓ excess D
⇒ ↑ income	⇒ **$8b ↑ income**
⇒ ↑ consumption demand	⇒ $5.6b ↑ consumption demand
⇒ excess demand, but smaller	⇒ $5.6b excess D
⇒ ↓ inventories and so repeat process	⇒ $5.6b ↓ inventories, etc.
	⇒ $5.6b ↑ output ⇒ $5.6b ↓ excess D
	⇒ **$5.6b ↑ income** (so cumulative ↑ income is $13.6b)
	⇒ $3.9b ↑ consumption demand
	⇒ $3.9b excess D
	⇒ $3.9b ↓ inventories, etc.
	⇒ $3.9b ↑ output ⇒ $3.9b ↓ excess D
	⇒ **$3.9b ↑ income** (so cumulative ↑ income is $17.5b)
	⇒ $2.7b ↑ consumption demand
	⇒ and so on until cumulative ↑ income reaches $26.7b

Figure 5.1   The Multiplier Process

In the numerical example, a dollar increase in income increases consumption by 0.7 dollars. The original increase in government spending of $8 billion leads to an ultimate increase in income of $26.7 billion, implying a multiplier of 3.33.

For the reader interested, this process can also be illustrated on a classic macroeconomic diagram, the 45 degree line diagram, shown in appendix 5.3 at the end of this chapter.

At first glance it seems as though the process outlined in figure 5.1 could go on forever, but it does not. Although the excess demand is continually being renewed, the magnitude of this renewal is shrinking, so this iterative process eventually dies out. The numerical example began with $8 billion excess demand. This led to an income increase of $8 billion, which in turn caused aggregate demand to increase, but by less than $8 billion. Why? Consumers use part of any increase in income to pay extra taxes and augment savings, causing the increase in consumption demand to fall well short of $8 billion. In this numerical example, consumption increases by 70 percent of the income increase. The next time the economy cycles through this iterative process, income increases again, but by less than $8 billion, and the third time through it increases by still less, as shown in the numerical example.

This process is also illustrated in figure 5.2 where the economy begins at income level $700 billion, experiences an increase in government spending of $8 billion, and then moves over time to a higher income level, eventually reaching an income of $726.7 billion.

Because of the renewal of aggregate demand, the ultimate increase in national income resulting from the $8 billion increase in government spending is more than $8 billion. If we had continued the iterative calculations in our numerical example, the ultimate cumulative increase in income would have turned out to be $26.7 billion. In this example each dollar increase in government spending serves eventually to increase income by 3.3

Income ($billion)

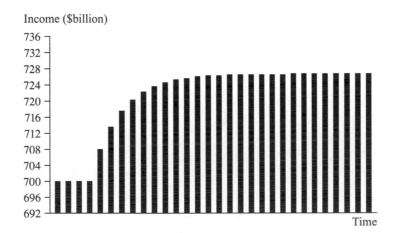

Figure 5.2   The Multiplier Process
The economy is initially in equilibrium at income level $700 billion when in the fifth time period government spending is increased by $8 billion, increasing income to $708 billion. As the multiplier process continues, income increases in each period by lesser and lesser amounts until it settles at $726.7 billion.

Curiosity 5.2: What Is the Multiplier?

A formal definition of the multiplier is the change in the *equilibrium* level of income per change in government spending. (The equilibrium level of income, discussed in Chapter 1, is that income level at which aggregate demand for goods and services equals aggregate supply of goods and services.) It is calculated as

$$\text{Multiplier} = \frac{\Delta \text{GDP}}{\Delta G}$$

where ΔGDP is the change in equilibrium income resulting from a change in government spending of size ΔG. A common use of the multiplier is to enable calculation of the increase in government spending that is needed to push the economy to a desired income level. Suppose, for example, that we wish to increase the income level by $10 billion, and the multiplier is 4. From the definition of the multiplier we obtain $4 = 10/\Delta G$, implying that the required $\Delta G = \$2.5$ billion.

This example of a multiplier of 4 should not be taken literally. The multiplier value varies across countries and within a single country over time. Furthermore its actual value is difficult to measure. Some economists believe its value is very small, perhaps less than one, depending on the current state of the economy. For example, in 2009 the government was increasing spending dramatically, trying to stimulate the economy through the multiplier process. But because of the subprime mortgage problem and bankruptcies of large financial corporations, the 2009 recession involved a lot of uncertainty. The extra government spending was creating income, but people were not spending that income as the multiplier process requires; instead, they were paying down debt, or saving to create a backup should they lose their jobs. Because of this the multiplier in 2009 was very small.

To be careful, we should really call the multiplier "the income multiplier with respect to government spending," so as not to confuse it with other multipliers, but we follow tradition and call it "the" multiplier, seldom using the quotes. Many other multipliers exist, all giving the change in something of interest per change in something over which we have control. Some examples are the income multiplier with respect to the money supply, giving the change in equilibrium income per change in the money supply, and the employment multiplier with respect to the tax rate, giving the change in equilibrium employment per change in the tax rate. The latter multiplier should be negative because an increase in the tax rate should decrease disposable income and thus lower consumption demand, decreasing aggregate demand for goods and services.

It is possible to derive an algebraic formula for the multiplier, but this is not very useful because the formula depends on the algebraic model being used to represent the economy. The more complicated the model, the more complicated is the formula for the multiplier.

dollars. In this case the *income multiplier with respect to government spending*, or the increase in equilibrium income due to a dollar increase in government spending—referred to casually as "the" multiplier—is said to be 3.3. The iterative process whereby an increase in government spending leads to an extended increase in income is called the *multiplier process*.

The heart of the multiplier process is consumption demand induced by income increases. These consumption demand increases keep the multiplier process going. A government decision to build an airplane-producing plant in a small town should have a significant multiplier effect on that town as incomes earned by those building the plant and employed in the plant are spent in town shops and restaurants. In turn these businesses and new businesses drawn in by the prosperity will need to hire more workers who will spend part of their incomes in local shops, and so on, expanding this prosperity through the multiplier process.

The value of the multiplier in the real world is subject to much debate, with estimates ranging from about 2.6 to about 0.6. Anything that reduces the increase in domestic aggregate demand for goods and services caused by an increase in income will slow the multiplier process down and decrease the value of the multiplier. A lower MPC, a higher tax rate, and a higher marginal propensity to import are examples.

> **Sample Exam Question 5.3:**
> Suppose that a dollar increase in income increases aggregate demand for goods and services by 60 cents.
>
> If the government increases its spending by $10 billion, after three rounds of the multiplier process by how much will the level of income have increased?

5.4   How Big Is the Multiplier?

Is it better to have a large or a small multiplier? In some circumstances a large multiplier is desirable. In 2009, for example, Barak Obama was faced with a recession of immense scale; it was obvious that a huge economic stimulus was needed, and because government spending was constrained by deficit spending worries and political disagreements, a large multiplier was needed to provide this stimulus. But in general it is better to have a small multiplier, for two reasons:

1. Our knowledge of the economy and how it operates is imperfect, so deciding when and by how much to change government spending is not an exact science. A large multiplier magnifies any mistake by the government.

2. A large multiplier means that *any* change in aggregate demand, not just a change in government spending, has a substantive impact on economic activity. All economies

are subject to irregular changes in aggregate demand, such as changes in export demand due to changes in foreign economies, or changes in investment demand due to new inventions. With a high multiplier these changes have a large impact on economic activity, creating instability.

In light of these two problems, anything that causes the multiplier to become smaller is considered desirable because it insulates the economy from the effects of policy errors and aggregate demand shocks. Government policies that serve to reduce the multiplier without any need for time-consuming legislative action are called *automatic stabilizers*. Government transfer payment programs such as unemployment insurance and welfare are good examples of this. As the economy is stimulated, for example, some of the people who receive unemployment insurance will find jobs. The increase in their income is partially offset by lost unemployment insurance payments. Consequently the increase in their consumption demand is smaller than if there had been no unemployment insurance, so the strength of the multiplier process is weakened. Similarly a negative shock to the economy is cushioned because those losing their jobs collect unemployment insurance and so do not decrease consumption demand by as much as they would otherwise.

Automatic stabilizers make the multiplier smaller than it would otherwise be, but there are many other phenomena that also lower the value of the multiplier. Two of the more obvious of these are income taxes and imports. An increase in income at each stage of the multiplier process is not all available for spending; some is required to pay income taxes on the extra income earned. Because taxes inhibit the rise in consumption spending, aggregate demand does not increase by as much at each stage of the multiplier process, so the multiplier process is weaker. The increase in consumption demand at each stage of the multiplier process is not all on domestically produced goods and services. Some demand goes to imports. At each stage of the multiplier process, therefore, aggregate demand for domestically produced goods and services does not increase by as much, so the multiplier process is weaker.

A less obvious factor weakening the multiplier process is the interest rate. As income increases, people like to hold more money (cash) for two reasons. First, more money is needed to facilitate a higher level of production. (Although money is not a physical input to the production process, just try producing anything without money on hand! The banking crisis in 2008 to 2009 made this painfully evident.) And second, more money is needed to facilitate the higher consumption spending induced by the higher income. This extra demand for money, if not met by the monetary authorities, causes the price of money, the interest rate, to rise. (Chapter 10 discusses the interest rate.)

A higher interest rate reduces all four of the major types of aggregate demand:

1. Consumption falls because a higher interest rate tempts people to save rather than consume. Moreover monthly payments on loans to purchase major consumer durables become too high for many would-be buyers.

Curiosity 5.3: What Is a Leading Indicator?

Inventory behavior is an example of a leading indicator—a variable that consistently changes a few months in advance of changes in macroeconomic activity and so can be used to forecast business cycles. Experience has shown that depending on a single leading indicator is unwise, but combining several leading indicators into a composite index produces much better forecasts of business cycles. One such composite is the *Leading Economic Index*, compiled monthly by the Conference Board, a private, not-for-profit, nonadvocacy organization that publishes several other statistical series including coincident, lagging, help-wanted, consumer confidence, and business confidence indexes. Check www.tch-indicators.org.

This composite index provides on average about twelve-month advance warning of an impending recession. The indicators that make up the index vary as improvements are made; its components in 2009, in order of importance (with weights in parentheses), were as follows.

1. M2 money supply in real dollars (0.358) (explained in chapter 8).

2. Average workweek in manufacturing (0.255).

3. Spread between long-term and short-term interest rates as measured by the difference between the ten-year Treasury and the federal funds rate (0.099) (interest rates are discussed in chapter 10).

4. Manufacturers' new orders for consumer goods in real dollars (0.077).

5. Vendor performance as measured by percentage of companies reporting slower deliveries from suppliers (0.068).

6. Standard and Poor's index of 500 common stock prices (0.039).

7. Average weekly initial unemployment claims (inverted to produce a number that increases during expansions) (0.031).

8. University of Michigan index of consumer expectations (0.028).

9. New private housing authorized by local building permits (0.027).

10. Manufacturers' new orders for plant and equipment in real dollars (0.018).

A weighted average of the percentage changes in each of these components produces the percentage change in the index each month. (An odd thing about these weights is that they reflect the variability in the respective measures, as opposed to their relative success in forecasting a recession.) A simple rule of thumb often used is that three consecutive months of decline in the index are a sign that the economy will fall into recession.

2. Investment falls because the higher costs of borrowing money to undertake an investment project may make that project unprofitable. Moreover some firms with money to
   invest discover that they can earn a higher return from loaning it out than from investing it in new equipment.

3. Government spending falls because local governments may decide to wait for lower
   interest costs before borrowing to finance projects such as a library or a swimming
   pool.

4. Export demand falls because the rise in interest rates causes foreigners to buy more of
   our financial assets, increasing the demand for our dollars on the foreign exchange
   market. This higher demand increases the value of our dollar, making it more expensive
   for foreigners to buy our exports. (See chapter 13 for more on this international
   phenomenon.)

The interest rate can play a strong role in reducing the size of the multiplier. One economic model has estimated the multiplier to be about 2.0 if the interest rate is held constant,
but only about 0.6 if the interest rate is allowed to rise.

All four examples of reactions that lower the multiplier value operate regardless of
whether the initial stimulus to aggregate demand takes the form of an increase in government spending or an increase in some other form of aggregate demand. In the case of an
increase in government spending, however, the means used to finance that spending can
have an additional offsetting impact on aggregate demand, referred to as *crowding out*.
This terminology comes about because if the government is to gain control over more
resources, it may in part need to do so by shouldering aside, or crowding out, others who
were controlling those resources.

The Keynesian story of the multiplier phenomenon traditionally sweeps under the rug
the fact that the government must somehow finance an increase in spending. This is
important because the means chosen to finance spending may have an influence on aggregate demand that to some extent could offset the stimulus of the fiscal action. An increase
in government spending can be financed in three basic ways: raising taxes, selling bonds
to the public, and selling bonds to the central bank (often referred to as *printing money*).
Let us look at the crowding out that may occur with each of these three financing
means.

Taxation

If taxes are raised to finance an increase in government spending, disposable income falls
and so consumers reduce consumption. The decrease in consumption demand partially
offsets the increase in government spending, reducing the size of the multiplier. The offset
is only partial because an increase in government spending of one dollar increases aggregate demand by one dollar, but an increase of taxes by one dollar decreases aggregate
demand by less than one dollar—the extra dollar for taxes comes partly from reducing

saving. When the increase in government spending is financed by raising taxes, the multiplier is called the *balanced-budget multiplier*. This name reflects the fact that in this case the policy action has no impact on the size of the government's budget deficit or surplus.

Selling Bonds to the Public

Keynesians implicitly assume that the government sells bonds to the public to finance an increase in its spending, so the usual multiplier concept refers to this context. Crowding out comes about in two ways:

1. *Raising interest rates.* To sell bonds, the government must make them attractive, so it must raise the interest rate. The higher interest rate crowds out all types of spending, as explained earlier.
2. *Smoothing consumption.* When the bonds mature, interest and principal must be paid to the bondholders. People may believe that future taxes will be higher as a result and react by increasing saving (decreasing current consumption demand) to build up a reserve so that those anticipated higher taxes can be paid without disrupting future consumption levels. This phenomenon is usually attributed to David Ricardo.

Printing Money

Financing increases in government spending by raising taxes or by selling bonds to the public leaves the supply of money in the economy unchanged. In contrast, financing by selling bonds to the central bank increases the money supply. When buying a government bond (or any bond, for that matter), the central bank writes a check against itself and thereby creates money out of thin air. This fact explains why this means of financing is referred to as *printing money*. The U.S. central bank is often referred to as "the Fed," short for the Federal Reserve System. (Chapter 8 explains the money creation process.)

Although printing money seems like an attractive way for a government to finance its spending, the reader should be warned that printing too much money creates inflation. In the absence of an independent central bank, politicians tend to print too much money, explaining why many countries experience high inflation rates. Chapter 9 explains the link between inflation and money creation.

Financing by printing money mixes a *fiscal* policy of increased government spending with a *monetary* policy of increasing the money supply. In this case there are no crowding-out effects due to the financing means. The operation of the multiplier is in fact strengthened by the increase in the money supply because (as explained in chapter 9) an increase in the money supply also stimulates the economy.

Monetarists are prominent critics of the Keynesian approach. They claim that crowding-out forces are strong, rendering fiscal policy weak. They also claim that financing fiscal policy by printing money is the only way any substantive impact can be made on GDP, and that the impact is due not to the increase in government spending but rather to the increase in the money supply. In their view the quantity of money in the economy is the proper focus of attention in analyzing the macroeconomy, something that so far has been ignored. We will return to this issue in chapters 8 and 9.

Sample Exam Question 5.4:
"Of course, if Washington needed less cash it would undoubtedly ease the strain on the states and the corporate sector."

(a) What does Washington needing cash mean? (b) What is the strain on the states and the corporate sector that is referred to?

5.5   Inventories and Forecasting

In figure 5.1 inventory changes play an important role, mainly serving as a signaling device that alerts producers to changes in aggregate demand. They also have two other important roles in macroeconomics.

First, desired inventory changes are a component of aggregate demand that affects the dynamics of an economy's reaction to disequilibrium, thereby playing an important role in the propagation and maintenance of business cycles. Consider a stimulating dose of fiscal policy. As the economy goes through the multiplier process, inventories are constantly falling because aggregate demand is continually a bit higher than output. Suppose that firms do nothing about these reductions. Then, after the multiplier process has worked itself out, inventories will have fallen to an undesirably low level. To prevent this result, firms must produce some extra output during the multiplier process. The time path followed by the economy during the multiplier process is affected by when and how quickly the firm decides to do so. If, for example, the firm elects to increase output to restore inventory levels at a late stage in the multiplier process, the level of national income could temporarily overshoot its final level.

Second, inventory changes can help in forecasting the direction of the economy. Their use in this regard occurs frequently in newspaper commentary, where they play a more prominent role than complex economic models built expressly for forecasting purposes.

When inventory levels are unusually high or are rising rapidly, firms should react by cutting back on production—meeting demand out of inventory—to decrease inventory levels to a more desirable level. This production cutback decreases income, however, setting the multiplier process in motion and pushing the economy toward a recession. We should forecast a downturn in the economy.

When inventory levels are unusually low or are falling rapidly, firms should react by increasing production to build inventories up to a more desirable level. The production increase also increases income, however, setting the multiplier process in motion and thereby pushing the economy to an even higher level of income. We should forecast an upturn in the economy.

> **Sample Exam Question 5.5:**
> "The recent fall in aggregate demand caused a buildup in inventories, pushing us currently into an inventory correction which will _____ GDP."
>
> (a) What is an inventory correction? (b) Fill in the blank and explain your reasoning.

5.6   Policy Implications

Although our earlier example of the multiplier process was couched in terms of a policy of increasing government spending, any policy that influences aggregate demand has similar effects. An alternative way of increasing aggregate demand is to decrease taxes, which increases aggregate demand indirectly by increasing consumers' disposable income, thereby enticing them to increase consumption demand C.

Changing government spending or taxation is referred to as *fiscal policy* because each involves a direct change in the government budget deficit, calculated as government spending G less tax receipts T. (*Fiscalis* is Latin for "pertaining to the public purse.")

In particular, an *expansionary fiscal policy* (an increase in government spending or a decrease in taxes) creates a government budget deficit. Keynesians believe this is a natural side effect of a fiscal policy designed to maintain an economy at full employment—a side effect that should be reversed when in boom times governments cut back on spending or increase taxes to cool off the economy. In the Keynesian view, running a deficit is a small price to pay for jump-starting the economy so that the multiplier process can pull it out of a recession. They believe that the deficit can be offset later by a budget surplus when the economy is strong.

Keynesians also believe that an economy can become stuck in a recession when its natural recovery forces operate far too slowly, creating prolonged periods of high unemployment. They further believe that the government is able to move the economy out of a recession through fiscal policy and that it should do so. This advocacy of government intervention in the economy has been opposed by others who believe that as a matter of principle the government has no business interfering in the economy, and that government intervention, however well-intentioned, too often makes things worse, not better.

Curiosity 5.4: What Is the Full-employment Budget?

When tax revenues fall as the economy enters a recession, the government budget moves automatically toward deficit. Two implications of this process are of note:

1. Many years ago, when politicians feared deficits, such a deficit triggered calls from politicians to decrease government spending or raise taxes to eliminate this deficit. This contractionary fiscal policy would be inappropriate because it would make the recession worse.

2. The budget deficit is misleading as an indicator of government discretionary fiscal policy because it is not necessarily caused by a conscious government policy action of increasing spending or decreasing taxes. Consequently any effort to measure the strength of fiscal policy by matching up budget deficits with economic activity would be inaccurate.

   The full-employment budget is actual government spending minus tax revenues that would be generated by a fully employed economy. This concept was developed to deal with the two problems that we have noted:

1. Although a recession decreases tax revenues and pushes the actual budget toward deficit, it does not change the full-employment budget (because, when calculating the full-employment budget, full-employment tax revenues are used). Consequently politicians averse to budget deficits could be persuaded to permit an actual budget deficit on the grounds that the full-employment budget is in balance. This argument was used during the early 1960s when the Keynesian policy view reached the height of its popularity.

2. By eliminating automatic tax revenue changes caused by income changes, the full-employment budget allows fiscal policy initiatives to be measured accurately by changes in the full-employment budget. We can thus see more clearly what is happening with fiscal policy and more accurately measure the influence of fiscal policy.

Another facet of this debate concerns the issue of whether fiscal policy should be undertaken through increases in government spending or decreases in taxes: the former involve more government influence over the production and distribution of goods and services in the economy, whereas the latter involve less. Those on the left of the political spectrum—liberals, socialists, and Democrats—believe that more control by the government over resource allocation in the economy is a good thing because they do not believe that market forces produce the right kind of outputs or distribute them fairly. Those on the right of the political spectrum—conservatives and Republicans—believe the government already plays too big a role in the economy, that it is an inefficient allocator of resources, and that individuals, through their spending financed by tax reductions, can cause the market to produce and distribute more desirable outputs in a more efficient fashion.

This is a sensitive issue. Everyone agrees that there is a prominent role to be played by government spending—on education, on infrastructure, on parks, and on operating things such as a legal system and an army. The disagreement comes from differing opinions about what the extent of the role of government should be.

Keynesians and their modern counterparts, New Keynesians, believe that judicious government intervention in the economy is appropriate. Classical economists (see appendix 5.1), monetarists (see chapter 9), and their modern counterparts, New Classicals, believe that government intervention is to be avoided. This issue is revived in chapter 9 when discussing the "rules-versus-discretion" debate: Should policy authorities be permitted to enact policy as they see fit?

> **Sample Exam Question 5.6:**
> "Countercyclical policy is about filling in holes and shaving off peaks, exactly what Keynes prescribed."
> Exactly what "filling in holes and shaving off peaks" did Keynes prescribe?

5.7   Deficit Spending

When government spending exceeds tax revenues, there is a government *budget deficit*, which is financed by selling bonds. The sum of all outstanding government bonds is called the *national debt*, which grows each year by the amount of the budget deficit. (It would shrink if there were a budget surplus.) Some bonds are sold to the central bank, an agent of the government, so this part of the national debt the government owes to itself; consequently no one worries about it. The remaining bonds are sold to the public, augmenting the publicly held national debt. Figures 5.3 and 5.4 provide a sense of the historical magnitude of these measures, along with some (optimistic!) projections from the Congressional Budget Office for their magnitudes beyond 2009.

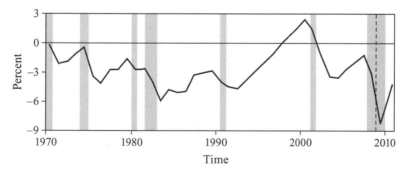

Figure 5.3   Government Deficit or Surplus as a Percentage of GDP
Shaded areas denote official recessions. Source: www.cbo.gov.

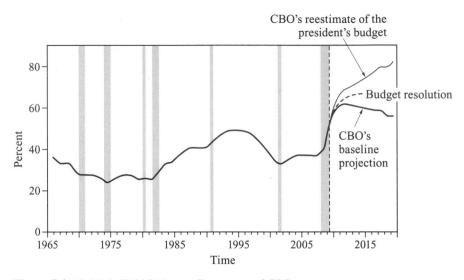

Figure 5.4   Publicly Held Debt as a Percentage of GDP
Shaded areas denote official recessions. Source: www.cbo.gov.

An important legacy of Keynes is that budget deficits became respectable side effects of efforts to keep an economy operating at full employment. Keynes's intention was that deficits required to stimulate the economy when it is in recession would be offset by budget surpluses in times of full employment—ensuring that in the long run the national debt would not continually grow.

History has not treated this Keynes legacy kindly. Once initial fears of budget deficits were overcome, politicians went overboard, producing deficits in both good times and bad. There are two main reasons for this, both at heart due to reluctance on the part of politicians to levy taxes. First, by world standards Americans are lightly taxed. The ratio of tax revenue to GDP is about 30 percent in the United States, the lowest of all OECD countries. Canada's ratio is about 40 percent, and Sweden's is about 50 percent. Second, social security and Medicare expenditures cannot easily be controlled because anyone eligible is entitled to coverage. As our population ages, spending in these two categories continually increases.

Sample Exam Question 5.7:
Suppose that the income multiplier with respect to government spending is 3 and the marginal tax rate is 20 percent.

If the government increases spending by $10 billion, what will happen to the budget deficit?

Curiosity 5.5: What Is Generational Accounting?

The size of our national debt is a misleading measure of possible burdens on future generations, mainly because the national debt measure does not incorporate financing obligations associated with promises the government has made regarding future spending.

Most prominent among these promises are future expenditures on social security (i.e., pension payments) and Medicare (i.e., subsidies for medical costs). These programs are financed on a pay-as-you-go basis, which means that the current, working generation pays for benefits being enjoyed by older generations who have retired. (Since 1983 the working generation has through extra payroll taxes been building up a fund to help pay for its future benefits, but this fund is far too modest; in effect we continue to operate on a pay-as-you-go basis.) The current generation has been promised that its benefits will be paid for by the following generation of workers. Notice that each generation is being taxed to pay for the preceding generation's benefits, rather than being taxed to pay for its own expected benefits. This system works well if the later generation can easily produce sufficient income to finance these promised benefits.

In the past it has been easy for later generations to meet this promise, primarily because later generations have always had more—and more productive—workers than earlier generations. But what if there is a slowdown in population and productivity growth so that a later generation finds itself unable to meet this promise easily? This possibility might imply that the earlier generation is placing a burden on the later generation.

Generational accounting is the name given to calculations designed to measure future taxes required to meet promised future government spending. These calculations suggest that the United States is facing a big problem. The demographics are such that when the current working generation (the baby boomer generation) retires, there will not be enough workers in the following generation to make the financing of this promise realistic. If the current generation continues to pay only about a third of its lifetime income in taxes, future generations will have to pay over 80 percent of lifetime income in taxes to meet the intergenerational promises we have described!

There is some justice in an intergenerational transfer if the higher productivity of the later generation is in part due to the higher capital stock passed on by the earlier generation. The numbers given here are too extreme to be justified on these grounds, however, especially given the recent slowdown in productivity growth. Clearly, such high taxes are not collectible, implying that some change is necessary: (1) tax the current generation more heavily so that it is forced to pay for much more of its own future benefits, (2) increase the age at which people become eligible to receive retirement benefits, (3) increase immigration dramatically to increase the number of people working to produce the income required to meet these promises, or (4) do not meet the promises—the most likely scenario.

Curiosity 5.6: What Is the Structural Deficit?

An implication of financing a budget deficit by selling bonds to the public is that as the budget deficit continues, the national debt grows. How worried should we be about this growing debt? Although there is no unique answer to this question, there is some consensus that we should worry about a budget deficit only if its size is such as to cause a long-run rise in the ratio of the publicly held national debt to nominal GDP. This ratio is a crude measure of our capacity to service the national debt. If it continues to grow, at some stage the economy will not have enough GDP to be able to service the debt, so a major crisis will ensue.

An economy is said to have a *structural deficit* if the current government spending and tax structure in the long run will continually increase the ratio of national debt to GDP. Put another way, the structural deficit is the deficit above and beyond the deficit that keeps the publicly held debt to GDP ratio constant in the long run. Several adjustments to the current deficit are made to calculate the structural deficit. The most prominent is a correction for cyclical effects that hinder the current deficit's ability to reflect accurately any long-run trend. For example, if GDP drops below its long-run trend average by $100, it is estimated that tax receipts fall by $25 and government spending on transfers increases by $8, so that $33 of the deficit does not correspond to long-run behavior. A second correction is needed to account for growth in GDP. This increases the denominator of the debt/GDP ratio and so eliminates some influence of the current deficit on this ratio. A third correction adjusts for that part of the deficit financed by selling bonds to the central bank and so not part of the publicly held national debt. This phenomenon, called seigniorage, is discussed in chapter 9.

5.8 Burdening Future Generations

These budget deficits are increasing the national debt, prompting many to claim that a burden is being placed on future generations. Whether or not a burden is imposed depends on the nature of the deficit spending, best analyzed by examining the capital stock that is being passed on to future generations. Two cases arise—domestic borrowing and foreign borrowing.

Domestic Borrowing

If the borrowing is domestic, then we owe the debt to ourselves, and it seems that overall there is no intergenerational burden. This reasoning is misleading, however. Domestic borrowing to finance a deficit crowds out some investment spending. If the deficit spending is on capital assets such as roads and airports, it is possible that the capital stock passed on to the future generation is of more value than the investment spending that is crowded out.

However, if the deficit spending is on things other than capital assets, such as Medicare and unemployment insurance, then the future generation will receive a smaller capital

Curiosity 5.7: How Big Is the Deficit?

Before the Great Depression of the 1930s, federal government spending was less than 5 percent of GDP. Introduction of the "New Deal" during the depression doubled this percentage, and since then it has increased to about 20 percent of GDP, a level maintained since the mid-1970s. About 45 percent of the federal government's revenue comes from individual income taxes, about 12 percent from corporate income taxes, about 5 percent from sales taxes, and about 36 percent from Social Security payroll taxes, accounting in 2008 for over 2.5 trillion dollars of tax receipts. About 22 percent of the federal government budget is spent on defense, about 35 percent on income and Social Security, about 23 percent on health and Medicare, and about 7 percent on interest payments on the national debt. Other areas of expenditure are much smaller: welfare and foreign aid, for example, are together less than 3 percent of total federal government spending. In 2008 these expenditures amounted to over 3.1 trillion dollars, implying a budget deficit of 482 billion dollars. These numbers are misleading, however, because state and local governments account for a huge amount of government spending and taxation (about 13 percent of GDP, on things like education, welfare, highways, fire and police protection, health, hospitals, prisons, and sanitation, although none of the deficit because they are not allowed to run deficits). Note that a large amount of this government outlay takes the form of transfer payments as opposed to spending on goods and services, the *G* that we have been using as a part of aggregate demand for goods and services. In 2007 the size of government in the United States was about 33 percent of GDP, compared to about 40 percent in Canada, 60 percent in Sweden, and 47 percent on average in the EU countries.

As a percentage of GDP, deficits were very modest in the early 1960s, less than 1 percent. By the late 1970s this had risen to about 3 percent, then 5 percent during the mid-1980s. Large deficits, about 3 or 4 percent of GDP, continued until the mid-1990s when they fell markedly and a series of budget surpluses arose from 1998 to 2002. Since then deficits have escalated to about 3 percent of GDP, with dramatic increases occurring in 2009 as the government used fiscal policy to battle the recession caused by the subprime mortgage problem. Consistent with all this, the ratio of the publicly held national debt fell from about 46 percent in 1960 to a low of about 24 percent in the mid-1970s, rose to about 49 percent in the mid-1980s, fell to about 33 percent in the early 2000s, and has risen since then, to about 38 percent in 2008. This amounts to about $30,000 per person.

stock. If the economy is at full employment, more crowding out occurs, increasing the likelihood that future generations will be made worse off. The key feature clearly is the nature of the deficit spending. If the deficit spending is on consumption items rather than investment items, the present generation is "living it up" at the expense of a future generation that will receive a smaller capital stock.

Foreign Borrowing

The great advantage of borrowing from foreigners is that crowding out can be avoided. The foreign exchange obtained by the borrowing can be used to import more goods and services, allowing the economy to have extra output to distribute to its citizens. In this case, however, future generations must pay interest and principal to foreigners, so it looks as though they are being burdened. Once again, this conclusion depends on the nature of the deficit spending. If the government has borrowed to invest in social infrastructure that increases the economy's productivity by enough to create additional annual income sufficient to pay off the interest and principal of the debt, then the deficit cannot be said to burden future generations.

A good example of "investment borrowing" is the foreign borrowing done by the United States that allowed it to build railroads and steel mills during the nineteenth century. If the deficit arises because the government has borrowed to spend on overly generous social security or Medicare, or unnecessary military hardware, future generations will be asked to reduce their consumption to repay the principal and interest. In this case a burden is placed on future generations.

> **Sample Exam Question 5.8:**
> "The debt buildup is worrisome because it is not financing. . . ."
>   Complete this clipping.

Media Illustrations

Example 1
All this frugality is producing a consumer-generated recession. What is needed is some policy action to stimulate consumer spending to move the economy out of its current lassitude. Consumer attitude surveys indicate that the time is ripe for such a move, and the high savings rate of recent years has led many economy watchers to predict an upturn.

What is a consumer-generated recession?
There has been a fall in consumer spending, decreasing aggregate demand and, through a contractionary multiplier process, causing a recession.

What kind of policy action could stimulate consumer spending?
A decrease in taxes could increase consumer spending.

How would stimulating consumer spending move the economy out of its current lassitude?
Stimulating consumer spending would increase aggregate demand; through a multiplier process, greater demand would move the economy to a higher level of income.

What is the relevance of consumer attitude surveys?
If consumer attitudes toward spending are negative, policy actions to increase consumer spending, along with the multiplier process that relies on higher incomes increasing consumption demand, may not work.

Why has the high savings rate of recent years led to a prediction of an upturn?
The high savings rates have increased people's wealth. Feeling wealthy, consumers may increase their spending.

Example 2

Under present circumstances there is such a thing as a "free lunch." In effect all the ingredients of that lunch are already there—the people who want to work, the factories and equipment standing idle, and the raw materials not being used. It is just a question of injecting a little spending power to prevent the free lunch from going to waste.

What kind of government policy is this a plea for?
The statement "injecting a little spending power" suggests it is a plea for a stimulating dose of fiscal policy—increasing government spending or reducing taxes.

Explain how it would work to create a free lunch.
By increasing aggregate demand, firms would be motivated to use the idle resources to produce output to meet this aggregate demand.

What would happen if this policy were undertaken without the ingredients listed in the example?
The list of ingredients indicates that the resources needed to produce the extra output are now idle—the economy is operating at less than full capacity. Were this not the case, price increases rather than output increases would result from the stimulating fiscal policy.

Example 3

Most economists these days are preaching that consumers had better start spending. Fears of unemployment have curtailed consumer spending and starved the federal government of tax revenues needed to reduce the deficit.

Why would economists urge consumers to start spending?
If consumers increase their spending, the increase in aggregate demand will set in motion the multiplier process that would move the economy out of recession.

Does the fact that unemployment fears curtail consumer spending serve to stabilize or destabilize the economy? Explain.
If consumer spending drops as unemployment increases, then aggregate demand falls, setting in motion a multiplier process pushing the economy to an even lower level of output and employment, destabilizing the economy.

How has a curtailment of consumer spending starved the government of tax revenues?
By curtailing consumer spending a multiplier process pushing the economy to a lower level of income is set in motion. The lower level of income automatically reduces the government's income tax receipts.

Example 4
Changes in inventories go a long way, for instance, toward explaining why first-quarter real GDP was ahead of a year earlier by a meager 1.7 percent.

What must have been happening to inventories during the first quarter?
The adjective "meager" suggests that GDP did not grow by as much as one would normally expect. One cause for this result could be firms cutting back production to decrease inventories. So a good guess here is that inventories were falling.

Example 5
Economists expect to see some further liquidation of inventories this quarter, but at a slower rate. And that change from rapid to slow—from negative to less negative—shows up as a plus for the economy.

What is a liquidation of inventories, and how would it be accomplished?
Liquidation of inventories is getting rid of inventories, accomplished by decreasing production levels to have more sales met by inventories.

Why would a slower rate of inventory liquidation be a plus for the economy?
To slow down the rate of inventory liquidation, a firm would have to increase production so that not quite so many sales would be met by inventories. This increase in production increases income and sets in motion the multiplier process, stimulating the economy.

Example 6
I think a lot of people, particularly in the business community and among economists, have realized that much of the present deficit is of a purely cyclical nature. It's resulting from what they call the automatic stabilizers.

What is a deficit of a purely cyclical nature?
A cyclical deficit is created by an automatic fall in tax revenues and rise in certain types of government spending (e.g., unemployment insurance payments) during recessions.

From what kind of deficit should it be distinguished?
It is to be distinguished from a budget deficit that has arisen due to a discretionary change in government spending or taxing.

What is an automatic stabilizer?
An automatic stabilizer is an increase or decrease in spending that kicks in automatically to stabilize the economy whenever it moves into a recession or a boom.

Example 7

One question is whether the government can steel itself to bring its fiscal policy into line with the central bank's monetary policy. Will the government be able to borrow the funds it will need to cover this year's deficit out of the existing money supply, which the Fed is trying to restrict?

Of what relevance is the Fed's monetary policy here?
If the Fed is restricting the money supply, it will not be willing to buy any of the government's bonds, so all these bonds must be sold to the public.

How can the government make sure it can borrow the funds it needs if the Fed refuses to increase the money supply?
By raising the interest rate high enough the government can ensure that it obtains the funds it needs. This result occurs for two reasons. First, a higher interest rate causes savers to increase their saving. Second, a higher interest rate causes some firms to cut back on investment so that funds that would have been used for this purpose are now available to buy government bonds.

Example 8

As to how the federal deficit would be cut back, the economists rule out tax increases. Instead, the cuts must come on the expenditure side with the average growth of federal expenditures—including interest payments on the national debt—kept below average growth of GDP.

Why would these economists favor cutting back government spending over raising taxes?
This view is purely a value judgment on the part of these economists. They are conservatives in that they feel that the level of government spending is already too large. Liberal economists would take the opposite view, favoring more government involvement in the operation of the economy. Most economists are conservatives in this respect because through studying economics they have come to respect the efficiency of the free market. They do not believe that government-directed spending creates extra benefits as great as those that would be created by private spending.

Example 9

First, a rise in the debt/GDP ratio means that the current generation is consuming goods and services at the expense of future generations. We are in effect stealing from the future by consuming more than we can produce.

How can we possibly consume more than we can produce?
By borrowing from foreigners we can pay for imports, augmenting the output we produce for distribution to our citizens.

Does this borrowing necessarily imply that we are stealing from future generations?
If the borrowing is to finance consumption goods, then future generations will pay. But if the borrowing is to finance investment goods, it is possible that future generations will be better off—the investment goods may make future generations much more productive.

Chapter Summary

- In a major break with tradition, Keynes focused on aggregate demand as the primary determinant of economic activity, illustrated in this chapter by assuming that producers were quantity rather than price adjusters.

- An increase in aggregate demand, created, for example, by an increase in government spending, induces producers to increase output to restore fallen inventories. The resulting increase in income causes consumption demand to increase, thus extending the expansion. This is the essence of the multiplier process, whereby an increase in government spending leads eventually to a much larger increase in income. The strength of this process is captured by the multiplier, which tells us the increase in equilibrium income caused by a dollar increase in government spending.

- Inventory changes send signals to producers that indicate what is happening to aggregate demand and foretell subsequent changes in output and employment. Consequently they are often used for forecasting purposes.

- Automatic stabilizers, some created deliberately by government policy, decrease the multiplier magnitude, alleviating business cycles

- The means chosen to finance an increase in government spending markedly affects the multiplier magnitude through crowding-out forces; the usual means of financing, selling bonds to the public, crowds out through higher interest rates

- An increase in the national debt through government deficit spending can be a burden on future generations if a larger capital stock is not passed on to them; the key factor here is the purpose of the government deficit spending, transfer payments versus infrastructure spending, for example.

Formula Definition

$$\text{``The'' multiplier} = \frac{\text{Change in equilibrium income}}{\text{Change in government spending}} = \frac{\Delta GDP}{\Delta G}$$

Media Exercises

(Group B questions require more thought.)

A1. There are specific reasons, of course, why a downturn may have been aborted in the past few months. With the Russian invasion of Afghanistan and the long confinement of American diplomats as hostages in Iran, the United States

began to strengthen the armed forces. Defense contracts work in the old-fashioned Keynesian way to stimulate the economy.

Explain how this old-fashioned Keynesian way operates to stimulate the economy.

A2.   The federal government will be prevented by the size of the deficit from taking any action to stimulate the economy. The only possible source of stimulus is a decrease in the personal savings rate.

a. What action could the government take to stimulate the economy? Explain why the size of the deficit may prevent this.

b. How would a decrease in the personal savings rate serve as a source of stimulus?

A3.   We saved 17 percent of our disposable income during the recession, the highest rate since World War II. The level of savings has fallen off since then to less than 10 percent of disposable income.

Would the higher savings rate have eased or exacerbated the recession? Explain how. (The U.S. savings rate in 2008 was only about 1 percent!)

A4.   The only other potential bright spot observers spy on the horizon is lower personal tax rates and higher take-home pay under the federal tax reform package, which will begin in July.

Why would this be viewed as a "bright spot"?

A5.   Weak markets will lead to a rapid drop in the rate of business capital spending during the next year, which in turn will increase unemployment.

Explain how a drop in capital spending will increase unemployment.

A6.   In a loose sense we are all Keynesians now—all of us, at any rate, who reject the notion that a sick economy heals itself by "natural" recuperative powers, without government action.

a. Explain why rejecting this notion makes us Keynesians.

b. What kind of government action is being referred to at the end of this clip?

A7.   For Canada, the demand pressures generated by the U.S. tax cut and the spillover effects of increased U.S. defense spending will push the Canadian economy further into an excess demand situation.

a. How will the U.S. tax cut and the increased U.S. defense spending influence the U.S. economy?

b. What name do economists give to this kind of government action?

c. How would this effect influence the Canadian economy?

A8. The report attributed the strength of the recovery during the first three months of this year to increased consumer spending and residential construction, as well as a reduced rate of inventory liquidation.

a. Explain how increased consumer spending contributes to the recovery.

b. Explain how a reduced rate of inventory liquidation contributes to the recovery.

A9. Manufacturers ended last year on a strong note with both shipments and orders rising to record levels in December. At the same time there was an ominous buildup of inventories, which also rose to a record level.

Why is the buildup in inventories described as "ominous."

A10. There have been times when the federal government has kept pumping fiscal stimulus into the economy when it was already growing vigorously and did not need the boost. The result was. . . .

a. What is meant by fiscal stimulus?

b. Complete the last sentence.

A11. When the news of Wednesday's numbers on GDP was made public, stocks and bonds immediately rose and the U.S. dollar strengthened. Then, when analysis of the numbers came in, the markets went into reverse. The reason was that the greater part of the improvement in the quarter—$33.7 billion out of a total GDP advance of $39.2 billion—came from additions to business inventories.

Explain why markets would go into reverse upon learning about the additions to inventories.

A12. But as consumer spending slackened, stocks began to pile up. So an inventory correction is under way, and it will reduce this quarter's real GDP by more than 10 percent at an annual rate.

a. What is an inventory correction?

b. Why would an inventory correction cause GDP to fall in this case?

A13. The U.S. Department of Commerce has estimated that if U.S. manufacturers use metric measures, their increased ability to compete on world markets

should increase exports by about $600 million and thus benefit the U.S. economy by between $1.2 billion and $1.8 billion.

Where are the $1.2 billion and $1.8 billion numbers coming from?

A14. **Unemployment is contagious: people who lose their jobs cut their spending, causing other workers to be laid off. With sales lagging, business firms lose confidence; they cut back on investment, so more people are out of work.**

What terminology do economists use to describe this phenomenon?

A15. **The Japanese economy is putting on the brakes, and this should inhibit our recovery.**

Why would a slowdown of the Japanese economy affect our recovery?

A16. **The U.S. economy should have enough vigor to continue growing for the rest of the decade, despite the braking effect of budget deficit reduction.**

Explain what the braking effect of budget deficit reduction is.

A17. **GDP grew at a much faster 4.8 percent rate in the October–December quarter, but analysts said that growth masked some dangerous imbalances that were not present in the first-quarter report. Almost all of the fourth-quarter increase in GDP wound up as unsold inventory sitting on shelves.**

a. If it doesn't get sold, how could it get counted into GDP?

b. Why is this phenomenon described as a "dangerous imbalance"?

A18. **The conference was told that the country is headed for a big inventory liquidation that will keep the recession going well into the next year.**

Explain how an inventory liquidation will keep the recession going.

A19. **The strong industrial production report seemed to contradict last week's report on retail sales, which showed that sales declined. Analysts point out, however, that production schedules for December were planned several months in advance, and were likely set before consumer spending began to show signs of weakness.**

What would likely happen if strong industrial production and weak sales continued?

A20. **Business inventories could have accumulated because sales fell below expectations. On the other hand, firms could have stockpiled inventories because they anticipated a surge in sales. The distinction is important because 87** percent of the stronger than expected 3.4 percent annualized growth in real GDP in the second quarter came from inventory accumulation. Those going with the first explanation are forecasting _____ while those who go with the second explanation are forecasting _____.

Fill in the blanks.

A21. The trend probably will continue through the autumn, analysts said, as auto makers continue trying to keep inventory levels in check through a mix of _____ and sweetened cash rebates.

Fill in the blank.

A22. The world has been hit with its biggest scare since the Great Depression first inspired Lord Keynes to urge the use of public coffers to manage demand.

What terminology do economists use to refer to "the use of public coffers to manage demand"?

A23. There are enough programs so that the federal deficit will swell as existing programs are maintained while tax revenues fall as a result of the weak economy.

Do these two phenomena serve to stabilize or destabilize the economy when it moves into recession? Explain.

A24. Fears had been expressed that financing of the federal deficit might squeeze private borrowers out of the market.

By what mechanism are private borrowers squeezed out of the market?

A25. Clinton has promised to get the economy moving strongly again, but if that effort requires increased government spending, financial markets may insist on an interest rate premium in anticipation of problems funding an even larger U.S. public debt. And those higher money costs could offset any benefit of higher government spending.

a. Explain the rationale behind the last sentence.

b. What terminology would economists use to refer to this?

A26. About the only benefit ever claimed for the deficit is that it will bring an increase in the level of aggregate demand and therefore a reduction in unemployment. In recent years, however, this very Keynesian notion has begun to be doubted by many economists. The main worry is crowding out.

Explain how crowding out can discredit the Keynesian view.

A27. The slack exists, of course, because people continue to save even when the private sector demand for loans ebbs away. And they tend to save more, not less, in scary times.

Does the phenomenon referred to in the second sentence serve as an automatic stabilizer or destabilizer?

A28. One good thing about financing by printing money—the crowding-out problem disappears.

a. What is the rationale behind this statement?

b. What problem might there be with this approach to financing?

A29. In general, the Treasury is doing less to "crowd out" private debtors, a phenomenon long considered to be one of the economy's weak points. Savings that would previously have gone into sterile government paper is instead available to. . . .

Complete this clipping.

A30. And as soon as the budget is produced, we're likely to hear a lot about the danger that government borrowing will "crowd out" private borrowing.

How does government borrowing crowd out private borrowing?

A31. U.S. Federal Reserve Board chairman Paul Volcker told senators Thursday the huge federal budget deficit is causing "disturbing pressures" on interest rates.

Explain in what direction and how pressure is placed on interest rates.

A32. This is the "crowding-out" theory: Increased government borrowing crowds household and business investment out of limited savings, driving up _____ but not raising total demand.

Fill in the blank.

A33. The government's deficit-reduction policies are "eerily reminiscent of the 1930s" and will only drive the economy deeper into recession and push up unemployment, says a report issued Monday by a private think tank.

Explain the rationale behind this thinking.

A34. The arithmetic is straightforward. If growth falls one percentage point below the government's 3 percent forecast, the deficit would widen by about $15 billion.

How does growth affect the budget deficit?

A35. Budget deficits are sometimes useful to spur consumption and thus encourage investment in business plant and equipment, but more generally they discourage rather than encourage investment because. . . .

    a. Explain how budget deficits could spur consumption and encourage investment.

    b. Complete this clipping.

A36. Both research groups said last week that the deficit has bottomed out and will begin to rise next year. They predicted that economic growth would slow this year to 2.5 percent in real terms, from a robust 3.7 percent last year.

What connection, if any, is there between the predictions in the first and second sentences?

A37. Already the electronics retailer Circuit City has filed for bankruptcy, and General Motors has said that it is in danger of running out of cash. If the consumer slump continues, there is a potential for a dangerous feedback loop, in which spending cuts and layoffs reinforce each other.

What terminology do economists use to refer to this phenomenon?

A38. It appears that the policy of sending out tax credits has not worked because households are using the tax credits to offset the higher gasoline prices and anything left over is being saved rather than being spent.

    a. How were the tax credits supposed to work to stimulate the economy?

    b. Explain why they do not appear to be working as planned.

A39. Keynesian theory says stimulate by lowering taxes. But what do you think a typical worker, given a thousand-dollar tax break during a major recession, will do with it? Spend it? Not likely.

Explain the thinking that lies behind this view.

A40. The federal government is piling up larger deficits than estimated in February as the recession. . . .

Complete this clipping and explain your reasoning.

A41. In a recent interview the central bank chairman said that the paring back of inventories, along with the fiscal and monetary policies now in place, are the key drivers that will. . . .

Complete this 2009 clipping and explain your reasoning.

A42. Businesses are quickly moving to cut inventory levels—a key development that will set the stage for. . . .

    a. Will cutting inventory levels push the economy toward recession or boom? Explain your reasoning.

    b. Complete this clipping and explain your reasoning.

A43. In an endeavor to minimize the worst of the downturn, governments worldwide are running up huge debts. This has led to the charge of generation theft— lumbering future generations with today's debt liability. It is an absurd accusation. Generation theft already exists, only in reverse. A child born today inherits a massive infrastructure, built and paid for by past generations.

    a. What name would economists give to this policy of running up large public debt?

    b. Does this imply that future generations are being exploited?

A44. The White House recently said that without the tax cuts in 2001 and 2003, there would currently be 1.5m fewer jobs in the United States.

What logic lies behind this claim?

A45. In the face of the major recession that seems certain to follow the financial crisis sparked by the sub-par mortgage fiasco, the responsible thing now is to give the economy the help it needs. Now is not the time to worry about the deficit.

What is this a plea for?

B1. For the people around here the $1 million increase in government spending means 42 direct jobs and, depending on the employment multiplier you prefer, another 120 or 160 indirect jobs. In the bush. In motels. On the highways. In the drugstore down the street.

    a. What is meant by an "employment multiplier"?

    b. Calculate the magnitude of this multiplier.

B2. The extent of the downturn surprised many analysts. Real GDP fell at an annual rate of 4 percent, but if an apparently unplanned buildup of inventories is taken into account, the rate of decline is estimated at 7.6 percent.

    a. Explain what logic is being used to get the 7.6 percent figure.

    b. What is the relevance of the buildup of inventories being unplanned?

B3. **What cannot be done, various reformers in the United States notwithstanding, is to impose on any government the obligation to balance its budget annually. Consider the consequences. If it did work, it would introduce a major destabilizing element.**

Explain how forcing the government to balance its budget would be destabilizing.

B4. **Adam Smith said 200 years ago, "What is prudence in the conduct of every private family can scarce be folly in that of a great kingdom." With the advent of a "Keynesian revolution" since World War II, principles of fiscal responsibility were abandoned—in fact they were reversed. The message of Keynesianism might be summarized as, "What is folly in the conduct of a private family may be prudence in the conduct of the affairs of a great nation."**

a. Exactly what is the "folly" referred to here?

b. Explain the rationale behind the "message of Keynesianism" given here.

B5. **Some claim that the fact that both deficits and unemployment have increased together since 1979 proves that fiscal stimulus doesn't work. It's true that our jobless rate rose from 1979 to 1984 while the federal deficit doubled as a percentage of GDP. But the inference about the ineffectiveness of fiscal stimulus is nevertheless wrong, because. . . .**

Complete the argument about to be developed here. Hint: What is happening to tax revenues?

B6. **In the first two quarters of the year, consumer spending was somewhat sluggish, but there was a strong buildup of inventories by business that boosted economic output.**

a. Are weak consumer spending and strong inventory buildup consistent with one another? Explain why or why not.

b. Does it matter if output is boosted by strong consumer spending or by strong inventory buildup? Explain why or why not.

B7. **The inventory buildup, the major source of strength in the first quarter, will not be repeated and will actually be a source of weakness as production is reduced to work down unwanted stockpiles in the face of slumping sales, analysts said.**

How can an inventory buildup be both a source of strength and a source of weakness?

B8. **The Commerce Department has just reported that manufacturers' stock of raw materials, goods in process, and finished items fell by 1 percent in May, the**

latest month for which figures are available. It was the biggest drop in seventeen years. But it isn't just the sheer size of the May decline that excites the experts. Rather, it is the fact that the figure extends a trend that has been going on for most of the year. The cumulative impact has now reached the point where it has become a more potent force for recovery.

a. Does the 1 percent fall in May imply that aggregate demand and income are the same, demand exceeds income, or income exceeds demand?

b. Why should this May decline "excite the experts"?

c. What is the cumulative impact referred to in the final sentence, and why is it a potent force for recovery?

B9.   The extent to which the economy slows depends in part on inventories. Businesses added $10.8 billion to their stockpiles in the fourth quarter. It's unclear whether that buildup was voluntary or involuntary.

a. What could cause the buildup to be voluntary?

b. What could cause it to be involuntary?

c. What difference would it make if the inventory buildup was voluntary or involuntary?

B10.   Economists at the seminar agreed that the U.S. deficit of about $180 billion is severely straining domestic capital markets because private-sector capital demand is proving to be exceptionally bouyant. The result is a classic "crowding-out" situation.

a. What is meant by "severely straining"?

b. What is the main category of aggregate demand that is being crowded out here? Explain your reasoning.

B11.   The bang from a buck of direct government spending—say, highway construction—is far greater than the punch from a tax cut of equal dollar magnitude.

Explain why this statement is true.

B12.   The OECD (Organization for Economic Cooperation and Development) data also indicate, for example, that the stimulative effects of tax reductions are considerably smaller than those triggered by government expenditure increases—a fact of life long recognized by economists.

Explain why this is so.

B13. A second reason for questioning the employment-generating abilities of the deficit involves how consumers respond to an increase in government borrowing. Rational consumers realize that a higher deficit now means higher taxes in the future. If people. . . .

Complete this clipping to explain what people will do to cause the employment-generating abilities of the deficit to be weak.

B14. In a closed economy, government borrowing "crowds out" household and business investment by pricing them out of available savings, namely by _____. So fiscal stimulus has no net impact on the economy. But in an open economy, excess demand for capital is met from. . . .

a. Fill in the blank.

b. Complete this clipping.

B15. This theory, called "Ricardian equivalence" by economists, claims that crowding out is the same whether higher government spending is financed by selling bonds or by raising taxes. It's all very complicated, but the essence seems to be that we all live in great fear of future taxes!

What would fear of future taxes have to do with crowding out?

B16. One of the professors' more controversial findings is that public investment in physical capital (as opposed to human capital) in the last forty years has had a negative effect on economic growth. The researchers speculate that this is because public investment has "crowded out". . . .

a. What is meant by investment in human capital?

b. Complete this clipping.

B17. However, there are some important differences in the relative situations in the two countries that suggest that the urgency of reducing the federal deficit right now is not as great in Canada as it is in the United States. This conclusion follows from Canada currently being much further below its potential output than is the United States.

Explain the rationale behind this view.

B18. Consumer spending will also have to contend with a jump in mortgage rates as Treasury yields rise. Fixed mortgage rates rose to the highest level since November (2008) yesterday with the average 30-year rate up to 5.59 percent

from 5.29 percent a week earlier, figures from mortgage insurer Freddie Mac showed.

Why would consumer spending be affected by mortgage rates? Isn't housing considered an investment item, not a consumption item?

B19. **There is growing optimism that the economy is heading for recovery, based on a slowing decline in inventories.**

Why would a slowing decline (as opposed to just a decline) in inventories create optimism here?

B20. **Movement out of the 2008–9 recession will be slowed because of concerns about higher taxes to pare down mounting debt.**

Explain the logic of this thinking.

B21. **Hammered by the 2008 downturn, Americans have boosted the U.S. savings rate from zero to 5 percent in the past year. They have a long way to go to match China, however, where the current savings rate is in excess of 30 percent!**

What has caused the marked increase in the U.S. savings rate? Explain your reasoning.

B22. **The hero of every major recovery since the end of the Second World War, the American shopper is ratcheting down spending amid the brutal housing and financial crisis. As the mighty American consumer saves, the United States is looking to China as it economic savior.**

How could China be the savior of the American economy?

B23. **As profits increase, there's going to be a need for a capital rationing process.**

a. Why would capital need to be rationed?

b. What is the usual capital rationing process in our economy?

B24. **One piece of the $787 billion Obama economic recovery package is an experiment in consumer behavior. The $116 billion in tax credits for 95 percent of Americans will come largely through reduced tax withholding (about $8 per week) from paychecks, over two years, rather than one-time payments. When the government sent lump-sum checks for the 2001 and 2008 stimulus packages, Americans stashed most of the cash in savings or paid off debt.**

a. Why would there be complaints about stashing cash in savings or paying off debt?

b. Explain the nature of, and rationale behind, the "experiment in consumer behavior."

B25. Efforts to encourage spending during a downturn are not usually successful because _____, and so an increase in government spending would have to be exceptionally large.

a. Fill in the blank.

b. What does the last part of the statement imply about the magnitude of the multiplier? Explain your reasoning.

B26. Everyone tightens their belts during a crisis, even though they may know that collectively this will lead to economic disaster.

a. What does tightening belts mean in this context?

b. Why might it lead to an economic disaster?

c. What name do economists use for this phenomenon?

B27. And this is also a good time to engage in some serious infrastructure spending, which the United States badly needs in any case. The usual argument against public works as economic stimulus is that by the time you get around to repairing the bridges. . . .

a. Complete this clip.

b. This clip was written in October of 2008 when the world was dealing with the big 2008 financial crisis. In this context why would the usual argument not be convincing?

B28. Research suggests that when the ratio of public debt to GDP is high, the multiplier effect of fiscal stimulus is low.

What reasoning lies behind this statement?

B29. People's reluctance to spend, according to Ricardo, stems from a lack of faith in the government's ability to manage stimulus, and a belief that they will eventually be hit by. . . .

a. What does "manage stimulus" mean here?

b. Complete this clipping.

Numerical Exercises

AN1. Suppose that you notice that a $7 billion tax cut was accompanied by a $9 billion increase in consumer spending in the same year. How would you explain why consumer spending increased by more than the tax cut?

AN2. Suppose that the government increased spending by $14 billion and this resulted in an increase in equilibrium income of $35 billion. What is the value of the multiplier?

AN3. Suppose that the income multiplier with respect to government spending is 3. What increase in government spending is required to increase equilibrium income by $12 billion?

AN4. Suppose that the income multiplier with respect to government spending is 4. If the government increased spending and thereby increased equilibrium income by $60 billion, what must the increase in government spending have been?

AN5. Suppose the multiplier is 3, the marginal tax rate is 25 percent, and the government increases spending by $8 billion. In the new equilibrium position by how much are tax revenues changed?

AN6. Suppose that the income multiplier with respect to government spending is 2.5 and the marginal tax rate is 25 percent. If the government increases spending by $8 billion, what will happen to the budget deficit?

AN7. Suppose the current level of income is $600 billion, "the" multiplier is 4, the marginal tax rate is 20 percent, and the current budget deficit is $20 billion.

   a. What change in the level of government spending would be required to push the economy to an income level of $630 billion?

   b. What impact would this have on the budget deficit?

AN8. Suppose that the government increases its spending by $10 billion but will not allow a deficit so at the same time it increases taxes by $10 billion. Will the equilibrium level of income rise, fall, or stay the same? Explain your reasoning.

AN9. Suppose that the government has decided to increase spending by $5 billion to buy some helicopters. To prevent this action from having any impact on GDP, must taxes be increased by $5 billion, more than $5 billion, or less than $5 billion?

BN1. Suppose that "the" multiplier is 4 and the government increases spending by $5 billion, but the economy is at full employment at nominal income level $600 billion.

So the increase in government spending elicits price increases rather than output increases.

a. By how much will the price level increase?

b. By how much will nominal income increase?

c. By how much will real income increase?

BN2. Order the following policies by the magnitude of the increase in equilibrium income they generate. Explain your reasoning.

a. A tax cut of $200.

b. An increase in transfer payments of $200.

c. An increase in government spending of $200.

d. An increase in government spending of $200 along with a tax increase of $200.

BN3. The data in table 5.1 tell us the levels of various types of aggregate demand corresponding to the income levels given in the first column. When the level of income is 350, what will be happening to inventories?

BN4. What is the equilibrium level of income for the economy described in table 5.1?

BN5. Using the data in table 5.1, by how much should the level of income have increased after two rounds of the multiplier process if the economy begins at its equilibrium position and increases government spending by $50 billion?

Table 5.1   Output and Expenditure ($ billions)

Output	Consumption	Investment	Government spending	Net exports
100	80	26	20	10
150	120	26	20	8
200	160	26	20	6
250	200	26	20	4
300	240	26	20	2
350	280	26	20	0
400	320	26	20	−2

Note: Interpret these numbers as follows: The income level given in the output column gives rise to the sector demands shown in the other columns.

BN6. The Treasury plans to pay down $1.85 billion on the public debt with the sale Monday of about $13 billion in short-term bills. Maturing bills outstanding total _____.

Fill in the blank and explain your reasoning.

BN7. Suppose that last year consumption was $570 billion, tax receipts were $240 billion, and income was $900 billion. The corresponding numbers for this year are $600 billion, $250 billion, and $950 billion.

a. What is the MPC (marginal propensity to consume out of disposable income)?

b. What is the marginal tax rate?

Appendix 5.1   Macroeconomics before Keynes: The Classical School

The classical school dominated macroeconomic thinking before Keynes published his famous book *The General Theory of Employment, Interest, and Money* in 1936. The purpose of this appendix is to lend some perspective to this chapter's exposition of the Keynesian approach by providing a brief description of the classical view, which has three distinguishing characteristics, and by contrasting them with Keynes's view.

Wage and Price Flexibility

Classical economists believed that prices and wages were quite flexible, so disequilibria were uncommon. They explained unemployment, a disequilibrium in the the labor market, as a temporary reluctance of wages to fall. This view of wages and prices as flexible was reinforced by a tendency to focus on the long-run equilibrium of the economy with little regard for how the economy might behave when out of equilibrium. Implicitly they assumed that disequilibrium forces operated reasonably quickly to prevent phenomena such as prolonged recessions. A crucial policy implication of classical economics is that there is no need for government intervention by means of fiscal or monetary policy. (Monetary policy is discussed in chapter 8.)

Keynes, in contrast, claimed that it was the failure of disequibrium adjustments to occur speedily that explained phenomena such as the Great Depression. He complained that the classical economists' tendency to focus on long-run equilibrium had led them to overlook the important role of short-run disequilibrium dynamics in explaining economic phenomena. He concluded that there was a need for government policy intervention to speed the adjustment process.

Say's Law

The classical school believed that supply creates its own demand, a claim known as *Say's law*. The rationale behind Say's law is that production of a billion dollars of output (supply) creates exactly a billion dollars of income payments that end up financing a billion dollars of spending. This process causes aggregate demand automatically to match aggregate supply.

How does this happen? Any income not spent is saved and so is available to finance investment spending. Suppose that there is an increase in saving, which causes aggregate demand to fall short of aggregate supply. The higher saving increases supply in the market for investment funds, causing the interest rate (the "price" of such funds) quickly to fall (classical economists believed market adjustments were swift) and thus increasing investment demand because it is now cheap for firms to borrow to undertake investment projects. This outcome ensures that any fall in aggregate demand due to higher saving is offset by extra investment demand. The result suggests that deficient aggregate demand should never be a concern, one reason why Keynes's focus on aggregate demand was so innovative.

Keynes did not believe in Say's law. One of his major objections is that a fall in the interest rate causes people to increase the amount of cash they wish to hold in their pockets and in their checking accounts. With a lower interest rate, a smaller interest return is forgone by holding more wealth in the form of cash, so people hold more cash for the convenience it provides. Consequently not all of an increase in saving makes its way to financing higher investment; some is siphoned off into people's cash holdings. In short, according to Keynes, it is quite possible that aggregate demand falls short of aggregate supply, implying a need for monetary or fiscal policy to boost aggregate demand.

Money Is Neutral

Classical economists believed that the quantity of money created by the economy's central bank (see chapter 8) has no long-run influence on real variables in the economy, such as the level of output. Instead, they believed that money supply increases in the long run cause only price increases. This belief is often referred to as the *money neutrality* proposition. This view is formalized in the quantity theory of money equation, discussed later in chapter 9. In this theory the relationship between money and income is captured by the formula $Mv = PQ$, where M is the money supply, v is a constant called *velocity*, P is the overall price level, and Q is output. The classical economists viewed output in the long run as being maintained at its full-employment level by the flexing of wages, so Q is considered fixed. Velocity also was thought to be fixed, reflecting the nature of the economy's payments system. Because v and Q are fixed, a doubling of the money supply by the quantity theory equation in the long run merely doubles the price level: money is neutral, playing no role in affecting the real dimension of the economy, such as output and employment levels.

Keynes did not agree that it was legitimate to view output Q as constant. Although Q may be constant in the long run, movement to that long-run position may be so slow that prolonged recessions develop, permitting an increase in the money supply to affect output. (This process is described in chapter 9.) Furthermore, because the interest rate can affect people's desired cash holdings, velocity should not be considered constant.

Modern schools of economic thought do not ignore the short run and its associated dynamics. They do not believe in Say's law, and they have reinterpreted the quantity theory to make it more palatable. But one difference between the classical and Keynesian views described earlier continues to divide modern macroeconmic theorists: the classical school believed that wages and prices are flexible and that, as a result, government should not intervene in the operation of the economy, whereas Keynes believed the opposite. The same difference characterizes New Classicals and New Keynesians, the modern counterparts to the classical and Keynesian schools, discussed later in curiosity 12.1 in chapter 12.

Appendix 5.2   The Circular Flow of Income

A popular way of illustrating the Keynesian analysis of aggregate demand is through the circular flow diagram. This diagram shows how from year to year the income earned producing things enables people to buy these things and thereby permits the process to continue in a never-ending circular flow of income earning and spending.

The flow of income and spending is shown circulating clockwise in figure 5.5. In the bottom box are producers who pay income in the form of wages, profits, interest, and rent, which flow up to the left to households in the top box. These households use this income to finance spending, which flows down to the right to the producers, providing them with the means to continue producing and paying incomes. Along the route of this circle, however, are several leakages from and injections into this circular flow.

The first leakage is taxes taken from income as it flows to households. A second leakage is saving, which goes to financial markets where it is made available to investors. (Saving is also made available to governments selling bonds to finance budget deficits. To keep figure 5.5 simple, however, this and other complications are omitted.) A third leakage is spending on imports, a demand for goods and services that never reaches domestic producers.

Offsetting the leakages are injections into the circular flow, shown in figure 5.5 as investment, government spending, and export demand for goods and services. When these injections equal the leakages, aggregate demand for goods and services equals aggregate supply of goods and services, and the economy is thus in equilibrium. Keynes argued that

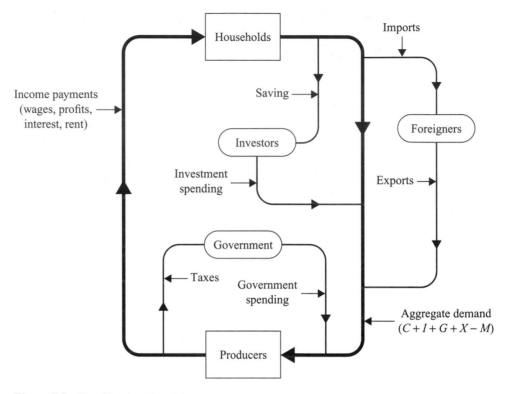

Figure 5.5 The Circular Flow Diagram
Income flows up to the left to households. It circulates back down to producers through a variety of
spending channels.

when leakages are greater than injections, an increase in the government spending injection
can restore equilibrium.

Another purpose played by the circular flow diagram is to illustrate the equality between
national income and output stressed in chapter 3. In the bottom box producers produce
national output (GDP). The entire value of this output is paid out in income of one kind
or another, going up to the left on the diagram. It is also sent up to the right on the diagram
to those demanding it. To measure national income, then, one can either add up all income
payments or add up all spending on domestically produced goods and services.

Appendix 5.3   The 45-Degree Line Diagram

The first of the infamous curve-shifting diagrams to which macroeconomics students are
introduced is the 45-degree line diagram, designed to illustrate the elements of Keynesian
analysis. All points on a 45-degree line are equidistant from both axes. In figure 5.6 the

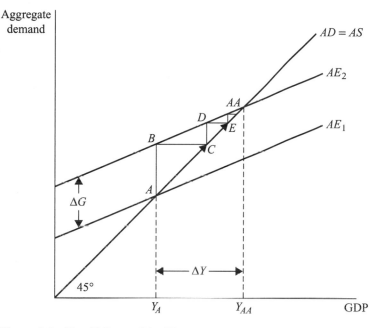

Figure 5.6   The 45-Degree Line Diagram
Government spending is increased by ΔG, shifting AE_1 up to AE_2, moving the economy ultimately from *A* to *AA*, increasing income by ΔY.

45-degree line is labeled $AD = AS$ because everywhere along that line aggregate demand for goods and services (measured on the vertical axis) is equal to aggregate supply of goods and services (measured on the horizontal axis). Such points are possible equilibrium positions.

We begin with an economy represented by the aggregate expenditure line AE_1, showing how increases in income (Y) increase aggregate demand for goods and services through the consumption function (i.e., as income increases consumption, demand increases). This implies that the economy will be at position *A*, corresponding to income level Y_A.

This result can be verified by choosing an income level smaller than Y_A and seeing that aggregate supply will be smaller than aggregate demand (because at that income level the AE_1 line is above the 45-degree line), so that income will rise. Similar reasoning shows that at an income level greater than Y_A aggregate supply exceeds aggregate demand and income will fall. It may seem odd to call the *AE* line an aggregate expenditure line rather than an aggregate demand line. The reason is that economists reserve the adjective "demand" to characterize curves drawn as a function of price.

Next increase government spending by ΔG, shifting the AE_1 line up by ΔG to AE_2, creating a new equilibrium at *AA* corresponding to income Y_{AA}. The change in equilibrium income resulting from this jump in government spending is $\Delta Y = Y_{AA} - Y_A$, and the multiplier is given by $\Delta Y/\Delta G$; if the change in government spending were one dollar, ΔY would portray the magnitude of the multiplier. The movement from *A* to *C* to *E* and so on portrays the adjustment process from *A* to *AA*, as described earlier in figure 5.1. The initial increase in government spending creates an excess demand of *AB*, so output increases by this amount, moving the economy to *C*. At position *C*, however, there continues to be excess demand, given by the smaller amount *CD*. Output increases by the amount *CD*, thus moving the economy to *E*. This process continues until the economy reaches position *AA*, where the excess demand has finally been squeezed off.

6   The Supply Side

In microeconomic analysis, economists rely heavily on supply and demand curves. They would never attempt to explain an economic phenomenon or offer policy advice without examining both the supply and the demand side of the market. In light of this fact, it is remarkable that the Keynesian view of the macroeconomy, which focused almost exclusively on the demand side, was accepted so completely by the profession. In retrospect, this exclusive focus was a grievous error for three main reasons:

1. When the large supply-side shocks of the early 1970s, such as OPEC-enforced increases in the price of oil, hit the economy, the Keynesian analysts were caught unprepared. Their economic models could not be employed to analyze the macroeconomic problems created by these shocks, so they were not able to offer useful advice.

2. Without the supply side of the economy, economists could not produce convincing analyses of business cycles; nor could they explain anomalous facts such as simultaneous increases in inflation and unemployment.

3. Neglecting the supply side deflected economists' attention from economic growth and increasing living standards—from what is happening to aggregate supply in the very long run. In the early 1970s, when the economy's growth rate slowed dramatically, they were inadequately prepared to analyze this phenomenon or prescribe policy to deal with it.

The purpose of this chapter is to discuss the supply side of the economy and how it can be integrated into macroeconomic analysis in the short and long runs. Discussion of the very long run, the topic of economic growth, is postponed until the next chapter.

Upon completion of this chapter you should

- understand how an aggregate-supply/aggregate-demand diagram can be used to portray business cycle behavior,
- be able to analyze a supply-side shock, and
- be familiar with "supply-side economics."

6.1   The Aggregate Supply Curve

The supply side in the Keynesian analysis introduced in the preceding chapter can be represented by an aggregate supply curve with three distinct zones, as illustrated by *AS* in figure 6.1. This curve shows how the quantity of output from firms increases as the overall price level increases.

1. At low levels of output, with excess capacity, firms are able to increase output without requiring price increases. Hoarded labor and idle machinery can be used to increase output without any increase in per unit costs. In this zone the aggregate supply curve

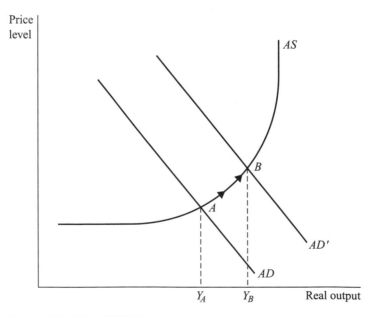

Figure 6.1   The *AS/AD* Diagram
An increase in government spending shifts *AD* to *AD′*, moving the economy from *A* to *B*.

is flat, corresponding to the flowchart explanation given in figure 5.1 in the previous chapter.

2. At intermediate levels of output, firms find that to produce more output they must pay current workers overtime, hire inexperienced, less productive workers, pay higher wages to attract additional workers, and use older, less efficient machinery. Consequently they increase output only if prices increase to cover higher per unit costs. The aggregate supply curve becomes upward sloping.

3. At some very high level of output, firms can no longer increase output because they have reached the physical limit of their capacity to produce output. The aggregate supply curve becomes vertical.

Anything that increases firms' costs shifts the *AS* curve in the upward direction. This result occurs because firms will supply the same output only if they are compensated for their higher costs by a higher price. A wage increase is an example of an increase in an input cost shifting the *AS* curve upward. Oil price increases engineered by OPEC in the 1970s constitute another prominent example. Readers are reminded that a change in the price level moves the economy along the *AS* curve; changes in all other variables cause shifts.

> **Sample Exam Question 6.1:**
> "Hoarding labor is not profit-maximizing behavior by firms—they could lay off these workers and output would not be affected."
>   (a) Is it true that hoarded workers could be laid off without affecting output? (b) Is it true that this is not profit-maximizing behavior by firms?

6.2   The Aggregate Demand Curve

To be useful, a supply curve must be paired with a demand curve. In this case an aggregate demand curve is developed by specifying that when the overall price level decreases, real demand for goods and services increases. The negative relationship between the overall price level and aggregate demand for goods and services comes about for three reasons:

1. *The wealth effect.* Some of people's wealth is held in the form of financial assets such as cash or bonds. A fall in prices of goods and services means that the purchasing power of these financial assets increases. This rise in people's wealth may cause them to increase their consumption spending. Suppose, for example, that you own a bond worth $10,000. If the price level fell so dramatically that a sports car originally costing $50,000 now only cost $5,000, wouldn't you feel wealthy enough to buy such a car?

In general, a fall in the price level causes the wealth of those who have loaned money to rise, inducing them to increase their consumption spending. Conversely, borrowers experience a decrease in their wealth and, feeling poorer, decrease their consumption. The decrease is quite small, however, because the dominant borrower, the government, is assumed not to change its spending. Consequently the lenders' reaction generates a net wealth effect on consumption.

2. *International forces.* Other things equal, a fall in the price level causes our goods to be cheaper to foreigners and foreign goods to be more expensive to us. Consequently demand for our exports increases, and we shift some of our demand for imports to domestically produced goods and services that compete against imports.

3. *The real money supply.* A fall in the price level causes the real supply of money in the economy to rise. As we will see in chapter 9, this increase in money serves to increase aggregate demand through several channels. For example, a rise in the real supply of money causes its price, the interest rate, to fall. Lower interest rates, in turn, cause people to increase spending because borrowing costs have fallen.

A fall in the price level causes an increase in aggregate demand. The Keynesian multiplier effect is thus invoked, further increasing aggregate demand. As a result a modest fall in the price level ends up increasing aggregate demand by a substantial amount, creating the downward-sloping aggregate demand curve *AD* portrayed in figure 6.1. For the interested reader, a graphical derivation of this curve appears in appendix 6.1 at the end of this chapter. The intersection of *AD* and *AS*, point *A*, is an equilibrium for the economy, so we visualize the economy as being at price level P_A and at corresponding output level Y_A.

An increase in aggregate demand for goods and services due to government policy shifts the *AD* curve horizontally to the right by an amount equal to the multiplier times this increase. A prominent example of such policy shifts is an increase in government spending—an expansionary fiscal policy. Tracing the economy's reaction to such a shock can illustrate how the aggregate-supply/aggregate-demand diagram is used.

Sample Exam Question 6.2:
If we are to the right of (above) the *AD* curve, there is _____ in the goods and services market, whereas if we are to the left of (below) the *AD* curve, there is _____ in the goods and services market.

Fill in these blanks.

6.3   Using the Aggregate-Supply/Aggregate-Demand Diagram

The aggregate-supply/aggregate-demand diagram is used in this book as a visual aid to understanding the stories we tell about how and why an economy reacts to a shock. Because curve-shifting is not an objective of this book, the derivation of the *AD* curve is placed in appendix 6.1 to this chapter; the rationale behind the *AS* curve is discussed in this appendix, but no formal derivation is provided. Despite their appearances these curves are quite different from microeconomic supply and demand curves. The correct way to think about these curves is as representing equilibrium behavior—points on the *AD* curve are potential equilibria in the goods and services market, and points on the *AS* curve are potential equilibria in the labor market. (They should have been called the "goods and services market equilibrium" curve and the "labor market equilibrium" curve!) From a practical point of view, whenever the economy is on the *AD* curve, we know that the goods and services market is in equilibrium—aggregate demand for goods and services equals aggregate supply of goods and services—and whenever we are on the *AS* curve, the labor market is in equilibrium—aggregate demand for labor equals aggregate supply of labor. At their intersection both markets are simultaneously in equilibrium. One consequence is that when telling stories about macroeconomic reactions, if we are on one of these curves but not the other, we know where to look for disequilibrium forces.

An increase in government spending of ΔG increases spending in equilibrium at every price level by ΔG times the multiplier, so the entire *AD* curve shifts to the right by this amount, as shown in figure 6.1 by the shift to *AD'*. The equilibrium moves to point *B*, and real income increases from Y_A to Y_B. Notice that the new equilibrium position involves a rise in the price level, and through wealth effects, international effects, and a fall in the real money supply, real aggregate demand decreases, causing the change in income $(Y_B - Y_A)$ to be smaller than would have been the case had the price level not risen. In real terms the multiplier becomes smaller than the multiplier of the previous chapter. This process is illustrated in figure 6.2, an updated flowchart incorporating the role of the price level.

Now the initial excess demand is squeezed off through two sources: increases in output and increases in prices. Consequently the multiplier in real terms is smaller than when we did not recognize the role of the price level.

The three zones of the *AS* curve give rise to three different reactions to a dose of fiscal policy. When the *AS* curve is flat, the economy reacts primarily by increasing output; in the intermediate range, both output and prices increase; and when the *AS* curve is vertical, only price increases follow expansionary fiscal policy. The lesson should be clear. Expansionary policy is appropriate when the economy is in a severe recession but inappropriate in a boom.

↑G ⇒ ↑ agg D for g & s
    ⇒ excess D for g & s
    ⇒ ↓ inventories or lost business
    ⇒ signal to firms
    ⇒ ↑ **prices**   ⇒ ↓ **excess demand**
    ⇒ **profitable to increase output**
    ⇒ ↑ output   ⇒ ↓ excess demand
    ⇒ ↑ income
    ⇒ ↑ consumption demand
    ⇒ excess demand, but smaller than before
    ⇒ ↓ inventories and so repeat process

Figure 6.2   The Multiplier Process with Price Changes
Incorporating price changes into the multiplier process makes the multiplier smaller in real terms. This process is illustrated in figure 6.1.

Sample Exam Question 6.3:
"The capacity constraints argument suggests that now is not a good time to pump up government spending."

    (a) What is the "capacity constraints" argument? (b) Why is this not a good time for stimulating fiscal policy?

6.4   Where Is Full Employment?

The analysis of the preceding section is antiquated and misleading, mainly because it contains a very naive view of what is happening in the labor market. In particular, there is no indication in figure 6.1 of the output level that would be generated by an economy at its natural rate of unemployment (NRU), which economists call full employment. Let us remedy this lack by drawing in figure 6.3 a vertical line at the level of output Y_{NRU} that the economy would produce if it were at its natural rate of unemployment. This line is labeled *LRAS* because, as will be seen shortly, it represents the aggregate-supply curve of the economy in the long run when contractual and informational barriers to adjustment no longer exist. The upward-sloping line *SRAS*, akin to the intermediate section of the *AS* curve in the preceding section, is the short-run aggregate-supply curve. For convenience the *AD* curve is drawn to pass through point *A*, the intersection of *LRAS* and *SRAS*.

    Placing the full-employment position on this diagram allows a more realistic portrayal of an economy's reaction to a spending shock. Two such shocks are of interest: (1) an increase in aggregate demand for goods and services pushing the economy into a boom and (2) a decrease in aggregate demand for goods and services pushing the economy into recession. Analyzing each of these shocks permits exposition of the modern view of the

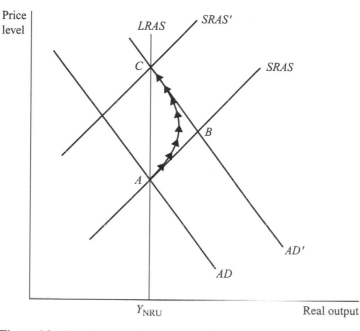

Figure 6.3   Reaction to an Expansionary Shock
The shock shifts *AD* to *AD'*, and the economy reacts by moving from *A* toward *B* as prices rise, decreasing the real wage and enticing firms to hire more workers. When workers become aware that their real wage has fallen and are able to do something about it, the economy moves toward *C*. Higher wages shift *SRAS* up to *SRAS'*.

economy's supply side and how the aggregate-supply/aggregate-demand diagram is used to portray business-cycle behavior.

> **Sample Exam Question 6.4:**
> If we are to the right of the LRAS curve, there is _____ in the long-run labor market, whereas if we are to the left of the LRAS curve, there is _____ in the long-run labor market.
>   Fill in these blanks.

6.5   Moving into a Boom

Suppose that an exogenous increase in aggregate demand shifts the *AD* curve to *AD'*. (*Exogenous* means resulting from an action that is external to the supply and demand forces under investigation; government policy actions are exogenous.) Inventories fall and business in the service industry is turned away, indicating to firms that demand for their good or service has risen. How are firms likely to react? Near the NRU, firms are operating at a high-capacity level, implying that extra output will involve higher per unit cost. Consequently firms are likely to increase prices. Once this price increase is in place, however, it is profitable for firms to increase output, and new firms may be enticed to appear. As a result the demand for workers increases.

When firms try to hire these extra workers, however, they discover to their surprise that workers are hard to come by. Because the economy is at its natural rate of unemployment, a pool of unemployed eager to work at the going wage does not exist. To solve this problem, firms bid up the wage rate slightly, being careful to bid wages up by less than they increased prices. Higher wages induce some students to quit school, some homemakers to leave home, and some job searchers to find more quickly a job with the wage they feel they deserve. This way firms are able to hire more workers and increase output. This combined increase in price and output is shown in figure 6.3 by a movement from *A* out toward point *B*. The wage increase shifts the *SRAS* curve up a bit, so the movement out toward point *B* turns slightly in an upward direction.

In essence, firms are willing to employ the extra workers because the rise in price is greater than the rise in wages—the real wage has fallen—making this venture profitable for firms. Ordinarily workers would not put up with it. At a lower real wage some workers would withdraw their services, choosing instead to become students or homemakers or to search the job market for a better job. Consequently, for the movement out toward

Curiosity 6.1: Are Real Wages Countercyclical?

Some economists have claimed that the theoretical arguments of this chapter can be checked by seeing whether real wages are countercyclical: do they rise during recessions and fall during booms? A key ingredient of this theory is that a fall in real wages induces firms to hire more labor, decreasing unemployment, increasing output, and pushing the economy into the expansionary phase of the business cycle, a series of events that suggests real wages to be countercyclical. But these events do not necessarily happen in sequence.

Other arguments have suggested that firms are primarily quantity adjusters, increasing output by means of overtime as the economy goes into a boom, and decreasing output through labor hoarding and layoffs as the economy enters a recession. Price reactions take place only after the boom or recession has continued for some time, with price changes preceding, matching, or following wage changes, depending on circumstances. Firms in perfectly competitive industries, for example, are likely to have price changes precede wage changes; firms in imperfectly competitive industries may follow a markup pricing strategy and so may not increase prices until wages increase. Furthermore cyclical movements initiated by aggregate demand shocks will have different characteristics from movements initiated by supply-side shocks, so there is no guarantee that real wages are countercyclical. The empirical evidence suggests that they follow no consistent pattern over the cycle.

point *B* in figure 6.3 to be maintained, workers must for some reason be willing to supply more labor at a lower real wage. Economists offer two main explanations for this phenomenon:

1. *Information problems.* Workers may not realize what is happening, genuinely mistaking a higher money wage for a higher real wage. They know exactly what the money wage is but do not have a clear idea what is happening to the overall price level.

2. *Contract obligations.* Workers may be obliged by a formal or informal contract to supply labor at a fixed money wage until the expiration of that contract. Some contracts are renegotiated sooner than others, implying that overall wages do not rise in step with overall price increases. Formal contracts last on average about three years. Those covered by informal contracts typically experience a wage increase once a year.

What is notable about both of these explanations is that they explain only a temporary fall in real wages. Workers eventually realize that their real wage has fallen and demand a rise in the money wage to compensate them fully for higher prices, and eventually all contracts are renegotiated, bringing the real wage back to its original level. Consequently the economy's movement toward point *B* is only temporary. In time, money wages rise as much as prices. As money wages rise, the *SRAS* curve shifts upward, reflecting firms' increased costs. So the economy moves along the curved arrowed line from *A* out toward *B* but eventually back to the NRU at point *C,* and the *SRAS* curve ends up eventually at *SRAS'*. (A common student mistake here is to think of movements to the right on this diagram as corresponding to a higher unemployment level; movements to the right correspond to higher output and *lower* unemployment.)

By now it should be clear why the vertical line at the NRU is called the long-run aggregate supply curve. An important policy lesson should also be evident. Any policy designed to move the economy below its NRU can succeed in the short run, but in the long run the economy will return to the NRU, leaving a higher price level as a legacy. Notice also that during the second half of this movement toward *C,* the economy experiences simultaneous price increases and output decreases/unemployment increases, something that the original Keynesian analyses claimed would not happen.

Another policy lesson might not be so evident. Suppose that the government underestimates the NRU, believing that it is 5 percent when it is actually 6 percent. A 5 percent unemployment rate corresponds to a higher level of output than a 6 percent unemployment rate, so the government thinks that the *LRAS* curve lies to the right of the actual *LRAS* curve. Policy designed to push the economy to this underestimated NRU (and corresponding higher output level) requires continued rightward shifts of the *AD* curve to counteract the economy's movements back to the actual *LRAS* curve. This process creates continued price increases—an inflation—and is the first of several examples we will encounter of how inappropriate government policy can lead to inflation.

6.6   Moving into a Recession

Let us now look at an economy in equilibrium at point *AA* in figure 6.4 and postulate an exogenous fall in aggregate demand for goods and services shifting *AD* to *AD′*. If the economy's reaction were a mirror image of the reaction described earlier for a move into a boom, the fall in aggregate demand should lead firms to lay off workers to avoid accumulating inventories and to cut prices to stimulate demand for their products. Laid-off workers may bid down the wage rate in an effort to regain employment, and this fall in

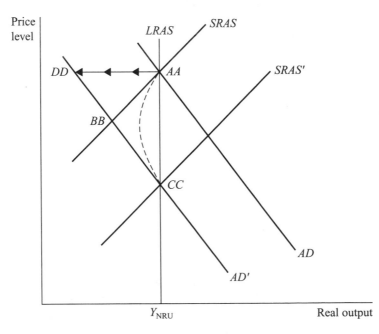

Figure 6.4   Reaction to a Contractionary Shock
The shock shifts *AD* to *AD′*, and economy reacts by moving via quantity adjusting to *DD* where it is stuck in a less-than-full-employment equilibrium. The dotted line shows what would happen if this reaction were the mirror image of the reaction to an expansionary shock.

cost may be passed on by firms through a further lowering of price. In figure 6.4 the economy would follow the dotted line from *AA* out toward *BB* and then down to *CC* as the falling wage shifts the *SRAS* curve down to *SRAS'*.

Unfortunately, this mirror image is not realistic. The reaction of an economy entering a boom can reasonably be expected to occur fairly quickly—the economy in figure 6.3 moves from *A* toward *B* and then up to *C* back at the NRU within about three years because few labor contracts in the United States are for longer than three years and may be shorter if labor unions are worried about such shocks and sign only short-term contracts.

The reaction of an economy entering a recession is much different in that although wages and prices may eventually fall, they do so very reluctantly. Their decline is so gradual that it is more reasonable to postulate that the economy initially moves not toward point *BB*, as the dotted line would suggest, but to point *DD* and stays there for a long time before wages and prices eventually fall, slowly moving the economy down toward point *CC*, where full employment is recovered. The movement to *DD* comes about because in the short run the economy quantity-adjusts rather than price-adjusts—rather than adjusting price in the face of excess supply, firms adjust quantity by laying off workers. Although wages and prices fell during the Great Depression, during ordinary recessions falls in wages and prices have not been experienced on any significant scale. It seems that recoveries from recession happen not because prices and wages fall but rather because of a major stimulus to aggregate demand—such as a war increasing government spending, a technological innovation increasing investment spending, or a buildup of saving increasing consumption spending—all of which lead to multiplier effects.

Why are wages and prices "sticky" downward? This is a crucial question, because its answer goes a long way to explaining why firms are quantity adjusters rather than price adjusters, using layoffs rather than price/wage adjustments when the economy moves into recession. Firms are reluctant to decrease prices because of fears of price wars with competitors and because of incurring "menu costs" such as printing new catalogs. Wages are sticky downward for several reasons:

1. *Contracts.* Union contracts are fixed until expiration, so wages will be sticky for that reason. More important are "implicit contracts," informal understandings firms have with their workers that wages will be steady through both good and bad times unless such changes are proved to be permanent, with deficient demand met by laying off temporary workers, part-timers, and recent hires. Most workers and all firms find this agreement advantageous. Most workers get income security and, in exchange, are willing to accept a slightly lower wage than the firm would otherwise have to pay; firms are assured of keeping their best workers. Temporary workers, part-time workers, and recent hires (sometimes called "outsiders" as opposed to the "insiders" who have the attractive implicit or union contract) are willing to put up with this layoff system for two reasons. First, being for a time subject to layoff may be part of the price one pays to become an insider eventually. Second, some of these people believe that their

skills are not attractive enough to secure a good job elsewhere. They may feel better off with this job even if it is subject to layoff. Both of these reasons are strengthened by the existence of unemployment insurance, which cushions the financial shock of being laid off.

2. *Relative wages.* Workers are concerned about relative wages: how their wages stand in relation to those of friends and workers in other occupations. Consequently no one is willing to be the first to agree to work for a lower wage for fear of moving to a lower rung on the ladder of relative wages. If everyone were to agree in unison to lower wages, a speedy fall in wages might be possible. This could happen, for example, in a country such as Japan where each year there is a coordinated, economywide wage determination process. In the United States only the pain of a prolonged period of high unemployment is likely to force unions and individual workers to agree to wage reductions.

3. *Temporary recession.* Workers may believe that the recession is temporary and decide to get by on unemployment insurance or welfare until the economy recovers, rather than agree to work for a lower wage. This belief has been reinforced over the years by government commitment to full employment. Workers have been led to believe that soon the government will take policy action to pull the economy out of recession.

4. *Efficiency wages.* Firms are afraid of alienating their workers. They find it in their profit-maximizing interest to pay a real wage higher than the real wage that is consistent with full employment, so in the face of deficient demand they do not press workers for lower wages. There are several reasons for this policy: First, by paying an abnormally high real wage a firm may be able to hire a better quality of worker. Second, workers may react by putting forth more work effort, either because they feel morally bound to do so or because they could be fired from an attractive insider job if they are caught shirking. Third, the high wage should reduce labor turnover, lowering hiring and training costs. The classic example of such behavior is Henry Ford's 1914 successful offer to his workers of $5 per day, a huge jump in the going wage.

All this suggests that a negative demand shock will most likely move the economy to point *DD* in figure 6.4 where the goods and services market is in equilibrium but the labor market is not. (A reminder: The goods and services market is in equilibrium because we are on the *AD* curve; the labor market is not in equilibrium because we are not on the *AS* curve.) If the unemployed workers do not cause wages to fall, no forces are set in motion to push the economy back to full employment. Keynes explained this result simply by stating that the unemployed do not bid down wages, so the economy is stuck at point *DD,* sometimes called a less-than-full-employment equilibrium. Modern interpreters draw the same conclusion but provide reasons why economic agents act in rational, maximizing ways to cause wages to be sticky. This approach has earned them the name New Keynesians.

The upshot of all this is that although the economic forces of supply and demand may eventually operate to bring an economy out of recession and back to full employment, they operate too slowly to satisfy participants, so there is a need for policy action. This is the essence of the Keynesian message.

Sample Exam Question 6.6:
"The insider–outsider story is another reason why Keynes is right—we need an active fiscal policy."

(a) What is the "insider–outsider" story? (b) How does it support the Keynesian view?

6.7   Analyzing Supply Shocks

Although we can now recognize that Keynesian analysis did contain an implicit supply curve, prior to the 1970s this supply curve was kept hidden. Rather than using an aggregate-supply/aggregate-demand diagram such as those portrayed in figures 6.3 and 6.4, economists used alternative diagrams that did not explicitly show the supply side of the economy. As a result they tended to forget about or unintentionally denigrate the role of the supply side in affecting economic activity.

The suppression of the role of aggregate supply became painfully evident when Keynesian analyses were unable to suggest appropriate policies to deal with the major supply shocks of the early 1970s. With the aggregate-supply/aggregate-demand diagram, the impact of a supply-side shock can be analyzed more easily. Suppose the economy is at position A in figure 6.5, and a negative supply-side shock—perhaps an increase in the price of energy—hits the economy. Since 1970 the world has experienced four major energy price shocks, resulting from the following events: 1973 OPEC oil embargo (causing oil prices to triple), 1979 Iranian revolution, 1985 OPEC price crash, and 1990 Iraq–Kuwait war. The resulting higher production costs cause the $SRAS$ curve to shift upward to $SRAS'$. (A reminder: An increase in the cost of producing output shifts the $SRAS$ curve upward because firms will continue to produce the same output only if the price is higher to cover the extra costs.)

The $LRAS$ curve should also shift slightly to the left to $LRAS'$, for two reasons. First, because energy is now more expensive, less energy will be used per worker, so workers will become less productive, implying that output produced by a given quantity of labor will be less. Here is an example to illustrate this phenomenon. Suppose that electricity becomes extremely expensive. To save electricity costs, a car repair shop will now hire an extra worker to open and shut the garage doors instead of using an electric garage door opener. Or the mechanics will need to spend time opening and closing doors instead of

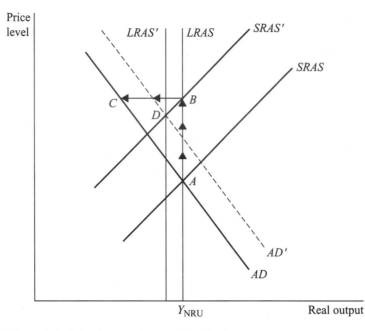

Figure 6.5   Reaction to a Supply-Side Shock
The shock of higher energy costs shifts *SRAS* to *SRAS′* and *LRAS* to *LRAS′*. Firms pass on the higher cost by increasing prices, moving the economy from *A* to *B*. The price rise lowers demand, and firms cut output, moving the economy to *C*. Further reaction depends on how workers respond to the fall in their real wage and nature of government policy action.

fixing cars. Per worker output falls. Second, the fall in worker productivity causes the real wage corresponding to equilibrium in the labor market to fall, prompting some workers to leave the labor force. In the new long-run equilibrium the number of workers becomes smaller. The *LRAS* curve reflects long-run activity in the labor market. In the long run a smaller number of less productive workers corresponds to equilibrium in the labor sector, so the *LRAS* curve must be further to the left. An alternative way of viewing this fall in worker productivity may be helpful: the higher price of energy requires that more output be sent abroad in payment to oil producers, implying that there is less output left over to be distributed to workers. (If energy were produced domestically rather than imported, the result would not be so clear—the fall in output noted earlier would be offset by the rise in the value of our energy output.)

In this situation firms may begin by increasing prices to pass on the higher cost of energy, moving the economy to point *B*. The higher price lowers aggregate demand, and firms react by cutting back production, laying off workers, and moving the economy over to point *C*. At this stage the government may adopt a fiscal policy that shifts *AD* rightward to *AD′*.

Care must be taken not to overstimulate and try to push the economy all the way back to the original *LRAS*—this response would create further price increases. The biggest complication, however, arises from workers' reaction to the price increase. If workers recognize their decreased productivity and accept the fall in their real wage, the economy could settle at *D* in figure 6.5. More realistically, however, workers may demand wage increases to prevent their real wage from falling. This would shift the *SRAS* further upward (not shown in figure 6.5), leading to more price increases and frustrating the fiscal policy. Unemployment will be maintained (i.e., the economy will remain to the left of *LRAS'* at a position like *C*) as long as employed workers prevent the real wage from falling to reflect their decreased productivity.

Sample Exam Question 6.7:
"The trouble is that workers became accustomed to real wage increases of about 3 percent a year, and when productivity growth crashed in the 1970s, they refused to cooperate by lowering real wage growth. Then firms acquiesced to avoid lower productivity due to worker dissatisfaction. The end result was similar to that of the oil price increases."

  (a) How would this situation be portrayed on an *AS/AD* diagram? (b) What terminology do economists use to refer to the phenomenon described in the second sentence?

6.8   Supply-Side Economics

Some economists came to believe that economic forces springing from the supply side were strong enough to play a major role in determining the level and character of economic activity. Such economists developed what has become known as *supply-side economics.*

The most distinguishing characteristic of supply-side economics is the importance placed on economic incentives. For example, a rise in the tax rate is thought to influence significantly the work/leisure decision, the consumption/saving decision, the investment decision, and the market/nonmarket activity decision. These decisions in turn affect the quantity of goods and services supplied in the economy in both the short and the long run. Economists believing that the strength of economic incentives is considerable are called *supply-siders.* They advocate the adoption of supply-oriented policies that operate through changing incentives.

Supply-side economics forces economists to rethink their advocacy of traditional policies in three ways:

1. When an economy is subjected to a supply-side shock, such as an increase in the price of oil, the traditional demand-oriented remedies for economic problems may be inap-

Curiosity 6.2: What Is Real Business-Cycle Theory?

Another legacy of economists' revitalized interest in the supply side of the economy is real business-cycle theory. In this view there is an unknown "natural" level of output that is affected by "real" changes (as opposed to nominal changes that involve only changes in dollar values) such as technological innovations, new products, new government regulations (regarding such things as pollution), weather changes, changes in consumer preferences, natural resource discoveries, labor supply changes, tax rate changes, changes in international relations, large changes in relative prices (especially that of oil), and other supply-side factors. Business cycles arise as the economy moves toward its new equilibrium in response to these "real" shocks. In this view, business cycles are primarily due to these supply-side effects, rather than due to transitory demand-side effects coupled with dynamic rigidities as argued by the Keynesians. A dramatic policy implication is that contrary to the Keynesians, the government should not try to smooth out these movements with policy action—doing so would prevent the economy from moving to its true equilibrium. (An analogy may make this point more clearly: when we move from summer to winter, we should not try to use government policy to offset the reduction of agricultural output that comes with winter.)

Although few economists feel that business cycles can adequately be explained by such supply-side phenomena alone, real business-cycle theory has undoubtedly improved our understanding of business cycles by drawing economists' attention to the wide range of real phenomena that affect the economy and forcing them to think carefully about how they should be incorporated into an overall theory of how the macroeconomy operates.

There is actually more to real business-cycle (RBC) theory than explained above, although discussion of this goes beyond the scope of this book. In addition to its focus on the supply side, it views economic fluctuations as the outcome of the decisions of individual agents operating in competitive markets with flexible prices. Recent advances using this methodology (e.g., relaxing the assumptions of competitive markets and flexible prices) have led to a change in name—dynamic stochastic general equilibrium (DSGE) theory. (See also curiosity 12.1.)

propriate. Consider, for example, a negative supply-side shock making the economy less productive, such as the example analyzed in figure 6.5. An increase in government spending to move the economy back to its original level of income would only serve to increase prices.

2. Traditional demand-oriented policies have impacts on the supply side that can alter substantively their influence on the economy. Consider, for example, an increase in taxes enacted to decrease aggregate demand and fight inflation, traditionally captured by a leftward shift of the *AD* curve. But higher taxes also shift the *AS* curve upward/leftward, by raising costs and reducing incentives: firms view taxes as costs to be passed on, and workers supply less labor when after-tax remuneration falls, compounding the impact on income and making the impact on the price level uncertain.

3. Previously neglected policy options, which affect mostly the supply side, are being reconsidered. Such options include reducing import tariffs on intermediate goods;

deregulation; preventing generous wage increases in the public sector from acting as a standard for the private sector; encouraging expansion of the capital stock through investment tax credits, accelerated depreciation allowances, and lower interest rates; increasing worker productivity by means of government spending on social overhead such as transportation systems, communication infrastructure, and basic research activity; and eliminating or reducing unnecessary health, safety, or environmental regulations.

The greatest attribute of these supply-side policies is that they can raise output and employment while lowering the price level, whereas demand-side policies must raise the price level when increasing output and employment. Supply-siders make much of this difference, claiming that its exploitation can create policy actions capable of attacking "stagflation," the simultaneous occurrence of high inflation and high unemployment.

The spirit of supply-side economics has come to be represented by the Laffer curve, illustrated in figure 6.6, which shows how the tax rate affects tax receipts. With a zero tax rate, tax receipts are also zero. Increasing the tax rate at first increases tax receipts, but eventually a fall in tax receipts occurs as the disincentive effects of higher taxes cause people to work and invest less and participate more heavily in the underground economy. Supply-siders believed that the U.S. economy in the early 1980s was at a point like *A*, so that a reduction in the tax rate would lead to a rise in tax receipts. This belief was part of the rationale behind the tax cuts enacted under President Ronald Reagan.

The enthusiasm of the supply-siders is not shared by many economists, for several reasons:

1. Although incentives matter in theory, in practice their empirical magnitude has been shown to be very small.

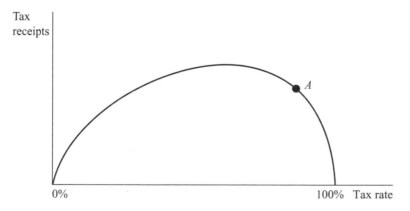

Figure 6.6   The Laffer Curve
An increase in the tax rate initially increases tax receipts, but the disincentive effects of higher taxes eventually cause a fall in tax receipts. Note that at point *A*, lowering the tax rate would increase tax receipts.

2. Many supply-side policies, such as changing tax rates, have minor effects on aggregate supply but major effects on aggregate demand, shifting the *AD* curve by more than the *AS* curve, creating results very similar to those of traditional demand-side policies.

3. Supply-side tax cuts have led to dramatic increases in the government budget deficit and the national debt. In figure 6.6 the economy was to the left of the hump when the Reagan tax cuts were enacted, and thus tax receipts actually decreased.

4. Many supply-side policies, such as lowering import tariffs or reducing taxes on the rich, are politically unacceptable or have undesirable distributional effects.

Because of these objections, supply-siders are not viewed with favor in the economics profession. They have left an important legacy, however—that the supply-side should not be ignored in macroeconomic analyses. Indeed many recent policy actions, such as education tax credits and government funding for the World Wide Web "information superhighway," have been inspired by supply-side considerations.

> **Sample Exam Question 6.8:**
> Suppose that an increase in the tax rate leads to a decrease in tax receipts. Where on the Laffer curve would this economy have been located? Explain your reasoning.

Media Illustrations

Example 1

Michael Spence of Harvard University cautioned about the high risks involved in some supply-side policies: "The Reagan people are currently arguing over what level of tax cuts should be implemented. What if they're wrong? What if the supply side doesn't respond enough to at least take care of the forgone revenues?"

Why can tax cuts be viewed as a supply-side policy?
Cutting tax rates causes people's after-tax return from working and investing to be greater, so there is greater incentive to work harder and invest more. This should increase aggregate supply.

What are the "forgone revenues"?
Forgone revenues are the reduction in tax revenues from the original income level due to the lower tax rate.

What is meant by the supply side responding by enough to take care of the forgone revenues?
The tax cut would need to cause a sufficiently large increase in income to make the rise in tax revenues due to higher income offset the fall in tax revenues due to the initiating tax cut.

What is the specific high risk that Spence is worried about here?
The risk that the tax cut will increase the budget deficit.

Example 2

Arthur Laffer's famous freehand curve showing the effect of tax reduction on tax revenue, the magic logo of the supply-siders, was also not taken seriously by the profession. For some, Laffer was a figure of fun. Most others held that the Kleenex, paper napkin, or toilet paper on which, according to varying legend, the curve was first drawn, could better have been put to its regular use.

Where on this curve is illustrated the possibility of tax rate reduction increasing tax revenue?
Consider any tax rate to the right of the top of the hump on this curve. A reduction in this tax rate moves the economy up toward the top of the hump and thus to a higher tax revenue.

What reasoning creates this possibility?
Lower tax rates increase after-tax income. This increase should stimulate consumption demand and through the Keynesian multiplier process further increase income. This growth increases tax revenue, but ordinarily not by enough to offset the original reduction in tax revenue due to the lower tax rate. But the supply-siders noted that lower tax rates create incentives for work that cause aggregate supply to increase. This extra force increasing income could create extra tax revenues sufficient to cause net tax revenues actually to increase.

Example 3

Secretary of the Treasury William E. Simon on behalf of President Gerald Ford's administration has submitted a proposal to the House Ways and Means Committee to reduce taxes on corporate profits. It seems the nation is faced with a trade-off between growth and redistribution: Does it want to split a smaller pie equally or a larger pie less equally? The "difference principle," advocated by Harvard philosopher John Rawls, in his book *A Theory of Justice*, holds that inequality can be justified only if it works to the absolute benefit of the least advantaged.

Explain the rationale that must lie behind Simon's proposal and how it gives rise to the trade-off mentioned.
Simon must feel that reducing taxes on corporate profits will cause corporations to respond by increasing investment spending, increasing both aggregate demand and the economy's productive capacity, stimulating growth. The trade-off is between this growth and the redistribution of income toward the wealthy owners of corporations.

Under what circumstances would Rawls's difference principle be met in this context?
The difference principle would be met if the inequality created by the lower profits taxes causes the low-income workers and unemployed in the economy to benefit. Such benefits could come about because of higher employment and higher real wages due to productivity increases.

Chapter Summary

- Keynesian neglect of the supply side of the economy handicapped analysis of supply-side shocks, business-cycle behavior, and long-run economic growth.

- The *AD* curve is most appropriately interpreted as a series of possible equilibrium positions for the economy in which aggregate demand for goods and services matches aggregate supply of goods and services. The *AS* curve is most appropriately interpreted as a series of possible equilibrium positions for the labor market. Short-run equilibria in the labor market differ from long-run equilibria because of contract obligations and information failures, so short- and long-run *AS* curves differ. The long-run *AS* curve is a vertical line at the level of output corresponding to the NRU.

- An expansionary policy at full employment moves the economy in the short run to a higher price level and a higher output level, but in the long run the economy returns to its original full-employment (NRU) level of output, implying that in the long run the only effect of this policy is to raise the price level. The temporary increase in output occurs because workers are induced temporarily to provide more labor at a lower real wage; formal or informal contract obligations may prevent them from quickly adjusting their money wage to offset price level increases, or they may not quickly perceive that these price increases have lowered their real wage. Two results of note are that (1) during the second half of this reaction, the economy is moving back up to the NRU while continuing to experience price increases (unemployment and prices are increasing together), and (2) if the government tries to maintain the economy at an unemployment level below the NRU, a continually rising price level will develop.

- A contractionary policy at full employment moves the economy into a recession made worse by "downward-sticky" wages and prices. Modern Keynesians, called New Keynesians, have provided several reasons why this is consistent with rational maximizing behavior. The wage and price stickiness exacerbates and prolongs the recession, causing Keynesians to call for government policy action.

- A negative supply-side shock can make the economy less productive and thus require a fall in the real wage if full employment is to be maintained. The economy's reaction to such a shock depends on how workers react to price increases that lower their real wage, and on whether government recognizes any change in the full-employment level of output.

- Supply-side economists stress the role of incentives (and disincentives) created by policies. An infamous example is the Laffer curve, which shows how disincentives cause tax revenues eventually to decrease as the tax rate increases. Supply-side economics has been discredited mainly because the empirical magnitude of the incentive effects is so small.

Media Exercises

(Group B questions require more thought.)

A1. For years the scale has tipped toward controlling the economy by controlling federal spending and consumption. Now It may begin to lean toward stimulating production through incentives.

What names are usually given to these policies?

A2. Inevitably, says Laffer, this economic growth will raise enough tax revenues to more than offset the original tax cut, thus shrinking the federal deficit.

Where on the Laffer curve must Laffer believe the economy is located?

A3. If it were a "stimulative deficit" that was deliberately undertaken to prime the pump of the economy, then the debt might liquidate itself.

a. How could a deficit "prime the pump" of the economy?

b. How could this cause the debt to liquidate itself?

A4. Indeed there was a remarkable consensus among economists at the conference that most of the rise in unemployment over the past two decades does not reflect deficient demand, but rather a rise in the. . . .

Complete this sentence.

A5. Supply-side economics, packaged and popularized as "Reaganomics," has become a big deal in the current policy debate over the fight against stagflation. To counteract this phenomenon of persistent high inflation, unemployment, and stagnant growth, supply-side policies emphasize _____ to take the pressure off prices.

Fill in the blank.

A6. The calculations governments make about tax revenues are always based on the assumption that taxpayers are dutiful sheep who will raise not a bleat as they are led to the fleecing pen. They will all continue to stay where they are, work just as hard, produce just as much, and pay their taxes on the same basis as they always have.

Does this comment imply that a government will underestimate or overestimate the extra tax revenue that a tax increase will generate?

A7. One striking challenge came from "supply-side" economists who contended that the sheer waste and perverse incentives associated with high tax rates created opportunities to cut tax rates without cutting. . . .

Complete this sentence.

A8. If adverse supply shocks (escalating oil prices, crop failures) were so influential in creating stagflation in the 1970s, it is difficult to believe that we cannot create favorable supply shocks in the 1980s.

How would adverse supply shocks create stagflation (rising prices and rising unemployment)?

A9. With the economy mired in recession, it is almost a classic case of room for government stimulus without damage.

What is meant here by government stimulus "without damage"?

A10. The net effect of the proposed Clinton taxes would be to raise the marginal tax rate of typical employees by more than 15 percentage points. The White House appears unaware that taxes do more than transfer money from individuals to the government. High marginal tax rates also distort _____.

Fill in the blank.

A11. Several economists argue that positive supply shocks—especially falling import prices—account for all of America's disinflation over the past couple of years.

How are falling import prices a positive supply shock?

A12. This month's slight uptick in the Australian unemployment rate to 4.5 percent shouldn't be taken too literally. It's probably just a blip. But it's a timely reminder that unemployment shouldn't fall much lower. If it does, it won't be a good sign.

a. Why would we not want unemployment to fall much lower?

b. What name do economists give to the level below which they do not want the unemployment rate to fall?

B1. The share of taxes paid by the top 0.5 percent of income earners rose to 18 percent in 1984–85 from 14 percent in 1981 despite (or rather because of) the reduction in the top marginal tax rate.

Explain the rationale that lies behind the "or rather because of" comment.

B2. **The European Union's jobless rate, by contrast, is nudging 12 percent. A few die-hard Keynesians might reckon that this leaves room for a demand stimulus to create jobs, but most economists believe that. . . .**

  a. What is the logic of the die-hard Keynesians?

  b. Complete this clipping to explain why most economists do not agree with the die-hard Keynesians.

B3. **When the British in 1979 cut top tax rates of 83 percent on earned income and 98 percent on investment income to 60 and 75 percent, respectively, they were accused of hugely reducing the share of tax paid by the rich. Instead, the top 5 percent of British taxpayers today contribute a third as much again in real terms as they did in 1978. This is because. . . .**

  Complete this clipping.

B4. **At a pragmatic level, my colleagues take the view that if a rich man paying a lower tax rate makes it possible for a low-income family to have a good house to live in, useful and secure employment, access to quality, affordable medical care, and a good education for their children, then society as a whole is richer.**

  a. What great trade-off is being described here?

  b. What name might economists use to describe this spokesperson and her colleagues?

B5. **We have a high minimum wage here in France, and quite frankly, we do not want the low-paid McJobs that proliferate in the United States.**

  What is the cost of this policy?

B6. **The main reason why French labor productivity is so high is that companies do not employ a lot of people. They prefer to grow by investing in machines.**

  a. What kind of supply-side policy may have brought this preference about?

  b. What undesirable side effect does it have?

B7. **Economists said that even after taking hurricane and strike distortions into account, industrial production data signaled that manufacturers were bracing for tougher conditions.**

  a. What name would economists give to "hurricane and strike distortions?"

  b. What must have happened in the industrial production data here?

B8. **With the economy already running a negative output gap of 6 percent, a lack of government stimulus will likely only result in. . . .**

a. What is a negative output gap?

b. Complete this clipping.

B9. **The same study finds that it is quite likely that the lower rates have generated significant Laffer curve effects—meaning the government. . . .**

Complete this statement.

Appendix 6.1   Deriving the AD Curve

The purpose of this appendix is to present the graphical derivation of the *AD* curve in its simplest form. This derivation utilizes the 45-degree line diagram (expounded in appendix 5.3) in figure 6.7 to derive the *AD* curve in figure 6.8.

In figure 6.7 we begin with price level P_A, which gives rise to aggregate expenditure line AE_{PA} putting the economy at equilibrium point A. At point A the price level is P_A and

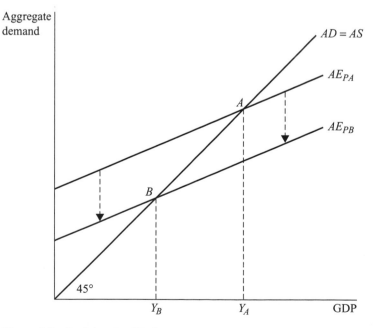

Figure 6.7   Deriving the *AD* Curve
A rise in price from P_a to P_b shifts the *AE* curve down to AE_{PB}, changing the equilibrium point from *A* to *B*. The higher price level P_b is matched with the lower income level Y_b in figure 6.8.

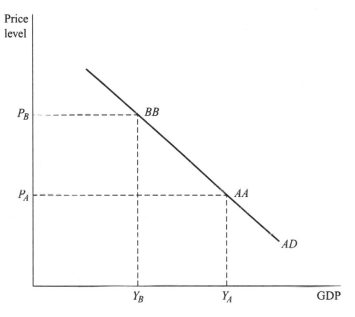

Figure 6.8   Deriving the *AD* Curve
The movement from *A* to *B* in Figure 6.7 corresponds to a movement from *AA* to *BB,* producing a downward-sloping *AD* curve.

income is Y_A, shown in figure 6.8 as point *AA*. Suppose now that the price level increases to P_B. This increase causes the wealth effect and other phenomena to operate to decrease aggregate demand for goods and services, shifting the *AE* curve down to AE_{PB}, lowering equilibrium income to Y_B. Thus the higher price level P_B corresponds to lower equilibrium income level Y_B, shown in figure 6.8 as point *BB*.

Figures 6.7 and 6.8 show that the *AD* curve is downward-sloping. They also make clear that the *AD* curve is better described as an "equilibrium" curve: for each price level it tells us what level of income would have to prevail to create equilibrium in the goods and services submarket of the macroeconomy. This version of the *AD* curve is very simple; it represents equilibrium in only one macroeconomic submarket, the goods and services market; more elaborate versions of the *AD* curve also represent equilibrium in the money market, or in both the money and the foreign exchange markets. The key thing to remember is that whenever the economy is on the *AD* curve we have equilibrium in the goods and services market, so there will be no pressure for change from this market.

The *AS* curve is also an "equilibrium" curve, representing equilibrium in the labor market. *The aggregate supply curve consists of combinations of price and income that correspond to equilibrium in the labor market.* It builds into its derivation (not presented here) the fact that workers demand wage increases when the price level increases. In the short run, workers may misjudge what is happening or be constrained by contracts, so price increases may not be matched by wage increases, allowing firms to increase profit by increasing output; because of the misjudgement or the contract constraints, a temporary equilibrium in the labor market occurs—the *AS* curve is upward-sloping in the short run. In the long run, however, workers should be successful in increasing wages by enough to offset fully the original increase in prices, pushing the equilibrium level of employment back to its original level. This result implies no long-run change in income, so the long-run AS curve is vertical. This is the rationale behind the *SRAS* and *LRAS* curves introduced in section 6.4. The key thing to remember is that whenever the economy is on the long-run AS curve, we have equilibrium in the labor market, so there will be no pressure for change from this market. Whenever we are on the short-run *AS* curve, there is temporary equilibrium in the labor market, so there is temporarily no pressure for change from this market.

The intersection of *AS* and *AD* is a combination of price and income that corresponds to simultaneous equilibrium in the both the goods and services market and the labor market. Whenever the economy is not located on both of these curves, disequilibrium forces should act to push the economy in one direction or another. Much of the macro-economic analysis in this book consists of stories about disequilibrium reactions, utilizing the *AS/AD* diagram to picture the equilibrium character of the economy.

7   Growth and Productivity

In the 1950s and 1960s the rate of growth of U.S. productivity, and hence of the domestic standard of living as measured by per capita output of economic goods and services, was between 2.5 and 3.0 percent per year. In the 1970s and 1980s, however, this rate fell to less than half its former level. At the higher rate of growth, the standard of living doubles every generation, about every twenty-five years, but at the lower rate the standard of living increases only by half during a generation. What appears to be a small difference in growth rates has surprisingly dramatic implications for the standard of living in the long run.

It is hard for politicians and even policy makers to become excited about doing something to raise the rate of productivity growth by, say, 0.7 percentage points. Doing so would double per capita real income over 100 years from what it would otherwise be. But the percentage seems so small, and the payoff so far away, that politicians are easily distracted by issues with bigger numbers and more immediate payoffs, such as keeping the economy at full employment. The misery of unemployment and the drama of short-run swings from recession to boom can seduce policy makers into focusing on unemployment issues and theorists into concentrating on business-cycle fluctuations. Both groups too easily forget that our material standard of living—which many believe to be the most important dimension of economics—is determined by forces only peripherally associated with the issue of full employment.

The previous chapter discussed the supply side of the economy, emphasizing the distinction between the short and long runs, but focused on the business cycle—fluctuations of output around potential output. The purpose of this chapter is to discuss how potential output is itself growing, a supply-side phenomenon of a different sort, and to try to understand what determines the rate of growth of potential output and what determines productivity growth, which is the prime determinant of our material standard of living.

Upon completion of this chapter you should

- realize that most of macroeconomics focuses on what keeps the economy operating at its potential output rather than on what causes potential output to grow rapidly;

- know the main determinants of economic growth, as well as possible explanations for an historical slowdown and subsequent revival of productivity growth; and

- understand the important role played by the nation's saving rate, and how it is affected by the government budget deficit.

7.1   The Determinants of Growth

The rate of growth of output varies dramatically over the business cycle. As we emerge from a recession, the economy can grow very quickly, at rates exceeding 5 or 6 percent a year, as unemployed labor and idle plant and equipment are put to work. "Economic growth" refers not to such short-run spurts in an economy's growth rate but to growth in an economy's *potential* or full-employment output, measured over quite long periods of time. Economic growth depends on increases in the quantity and quality of the two basic inputs of the macroeconomic production process—capital and labor—and on improvements in the way in which they are combined. The following are the five main sources of GDP growth:

1. *An increase in the size of the labor force.* Examples of supply-side policies that affect the size of the labor force are immigration regulations, day-care subsidies, retirement benefits, and tax incentives.

2. *An increase in the quality of the labor force.* Examples of supply-side policies that influence labor quality are subsidies for retraining programs and the development of technical schools oriented more closely to the needs of industry. The quality of the labor force is sometimes referred to as *human capital.*

3. *An increase in the size of the stock of physical capital.* Physical stock equals the number of buildings and the amount of equipment firms have to work with. Examples of supply-side policies that affect the size of the capital stock are tax incentives for investment and saving.

4. *An increase in the quality of the capital stock.* Examples of supply-side policies that influence the quality of capital are tax incentives for research and development, and promotion of competition.

5. *Improvements in the way in which capital and labor are combined to produce output.* Improvements could be due to better worker/management relations, just-in-time inven-

tory policies, greater division of labor (specialization), economies of scale, or the migration of workers from areas of low productivity to areas of high productivity, such as movement of farm workers to the cities.

Technological change, thought by many to be the most important determinant of per capita income growth, is embodied in labor and capital, so it is included with the improvements in their quality.

The middle column of table 7.1 shows the relative contributions to actual growth in the United States during the 1929 to 1982 period. The negative contribution of changes in legal and human environment is due to regulatory legislation involving worker safety and environmental protection, which direct resources away from the production of output counted in the GDP measure. The category "advances in knowledge" is calculated as a residual; it represents technical change.

Associated with the concept of economic growth is an increasing material standard of living enjoyed by people in the economy, the main determinant of which is an economy's *productivity*, usually measured as output per working hour. Growth in productivity results from increases in physical capital, higher quality of labor and capital, and improvements in how capital and labor are combined. The role of each of these is affected by institutional features of the economy such as the work ethic of the culture, the entrepreneurial drive of the populace, and its ability to adapt to change. For more on this see curiosity 7.2. The right-hand column of table 7.1 offers some insight into past contributions to productivity growth. The negative number for labor input reflects decreases in hours worked per week. This change reflects a substantial gain in our standard of living—during the 1970s and 1980s, a period in which low productivity gains were plaguing the economy, workers on

Table 7.1 Relative Contributions to U.S. Growth, 1929 to 1982

Source	Percent contribution to total growth of 2.9% per year on average	Percent contribution to perperson growth of 1.5% per year on average
Labor input except education	32	−12
Education per worker	14	27
Capital	19	20
Advances in knowledge	20	38
Improved resource allocation	8	16
Economies of scale	9	18
Land	0	−3
Changes in legal and human environment	−1	−3

Source: Edward F. Denison, *Trends in American Economic Growth, 1929–1982*, Washington, DC: Brookings Institution, 1985.

Curiosity 7.1: What Is Endogenous Growth Theory?

Keynesian analysis viewed investment spending as a component of aggregate demand and focused on its multiplier impact on income. A longer run view, however, recognizes that investment affects the supply side of the economy by increasing the capital stock and making the economy more productive. In round terms, 60 percent of investment offsets depreciation of existing plant and equipment, 20 percent increases capital in line with annual labor force growth, and the remaining 20 percent serves to increase capital per worker, thus enhancing productivity.

   Early attempts to formalize this role of investment viewed GDP as being determined, through an algebraic formula, by the stock of labor, the capital stock, and a term representing productivity. GDP grew because each year the labor force grew thanks to population growth, the capital stock grew thanks to investment, and productivity grew each year (by about 2 percent) thanks to technical change brought about by a continuous stream of innovations. A key assumption was that this rate of technical change is unaffected by the saving and investment levels it helps determine through its influence on the growth rate. The independence of the rate of technical change from investment and saving activity is what is meant by the statement that technical change is exogenous. The lack of such independence means that technical change is determined endogenously by the interaction of saving, investment, growth, and technical change.

   Modern growth theory questions this exogenous view of technical change, claiming that technical change is determined endogenously: the level of technical change can be influenced by investment in education to improve the quality of labor and by investment in research and development to improve the quality of capital. Furthermore the success of such investments could induce more such investment and higher saving to finance it. It is therefore possible for a virtuous circle to develop in which investment creates more knowledge, which in turn spurs more investment. Some have claimed that the United States was experiencing such a virtuous circle during the late 1990s. This endogenous growth theory raises the profile of national saving and investment.

average added almost five years of waking leisure to their lifetimes! Note how large is the unexplainable residual "advances in knowledge," which reflects technical change.

   An interesting way to measure productivity improvements is to calculate the number of hours of work required to earn enough money to pay for the goods and services we purchase. Over time we need to work fewer and fewer hours at the average wage to buy things. Many examples are quite spectacular because they refer to items that have experienced actual decreases in price over time, such as color TVs, computers, and microwave ovens. In 1984, for example, a VCR cost 54 hours of work, but in 1997 it cost only 15 hours. In 1900 a bottle of Coke cost 5 cents, 20 minutes of wages; today it costs less than 1.5 minutes of wages. Other examples are more modest, such as a large pepperoni pizza in 1980 costing 66 minutes of work but in 1997 costing 50 minutes. For an excellent discussion of this topic with plenty of examples, point your browser at www.dallasfed.org and search for the 1997 annual report. (These comparisons can be tricky. The real wage

Curiosity 7.2: Why Does the Standard of Living Vary So Much across Countries?

Natural resources play a big role in explaining differences in the standard of living across countries, but the economics profession has come to believe that the main reason for differences in living standards across countries is institutional differences. In particular, some countries have evolved institutional arrangements that create incentives for individuals to channel effort into activities (investment, saving, entrepreneurship, etc.) that bring about economic growth. "Institutions" is a general term that encompasses a broad range of phenomena such as a fair and efficient judicial system, an educated populace, market incentives, openness to international trade (allowing economies of scale), secure property rights, protection against theft, political stability, mutual trust in business transactions, and a government with competent officials minimizing corruption, red tape, frivolous regulations, confiscatory taxation, and unjustified expropriation. Note the major roles of government, the rule of law, and economic freedom. (Check www.freetheworld.com for more information on economic freedom.) *Rent seeking* is terminology often encountered in this context. People can earn income by producing output, or by taking/diverting the output others have produced; the latter is called rent seeking, an example of which is corruption. Rent seeking absorbs labor that would otherwise go into productive activities, and by taking some of the output of entrepreneurs rent seekers act as a tax on entrepreneurs, reducing their growth-enhancing activities. Unfortunately, institutions in some nations favor diversion over production.

West versus East Germany, and North versus South Korea, are dramatic examples confirming the role of institutions in affecting growth and prosperity. Another example is China, which at the end of the fourteenth century had a marked technological advantage over other countries, having invented paper, movable type, the compass, the clock, gunpowder, iron casting, and the spinning wheel. But China lacked institutions supporting entrepreneurship; rulers preferred a stable and controllable environment and so suppressed innovators. Additional evidence comes from studies in which measures such as the length of time it takes someone to start up a new business are shown to be highly correlated with standards of living across countries. For example, in the United States it takes 5 days to start a new business, 250 days to resolve a dispute in court, and costs 8 weeks wages to fire a worker; the numbers for Brazil are 152, 566, 165!

Because different countries have different institutions, steady-state (achievable) standards of living vary across countries, even when all countries have access to the same technology. An important consequence here is that there is no reason to expect countries to be converging over time to the same standard of living; each country should over time approach its own steady-state standard of living. (We do observe *conditional convergence*, however—convergence among countries thought to have similar steady states.) Because of this growth rates across countries can vary markedly; countries at their steady-state per capita income level should grow at a rate determined primarily by technological change, whereas countries below their steady-state per capital income level are capable of growing much faster. Another important consequence here is that foreign aid cannot be expected to be successful if the recipient country has poor institutions.

actually fell slightly from 1970 to 2002, but when nonwage compensations, such as insurance and pension contributions, and payroll taxes, are accounted for, total compensation rose by about 45 percent.)

Productivity growth in the United States slowed dramatically from the early 1970s to the mid-1990s. (During this period productivity growth was about 1.4 percent compared to the historical average of about 1.8 percent and the remarkable surge of about 2.3 percent during the late 1990s.) Several explanations have been offered for this slowdown:

1. *A return to normal.* The rate of productivity growth experienced during the thirty years after World War II was anomalously high when viewed in a broader historical context. It may be that during this period we fell back to a more normal rate of productivity growth or are experiencing a normal cyclical downturn in the rate of discovery of new technology.

2. *Decreases in investment.* A smaller rate of investment implies lower growth in the amount of capital (plant and equipment) with which each worker has to work, as well as a slower rate at which technical change becomes embodied in the capital stock. It also implies lower spending on research and development, decreasing the rate at which technological innovations are developed. Decreases in government investment in infrastructure (roads, airports, water supply systems, etc.) affect the productivity of private capital and thereby affect growth. A decrease in the national rate of saving affects the amount of funding available for investment.

3. *Measurement problems.* Many productivity increases manifest themselves in a higher quality of output rather than in a higher quantity of output per worker. If quality changes are not measured properly, which is often the case, the growth slowdown may be an illusion. Increases in government regulations to enhance worker safety and environmental protection are another source of measurement problems. To the extent that such regulations achieve their desired ends, traditional measures of productivity are usually underestimates, and thus the productivity growth slowdown is an illusion, but if they reflect unnecessary bureaucracy, productivity growth is dissipated. Home production fell steadily from about 45 percent of GDP at the end of World War II to about 33 percent of GDP in 1973, exaggerating measured GDP growth during this period as more and more household activity became measured in the market. After 1973 this movement of household activity to the marketplace ceased, suggesting that the perceived slowdown was due to an exaggerated growth rate during the earlier period.

4. *Inflexibilities.* For productivity increases to occur, both labor and output markets must be flexible, allowing competition to force old, inefficient industries to die out and new, more efficient industries to replace them. In Europe, many countries have enacted policies to protect existing industries and jobs, making the introduction of technological change very costly. The United States is thought to have a relatively flexible labor market in this respect. From 1973 to 1983 the U.S. economy created 18 million jobs, whereas the German economy lost almost a million jobs.

5. *Structural changes.* Over time, changes in tastes and technology affect what is produced, where it is produced, how it is produced, and the skills required of the labor force. Although such structural changes reflect the needed flexibility noted earlier, they can lead to slowdowns in further growth. Examples of such changes include a shift of economic activity into the service industries where productivity increases are more difficult to attain; a change in the composition of the workforce, including more young people and former homemakers with less experience and fewer market-oriented skills; and a slowdown in the movement of labor from the farm to the city as the great technological advances in agriculture become fully integrated into the economy. Increases in energy prices require that the economy shift to a new profit-maximizing mix of inputs, reflecting their new relative prices, during which time productivity growth will be inhibited. Moving toward the new IT world required huge investment without an immediate payoff.

6. *Incentive effects.* Supply-siders claim that we have been taxing work, saving, and output while subsidizing consumption, leisure, unemployment, and retirement. The remarkable economic growth of Japan and the four "tigers" (Hong Kong, Singapore, Taiwan, and South Korea) has been based on allowing free markets to operate—permitting entrepreneurs to reap the fruits of their risk and labor. This experience has led many economists to believe that although the supply-siders' incentive effects may not have much impact in the short run, they can be of considerable importance in the long-run-growth context.

> **Sample Exam Question 7.1:**
> "The average work week was 76 hours in 1830, 60 hours in 1890, 39 hours in 1950, and about 34 hours today. This surely must mean that less output is being produced per worker, so productivity must be falling."
>
> How would you respond to this comment?

7.2   The Productivity Growth Process

Unfortunately, the process by which productivity increases are incorporated into the economy is not a comfortable one. In 1942 economist Joseph Schumpeter described the essence of capitalism as the continuous mutation of the firm and market, as old industries prospered and then died, and were replaced by new industries. He named the process *creative destruction.* It is sometimes referred to as the *churn.* In the United States approximately one in twenty jobs disappears each year (about 7 million!); the most economically thriving U.S. regions tend to have the greatest job loss but also the greatest job creation, so there is plenty of churn.

New technology invariably destroys many more jobs than it creates. This fact is indeed the essence of how productivity increases are injected into the economy. Fewer workers are needed to produce the same output, with the surplus workers put to work producing a bonus (extra output) that would not be possible without the new technology. For example, manufacturing output almost doubled from 1980 to 2003, but employment in manufacturing actually declined! This process can be far-reaching. In 1800 nearly 90 percent of the U.S. population was on farms, but today that figure is less than 3 percent. An unfortunate side effect of this process is that new technologies usually require workers with new skills, so those with old skills become unemployed. For example, blacksmiths cannot easily get jobs as auto mechanics. These unemployed find that sweeping technological and institutional change has wiped out firms and entire industries, revolutionized products and human skills, and altered dramatically the nature of the workplace itself. The past few decades have seen dramatic growth in DVD rental, software, carpet cleaning, and movie production businesses and significant decreases in activity associated with fur goods, barbershops, leather products, and drive-in theaters. Railroad employees, cobblers, and switchboard operators have diminished dramatically in numbers, while occupations like medical technician, computer programmer, and professional athlete have mushroomed. Understandably, workers find it difficult to adapt to such changes, producing long-term unemployment, recession, and slow growth.

Although this process is ongoing as a continual stream of innovations occurs, some innovations are of such importance that they exaggerate any subsequent recession and growth slowdown. The Industrial Revolution is the best-known example. More recent examples include the period between 1880 and 1930, with the development of electric power, chemicals, the internal combustion engine, and the assembly line; the period between 1940 and 1970, with the creation of plastics, synthetic fibers, the jet engine, television, and multinational corporations; and most recently, the computer/information revolution based on the personal computer, biotechnology, telecom networks, and lean, flexible, decentralized, nonhierachical workplaces.

Such periods of great innovation give rise to a long-wave cycle. The recession created by significant innovations lingers—with stagnant growth, write-offs of dated capital stock, high structural unemployment, and social tension—until a new generation of workers arises, unencumbered by the old way of doing things. The economy rebuilds itself around the new technology and its associated new infrastructure, creating a protracted period of expansion, within which the normal business cycles occur. Some economists believe that the productivity slowdown that occurred from the early 1970s to the mid-1990s was in part due to the economy passing through the trough of a long-wave cycle, and that the apparent recovery of productivity growth during the late 1990s represented the beginning of a long-wave expansion period based on Internet, telecommunication, and computer technologies.

The creative destruction phenomenon is the process whereby productivity increases are implemented, increasing our standard of living. One policy implication is that government should not inhibit this process by forcing firms to bear high costs when laying off workers, subsidizing firms to protect jobs, or insulating firms from competition. Another policy implication is that governments should facilitate adjustment by organizing worker retraining programs.

Sample Exam Question 7.2:
"They don't seem to be getting the underlying message in the country's failures in domestic and international markets: America has been destroying too few jobs."
    What logic could lie behind this statement?

7.3   The Role of National Saving

No agreement exists about the causes of the productivity growth slowdown, but economists do agree that the level of investment is a crucial element in the productivity growth process. Figure 7.1 illustrates the connection between growth and investment for selected countries. The relationship between investment and growth is by no means exact, but it is apparent. A major determinant of investment is the level of national saving—that part of GDP not used for private or public consumption. A useful perspective on national

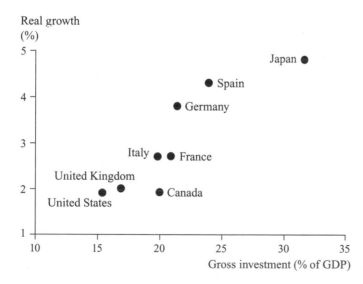

Figure 7.1   Real Growth and Investment
Real growth as measured on the vertical axis is average growth over the 1986 to 1991 period. Gross investment is for 1991. Source: OCED Economic Surveys, 1993–1994.

saving can be gained by looking at how the various categories of aggregate demand are financed.

Income earners allocate some of their income to pay for their consumption goods and services, and some of it to pay their taxes. What is left over is called *private saving*, which is used to buy financial assets, such as government bonds or stocks and bonds sold by businesses to pay for their investment in plant and equipment. What determines how much of the saving goes to the government and how much goes to business? The answer, in short, is the interest rate. The government needs to sell enough bonds to finance its deficit, so it bids up the interest rate to get the financing it needs. As the interest rate rises, some businesses decide that it is too expensive to undertake investment plans, and they abandon their plans. This way the rising interest rate squeezes business demand for financing down to what is left over after the government has financed its deficit.

This process can be illustrated by ignoring the international sector and writing GDP as

$$GDP = C + G + I$$

reflecting its aggregate demand components, and writing it again as

$$GDP = C + T + S$$

reflecting its use in financing consumption and paying taxes T, with what is left over called private saving S. This analysis gives rise to the portrayal in figure 7.2 of T and S serving as the financing sources for G and I.

Taxes are used exclusively to finance government spending, with the budget deficit financed by some of our private saving. The private saving that is left over is called *national saving*; it is used to finance private investment, so private investment ends up equal to private saving less the budget deficit. The lesson from this analysis is that there

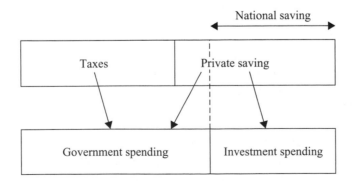

Figure 7.2   National Saving
When the government has a deficit, its spending is financed partially by taxes and partially by selling bonds to the public. The funds that the public have left over are used to finance private investment.

are two fundamental determinants of private investment: the level of private saving and the government budget deficit. Between them, they determine the interest rate that forces private investment to a level equal to national saving—what is left over after private saving has financed the budget deficit. In formal terms,

Private investment = National saving = Private saving − Government deficit

If there were a government budget surplus, as happened in the late 1990s, the government deficit would of course be negative in this relation—national saving would be larger. Instead of competing for financing, the government would be making additional financing available as it used its budget surplus to retire some of its debt.

A caveat should be added here. Notice that this relationship determines *I, private* investment. But the effectiveness of private investment is in part determined by *public investment*—government spending on infrastructure, such as highways and dams, and on education and health. Consequently it is misleading to identify growth with only national saving/private investment; public investment should be recognized.

During the 1980s the determinants of national saving changed markedly. Before 1980, U.S. private saving was about 9.6 percent of GDP, and the government budget deficit was about 1.4 percent of GDP, yielding a national saving rate of about 8.2 percent. By 1990, private saving had fallen to 6.6 percent and the government deficit had risen to 3.6 percent, dropping national saving to 3 percent. This rate of national saving was low not just in comparison to earlier years, but also relative to the 12 percent of most other industrialized countries, and the 17 percent of Japan. This trend to a lower private saving rate in the United States continued until in 2008 it had fallen to zero! (This was partly caused by people increasing mortgages on their homes to increase consumption.) Saving returned to more normal levels in 2009 as people recovered from the financial crisis and protected themselves in case of job loss.

Did the drop in U.S. national saving cause private investment in the United States to fall? Surprisingly, not much, mainly because of financing from foreign sources (see curiosity 7.3 on foreign financing). Prominent among these foreign sources was China, where the saving rate was over 30 percent. Reliance on foreign financing is not a good long-run strategy, however. It can disappear quickly, causing great disruption, and if it is continued, much of the benefit of the investment accrues to the new foreign owners of our businesses rather than to our own citizens. Consequently considerable interest has focused on ways to increase the national saving rate, such as by decreasing the government deficit, an obvious implication of the preceding analysis.

Sample Exam Question 7.3:
"Domestic investment did not fall as sharply as did national saving because. . . ."
  Complete this clipping.

Curiosity 7.3: What about Foreign Financing?

Domestic financing for private investment comes from national saving, which is private saving less the government deficit. Foreigners may also provide financing, which can be examined by including imports (M) and exports among the aggregate demand categories that comprise GDP.

GDP can be written as $C + I + G + X - M$, reflecting its aggregate demand makeup, or $C + T + S$, reflecting its breakdown for financing purposes. Equating these two expressions, we get

$$C + I + G + X - M = C + T + S$$

Cancel the Cs and move the $X - M$ to the financing side to get

$$I + G = T + S + M - X$$

This equation shows that financing for G and I comes from taxes, private saving, and foreign sources $M - X$, as illustrated in figure 7.3.

How does $M - X$ represent foreign financing? $M - X$ is the excess of U.S. imports over exports. In 2007 this was about $730 billion, representing US$730 billion left in the hands of foreigners after they paid for their imports. These dollars are available to be loaned to U.S. citizens, augmenting the sources of financing discussed earlier. This reflects the United States–China situation—the United States imports a lot more from China than it exports to China, with China using the net dollars it obtains to buy U.S. government bonds. More on this topic appears in chapter 14 where, when we discuss the balance of payments, this foreign financing is referred to as capital inflows. In formal terms we have

Private investment = National saving + Foreign financing

A final comment on the role of the foreign sector in growth is in order, to dispel an unfortunate myth that has misled debate on this issue. Growth in a country's standard of living is not affected by how "competitive" it is relative to other countries; as emphasized earlier, the key is domestic productivity growth. If two countries both improve their productivity by the same amount, they both improve their standards of living and their competitiveness is unaffected. Another country can increase its productivity by more than we increase our productivity, and so it will become more "competitive" relative to us, but our standard of living nonetheless increases according to our own increased productivity. Calls for increasing our international competitiveness are out of place; what is important is to increase our productivity regardless of what other countries are doing.

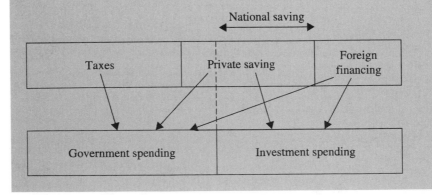

7.4   Policy for Growth

Policies to encourage growth and productivity increases fall into four broad categories:

1. Government should provide an institutional environment conducive to the efficient operation of private enterprise, including protection of property rights; maintenance of law and order; establishment of a sound monetary system; avoidance of excessive regulation; no protection of existing jobs, industries, or businesses; prevention of monopolies in major services such as transportation and communication; dedication of unemployment outlays to retraining programs; and liberalization of trade and investment so that the country does not miss out on new technologies.

2. Government should invest in growth-enhancing public goods. Such goods have overall returns to society that exceed the returns that can be captured by private enterprise. For example, private enterprise cannot collect payment from all those who benefit from a dam providing flood control. As a result such goods are not provided adequately by private enterprise. Other examples involve providing infrastructure, such as highways, and spending on education and health. Some economists have argued that such investment in public goods should be viewed as part of national saving because it augments the nation's stock of human and physical capital.

3. Government should provide appropriate incentives for savers and investors through favorable tax treatment of saving and investment, particularly investment in research and development, tax reductions for individual retirement accounts to increase saving, and lower taxes on capital gains to reward investment in entrepreneurial activities. Bringing private saving back up to earlier levels may be difficult, however. Personal savings have fallen for many reasons that government policy is not in a position to affect. For example, improved social security has reduced the need to save for one's old age; insurance and bank loans have reduced the need to save for rainy days; and changes in the age profile of the populace, from younger to older, and in social attitudes, toward self-gratification and less concern for future generations, have reduced saving. Most empirical evidence does suggest, however, that high-growth countries have lower tax rates on average than low-growth countries.

4. Government should ensure that fiscal policy does not create a large government deficit that reduces financing available for private investment—in other words, national saving. The reduction in national saving is particularly disadvantageous if the deficit corresponds to spending on things like transfer payments rather than infrastructure.

A prime objective of these policies is to increase saving and investment. The bottom line here can be expressed in cruder terms that may strike a reader with more force. Raising productivity requires that workers be given more and better capital and education. The only way these things can be done is by asking the present generation to sacrifice—

consume less to create capital and pay for education that in all likelihood will benefit only future generations. If the present generation has become more self-centered than its predecessors, it will be difficult for policy to make much headway in achieving this objective.

> **Sample Exam Question 7.4:**
> "There is some suspicion that what cuts inflation in the short run may make the economy more inflationary in the long run."
> Explain the logic of this statement.

Media Illustrations

Example 1

Economist McKenzie attacks both American political parties' attraction to what he calls "jobilism"—trying to create jobs mostly by protecting current jobs, thence reducing churn.

What is churn in this context?
Churn is another term for creative destruction. It refers to the turnover of jobs—elimination of jobs that have become obsolete because of technical advances and their replacement with new jobs in areas meeting new demands for goods and services and incorporating new technology. An example might be the invention of the automobile requiring the elimination of jobs in the buggy industry and creation of jobs in the automobile industry.

Why would reducing churn be viewed as undesirable?
It is churn that causes productivity to improve.

What implications does this comment have for one's view of the North American Free Trade Agreement?
One would have to recognize that this agreement would require the loss of many jobs offset by the creation of many new jobs as our economy specializes in what it does best, thereby improving our overall productivity.

Example 2

Richard Lipsey points to evidence that when demand is held too long below capacity output, "capacity itself may shrink (at least relative to the potential labor force) with disastrous consequences for the inflation–unemployment trade-off." This means that successive demand-induced recessions compound the problem and lead to ever-increasing levels of inflation and unemployment.

How and why would capacity shrink?

If demand is below capacity output, there is idle capital stock and thus no incentive for new investment. Over time the existing capital stock wears out and becomes obsolete. This depreciation of the existing capital stock shrinks capacity.

Why is the caveat "at least relative to the potential labor force" added?

The labor force continuously grows as population grows. This growing labor force requires a growing capital stock to work with. It is not enough for the capital stock to remain unchanged or to grow slightly—it must grow by enough to match the growth in the labor force.

Use an AS/AD diagram to illustrate the inflation/unemployment problem referred to in the clipping.

The fall in the capital stock makes the economy less productive, causing the *AS* curve to shift leftward/upward. This shift moves the economy to a lower level of income/employment and a higher price level.

Example 3

Personal saving habits peaked in the early 1970s, when the average American stashed away over 9 percent of take-home pay, and declined through the 1980s to a low of less than 3 percent. It seems that Americans prefer to cut down on their saving to maintain living standards; the catch is that a low saving rate makes it harder to increase living standards.

Explain this seeming paradox.

By decreasing saving to maintain living standards, we decrease the financing available for investment, causing investment in new plant and equipment and in research and development to fall, which inhibits increases in productivity that increase living standards.

Chapter Summary

- Most macroeconomic analysis is concerned with explaining business-cycle behavior and devising means of keeping the economy as close to full employment as possible without creating inflation. Comparatively little attention is paid to what many would claim are more important goals of macroeconomic analysis: explaining the process whereby our material standard of living increases and devising means of enhancing this process.

- GDP growth is due to increases in the quantity and quality of labor and capital, and improvements in the way in which they are combined to produce output.

- Productivity, measured as output per hour worked, is the prime determinant of our material standard of living. Productivity increases are incorporated into the economy through *creative destruction*, a process in which old industries are replaced by new ones, destroying more jobs than are created. Putting to work the resulting jobless creates extra output that produces the increase in our standard of living.

- Several explanations for the slowdown in productivity growth during the 1970s and 1980s have been put forward, but this slowdown remains a puzzle.

- *National saving*, the difference between private saving and the budget deficit, represents domestic financing available for investment. This pool of financing can be increased either by the current generation saving more (and thus sacrificing for the benefit of future generations) or by the government decreasing its budget deficit.

Formula Definitions

- National saving = Private saving – Government deficit
- Private investment = National saving + Foreign financing

Media Exercises

(Group B questions require more thought.)

A1. Annual growth will probably be 3 to 4 percent, rather than the more robust 5 to 6 percent typical after a recession.

Explain why an economy's growth rate is typically relatively high just after a recession.

A2. He believes that the nation's core economic problem remains slow growth in productivity—a condition that is worsened, if not caused, by Americans' historically low rate of. . . .

Complete this sentence, and explain the logic behind it.

A3. Although the Americans talked boldly about boosting investment, they mainly ducked the question of how to boost America's low rate of _____. To finance higher investment, America would have to increase _____ or slash _____.

Fill in the blanks here.

A4. Given the low level of savings and investment, some economists now fear that the United States will be lucky during the 1990s to match the record of the

1980s when the amount of goods and services produced by each worker rose a scant 0.8 percent a year.

a. What technical term do economists use to talk about the phenomenon being discussed here?

b. Why are savings and investment important in this context?

A5. Over the longer term business may be shooting itself in the foot by taking a hard line against government taxing and spending policies if this hard line causes a decline in public spending on the economy's infrastructure—roads, sewers, bridges, and other public works.

Explain the logic of this comment.

A6. Economists have traditionally concentrated on annual fluctuations in GDP and had little to say about _____. Questions such as why growth in per capita GDP in industrial economies slowed from an average of 3.5 percent in 1950–1973 to 1.9 percent in 1974–1990 have been mostly ignored. That is a shame. If growth had continued at its earlier pace, real incomes today would be a third higher. By comparison, the gains from _____ seem minuscule.

Fill in the blanks here.

A7. He claims that we must view the loss of hundreds of thousands of jobs in the U.S. textile industry over the past two decades as a positive measure of the success of the industry in dramatically improving. . . .

Complete this clipping.

A8. A popular view is that the best way for governments to stimulate growth is to improve the functioning of markets and adopt stable and credible macroeconomic policies that encourage firms to take a long-term view. The trouble with this view is that governments, like voters, are more interested in. . . .

Complete this clipping.

A9. He also admits that the budget deficit diverts domestic savings that could have been directed to productive investment elsewhere. During the 1960s the budget deficit absorbed about 2 percent of national savings, according to the General Accounting Office. By the 1970s it absorbed 19 percent, and by 1990 the figure was 58 percent.

How would budget deficits accomplish this diversion?

A10. Some economists believe the economy is able to grow without reigniting inflation because of strong improvements in _____ brought about by huge investments in new technology by business.

Fill in the blank.

A11. A key economic adviser to President George W. Bush said yesterday he believed that national saving was too low in the United States. But he agreed that encouraging consumers to save at a time when their spending was largely responsible for keeping the U.S. economic recovery on track could be risky. But in the longer term, he said, the rationale for increasing savings in the United States was clear.

    a. Explain the logic that lies behind the statement that encouraging saving could be risky.

    b. What is the rationale behind why increasing saving is good in the longer term?

A12. One way corporations justify growing debt is that it enables the expansion of markets and capital assets. But that isn't the case with the federal government. It produces nothing. Money tied up in the debt may go partially for necessities or entitlements that large segments of the population want to continue, but the debt itself is not an example of productive debt.

What is an example of government "productive debt"?

A13. Three-quarters of all Americans worked on farms in 1800. Only 40 percent did in 1900, and only 3 percent in 2000. This change was the best thing that could have happened to Americans.

Explain why this change was so desirable.

A14. The argument is simple and convincing: Driven by an inexorable urge to cut costs and boost profits, business buys the latest labor-saving technology and fires workers, leading to higher unemployment across the economy. The government needs to do something about this greedy behavior.

Evaluate this argument.

A15. A rapid, global, private sector shift to thrift is exactly what the world economy does not need, but it ought to be good news in the long term.

Explain the rationale behind this statement.

A16. The debt buildup is worrisome because it is not financing. . . .

Complete this sentence.

A17. Much more important than the size of the deficit is whether government resources are being used to. . . .

Complete this sentence.

A18. President Obama wants short-term personal consumption and long-term personal savings, he said. There are contradictions everywhere.

Why would Obama want short-term consumption? Why would he want long-term saving?

B1. On those rare occasions when the economic benefits of accelerated infrastructure spending are discussed, it is usually in the context of the countercyclical role assigned to such spending by John Maynard Keynes, leading to charges of make-work projects with little economic value. Precious little is said about the critical links that exist between quality infrastructure and. . . .

a. Explain what is meant by the countercyclical role and how it works.

b. In the context of the countercyclical role, are make-work projects of equal value to quality infrastructure? Why or why not?

c. Complete this clipping.

B2. The case for tax breaks for investment rests on the claim that because of big spillover effects, the return on investment in machinery and equipment to the economy as a whole is far greater than. . . .

Complete this clipping.

B3. Countries with a high level of education tend to absorb new technology more quickly and therefore grow more quickly. But one problem is that firms and workers cannot take account of external benefits from investing in education, which means that they. . . .

Complete this clipping.

B4. It may make more sense to remove some of the many disincentives to save and invest than to use the tax system to discriminate in favor of investment. For example, tax breaks on mortgage-interest payments diverts savings from. . . .

Complete this clipping.

B5. Yet Mr. Stein himself estimates that the growth of budget deficits during the 1980s cut 3 percent from the decade's GDP.

How would growing budget deficits lower GDP? Shouldn't they increase GDP through the multiplier effect?

B6.   Business productivity in the last quarter grew at its fastest pace in six years, offering another explanation for how the strong U.S. economy has kept inflation at bay.

Explain how higher productivity would keep inflation at bay.

B7.   The Opposition said that while it welcomed the high levels of growth, "it is low-quality growth because investment is a missing ingredient. This is simply recovery brought about by government pump-priming and some small contri- bution from consumption spending. This growth cannot be sustained."

a.   What is meant by government pump-priming?

b.   What reasoning lies behind the claim that this growth won't be sustained?

c.   What counterargument would you suggest the Australian prime minister use to respond to this claim?

B8.   Jorgenson said that the high cost of imported energy will cause business in general to substitute labor for energy in the production process and that this would likely have a number of harmful effects on the economy: reduced growth, lower productivity, and higher inflation.

a.   Since this phenomenon creates more jobs, how could it imply reduced growth?

b.   Since this phenomenon reflects firms trying to be more efficient, how could it imply lower productivity?

c.   Since this phenomenon is undertaken by firms to reduce costs, how could it lead to higher inflation?

B9.   We should expect that after a couple of years of very robust gains in productiv- ity (1.7 percent last year and 1.9 percent the year before, a substantial improve- ment on the 1 percent annual average over the 1974 to 1995 period), productivity gains would be more moderate.

Why would we expect more modest productivity gains in this circumstance?

B10. Since 1991 business-sector productivity has increased at a 1.3 percent annual rate, while the adult population has increased at a 1 percent annual rate. Mean- time, business output has risen 3.3 percent per year. The one percentage point gap between output growth and productivity-adjusted population growth has been filled by three things: . . . .

Complete this clipping. Hint: What has happened to employment?

B11. The Labor Department reported that output rose at a 3.9 percent annual rate, while hours worked were up 1.2 percent. The higher output, analysts said, was

largely a result of businesses working their employees longer rather than adding to payrolls.

a. How is productivity measured?

b. What can you say about productivity change from these figures?

B12. The main reason why French labor productivity is so high (higher than in Germany or America) is because employers in France have to pay higher social security charges, and spend more on redundancy pay, than in other countries.

a. How can this statement be true? Doesn't the higher cost of labor increase costs? Hint: How is labor productivity measured?

b. What is the drawback to this policy of high labor costs?

B13. This is particularly true in the service sector, which has been the motor of job creation in America over the past twenty years. Toys "R" Us, for example, employs 30 percent fewer people in its shops in France than it does in its U. S. shops. "At Club Med in the U.S.," says Philippe Bourguignon, "we employ more kitchen hands; in France, we. . . ."

Complete the Club Med president's statement.

B14. India, however, is strong in ways that are not always apparent. Although its savings rate is lower than China's, it uses investment more efficiently to produce economic growth."

What is meant here by "uses investment more efficiently"?

B15. The survey of global labour market trends from the Geneva-based International Labour Organisation (ILO) found that the United States surpassed Europe and Japan in terms of annual output per worker, partly because Americans worked longer hours than Europeans, clocking up an average of 1,825 hours last year, compared with 1,300 to 1,800 hours in leading European economies. While unemployment in the European Union as a whole was higher than in the United States, one key indicator, the employment-to-population ratio, rose from 56.1 to 56.7 percent between 1999 and 2002. The same measure fell from 64.3 to 62.7 percent in the United States during the same period.

a. Can you tell from this information if worker productivity higher in the United States or Europe? Explain why or why not.

b. Does the level of unemployment affect your answer to part a above? Explain why or why not.

    c. From the information in this news clip would you guess that per capita income in the United States is higher or lower than in Europe? Why?

    d. From the information in this news clip would you guess that the participation rate in the United States is higher or lower than in Europe? Why?

B16. Australia has passed the fruits of economic growth to working people through tax cuts, which encourages growth because. . . .

Complete this statement.

B17. Inequalities often lead to calls for government intervention to redistribute wealth. But history has shown the result is often not only less inequality but also less. . . .

Complete this statement.

B18. The economists argued that a program focused on stimulating investment would be healthy for the economy even if it increased the deficit in the short term, and that cutting income taxes would be exactly the wrong approach.

    a. What healthy things would higher investment engender?

    b. How might it not increase the deficit in the long term?

    c. How does cutting income taxes differ?

B19. Of course, if the government uses borrowed funds to invest in assets—hospitals, schools, roads, and dams—which themselves have large future returns, then any costs of crowding out will be. . . .

    a. What are the costs of crowding out?

    b. Complete this clipping.

Numerical Exercises

AN1. Suppose that income is $700 billion, consumption is $500 billion, taxes are $60 billion, and government spending is $80 billion. What is national saving?

AN2. Suppose that national saving is $150 billion, the government deficit is $30 billion, and gross investment is $170 billion. What is foreign financing?

AN3. Suppose that the multiplier is 3, the marginal tax rate is 20 percent, and the marginal propensity to consume out of disposable income is 0.9. If government spending increases by $10 billion, what happens to national saving?

AN4. An economy growing at x percent per year will take about $72/x$ years to double in size. Use this "rule of 72" to compute how long it should take an economy growing its per capita income at 1.8 percent per year (the historical average of U.S. per capita growth over the past hundred years) to double, compared to the comparable 1.4 percent figure for the 1970s and 1980s.

AN5. Suppose that national saving is $40 billion, foreign financing is $8 billion, and the budget deficit is $15 billion. What is private saving?

8   The Money Supply

Money plays an important role in the operation of the economy, illustrated by the following excerpt from a 1942 radio broadcast by Keynes:

For some weeks at this hour you have enjoyed the day-dreams of planning. But what about the nightmare of finance? I am sure there have been many listeners who have been muttering, "That's all very well, but how is it to be paid for?" Let me begin by telling you how I tried to answer an eminent architect who pushed on one side all the grandiose plans to rebuild London with the phrase "Where's the money to come from?"

"The money?" I said, "But surely, Sir John, you don't build houses with money. Do you mean that there won't be enough bricks and mortar and steel and cement?"

"Oh no," he replied, "of course there will be plenty of all that."

"Do you mean," I went on, "that there won't be enough labor? For what will the builders be doing if they are not building houses?"

"Oh no, that's all right," he agreed.

"Then there is only one conclusion. You must be meaning, Sir John, that there won't be enough architects." But there I was trespassing on the boundaries of politeness. So I hurried to add: "Well, if there are bricks and mortar and steel and concrete and labor and architects, why not assemble all this good material into houses?"

But he was, I fear, quite unconvinced. "What I want to know," he repeated, "is where the money is coming from."

To answer that would have got him and me into deeper water than I cared for, so I replied rather shabbily, "The same place it is coming from now."

He might have countered (but he didn't), "Of course I know that money is not the slightest use whatever. But, all the same, my dear sir, you will find it a devil of a business not to have any."

The message here is that although money is not a physical ingredient required for the production of goods and services, its presence greatly facilitates this production. Money serves as a lubricant for the economy, allowing greater specialization of production and labor and thus creating higher productivity. Imagine how inefficient it would be to do business by bartering one good or service for another!

By controlling the amount of money in the economy, the government can affect the operation of the economy. The purpose of this chapter is to explain how the banking system works and how the government, through its central bank—the Federal Reserve System—influences the supply of money in the economy. The role played by the financial system in channeling funds from savers to investors, an extremely important ingredient in the operation of our capitalist economy, is described in section 8.5. The subprime mortgage crisis of 2008 illustrates dramatically the important role in the economy played by the financial system; appendix 8.2 discusses this crisis.

Upon completion of this chapter you should

- know how the money supply is measured,

- understand how a fractional-reserve banking system operates,

- know how the government can influence the money supply,

- understand the concept of the money multiplier,

- know what a financial intermediary is, and

- be familiar with the essence of the subprime mortgage crisis.

8.1   What Is Money?

Money is defined as anything that is widely accepted in payment for goods and services and to pay off debt. Many things can serve this purpose, as evidenced historically by the use of cigarettes in prisoner-of-war camps and ownership titles to large stone wheels on the South Pacific island of Yap. This definition creates a serious problem in measuring a country's money supply. What should be counted as money? Should we count cigarettes and stone wheels? Different choices of what should be counted as money give rise to different measures of the money supply. These measures are called *monetary aggregates.*

In our society, dollar bills and coins in the hands of the public should definitely be counted as money because they are almost universally accepted as payment. Although not quite so widely accepted as cash, traveler's checks are sufficiently widely accepted as payment that it is reasonable to include them in our measure of money. Personal checks are also widely accepted as payment, suggesting that balances in checking accounts (often called *demand deposits* because balances in such accounts can be accessed on demand by writing a check) should be included when measuring money. There is little dispute about whether these three items—cash, traveler's checks, and balances in checkable accounts—should be included in our economy's measure of money. Adding these together produces the monetary aggregate M1, the narrow definition of money.

Money plays four main roles in our society: as a medium of exchange, as a unit of account, as a store of value, and as a standard of deferred payment. The key feature of money, as far as macroeconomics is concerned, is its use as a medium of exchange because it is through this role that control over the money supply is connected to spending and thus to overall economic activity. To be a good medium of exchange, money must be accepted by people when buying and selling their productive resources or goods and services. It should be portable, and it has to be divisible so that large and small transactions can be made. The aggregate M1 captures this dimension of money because it includes those items most widely used as media of exchange. (About 85 percent of household purchases are made using M1 balances, about 40 percent of which are made with cash.) The term *transactions balances* is often used to refer to money balances suitable for use as a medium of exchange.

Other items exist, however, that can be used as media of exchange, although they are not as close substitutes for cash as are traveler's checks and checking account deposits. Savings accounts at banks, for example, can be turned quickly into cash without incurring major cost, as can term deposits. (Term deposits earn higher interest but are not accessible for a specified time unless a penalty is paid.) Subject to some restrictions, checks can be written on accounts at brokerage firms and balances in money mutual fund accounts. If we want a measure of money that is closely connected with spending, we should therefore augment M1 to include all items that can quickly be used for spending. This is the rationale behind M2, the broad definition of money, thought by many to be more closely related to economic activity than is M1. It adds to M1 other assets with check-writing features, such as money market deposit accounts, and other assets that can be turned into cash quickly with very little cost, such as savings deposits. Such assets are described as being very "liquid." Table 8.1 documents the differences between M1 and M2. Figures

Table 8.1   M1 and M2 Monetary Aggregates ($ billions, not seasonally adjusted)

	Value, April 2009
M1 = Currency held by public	849
+ Traveler's checks	5
+ Demand deposits[a]	408
+ Other checkable deposits[b]	346
Total M1	1,608
M2 = M1	
+ Small-denomination time deposits[c]	1,328
+ Savings deposits[d]	4,403
+ Retail money funds[e]	1,019
Total M2	8,358

Source: www.federalreserve.gov.

a. Demand deposits are checking accounts that pay no interest.

b. Other checkable accounts are accounts that pay interest, such as ATA (automatic transfer from saving accounts).

c. Time deposits, also called term deposits, are deposits that are locked in for a specified length of time; an owner can access these funds only by paying a penalty. "Small" means less than $100,000.

d. Savings deposits include money-market deposits, deposits on which checks can be written, but with restrictions such as that the check be for at least $500.

e. Retail money funds are mutual funds (bought by individuals as opposed to institutions) that invest in safe short-term assets such as Treasury bills.

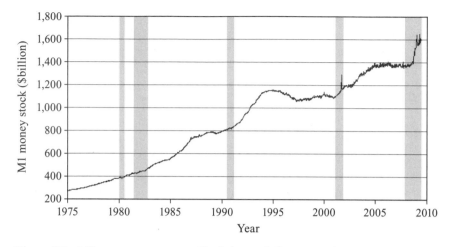

Figure 8.1   M1 monetary aggregate. Shaded areas indicate recessions. Source: Board of Governors of the Federal Reserve System.

8.1 and 8.2 graph the movements of M1 and M2 over time; notice the remarkable increases in both as the economy moves into the subprime mortgage crisis and its associated recession.

The official Fed aggregates, M1, M2, and M3 (M2 plus some less-liquid assets) are reported regularly in the business sections of many newspapers. Each Friday, for example, *The Wall Street Journal* publishes these data in a "Federal Reserve Data" column in its "Money & Investing" section. It must be noted that these measures are often revised substantially; short-run movements in monetary aggregates should not be taken too seriously.

The distinction between M1 and M2 has important policy implications. As discussed in the next chapter, monetary authorities sometimes use one of these measures to monitor monetary policy. An inappropriate choice of money supply measure can lead to policy errors; historically such errors frequently arose when M1 was being used to measure the money supply. There were several reasons for these errors:

1. *Interest rate changes.* Higher interest rates entice people to switch balances in checking accounts, which pay little or no interest, into savings accounts, which pay more interest. This activity causes M1 to shrink, but does not affect M2 because both these deposits are included in M2. If savings account balances can easily be mobilized to effect spending, as has become the case, M1 becomes misleading as a measure of transactions balances.

2. *Financial innovations.* Thanks in part to the computer revolution, the banking sector has been adopting many financial innovations. It used to be the case, for example, that the Fed prohibited interest payments on checking accounts and counted all interest-

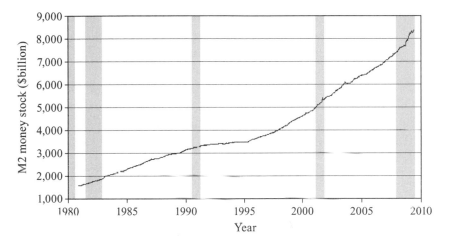

Figure 8.2   M2 monetary aggregate. Shaded areas indicate recessions. Source: Board of Governors of the Federal Reserve System.

Curiosity 8.1: What Is the Fed?

The United States does not have a single central bank like other countries. Instead, its central banking activities, which consist of participating in the money markets and regulating banking activity, are carried out by a group of twelve regional central banks called district Federal Reserve Banks, located in Atlanta, Boston, Chicago, Cleveland, Dallas, Kansas City, Minneapolis, New York, Philadelphia, Richmond, San Francisco, and St. Louis. Collectively they are known as the Federal Reserve System, set up in 1913 to regulate commercial banks, act as banker to the government, and, of most interest to economists, conduct monetary policy. This system in essence acts just like a single central bank because of its centralized power structure. The power lies with the Washington, DC–based Federal Reserve Board of Governors and the Federal Open Market Committee (FOMC). The former consists of seven members appointed by the president of the United States for fourteen-year terms (with a new term beginning every two years so that no one president can control the board). One of these members is appointed by the president to be chairman of this committee for a four-year period. He is called the "chairman of the Fed" (a woman has not yet filled this position) and is generally regarded as the most powerful person in the Federal Reserve System, if not the most powerful civil servant in the country. The FOMC consists of the seven governors plus five of the district Reserve Bank presidents. In practice, monetary policy decisions are made by the Board of Governors or by the Federal Open Market Committee, which is dominated by the governors. This structure makes the Federal Reserve System act as though it were a single central bank.

bearing accounts in M2 but not in M1. Banks found clever ways of getting around this regulation, however. For example, they created savings accounts that earned interest but whose balances were transferred automatically into checking accounts when needed. Consequently such savings accounts—called ATS (automatic transfer from savings) accounts—were really checking accounts and should have been counted in M1. As the use of ATS accounts grew, M1 balances became more and more misleading as a measure of transactions balances. Finally, the Fed recognized the existence of such accounts and included them in the M1 measure in the category "other checkable deposits."

3. *Financial deregulation.* Nonbank financial institutions—mutual savings banks, credit unions, and savings-and-loan associations—were at one time not allowed to have checking accounts, so their deposits were not included in M1. As these institutions circumvented this regulation in imaginative ways, M1—which only measured checkable deposits in commercial banks—became misleading as a measure of the nation's transactions balances. Current monetary aggregate measures include deposits at all financial institutions.

> **Sample Exam Question 8.1:**
> Suppose that you use $1,000 in your checking account to buy a term deposit.
>   What happens to M1 and M2 as a direct result of this?

8.2   Fractional Reserve Banking

Regardless of what measure of the money supply is employed, we must first understand how our banking system operates to understand how the central bank controls the money supply. The key thing to recognize is that banks can create money by extending loans. If a bank loans you $1,000, you sign a legal agreement with the bank, and it simply opens an account in your name with a balance of $1,000. This $1,000 is now counted as part of the economy's money supply: it has been created by this bank out of thin air!

When a bank creates money out of thin air like this, it is taking a chance, hoping that you and other depositors will conduct financial transactions by using checks rather than cash. If you wanted to withdraw the $1,000 in cash, it could be embarrassing for the bank. Because it created the $1,000 deposit out of thin air, it may not have $1,000 in cash to give you!

To guard against this kind of embarrassment, banks refrain from creating money (loans) in unlimited quantities. Most customers make transactions by writing checks so that banks are continually experiencing increases and decreases in deposit balances as checks clear, and increases and decreases in their vault cash as cash is deposited or withdrawn. They know from experience, however, that the amount of cash they must have on hand to deal with withdrawals of cash is a small fraction of total deposits, and so they limit the money they create (loans they make) to ensure that their reserves of cash are at least this fraction of total deposits.

The implication of all this for the money supply is best explained by means of an example. Suppose that banks figure their cash requirements to be 5 percent of total deposits. If the banking system's cash holdings are $40 billion, then the banks will increase loans until the amount of deposits, and thus the money supply, is $800 billion (5 percent of $800 billion is $40 billion). Because the central bank (the Fed) creates cash, any balances in the commercial banks' accounts with the Fed are just as good as cash. This fact implies that the reserves held by banks to handle possible cash disbursements can be either cash or balances in their accounts at the central bank. (Such balances are called *claims on the central bank.*) The money supply is thus a multiple of these reserves, which are controlled by the central bank. Because such reserves are a fraction of the total money supply, this banking system is called a *fractional-reserve banking system.*

There is an obvious danger inherent in such a banking system. Because a smaller percentage of reserves means a greater quantity of loans and therefore more profits, there is a temptation for banks to underestimate the fraction of reserves they should hold. This increases the chances of being unable to meet requests for cash, with the consequent financial ruin of the bank should depositors panic and create a run on that bank. Government regulation of banks, including deposit insurance and the setting of a *reserve requirement,* arose because of such banking disasters and because the government wanted to be

---

Curiosity 8.2: What Are the Legal Reserve Requirements?

In early 2009 the Fed reserve requirements for all depository institutions were zero percent on the first $10.3 million of checkable deposits, 3 percent on the next $34.1 million, and 10 percent thereafter. The Fed has the power to vary this rate between 8 and 14 percent. There are no reserve requirements on other deposits (e.g., term deposits). Overall, the reserve requirement averages about 8 percent. By changing the reserve requirements, the Fed can affect the money supply. Decreasing the required reserve ratio causes the commercial banks suddenly to find themselves with excess reserves, so they can increase loans and thereby expand the money supply. Increasing reserve requirements causes a contraction in the money supply. Changing the required reserve ratio is a very blunt way of affecting the money supply, however, so it is rarely used.

Many countries—such as Australia, Canada, and the United Kingdom—have no reserve requirements at all. Banks in these countries still hold reserves to deal with their everyday cash requirements and are immediately loaned extra reserves by their central bank (at a very high price) should they experience an embarrassing shortfall of cash, so there is no danger of banking disasters. By eliminating reserve requirements these countries strengthen their banks' ability to compete in a multinational banking environment.

able to control the total amount of money circulating in the economy to affect the pace of economic activity.

> **Sample Exam Question 8.2:**
> "Banks are very profitable. Having a license to be a bank is like having a license to print money."
>   How can banks "print money?"

8.3   Controlling the Money Supply

By changing the money supply, a central bank can influence economic activity through *monetary policy.* The central bank controls the money supply by controlling the *money base*—cash plus commercial banks' deposits with the central bank (claims on the central bank)—and thereby controlling the quantity of reserves in the banking system. Commercial banks can use as reserves any part of the money base in their hands. By increasing the money base, the Fed increases commercial banks' reserves, enabling them to increase their loans (and thus the money supply) while continuing to meet their reserve requirement. Note that an increase in reserves does not guarantee that the money supply will increase: for the money supply to increase, commercial banks must react by increasing loans. (For a spectacular example in which the commercial banks did not react by increasing loans, see curiosity 10.3 in chapter 10.) The central bank's control over the money supply is thus subject to some uncertainty.

The main way in which the central bank controls the money base is by buying and selling government bonds, a process referred to as *open-market operations.* It deals only in government bonds, not in any other types of bonds; it has a big stock of government bonds it has bought in the past. When it buys bonds, it augments this stock, and when it sells bonds, it diminishes this stock.

Suppose that the central bank buys a $1,000 government bond from you, paying you with a check drawn on itself. When you deposit this check in your bank account, your bank credits your account and ends up in possession of this $1,000 check, a claim on the central bank. This check could be taken to the central bank and exchanged for cash, so it is treated as cash for the purposes of satisfying the legal reserve requirement. It ends up increasing your bank's deposits with the central bank and thus your bank's reserves.

Therefore any bond purchase by the central bank increases reserves in the banking system, directly increasing the money supply and indirectly inducing banks to increase the money supply further by making it possible for them legally to make more loans. The ultimate increase in the money supply is therefore more than the original purchase of bonds.

> **Sample Exam Question 8.3:**
> "The Fed bought a huge number of bonds on the open market, but for some reason this did not result in the usual increase in the money supply."
> Why might the "usual" increase in the money supply not appear?

8.4   The Money Multiplier

It is instructive to trace through the process whereby an open-market bond purchase by the Fed increases the money supply. Suppose that the Fed buys a government bond from you for $4,000, paying you with a check for $4,000. When you deposit this check in your checking account, the money supply increases by $4,000 because your account balance has increased by $4,000 and nobody else's has decreased. When your bank (bank AAA) increases the balance in your checking account by $4,000, it now possesses a $4,000 claim on the central bank. Its balance with the central bank increases by $4,000, so its reserves increase by $4,000.

Now view this situation through the eyes of bank AAA. Its deposits are $4,000 higher, and it has $4,000 extra reserves. Suppose that the reserve requirement is 5 percent. Bank AAA must keep an extra $200 (5% of $4,000) on hand as extra cash holdings because of its higher deposits, leaving it with $3,800 *excess* reserve holdings. It can increase its profits by loaning out this $3,800, so it does so to stranger X, thereby increasing the money supply by $3,800. (Note that at this stage the total money-supply increase is $4,000 + $3,800 = $7,800.) Stranger X may write a check for $3,800 to firm W, which has an account in bank BBB. Firm W's account in bank BBB then increases by $3,800, and bank BBB has a claim of $3,800 on bank AAA. Bank BBB asks bank AAA to send it $3,800, accomplished when bank AAA transfers $3,800 from its account at the Fed to bank BBB's account at the Fed, increasing bank BBB's reserves.

Now look at the situation through the eyes of bank BBB. It has an extra $3,800 in reserves, and a corresponding extra $3,800 in deposits. It needs $190 extra cash (5% of $3,800) and so has $3,610 in excess reserves. It loans this out, the money supply increases by $3,610, and the same procedure is repeated over and over, with the money supply growing by progressively smaller amounts at each stage. This process is illustrated in figure 8.3.

This process of increasing money supply continues until ultimately it increases by $80,000, deduced by noting that $4,000—the original increase in the money base—is 5 percent (the assumed reserve requirement in this example) of $80,000. This phenomenon—that the money supply increases by a multiple of the increase in the money base—is formalized by the concept of the *money multiplier: the ultimate increase in the money*

Money multiplier process	Total money-supply increase
Fed buys $4,000 bonds	
⇒ ↑ bank AAA reserves by $4,000	
and ↑ money supply by $4,000	$4,000
⇒ $3,800 excess reserves in bank AAA	
⇒ ↑ loans by bank AAA by $3,800	
⇒ ↑ money supply by $3,800	$7,800
⇒ check for $3,800 to account in bank BBB	
⇒ $3,610 excess reserves in bank BBB	
⇒ ↑ loans by bank BBB by $3,610	
⇒ ↑ money supply by $3,610	$11,410
⇒ check for $3,610 to account in bank CCC	
⇒ $3,429.50 excess reserves in bank CCC	
⇒ ↑ loans by bank CCC by $3,429.50	
⇒ ↑ money supply by $3,429.50	$14,840
⇒ and so on until ultimately ↑ money supply by	$80,000

Figure 8.3   The Money Multiplier Process

supply per dollar increase in the money base. In this example, the money multiplier is 20. In formal terms it is written as

$$\text{Money multiplier} = \frac{\Delta \text{ Money supply}}{\Delta \text{ Money base}}$$

The calculation of 20 for the money multiplier is misleading, however. As deposits increase, you and others may wish to hold some fraction of these increased deposits in cash, draining reserves from the banking system. This response lowers the amount of

Curiosity 8.3: How Big Is the Money Multiplier?

The actual magnitude of the money multiplier is determined by both legal and behavioral factors. For M1 it is about 2, and for M2 it is about 12.

   Why is the M2 money multiplier larger? As loans are made and account balances rise, people have a tendency to keep most of those balances in term deposits to earn a higher rate of interest. Banks encourage this practice by offering higher interest rates on term deposits because required reserves on term deposits are zero; banks can make more loans, and thus more profit, if extra deposits are in term deposits rather than demand deposits. As a result, when the Fed increases the money base by buying bonds, M2, which includes term deposits, increases much more than M1, making the M2 multiplier larger.

extra loans the banking system can make, decreasing the magnitude of the money multiplier.

Other complications are possible. There are different legal reserve requirements for different types of deposits—10 percent for checking accounts, for example, and zero percent for time deposits—so the value of the money multiplier may depend on the mix of accounts into which the money-supply increase goes. Another possible complication is that banks may wish to hold reserves in excess of those they are legally required to hold as a safety precaution against having to pay a penalty should their reserves inadvertently fall below their legal requirement. (These are called *excess reserves*.) In general, the magnitude of the money multiplier is determined by the interaction of various legal requirements and behavioral reactions on the part of the public and commercial banks.

Sample Exam Question 8.4:
Suppose that the money multiplier is 6, and a purchase of bonds by the Fed ultimately increased the money supply by $300 billion.
How many bonds did the Fed buy?

8.5   The Subprime Mortgage Crisis

As Keynes pointed out in the introduction to this chapter, although houses are built with bricks and mortar, not money, you will have a devil of a time building without money. Money is the grease that lubricates the economy, and that grease is produced and allocated by the financial system. Appendix 8.1 discusses at length the role of financial intermediaries, the mechanism by which funds from savers are channeled to borrowers, in the process greasing the economy's production process and ensuring that those funds are allocated to their best end uses. Although economists knew that the financial/monetary sector was an important dimension of the economy, just how important was not fully realized until the subprime mortgage crisis triggered in late 2008 what has become known as the "great recession."

The subprime mortgage crisis, which began in late 2006, is a dramatic illustration of how important is the financial system to the overall health of the macroeconomy. The money multiplier process described in this chapter assumed that the banks had the good sense to make loans that would be repaid. During the early 2000s banks made a lot of loans—mortgages—to people who were "high risk" in that there was a high probability that they would not repay; these high-risk loans were called *subprime mortgages*. (A *mortgage* is a loan taken out to buy a house, which serves as collateral for the loan; if the monthly mortgage payments are not paid, the bank forecloses and becomes the owner of the house.) These loans were bundled together, transformed into *mortgage-backed securities* (a claim to the stream of monthly mortgage payments), and sold on to other banks and financial institutions. When it became apparent that these securities were worthless, institutions owning these securities were in danger of going bankrupt. Because there were so many institutions in this predicament, allowing them all to fail would have destroyed the economy's financial system, so the government stepped in to bail them out.

Two consequences of this pushed the economy into recession. First, the bad loans caused banks to lose a lot of their capital, so they stopped lending. And because of the huge uncertainty (and steady movement into recession) characterizing these times, those banks capable of loaning stopped loaning because they were worried that any institution (or individual) to whom they extended a loan might go bankrupt. Without access to loans, normal economic activity slowed dramatically. Second, the real estate market collapsed. With no new loans being made, demand for houses fell. And people who could not meet their mortgage payments lost their homes to the banks who sold them for whatever they could get. At the end of 2008 over 8 million households (20 percent of people with mortgages) owed more on their mortgage than their house was worth! All of this added up to a major fall in spending, setting in action a multiplier process that led to layoffs and further falls in spending. All of this pointed toward falling profits for corporations, so their share prices fell. The fall in the stock market (in the order of 40 percent!) made everyone feel less wealthy, causing a further fall in spending, aggravating the situation. Finally, although the subprime loan problem was mainly an American phenomenon, the associated mortgage-backed securities were sold worldwide, extending the crisis to the world economy.

Who is to blame here? An interesting thing about this crisis is that there are so many directions in which the finger of blame can be pointed:

1. Politicians had put in place "antidiscrimination" policies that encouraged making loans to poor people, following the view that everyone, rich or poor, should be able to own a home.

2. The banks made loans knowing they were risky—the borrower's ability to repay was not adequately investigated, and little or no downpayment was required for mortgages (some have claimed that there was a lot of fraudulent behavior going on here).

3. The banks were using incentive mechanisms that encouraged their employees to approve such loans—they were rewarded now for loans made, rather than being rewarded later if these loans proved to be profitable.

4. People taking out loans were gambling—they were betting that the value of the house they were buying would rise markedly, and they were hoping that the low, introductory interest rate that the bank had given them would be available when the loan had to be renewed (some have called this predatory behavior by the banks).

5. Rating agencies failed to classify the mortgage-backed securities (consisting of the subprime loans) as being very risky, and so misled potential purchasers of these loans.

6. Institutions purchasing these mortgage-backed securities should have done due diligence.

7. Financial institutions employed unsound risk management practices, using strategies that ignored low-probability events with catastrophic consequences—they bought huge quantities of mortgage-backed securities, financing them with bank loans (a process called *leveraging*). So when these mortgages turned bad, they found themselves with no assets but big debts.

8. Insurance against default of mortgage-backed securities became worthless when the insurer, American International Group (AIG), was unable to honor its contracts—it had issued the insurance not recognizing the high risk involved.

9. The financial services industry created very complex financial products that too few (including bankers!) could understand well enough to gauge their risk.

10. The Fed kept interest rates too low for too long, thereby encouraging people to take out loans (see chapter 10 for how the Fed controls interest rates).

11. The Fed's regulatory arm did not fully realize what was going on, in what magnitude (hundreds of billions of dollars!), and with what potential consequences.

12. Investment banks (which do not take deposits and so are not technically banks—like banks, they are financial intermediaries, described in appendix 8.1) are not subject to Fed regulation, but they played a major role in the mortgage-backed securities market. (For your interest, here is what happened to the investment banks: Lehman Brothers went bankrupt, Bear-Stearns and Merrill-Lynch were sold off to big commercial banks, and Morgan Stanley and Goldman Sachs became commercial banks subject to regulation.)

For more detail on all this, google subprime mortgage crisis. Readers may also wish to preview "quantitative easing" in curiosity 10.3 for discussion of how the subprime mortgage crisis affected Fed monetary policy.

Sample Exam Question 8.5:
"The subprime mortgage crisis has led to a situation in which everyone is nervous—the banks because they can't trust people to repay loans, and people because they can't assume they will have a job next year. As a consequence banks have stopped loaning and people have begun saving."

(a) What impact would this have on the money multiplier? Explain. (b) What impact would this have on "the" multiplier? Explain.

Media Illustrations

Example 1

M1 can be a slippery commodity. The central bank admits to having significantly underestimated the transactions money flying around the system. One reason is that banks' bigger corporate customers cottoned onto the advantage of so managing their moneys as to achieve, at a consolidated, central checking account, practically zero balances. For the banks promoting this switch of idle money to easily accessible interest-bearing deposits, there were similar economies: reserve requirements on such deposits are much lower.

What is meant by "transactions" money, as opposed to what other kind of money?
Transactions money is money used to pay for purchases (monetary transactions) as opposed to money used purely as a store of value.

What is the significance of underestimating transactions money?
Transactions money is thought to be connected to spending, so if it is underestimated, monetary policy will promote more spending than suitable, creating inflation.

Why would corporations want to achieve zero balances?
Checking accounts pay little or no interest. By keeping most of their transactions money in savings, or interest-bearing, accounts, which are easily switched into checking accounts, they can earn interest on most of their transactions moneys.

Explain how the banks gain from this corporate behavior.
Because the legal reserve requirement on interest-bearing accounts is lower (now it is zero, but when this clipping was written it may not have been zero), the banks are able to make more loans and thus more profits.

Example 2

In the process, the money multiplies, since the banks are allowed to lend more money than they actually have, within limits set by the Federal Reserve Board. The board tries to anticipate how much the money will multiply as this process unfolds. If its calculations are right, just enough money will be created to accommodate the growth it desires for the economy. If the calculations are wrong, it would make them right by pumping some money into the economy or pumping some out.

What money is being multiplied here?
The Fed has increased the money base, which is being multiplied.

What are the limits set by the board?
The board has a legal reserve requirement that must be met by the banks. This limits the amount of extra loans that banks can make.

What name do economists use to refer to "how much the money will multiply as this process unfolds"?
The money multiplier.

How does the board pump money into or out of the economy?
Money is pumped into the economy by buying bonds, and it is pumped out of the economy by selling bonds.

Example 3
The deficit will mainly be financed by selling bonds to the general public and not to the central bank.

What happens to the money supply if a deficit is financed by selling bonds to the general public?
The money supply decreases when bonds are sold to the public. When the government spends the proceeds, this money is injected back into the economy, so the net effect is no change in the money supply.

What happens to the money supply if a deficit is financed by selling bonds to the central bank?
The money supply increases if bonds are sold to the central bank. Whenever the central bank buys bonds, the money supply increases.

Chapter Summary

- Measuring an economy's money stock is challenging because so many different things can be used as a medium of exchange. The two most popular monetary aggregates are M1 and M2. Financial innovations and other changes have disrupted the connection between economic activity and these aggregates, especially M1.

- In a fractional-reserve banking system an economy's central bank can create a multiplied increase in the money supply by increasing the monetary reserves in the banking system. By buying a bond, for example, the central bank writes a check on itself, which a commercial bank comes to possess whenever the person who sold the bond deposits this check. This bank's account balance with the central bank therefore increases, giving it immediate access to cash if required. This increase in this bank's holdings of legal reserves permits it to increase loans and thereby to increase the money supply.

- The main way in which the central bank influences the money supply is by controlling monetary reserves (the money base) through buying or selling bonds, a process known as open-market operations.

- The money multiplier tells us by how much the money supply ultimately increases whenever the central bank increases reserves by a dollar (e.g., by buying a bond worth a dollar).

- Financial intermediaries (discussed in appendix 8.1) are institutions through which the savings of households are channeled to borrowers.

- The subprime mortgage crisis illustrates the importance of the financial sector to the health of the macroeconomy.

Formula Definition

$$\text{Money multiplier} = \frac{\Delta \text{ Money supply}}{\Delta \text{ Money base}}$$

Media Exercises

(Group B questions require more thought.)

A1. Bank reserves are created in the process, since the Fed can "pay" simply by crediting the amount of its purchases to the account of the bank involved in the transaction. As a result. . . .

a. What kind of a transaction is being discussed here?

b. Complete this statement.

A2. The annual growth rate in what had once been the officially watched aggregate, M1, was 4 percent last year, but for M2, the rate was 12 percent.

Why might M2 be growing so much faster than M1?

A3. Money deposited for a term is not left in bank vaults but is loaned out by the banks (subject to minimum cash reserve requirements). This means that a dollar on deposit can flow back into the banking system one or more times and that dollar can expand the money supply.

a. What is meant by the minimum cash reserve requirements referred to in this clip?

b. What terminology do economists use to refer to the process described in this clip?

A4. During May the rate of growth in the narrowly defined money supply, M1, moved below its current target range of between 5 and 9 percent annual growth. Two main causes were identified: the delayed impact of rising interest rates earlier this year, and the increasing use of daily-interest savings accounts by bank customers.

Explain how each of these two main causes contributes to a lowering of growth in M1.

A5. The impact on this monetary aggregate of extensive financial innovation—the changes in the kinds of deposits and services offered by banks—led the central bank to drop M1 as an intermediate target. With the changes in the way the public was holding payments balances, the M1 aggregate no longer had the same reliable link to. . . .

a. What impact would these financial innovations have on M1?

b. Complete this clipping.

A6. Because it is broader in coverage than M1, M2 is less prone to the shifts resulting from financial innovation that caused difficulties in the interpretation of M1.

What are the "shifts resulting from financial innovation," and why do they cause difficulties in the interpretation of M1?

A7. Although the central banker didn't say so, this may ultimately compel him to resort increasingly to managing the money supply by managing banks' excess cash reserves—the stuff from which the banks create loans.

a. What are excess cash reserves?

b. Why are they called "the stuff from which the banks create loans"?

c. How would the central bank manage these excess reserves?

A8. A significant difference exists between the consequences of federal as opposed to state borrowing if the federal government borrows by selling bonds to the Federal Reserve. It alone can do so—the central bank buys only federal bonds.

What is this significant difference?

B1. Another potential thorn in the flesh of central bank money-measurers is the daily-interest savings account.

Why would daily-interest savings accounts be a thorn in the flesh of central bank money-measurers?

B2. America's broad money, M2, the Federal Reserve's preferred measure, rose by only 1.7 percent in the year to August, while America's narrow money, M1, jumped by 12.3 percent. The money supply is a useful guide for policy makers only if it has a predictable relationship with GDP. In practice, the link is fickle. The biggest problem is that the various measures are sensitive to shifts within portfolios. The recent sharp drop in short-term interest rates may explain this.

Explain how a fall in interest rates could explain the disparate rates of growth of M1 and M2.

B3. If I ask a worker to get me a spare part for my car, he'll refuse to do it for money but will do it for vodka.

What must be happening in Russia to cause this phenomenon to occur?

B4. Monetizing the debt means that the Federal Reserve is not seeking buyers for all the government bonds, but is _____. This essentially means that the Fed is. . . .

Fill in the blank and complete this clipping. Hint: "Monetizing the debt" means turning debt into money.

B5. The earlier predictions underestimated currency in circulation and Treasury balances at the Fed, both of which drained reserves from the banking system.

a. Explain how these two things drain reserves from the banking system.

b. What is the main implication of draining reserves?

B6. In response to the financial turmoil in the wake of declining house prices, the Fed instituted a series of new lending facilities that increased the liquidity of participating institutions' portfolios without simultaneously increasing the total supply of liquidity in the financial market, at least before September 2008.

How would the Fed have accomplished this?

B7. It appears, however, that initially the Fed did not want to address the financial market turmoil by increasing the total amount of credit in the market. Rather, it chose to reallocate the credit in the market by providing loans to institutions that participated in its new lending programs, while offsetting the effect of this lending on total credit through. . . .

Complete this clipping.

Numerical Exercises

(Group B questions require more thought.)

AN1. Suppose that the central bank buys $4 billion of bonds on the open market.

   a. If banks wish to hold reserves of 6 percent, by how much can the money supply ultimately increase?

   b. What would the money multiplier be in this case?

AN2. Suppose that the money multiplier is 6. What happens to the money supply if the Fed buys $3 billion of bonds?

AN3. Say you sell a bond to the Fed for $10,000 and deposit the proceeds in your checking account. As a direct result of this transaction,

    a. What has happened to M1?

    b. What has happened to M2?

AN4. Suppose that the Fed buys $5 billion of bonds, and as result of this the money supply eventually increases by $20 billion. What is the magnitude of the money multiplier?

AN5. Say you withdraw $500 in cash from your checking account. As a direct result of this transaction,

    a. What has happened to M1?

    b. What has happened to M2?

AN6. Suppose that the money multiplier is 5. How many bonds should the Fed buy on open market to increase the money supply by $30 billion?

AN7. Say you use $1,000 from your checking account to buy a term deposit. As a direct result of this transaction,

    a. What happens to M1?

    b. What happens to M2?

BN1 In question AN1 above, suppose that when extra deposits are created, customers increase their holdings of cash by 3 percent of those extra deposits. Does the money multiplier become larger, become smaller, or stay the same?

BN2 Are your answers to parts a and b in question AN3 above different if you allow for indirect effects? If yes, in what way? Explain.

BN3 Are your answers to parts a and b in question AN5 above different if you allow for indirect effects? If yes, in what way? Explain.

BN4 Are your answers to parts a and b in question AN7 above different if you allow for indirect effects? If yes, in what way? Explain.

Appendix 8.1   What Is a Financial Intermediary?

A *financial intermediary* is a financial institution that pools the savings of households and lends them to others, either individuals or firms. *Commercial banks, credit unions,* and *savings and loan associations* are examples of financial intermediaries. Financial intermediaries render valuable services to both lenders and borrowers, for which they are paid by means of the difference between the relatively high rate of interest they charge borrowers and the relatively low rate of interest they pay lenders. These services are of several types:

1. *Lower transactions costs.* The borrower avoids having to deal with thousands of households, and lenders enjoy banking services that enable them to deposit and withdraw funds without negotiation.

2. *Lower information costs.* The financial intermediary specializes in collecting and analyzing information about borrowers to determine whether a loan is a wise undertaking.

3. *More liquidity.* Loans are unattractive to households because they are illiquid—they cannot quickly and cheaply be turned into cash. Financial intermediaries can offer savers the liquidity of a checking account because they are collecting payments on so many illiquid loans.

4. *Greater diversification.* Savers participate in all the loans extended by a financial intermediary and so enjoy the lower risk that comes from diversification.

Not all financial intermediaries offer banking services. *Insurance companies* and *pension funds,* for example, have funds from thousands of households available for investment. Because these funds are committed for a long period of time, these types of financial intermediaries can more safely make long-term loans. This situation contrasts with banking-type financial intermediaries, whose funding sources from savers can be withdrawn with little or no notice. Yet another type of financial intermediary is a *mutual fund,* which invests households savings in stocks and bonds. The stock market and the bond market are also financial institutions that channel funds from savers to borrowers.

A corporation can raise funds by selling additional shares in its company, the collective term for which is *stock*. This type of financing is called *equity* financing. The value of a corporation's shares is determined by the forces of supply and demand on a stock market, the most prominent of which is the New York Stock Exchange (NYSE). Buying and selling of stock is handled by brokerage firms that act as agents for buyers or sellers. Shares of smaller corporations are traded "over the counter" in a market among brokers called NASDAQ (National Association of Securities Dealers Automated Quotations). Today these markets all operate electronically. Information on stock prices appears daily in financial sections of newspapers, as shown in the following example:

52 Week					Yld		Vol				Net
Hi	Lo	Stock	Sym	Div	%	PE	100s	Hi	Lo	Close	Chg
67	$45^7/_8$	Goodyear	GT	1.20	2.1	17	5031	$58^1/_2$	$57^5/_8$	58	$-^3/_8$

This information pertains to Goodyear Tire and Rubber Company whose trading symbol is GT. Over the preceding year its stock price ranged from a low of $45^7/_8$ dollars to a high of 67 dollars. During the previous year it paid a dividend of $1.20 per share of stock, which is a yield of 2.1 percent of the current share price. The price of this stock is 17 times its annual earnings, and this day 503,100 shares were traded. During the day its price ranged from a low of $57\frac{5}{8}$ dollars to a high of $58\frac{1}{2}$ dollars, closing at 58 dollars, down $\frac{3}{8}$ dollar from its closing price the previous day.

To raise funds by selling new shares, typically a firm will sell all the new shares to an *investment bank,* or *underwriter,* who acts as an intermediary by in turn selling these shares to thousands of different investors, some of whom are individual households and others of whom are financial intermediaries such as mutual funds.

The owner of stock may cast one vote per share in the election for company directors, and each share participates equally in the profits of the firm. Stocks are quite liquid because they can be sold quickly on the stock market, but they are also quite risky, since the shares can change in value as the profitability of the company changes. By owning shares in many different types of companies an investor can reduce this risk through diversification, but this has high information costs for an individual. These costs explain why mutual funds have become such a popular financial intermediary—by investing in a mutual fund an individual investor can own part of a large, diversified, professionally managed portfolio of stocks.

A third major way in which savers can channel funds to borrowers is through the bond market. This type of financing is called *debt* financing. Bonds combine some of the characteristics of a loan with some of the characteristics of a stock. Like a loan, a bond is a promise by the borrower to make future payments. But like stocks, bonds are bought and sold at prices determined by supply and demand, and the borrower pays the owner of the bond rather than the original lender. Bonds can be risky—the borrower could go bankrupt and not meet the bond payments, or the price of the bond may change as a result of market forces—but they are not nearly so risky as stocks. It is mainly only governments and large, well-known corporations that issue bonds, since they are perceived to have a low risk of default. Smaller, less well known companies usually borrow directly from financial intermediaries that specialize in evaluating credit risk. During the 1980s, however, a lot of small companies issued what came to be known as *junk bonds.* When a company issues bonds, it typically sells them all to an underwriter who in turn sells them to thousands of households and financial intermediaries such as mutual funds. Investing in the bond market through mutual funds diversifies in exactly the same way that mutual funds allow investors to diversify stock holdings. More information on bonds is provided in appendix 10.1 of chapter 10.

All three of these means of allocating savings to borrowers—financial intermediaries, the bond market, and the stock market—involve a return to the lender, in the form of explicit payments or changes in financial asset prices. This aspect of investing will be discussed at greater length in chapter 10 when the interest rate is analyzed.

9   The Monetarist Rule

The purpose of this chapter is to examine the monetarist approach to macroeconomic analysis and discuss a major legacy of monetarism: the monetarist rule that the money supply should grow at a fixed rate equal to the real rate of income growth of the economy.

By the early 1960s the Keynesian view of the macroeconomy had become the conventional wisdom, evidence of which was its explicit use as the rationale for a proposed tax cut. Just as the Keynesian view was reaching the peak of its popularity, however, in 1963 Milton Friedman and Anna Schwarz published their book *A Monetary History of the United States, 1867–1960*, heralding the arrival of a competing view of the macroeconomy that has since come to be known as *monetarism*.

Monetarists deplored the way in which disciples of Keynes neglected the role of money, something that Keynes himself had stressed, and placed money at center stage of the macroeconomy, the position it had held in the classical view (see appendix 5.1), which was the conventional wisdom before the Keynesian revolution. In the late 1960s and early 1970s the monetarist view gained considerable popularity, primarily because during this time the money supply increased dramatically, causing monetarist predictions to be more accurate than those of the Keynesians. Monetarists claim that crowding-out forces are so strong that fiscal actions are completely ineffective, and that only money matters in determining the level of economic activity. Keynesians soon came to agree that money matters and modified their thinking to develop a more eclectic approach. Monetarists, however, insisted that *only* money matters. This dogmatism, at first very effective as an attention-getting debating tactic, has ultimately been a main reason for the decline of monetarism, as it became evident that several factors in addition to money play roles in the operation of the macroeconomy.

Upon completion of this chapter you should

- understand the quantity theory of money,
- know what is meant by velocity,
- understand the rationale behind the monetarist rule,
- know what is seigniorage, and
- be familiar with the rules versus discretion debate.

9.1   The Quantity Theory

In the classical school of thought, supplanted eventually by Keynesianism, a prominent role was played by the *quantity theory of money*, represented by the mechanical formula

$Mv = PQ$

Here P is the overall price level, and Q is the physical quantity of output produced. The right-hand side of this formula then is the money value of output, or, equivalently, nominal GDP. The variable M is the money supply, and v is the *velocity of money*, interpreted as the number of times in a year each dollar of money supply is used to buy a final good or service. This is usually expressed as the number of times the money supply "turns over" in supporting financially the production of output.

(Many students have difficulty with the velocity concept, so here is another view. Suppose that on average you hold $1,000 of money in its various forms, with actual holdings going up and down as you are paid income and as you buy things. And suppose that during a year you buy $15,000 of goods and services. To buy the $15,000 of goods and services you need to spend your average money holding 15 times during the year. Your personal velocity of money is thus 15. If your average money holding had been $500 instead of $1,000, your average money holding would have had to work much harder to facilitate your purchase of $15,000 of goods and services—its velocity would be 30. An economy's financial system is said to become more efficient as velocity increases because a smaller amount of money holdings can support/facilitate the same amount of spending.)

According to this quantity of money formula, if velocity is constant, a rise in M causes a rise in either P or Q, depending on whether or not the economy is at full employment. This result is easily seen from looking at the formula $Mv = PQ$. Clearly, the role of money is center stage in determining the level of economic activity. What is not so easily seen is what is going on in the economy to cause this result to hold, the greatest drawback of the quantity theory: it offers no explanation of how an increase in the money supply causes an increase in economic activity. The quantity theory formula seems to appear as gospel without any theoretical justification. Indeed, velocity is *defined* as the ratio of income to the money supply, making the quantity theory formula a mere tautology. (Take the equation and solve it for v, obtaining $v = PQ/M$. If this is how v is defined, then the quantity equation becomes true by definition—a tautology!)

The monetarists reinterpreted the quantity theory as representing an economy's demand for money, and with this reinterpretation they were able to structure an explanation for how an increase in the money supply caused an increase in economic activity. The result is referred to as the *modern quantity theory of money*, and it is a cornerstone of monetarism.

> **Sample Exam Question 9.1:**
> Suppose that an economy's money supply is $6,000 billion, its current income is $15,000 billion, and its real income is 12,000 billion year 2000 dollars.
>   What is velocity?

9.2   The Modern Quantity Theory

The original quantity theory formula is rewritten as $M = (1/v)PQ$ and is interpreted as a behavioral equation that reflects the economy's demand for money—as nominal income PQ increases, our demand for money increases. Individuals and firms demand money for the convenience it provides as a medium of exchange and a store of value. Individuals' money holdings increase and decrease as their bank accounts are augmented by paychecks and as they spend money between paychecks. Firms' money holdings increase and decrease as they receive payment for goods and services and as they pay out wages. How much money (cash and balances in bank accounts) do we collectively want to hold on average? This average is the economy's demand for money.

The modern interpretation of the quantity of money equation essentially says that the demand for money is higher when the level of nominal income is higher. Higher consumption spending associated with a higher level of income should cause individuals to hold more cash in their pockets and larger bank balances to facilitate this higher consumption spending. A person earning $30,000 per year may on average hold about $1,000 in money balances, for example, but a person earning $60,000 per year will on average hold considerably more, probably about $2,000. In general, as income/output increases producers require more money to support financially the higher level of production, and consumers require more money to facilitate their higher level of consumption. In this new interpretation, the parameter $1/v$ is not determined tautologically from the definition of velocity, but rather is viewed as reflecting the economy's money-demand behavior. Economists consider velocity *v* to be a function of other forces in the economy, such as the interest rate, but it is thought nonetheless to be quite stable.

How is this new interpretation of the quantity theory used to explain the reaction of the economy to an increase in the money supply? If the money supply increases, people find themselves holding more of their wealth in the form of money than they really want to hold in the form of money: the supply of money exceeds the demand for money. People are assumed to react by spending these excess cash balances in an effort to draw them down. This desire to spend increases aggregate demand for goods and services and sets in motion the traditional Keynesian multiplier process. Initially people's efforts to rid themselves of excess cash balances are unsuccessful because, by spending these balances, they are simply giving the excess balances to others, not eliminating them. As this process continues, however, the level of income rises, causing an increase in the demand for money. This reduces the excess cash balances and slows down the multiplier process. Eventually income increases to the point where the rise in demand for money exactly equals the original increase in the supply of money, stopping this multiplier process.

Curiosity 9.1: Does Excess Money Really Affect Spending?

Excess money can affect spending directly, as we have claimed in this chapter, or indirectly as will be explained in the next chapter when we examine the role of the interest rate. The following example of how an excess demand for money can directly decrease spending is informative. In the early 1970s in Washington, DC, a baby-sitting co-op club was formed in which parents baby-sat for club members and in turn could call on club members to baby-sit for them. The club began by giving each member several units of scrip, each worth one hour of baby-sitting time. This scrip served as the medium of exchange for baby-sitting services, thus playing the role of money in this baby-sitting economy.

The club was successful and grew, but then began to experience a mysterious decline in baby-sitting activity, but not because club members were unwilling to baby-sit. On the contrary, members very much wanted to baby-sit to obtain scrip to use to buy baby-sitting from other club members. The problem was that although everyone claimed to want to buy baby-sitting services, very few were actually buying. All of the available scrip was being held by club members for emergency baby-sitting needs, with no extra scrip left over for members to use to buy normal baby-sitting services. Everyone wanted to baby-sit to earn scrip to buy baby-sitting services, but no one could collect any scrip to spend because everyone else was also trying to accumulate scrip by not buying.

This baby-sitting economy was in a recession caused by a low demand for baby-sitting services, which was in turn caused by an inadequate supply of scrip. The club's growth had increased the demand for scrip, and without an equal increase in scrip supply, an excess demand for scrip developed. To accumulate scrip, members cut down on baby-sitting demand, creating the problem described. To an economist, the obvious solution is to increase the supply of scrip (money). This action was taken, and the baby-sitting club revived.

This story is sometimes told using the hot potato analogy. Suppose that the extra money takes the form of a hot potato, which nobody wants to hold because everyone currently has all the potato (money) they want to hold. Whoever has the hot potato wants to get rid of it and does so by using it to buy something from a neighboring merchant. This merchant now has the hot potato but doesn't want it, so does the same thing—namely gets rid of it by buying something from another merchant. This merchant does the same thing, and so on. As this process continues, the merchants notice that business has improved and that their income is higher. They require more money to lubricate a larger business and to facilitate their own higher consumption spending, so they say to themselves, "The next time that hot potato comes around I will slice a bit off to augment my potato (money) holdings," and they do so. Over time, the hot potato (excess money supply) gets whittled away to nothing.

This process is illustrated in figure 9.1. In the numerical example there is a money-supply increase of $6 billion, brought about by open-market bond purchases of $2 billion.

General process	**Numerical example**
Open-market operations	Open-market operations
⇒ Fed buys bonds	⇒ Fed buys $2b bonds
⇒ people trade bonds for money	⇒ people trade bonds for money
⇒ money multiplier operates	⇒ money multiplier (= 3) operates
⇒ ↑ money supply	⇒ $6b ↑ money supply
⇒ excess money holdings	⇒ $6b excess money
⇒ spend excess money	⇒ people spend excess money
⇒ ↑ agg D for g & s	⇒ $6b ↑ agg D for g & s
⇒ Keynesian multiplier process	⇒ Keynesian multiplier (= 2) process
⇒ ↑ income	⇒ $12b ↑ **income**
⇒ ↑ money demand	⇒ $2.4b ↑ money demand
⇒ smaller excess money holdings	⇒ ↓ **excess money supply** by $2.4b
	⇒ $3.6b excess money
	⇒ people spend excess money
	⇒ $3.6b ↑ agg D for g & s
	⇒ Keynesian multiplier (= 2) process
	⇒ $7.2b ↑ **income** (so cumulative ↑ income is $19.2b)
	⇒ $1.44b ↑ money demand (so cumulative ↑ money demand is $3.84b)
	⇒ ↓ **excess money supply** by $1.44b
	⇒ $2.16b excess money
	⇒ people spend excess money
	⇒ and so on until cumulative ↑ income reaches $30b to cause $6b ↑ money demand and thus eliminate completely the original $6b excess money supply

Figure 9.1 The Impact of Monetary Policy
In the numerical example the money multiplier is 3, "the" multiplier is 2, and a dollar increase in income increases money demand by 0.2 dollars. The multiplier process stops when money demand increases by enough to equal the new money supply.

We have assumed that the money multiplier is 3, that "the" multiplier is 2, and that a dollar increase in income increases money demand by $0.2.

The multiplier process causes the original increase in the money supply to lead ultimately to a "multiplied" increase in the level of income. The strength of monetary policy is usually measured by the *income multiplier with respect to the money supply: the increase in equilibrium income due to a unit increase in the money supply*. In the numerical example in figure 9.1, the $6 billion increase in the money supply leads eventually to an increase in income of $30 billion, so the income multiplier with respect to the money supply is 30/6 = 5. This multiplier should not be confused with the money multiplier, described in the preceding chapter (and assumed to be 3 in this example), or with "the" multiplier (the income multiplier with respect to government or other exogenous spending, assumed to be 2 in this example).

> **Sample Exam Question 9.2:**
> Suppose that "the" multiplier is 3, the income multiplier with respect to the money supply is 4, and the money multiplier is 5.
>
> If the Fed buys $8 billion of bonds on the open market, what ultimate effect on the income level will this have?

9.3   The Monetarist Rule

The essence of the story presented in figure 9.1 is that an increase in the money supply causes changes in the economy that increase the demand for money to equal the now higher supply of money. In the new equilibrium the change in the demand for money must equal the change in the supply of money. In the modern quantity theory the demand for money is given by $(1/v)PQ$, so there are three possible sources of change in demand for money—namely changes in v, P, and Q. The preceding exposition assumed that v and P were constant so that a change in M elicited an equal percentage change in real income Q.

If the economy is at full employment, real income does not change; instead, the extra money supply causes an increase in the price level. To be specific, if the money supply increases by 8 percent when the economy is at full employment, prices increase by 8 percent to increase the demand for money to its higher supply. If the monetary authorities adopt a policy of increasing the money supply at a rate of 8 percent per year, an inflation of 8 percent per year develops, reflecting the adage that inflation is caused by too much money chasing too few goods.

This result is too crude, however, because it does not recognize that the full-employment level of income in the economy is growing due to population changes and investment that

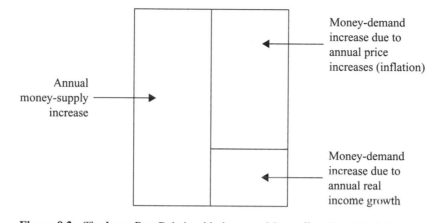

Figure 9.2   The Long-Run Relationship between Money Growth and Inflation
The height of the left-hand rectangle represents the rate of growth of the money supply. The right-hand rectangle, representing money-demand growth, must be of equal height to reflect equilibrium in the monetary sector. Money-demand increases come from two sources—increases in real income and increases in prices (inflation).

augments the nation's capital stock. Suppose that the economy's real income growth rate is 2 percent per year. This 2 percent real growth in income causes the demand for money to increase by 2 percent per year. If the money supply is growing at 8 percent per year, then prices will increase by only 6 percent per year because 2 percent of the extra money supply is needed by the increasing real income. Only money-supply growth rates in excess of the rate of real income growth of the economy should create inflation.

This relationship is illustrated in figure 9.2 where money growth is represented by the height of the left-hand rectangle; for equilibrium in the monetary sector, money-demand growth, represented by the height of the right-hand rectangle, must match money-supply growth. Some money-demand growth comes from the annual increase in real income; the rest must come from price increases—inflation.

The thinking that we have articulated gives rise to the following rule of thumb for predicting the economy's long-run annual rate of inflation:

Long-run rate of price inflation = rate of growth of the money supply
                              − Rate of real income growth

Warning! Students have a bad habit of memorizing this formula, losing sight of where it comes from. It comes from the fact that in the long run the monetary sector of the economy will move to an equilibrium in which the rate of growth of money demand equals the rate of growth of money supply. Money demand growth comes from two basic sources, growth in real income and growth in prices (inflation). Matching this up with money supply growth creates the long-run rule of thumb presented above.

The long-run qualification attached to this rule of thumb is important. In the short run we could be in a recession, in which case money-supply increases can elicit output increases rather than price increases. Several other short-run factors can play a role in influencing price increases, most notably aggregate demand shocks, energy price increases, and generous wage settlements. The rule of thumb says that although these other factors can influence prices, they will not create sustained price increases unless they are supplemented with money-supply increases. This is the basis for the monetarists claim that *in the long run inflation is always and everywhere a monetary phenomenon.*

Figure 9.3 presents evidence of this relationship for selected low-inflation countries. Data for 1971 to 1985, a period of relatively high money-supply growth worldwide, were averaged to produce the points plotted. Averaging should dilute the influence of short-run phenomena affecting inflation and allow the long-run relationship to be more apparent. This graph suggests that the monetarist equation is a good guide to long-run inflation behavior. Had we plotted figures for high-inflation (*hyperinflation*) countries, the graph would have been even more convincing. Brazil had money growth of 83 percent and inflation of 81 percent, Chile had money growth of 133 percent and inflation of 144 percent, and Argentina had money growth of 234 percent and inflation of 251 percent.

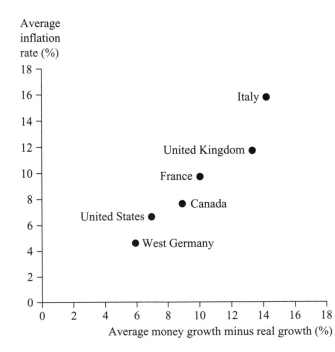

Figure 9.3 Money Growth and Inflation
To reflect the long-run nature of this relationship, data have been averaged for the 1971–1985 period.
Source: International Financial Statistics, 1974–1986.

Two implications of the inflation equation are that (1) an economy does not experience inflation if its money supply increases at a rate equal to the real rate of growth of the economy, and (2) an economy will experience a low, steady inflation in the long run if its money supply grows at a low, steady rate. This is part of the rationale behind the monetarists' belief that the monetary authorities should be replaced by a robot programmed to increase the money supply at a low, constant rate—a controversial prescription known as the *monetarist rule*.

Sample Exam Question 9.3:
Suppose that long-run real growth is 2 percent, the money growth rate is 5 percent, and the economy is operating at full employment.

(a) What should be the inflation rate? (b) If in the previous question the economy had been in a recession rather than at full employment, how would your answer differ?

9.4   Seigniorage

The government, through its agent the central bank, has the legal right to print money. The new money printed each year is a source of financing for the government. Seigniorage is the amount of financing made available to the government through printing money, currently about 2 percent of total government revenue. The term stems from the right of the lord of the realm (in French the seigneur) to coin money. Seigniorage is calculated by figuring out how much government spending can be financed by selling bonds to the central bank, bonds that will never be repaid. What limits this source of financing? Too much of this financing creates inflation!

A story is sometimes told to highlight this phenomenon. A wealthy American vacationed in a small island country, paying for all his costs with personal checks. The islanders were so impressed by the American that they chose not to cash the checks, instead using them as currency. Who paid for the American's vacation? Not the American, whose checks were never cashed. Not the islanders to whom he wrote the checks, because they were compensated when they used the checks as currency. Who then? The islanders collectively all paid for this vacation because by using the American's checks as currency their government did not receive the seigniorage that it would otherwise have enjoyed by increasing the island money supply.

Computation of seigniorage is undertaken in two steps. First, calculate the desired annual increase in the money supply. Our rule of thumb for inflation can be used for this purpose—the money supply should be increased by the real growth rate plus the desired inflation rate. And second, calculate how many government bonds the central bank needs

Curiosity 9.2: Should the Fed Be Independent?

Although not as independent as the Swiss National Bank or the Bundesbank of Germany, relative to most other central banks the Federal Reserve System is quite independent from political influence, mainly because its board members are appointed for long, nonrenewable terms and because it is financially independent. It does not have complete autonomy, however. Congress has the power to affect the Fed through legislation.

The strongest argument in favor of an independent Fed is that subjecting the Fed to political pressures would impart an inflationary bias to monetary policy as politicians use monetary policy to enhance their reelections. Indeed in countries with relatively independent central banks, such as the United States and Germany, inflation is relatively low, whereas in countries with less independent central banks, such as Italy and Spain, inflation is much higher. A related argument is that an independent Fed can resist financing large government budget deficits, which would also lead to excessive inflation. Many believe that politicians do not have the ability to make hard decisions on issues of great economic importance, such as reducing the budget deficit or reforming the banking system. An independent Fed can pursue policies that are politically unpopular yet in the public interest.

Those opposed to Fed independence claim that it is undemocratic to allow important economic decisions to be made by an elite group responsible to no one. Further, effective policy requires coordination from all policy makers. With an independent Fed, fiscal policy may be undone by contrary monetary policy.

The independence issue will never be settled. Those who like the Fed's policies will support its independence, but those who do not like its policies will not.

to buy to make the money supply increase by this amount. The money multiplier concept can be used for this purpose—seigniorage times the money multiplier should create the desired money supply increase.

Sample Exam Question 9.4:
Suppose that the money multiplier is 6, the money supply is $200 billion, long-run real growth is 2 percent, and inflation is 5 percent.
   What is seigniorage?

9.5   The Rules-versus-Discretion Debate

Monetarists advocate their rule for several reasons:

1. *It guarantees a low long-run rate of inflation.* This creates a stable economic environment conducive to long-term investment projects, a necessary ingredient in the promotion of long-term growth.

2. *It creates automatic stabilizing forces.* As the economy moves into recession, income and thus the demand for money grow more slowly. If money-supply growth is kept steady, the slowdown in money-demand growth causes an excess money supply that begins to stimulate the economy and pushes it out of recession. If the economy overheats and begins to experience high inflation, the higher prices increase the demand for money, and an excess demand for money develops. This cuts back aggregate demand (as people stop spending to accumulate more money), which puts a damper on the inflationary forces.

3. *It insulates monetary policy from politics.* Just before an election politicians are tempted to pump up the money supply, letting the later fallout of higher inflation appear after the election.

4. *It prevents the Fed from making mistakes.* History has shown that the Fed has made many mistakes in its efforts to use discretionary monetary policy to improve the economy. Although major mistakes—such as its failure to serve as a lender of last resort during the Great Depression and its overly expansionary monetary policy during the Vietnam war—have become less and less frequent over time as the Fed has learned, monetarists argue that even a clever and well-intentioned Fed is doomed to make mistakes continually because of the extreme complexity of the economy. For example, accurate information about the current state of the economy is unavailable; the magnitude of the income multiplier with respect to the money supply is uncertain and changing; the lags of monetary policy in affecting the economy are long, variable, and unpredictable; and forecasting the economy's behavior is difficult. Chapter 15 of Edward Leamer's *Macroeconomic Patterns and Stories: A Guide for MBAs* (Berlin: Springer-Verlag, 2009) discusses at length the claim that the Fed is responsible for recessions.

However, those who believe in the use of discretionary monetary policy offer cogent criticisms of this monetarist prescription:

1. *Unstable velocity.* Although most economists concur with the general logic of the inflation equation, they note that to make it operational, a specific measure of the money supply must be chosen—in particular one for which velocity is constant, or at least growing at a constant rate. As a result of banking innovations and financial deregulations, M1 velocity and, to a lesser extent, M2 velocity have behaved irregularly at times, as illustrated in figure 9.4 in the appendix to this chapter. This objection is summarized in amusing fashion by Goodhart's law: whatever measure of the money supply is chosen for application of the monetarist rule, it will soon begin to misbehave—it will no longer bear a stable relationship with income or inflation. One suggestion for overcoming this drawback is to change the rule to target on a nominal GDP growth rate equal approximately to the historical real rate of growth of GDP. When nominal GDP grows faster than the chosen target rate, cut back on money-supply growth; when

nominal GDP grows more slowly than the target rate, increase money-supply growth. Changes in velocity cause changes in nominal GDP, so they are automatically offset by this rule. An alternative rule is to target on an inflation rate.

2. *Lack of Fed control over money supply.* Even if velocity were constant, the Fed could not maintain close enough control over the money supply to effect the monetarist rule. This lack of control arises from several sources: the public's holdings of currency fluctuate irregularly, banks and the public shift deposits from one measure of the money supply to another, financial innovations are continually rendering money measures obsolete, and banks can choose to hold excess reserves. Unstable velocity and the lack of control over monetary aggregates have prompted suggestions that it is better to target monetary policy directly on the inflation rate rather than on a monetary aggregate.

3. *Short-run monetary shocks.* The economy is often hit with short-run increases in money demand that cry out for a temporary increase in the money supply. Turning the central bank into a preprogrammed robot would prevent the application of any such obviously correct policy. Examples of such situations are the Penn Central bankruptcy in 1970, the Franklin National Bank collapse in 1974, the near failure of the Continental Illinois Bank in 1984, the Hunt brothers silver speculation crisis in the 1980s, the stock market crash of October 19, 1987, and postal strikes in Canada. More recent examples are the Asian crisis/Russian default of 1998, the Y2K worry of late 1999, the 9/11 attacks of 2001, and the subprime mortgage crisis of 2008. By increasing the money supply markedly in these crises, the Fed can alleviate these shocks, and then when things settle down, they can decrease the money supply back to what its normal growth level would have produced, to avoid inflationary pressures.

4. *Inflexibility.* The Fed can achieve the benefits of a rule by following a rule on its own, without being tied to it. This policy would allow the Fed to retain flexibility should events require a deviation from the rule. The most dramatic example of this is the 2008 subprime mortgage crisis. This event has underlined how important it is for central banks to maintain the health of the economy's financial system, rules be damned. Section 8.5 in the previous chapter discusses the subprime mortgage crisis, and curiosity 10.3 in the next chapter highlights Fed policy in this crisis.

Sample Exam Question 9.5:
"One thing the subprime mortgage crisis made clear is that the Fed's control over the money supply is not as close as we had thought. Efforts to expand the money supply to stimulate the economy were frustrated by unanticipated commercial bank behavior."

What commercial bank behavior is being referred to here?

Media Illustrations

Example 1
The central bank claims that "there are no aggregate measures or indicators of the rate of monetary expansion that are sufficiently reliable at present to be used as targets for policy, or that are uniquely helpful in the task of explaining the impact of monetary policy." Accordingly, judgment about financial and economic conditions—rather than following a monetary rule—will continue to be the guiding force behind monetary policy. Thus, it appears that monetary targeting isn't in the cards.

What are the most popular "aggregate measures or indicators of the rate of monetary expansion"?
M1 and M2 are the most popular measures of the money supply.

What is the monetary rule that is being referred to here?
The monetary rule requires that the money supply be increased at a steady, preannounced rate, usually low enough to deliver an acceptable rate of inflation.

What does "monetary targeting" mean?
Monetary targeting means devoting monetary policy to achieving a specific rate of growth of a monetary aggregate.

What argument is being used to defend the decision not to adopt such a rule?
For this rule to work, the definition of the money supply used to measure the rate of money growth must be reliably connected to the level of economic activity. In more formal terms, its velocity must be roughly constant. It is claimed that no existing money supply measure qualifies in this respect.

Example 2
How can this be? How can the economy show just as much inflation with money growing only half as fast? After all, the growth of M1 has been cut to about six percent, which is close to the four percent that we were told five years ago would produce a stable price level.

How would one calculate the money supply growth rate that would be such as to "produce a stable price level"?
This rate would be equal to the long-run real rate of growth of the economy.

What answer would you give to the questions in the first two sentences of this clipping?
Although the growth of M1 has been cut to 6 percent, it is probably the case that an alternative measure of the money supply, say M2, which is more closely related to spending, is growing at a much higher rate.

Example 3

The rapid expansion of M2 occurred as inflation rates were at historically high levels. Instead of saving, people spent and turned money over quickly in the banking system.

This clip suggests that the historically high inflation rate has caused the rapid expansion of M2. Do you agree? Explain.

No. It is more likely that the rapid expansion of the money supply, as measured by M2, has caused the historically high inflation. (It is possible, however, that some other factor, such a surge in consumption demand, has caused a temporary increase in inflation which the monetary authorities have accommodated, by increasing the rate of growth of the money supply to avoid constricting the economy.)

What terminology do economists use to refer to "turning money over quickly in the banking system"?

This would be called a high velocity.

Why would velocity tend to be higher during an inflation?

When inflation is high, money holdings lose their value more quickly. To avoid this loss, people will try to get by with fewer cash balances, making this smaller level of cash balances work harder (turn over more frequently) to support their spending.

Example 4

The central bank has got it right. Its job is to take the punch bowl away just as the party gets roaring. And if you have 6 percent real growth a quarter like we did last year, it's quite a party you've got going.

What is the party being referred to?

The party is a recovery from a recession.

What is the punch bowl in this context, and what role does it play at this party?

The punch bowl is money-supply growth. It has served to stimulate, or at least accommodate, the economy's recovery from the recession.

Why is it necessary to remove this punch bowl?

Once the recovery is well under way, capacity output will soon be reached, implying that price increases rather than output increases will result from continued stimulation. To prevent this result, the central bank must lower the money-supply growth to a level consistent with full-capacity real growth.

Chapter Summary

- The original quantity theory, represented by $Mv = PQ$, was a tautology because velocity v was defined to be the ratio of PQ to M. If v is constant, an increase in the money supply M causes an equal percentage increase in the price level P for the economy at full employment, and an equal percentage increase in real output Q for the economy at below full employment.

- The modern quantity theory rewrites the quantity equation as $M = (1/v)PQ$ and interprets it as a money-demand equation, reflecting the fact that money demand increases as nominal income, PQ, increases. This behavioral relationship is used to develop an explanation of how the economy reacts to an increase in the money supply to move to a higher income level. The magnitude of this reaction is captured formally by the income multiplier with respect to the money supply.

- By equating growth in supply of and demand for money, monetarists developed a rule of thumb for predicting long-run inflation: money growth less real growth. In the short run, many things affect inflation, but in the long run, inflation is always and everywhere a monetary phenomenon because price increases through demand or cost increases can be sustained only if supplemented with money-supply increases.

- When the government creates money, it injects it into the economy by spending it. The amount of goods and services obtained in this way is called seigniorage, measured as the amount of government spending financed by selling bonds to the central bank.

- The monetarist rule—that the central bank be replaced by a robot designed to increase the money supply at a rate approximately equal to the real rate of growth in the economy—is designed to keep long-run inflation low. This proposal has spawned the very active rules-versus-discretion debate between those who believe that policy authorities should be replaced by policy rules and those who believe that policy authorities should be permitted to take discretionary policy action as they see fit.

Formula Definitions

- Velocity $= \dfrac{PQ}{M} = \dfrac{\text{Nominal GDP}}{\text{Money supply}}$

- Income multiplier with respect to the money supply $= \dfrac{\Delta \text{GDP}}{\Delta M}$

Rule of Thumb

Long-run inflation = Money growth rate − Real income growth rate

Media Exercises

(Group B questions require more thought.)

A1. **Of course, a large body of economists now believes that if the 1970s taught us anything it's that macroeconomic fine-tuning is more trouble than it's worth. In effect the economy's steering gears are so loose that unless you hit a very sharp curve, fiddling with the wheel is just as likely to do harm as good.**

a. What is macroeconomic "fine-tuning"?

b. What kind of monetary policy is this an argument for? Explain.

A2. **If the Fed's sole objective is going to be fighting inflation, it may as well be run by a computer, say critics of a proposal to change its mandate. The proposal to strip the Fed of its other economic jobs such as supporting the value of the dollar and promoting economic growth and employment is bringing to wider public attention a debate that has quietly gone on among economists for the past few years.**

a. Explain how a computer could be used to run the Fed's inflation-fighting policy.

b. What is the debate referred to in this clipping?

A3. **The introduction of daily interest saving accounts attracted a growing portion of funds away from checking accounts. The upshot was that a given amount of M1 supported a higher level of total spending, or in other words, its _____ increased.**

a. Fill in the blank in this clip.

b. Explain in your own words exactly why it increased.

A4. **Monetarism's recognition of the usefulness of monitoring the money supply was an important contribution to economics, they say. And policy makers accept the principle that eventually an economy that goes on producing more money than noninflationary growth requires will turn inflationary. "In the long run, monetarism has to be correct," said Richard Darman, the deputy secretary to the Treasury. Excessive money growth has to lead to inflation. "The problem with monetarism," he said, "is that its advocates have seen it as infallible over short periods of time and wish it to be rigid in its application over all periods of time."**

a. What level of money supply growth does "noninflationary growth" require?

    b. Why do the advocates of monetarism "wish it to be rigid in its application over all periods of time"?

    c. Why do others view this as a problem?

A5. **Most economists look for the Fed to adopt a more restrictive policy once the recovery _____ and the presidential election _____.**

    a. What is meant here by a more restrictive policy?

    b. Fill in the blanks and explain your reasoning.

A6. **I really don't believe monetary policy is a very useful tool for fine-tuning the business cycle or fighting unemployment directly. I do believe that what monetary policy can do is control the inflation rate.**

    a. Why might one believe that monetary policy is not useful for fine-tuning the business cycle?

    b. How can monetary policy be used to control inflation?

A7. **The broader measure M2, however, since it encompasses most significant forms of money individuals may hold, resolves the problem. The shifts in asset holdings take place *within* the broader measure. That doesn't make it impervious to distortion, but M2 velocity has shown substantial predictability for several years.**

    a. What is M2 velocity?

    b. Explain why M2 velocity should be more predictable than M1 velocity.

    c. What is the problem referred to at the very end of the first sentence, and exactly how does M2 solve this problem?

A8. **But the experience of M1 still unnerves: innovations in the banking system, especially interest-bearing checking accounts that at that time were not counted in M1, allowed the public to shift money holdings into and out of different instruments in such as way as to make the relationship between M1 and total spending in the economy unstable.**

    a. Explain what must have been the experience with M1 that was unnerving.

    b. What technical terminology would economists use to describe "the relationship between M1 and total spending"?

A9. A growing number of economists view the Fed's new willingness to take on more of the nation's debt as inflationary in the long run.

a. Explain the rationale for the inflation worry.

b. Why is the "long-run" qualification added?

A10. Far better for central bankers to get out of the fine-tuning business. Instead, they should try to keep. . . .

Complete this clip.

A11. In their study of ten European and North American countries, they found that democratically controlled central banks pursue less restrictive policies than do independent central banks, and are less likely to try to veto the expansionary policies of left-wing governments.

a. How do you think the authors of this study would have classified the Fed, democratically controlled or independent?

b. How would a central bank try to veto expansionary policies? Why would they want to do so?

c. Why do you think democratically controlled banks would in general pursue less restrictive policies?

A12. With financial deregulation changing the meaning of money, the Fed finally abandoned the monetarist prescription of targeting the money supply.

a. How did financial deregulation change the meaning of money?

b. Exactly what is the monetarist prescription of targeting the money supply?

c. Why would this monetarist prescription need to be abandoned?

A13. It is very difficult for politicians to take action—especially unpleasant action—against a problem until the problem seems compelling. By that time, though, action tends to be tardy. The point of economic management is to stabilize the economy, but a political system that requires signs of instability before it can act makes the process self-defeating.

In terms of classic debates over economic policy, what does this argument support?

A14. Inflationary policies can spur growth for a time, which is why politicians have often found them so tempting. This is the best argument for making central banks. . . .

Complete this clipping.

A15. **A small but vocal clique of Japanese politicians has floated the idea that the Bank of Japan might purchase government bonds directly from the Ministry of Finance as a way to fund the government's rapidly expanding deficit. The plan, which would essentially have the central bank _____ to finance government spending, is opposed by the Bank of Japan.**

a. Fill in the blank.

b. Why would this plan be opposed by the Bank of Japan?

A16. **The Fed has been criticized for raising interest rates before seeing any evidence of worsening inflation, but Fed chairman Alan Greenspan replied that "to successfully navigate a bend in the river, the barge must begin the turn well before the bend is reached," introducing a new monetary-policy metaphor.**

a. Is the Fed following a policy rule or policy discretion?

b. Spell out in your own words the meaning of the metaphor.

A17. **In the longer term, however, things will be different. It is worth recalling that seigniorage is no longer being exercised by all those seigneurs—emperors, kings, and imperial governments—who once possessed it. The reason is simple: seigniorage is such a tempting privilege that it always ends up being abused.**

What is meant by abusing seigniorage, and what consequences result?

A18. **This suggests a shift in the FOMC's assessment away from concern over economic growth toward concern over inflation.**

What is the implication of this shift for monetary policy?

A19. **While central bankers still accept that inflation is largely a result of money-supply growth, few target the money supply in practice because. . . .**

Complete this statement.

A20. **Subtle changes in the wording of the FOMC's statement suggest that the Fed is becoming more hawkish on inflation and so is probably near the end of its cycle of. . . .**

Complete this statement.

A21. **The Fed's statement is reminding us that it has provided a lot of stimulus but that it takes time for this action to work.**

a. How has the Fed provided stimulus?

b. How does this work to stimulate the economy?

c. Why does it take time? What is the major implication of this time lag?

A22. A single cigarette now costs Z$500,000. President Robert Mugabe of Zimbawa blames hyperinflation on exploitative businessmen who are part of a Western plot to destabilize his country. His critics point instead to widespread economic mismanagement, corruption, and the government's policy of. . . .

Complete this statement.

A23. It took Paul Volker, who became Fed chairman in 1979, to put the monetarist theory into practice, adopting money-supply targets that drove interest rates to double-digit levels, sent the economy into a deep recession, and ultimately brought inflation down.

What is this monetarist theory?

A24. Financial innovation and the spread of U.S. currency throughout the world have broken down the relationship of money to inflation and growth, making monetary gauges. . . .

a. Complete this statement.

b. What implications does it have for U.S. monetary policy?

A25. Whatever the reason, it now appears that the Fed has abandoned the strategy of offsetting completely the effects of its new lending programs. Instead, the Fed has injected historically large amounts of credit into the market. Such massive injections of base money have raised concerns about _____. However, provided the increase is temporary and is removed once the need for _____ is gone, as the Fed did in the _____ crises, there is no reason that a temporary increase in base money should cause _____.

Fill in these blanks.

A26. "The empirical relationship between money growth and variables such as inflation and nominal output growth has continued to be unstable," Mr. Bernanke said.

What implication does this have for monetary policy?

A27. It is the rare consumer or investor who would not conclude that where government debt was growing faster than GDP, tax increases and/or accelerated inflation could not be far off.

How can accelerated inflation be an alternative to taxation?

B1. **Followers of Milton Friedman of the University of Chicago were convinced that business cycles could be smoothed away simply by requiring that the Federal Reserve. . . .**

a. Complete this sentence.

b. Explain the logic of the smoothing away of business cycles.

B2. **A monetary rule need not mean a single, bald number. If the central bank fears velocity shifts, rules could be adopted for adjusting the target in the face of a trend change in velocity.**

a. What might cause a velocity shift?

b. What is the "target" referred to in this clip?

c. By means of a numerical example, explain how this target would be adjusted for "a trend change in velocity."

B3. **Jobs increased at a healthy pace last month, the unemployment rate fell, and the manufacturing sector stayed strong. As a result most analysts think that when the Fed meets later this month it will again _____ short-term interest rates in an effort to _____ economic growth and put off _____.**

a. Does this comment reflect a monetarist rule or discretionary monetary policy?

b. Fill in the blanks.

B4. **The chairman of the Federal Reserve Board stated that "I remain concerned that economic growth will run into constraints if job growth continues. If some slowdown doesn't bring labor demand into line with its sustainable supply, _____ is a real danger and _____ may be necessary."**

Fill in the blanks.

B5. **Rising productivity does not in itself spell the end of inflation. With enough _____ it would still be possible to whip prices into a froth.**

a. How would rising productivity affect inflation?

b. Fill in the blank.

B6. **The Federal Reserve itself noted that "trend increases in costs and core prices have generally remained quite subdued." But monetary policy must be forward-looking, taking action today to stem future inflationary pressure. That is why**

an analysis of why inflation is low should carry more weight than the numbers alone.

    a. Does this clipping advocate a rule or discretion?

    b. Interpret what is meant by the last sentence.

B7. **Governments increase the money supply too rapidly because it enables them to finance an expanding government sector without increasing taxes or borrowing from the economy's savings.**

    a. What is this means of financing usually called?

    b. What is its drawback?

    c. What is meant by "borrowing from the economy's savings"?

B8. **The Fed blames all problems on external influences beyond its control and takes credit for any and all favorable occurrences. It thereby continues to promote the myth that the private economy is unstable, while its behavior continues to document the reality that government is today the major source of economic instability.**

What view of economic policy does this clip promote?

B9. **Price-level targeting is the latest suggestion for monetary policy. This policy would target on an inflation rate measured over the next three years, say, rather than over the next year. Its advantage is that. . . .**

What advantage would this proposal have?

B10. **The biggest criticism of central bankers is that their confidence in the link between the inflation rate and economic stability caused them to underestimate the dangers of asset bubbles.**

    a. What policy would a central bank follow if it believed in this link?

    b. What is an asset bubble?

    c. How could an asset bubble be dangerous?

B11. **"The Federal Reserve must be conscious of the limits of its capabilities. We can try to provide a backdrop for stable, sustainable growth, but we cannot iron out every fluctuation, and attempts to do so could be counterproductive," Alan Greenspan, the Fed chairman, said.**

    a. How would the Fed provide a backdrop for stable, sustainable growth?

    b. What name is usually given to a policy of ironing out every fluctuation?

c. Give an example of how an attempt to iron out a fluctuation could be counterproductive.

B12. There is no direct connection between the deficit and inflation. If there were, why did inflation hit 14 percent in 1948, a year when the government had a spending surplus? And why has inflation continued to fall the past two years while the deficit has been rising?

a. What is the logic behind the view that there is a connection between the budget deficit and inflation?

b. Do the facts cited in this clip contradict this view?

Numerical Exercises

AN1. Suppose that the income multiplier with respect to the money supply is 4, the money multiplier is 3, and "the" multiplier is 2.5. Ignore growth.

a. If the central bank buys $2 billion worth of bonds, what increase in income should ultimately result?

b. If the economy is at full employment when this policy is undertaken, what fraction of this increase in GDP is an increase in real GDP?

AN2. Suppose that income is $800 billion, the price index is 120 (base year 1987), inflation is 10 percent, the long-run real rate of growth is 2 percent, and the current money supply is $200 billion.

a. What is the level of real income?

b. What is the velocity of money?

c. What is the rate of growth of the money supply?

AN3. Suppose that the current level of income is $600 billion, the long-run real rate of growth is 2 percent, the current money supply is $200 billion, and the rate of money-supply growth is 10 percent.

a. What is the velocity of money?

b. What long-run level of inflation is this economy experiencing?

AN4. Suppose that real GDP is $400 billion, the price index is 120, the money supply is $40 billion, and the money multiplier is 4. What is current velocity?

AN5. If "the" multiplier is 6, the income multiplier with respect to the money supply is 4, and the money multiplier is 5, then which of the following policies increase income by $50 billion dollars?

a. Increase in money supply by $2.5 billion.

b. Increase in government spending by $10 billion.

c. Fed purchase of $12.5 billion in bonds.

d. Increase in government spending by $3 billion and the money supply by $8 billion.

e. Fed sale of $2 billion in bonds and increase in government spending by $15 billion.

f. Fed purchase of $1 billion in bonds and increase in government spending by $5 billion.

AN6. Suppose that "the" multiplier is 3, the money multiplier is 4, and the income multiplier with respect to the money supply is 5. If the government increases its spending by $10 billion at the same time that the central bank sells $2 billion of bonds on the open market (beyond the bond sales involved in financing the government spending), what will happen to the equilibrium level of income?

AN7. Suppose that the income multiplier with respect to the money supply is 5. When the Fed bought $20 billion of bonds, income eventually increased by $400 billion. What is the money multiplier?

AN8. Suppose that the aggregate supply curve is vertical, velocity is 4, and the money supply increases by 3 percent beyond what is needed to meet long-run growth. Not counting the usual long-run growth, according to the quantity theory of money, what will be the percentage change in (a) real income, (b) the price level, and (c) nominal income?

AN9. Suppose that the money multiplier is 4, seigniorage is $6 billion, and the current money supply is $400 billion. Assuming that the central bank did not engage in any discretionary policy action, how many bonds did the central bank buy this year?

AN10. Suppose that the money multiplier is 8. When the Fed bought $15 billion of bonds the income level eventually increased by $360 billion. What is the income multiplier with respect to the money supply?

AN11. Suppose that "the" multiplier is 3.5, the money multiplier is 4.5, the income multiplier with respect to the money supply is 2.5, and the marginal tax rate is 20 percent. What ultimate change in the government's budget deficit would result if government spending increased by $10 billion and at the same time the central bank sold bonds worth $8 billion?

AN12. Suppose that the current level of income is $800 billion, the income multiplier with respect to the money supply is 4, the money multiplier is 5, the long-run real rate of growth is 2 percent, the current money supply is $200 billion, and the rate of inflation is 8 percent. What level of seigniorage is the government currently enjoying?

BN1. Suppose that "the" multiplier is 3, the money multiplier is 6, and the income multiplier with respect to the money supply is 4. The government increases spending by $12 billion, but because the economy is operating at full capacity, it wants to use monetary policy to offset the impact this increase will have on income.

a. Does the central bank need to buy or sell bonds to offset this fiscal policy?

b. How many bonds must the monetary authorities buy or sell to accomplish this end?

BN2. Suppose that the economy is at full employment with a real rate of growth of 3 percent. If innovations in the banking system are reducing, all other things constant, the need for money at 1 percent per year, what rate of growth of the money supply would you recommend to achieve a long-run inflation rate of 4 percent?

BN3. If the money supply is growing at 8 percent, the real rate of growth of GDP is 2 percent, and financial innovations are reducing the demand for money by 0.5 percent per year, what should the long-run inflation rate be?

BN4. Suppose that "the" multiplier is 4, the income multiplier with respect to the money supply is 2, the money multiplier is 3, and the government is obliged by an election promise to increase government spending by $5 billion but wants the level of income to grow by only $8 billion to avoid inflation. What open-market operation will accomplish this goal?

BN5. Suppose that the money multiplier is 8, the money supply is $400 billion, real growth is 2 percent, banking innovations are decreasing money demand by 1 percent per year, and inflation is 3 percent. What is seigniorage?

BN6. Suppose that the income elasticity of the demand for money (the percent rise in the demand for money due to a 1 percent rise in income) is less than one. Does this fact imply that the long-run inflation rule of thumb overestimates, underestimates, or remains an accurate estimate of inflation? Explain your reasoning.

BN7.   Suppose that the money multiplier is 5, the money supply is $200 billion, real growth is 2 percent, velocity is constant, and seigniorage is $4 billion. What is the rate of inflation?

BN8.   Suppose that the money supply is $500 billion, real growth is 2 percent, velocity is constant, inflation is 8 percent, and seigniorage is $5 billion. What is the money multiplier?

Appendix 9.1:   Changing Velocity

Implicit in our derivation of the formula for inflation is an assumption that velocity is constant, but in reality this is not so. There are two basic kinds of velocity changes, erratic changes and steady increases. The former, as described earlier in this chapter, is one of the main reasons for why the Fed does not base monetary policy on the monetarist rule. The latter requires an adjustment to our rule of thumb representing the link between money growth and economic activity.

Financial innovations have been steadily decreasing the demand for money. For example, the growing use of credit cards has made it possible for people to coordinate more closely their consumption payments and income receipts, reducing their need to hold money. The proliferation of automatic banking machines has allowed people to carry fewer dollars in their pocket. They are able to make a smaller amount of money holdings support the same amount of spending. This is what is meant by a higher velocity! (Students often miss this point, so it bears repeating: if, holding income constant, the demand for money decreases, people are making smaller money holdings work harder—velocity increases.)

Suppose, as was the case during the 1960s and 1970s (and as illustrated in figure 9.4), that financial innovations are decreasing the demand for money, and thus increasing velocity, at an annual rate of about 3 percent a year. If long-run growth is 2 percent, then there is a net decrease in money demand of 1 percent a year. If the supply of money is increasing at 8 percent a year a gap of 9 percent between money supply and money demand opens up, causing prices to rise by 9 percent. As a result we must modify our rule of thumb for long-run inflation. This equation comes from recognizing that for equilibrium to be maintained in the monetary sector a change in money supply gives rise to an equal change in money demand. So, to figure out the equation for inflation, add up the sources of money demand change and equate them to money supply change. Doing this, we get

Money-supply growth = Money-demand growth
= Real income growth + Price growth − Velocity growth

Rearranging we get

Long-run rate of price inflation = Money growth rate − Real income growth rate
+ Velocity growth rate

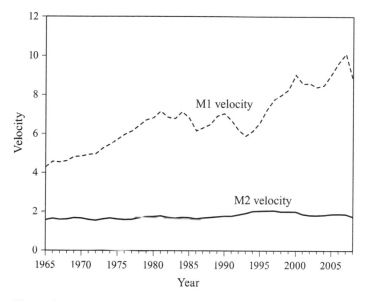

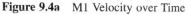

Figure 9.4a M1 Velocity over Time

M1 velocity steadily grows, then dramatically becomes irregular. Source: Economic Report of the President, 2009. www.gpo.access.gov/eop.

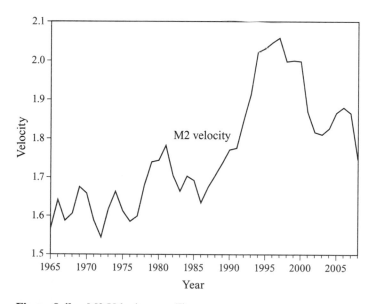

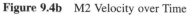

Figure 9.4b M2 Velocity over Time

In figure 9.4a, M2 velocity seemed much steadier, but this appearance is misleading because small changes are substantial percentage changes due to the low value of M2 velocity. Source: Economic Report of the President, 2009. www.gpo.access.gov/eop.

(For the mathematically minded, the modified inflation equation can be derived by using the quantity equation $Mv = PQ$ to obtain the approximate result that $\%\Delta M + \%\Delta v = \%\Delta P + \%\Delta Q$, implying that $\%\Delta P = \%\Delta M - \%\Delta Q + \%\Delta v$.)

From 1950 to 1980, M1 velocity climbed steadily from about 3 to about 7 but then fell dramatically (by about 7 percent) in the early 1980s and behaved irregularly thereafter. During this same period, M2 velocity held constant at about 1.7, but it fell markedly (by about 10 percent) in the early 1980s and has recently behaved irregularly. These velocity changes are illustrated in figure 9.4. A steadily growing velocity can be accommodated, as shown in our new equation for inflation, but an irregularly changing velocity implies that this equation is of less value as a summary of long-run economic behavior.

10   Monetary Policy and Interest Rates

It may be surprising that we have completed two chapters dealing with money and the role of the central bank but have only peripherally mentioned interest rates. This approach was chosen deliberately. The fundamental role of the central bank is to control the supply of money in the economy. Effects on interest rates are a product of this control, so a prerequisite to any discussion of interest rates is a knowledge of the role of money creation.

Monetary policy influences interest rates in two distinct ways, depending on whether or not the monetary policy affects inflation. The purpose of this chapter is to discuss how monetary policy affects the interest rate in a noninflationary environment and how the interest rate in turn affects the operation of the economy. Chapter 11 examines interest rates in an inflationary environment.

Upon completion of this chapter you should

- be able to explain the crucial role played by the inverse relationship between the interest rate and the price of bonds, and
- understand how monetary policy affects the economy through interest rates.

10.1   A Multitude of Interest Rates

Macroeconomists talk of "the" interest rate, but in fact a myriad of interest rates exist, depending on such variables as time to maturity of the financial asset, how the interest is taxed, how liquid the financial asset is, and what is known about the borrower (in particular, the risk of default). There are the interest rate you pay on a mortgage, the interest rate you pay on a consumer loan (e.g., to buy a car), the interest rate the bank pays you on a savings account, the interest rate the bank pays you on a term deposit, the interest rate a large corporation pays on loans from a bank, the interest rate paid to you on a bond due to mature in a year, the interest rate paid to you on a bond due to mature in ten years, the interest rate paid to you on a government bond, and the interest rate paid to you on a junk bond (issued by a high-risk company), to give but a few examples. Short-term debt instruments (a debt instrument is a financial asset, e.g., a bond, on which interest is paid), of maturity less than a year, are traded in what is called the *money market.* Longer term instruments are traded in the *capital market.*

Typical interest rates in the money market are T-bill rates (on U.S. government Treasury bills), commercial paper rates (on loans by financial institutions to large banks and corporations), the federal funds rate (on very short-term loans between banks of their deposits at the Fed), and the eurodollar rate (on U.S. dollars deposited outside the United States). Typical interest rates in the capital market are the mortgage rate, the corporate bond rate, the Treasury bond rate, and the municipal bond rate.

All these interest rates tend to move together, however, so little harm is done by analyzing the economy in terms of a single representative interest rate, as we do throughout the rest of this book. Two representative rates are graphed in figure 10.1. For those interested, the "Currency Trading" column in the "Money & Investing" section of *The Wall Street Journal* lists several key U.S. and foreign interest rates in about twenty categories.

> **Sample Exam Question 10.1:**
> "All these other interest rates are traditionally higher than the T-bill rate, for the same length of time to maturity."
> Why would the T-bill rate be lower than other interest rates?

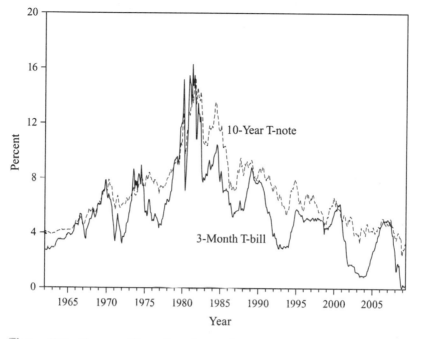

Figure 10.1   Short- and Long-Term Interest Rates
Monthly averaged rates are graphed from 1962–01 to 2009–05. The short-term rate (the 3-month T-bill rate) is more volatile than the long-term rate (the 10-year Treasury note rate) and is usually lower. Source: www.federalreserve.gov.

10.2   Interest Rates and the Price of Bonds

There is an inverse relationship between the interest rate and the price of bonds, the closest we come in macroeconomics to a "law," as opposed to the rules of thumb that we have been using elsewhere to represent important concepts. This inverse relationship is fundamental to understanding how monetary policy affects interest rates, so it is an important part of the stories we will tell about how the monetary sector plays a role in influencing the macroeconomy. It also explains why the financial pages of the newspaper are so full of speculation about the future course of the interest rate—if you can correctly predict that the interest rate will fall, say, you can make a lot of money by buying bonds because their price should rise as the interest rate falls—the inverse relationship described above!

There are two main types of bonds. A *coupon bond* pays the owner of the bond a fixed interest payment each year until the bond matures, when the *face value* (or *par value*) of the bond is paid. The name "coupon bond" comes from the fact that many years ago, the bond owner had to clip a coupon from the bottom of the bond each year to receive this fixed interest payment. Now these payments are made electronically. A *discount* bond has

Curiosity 10.1: What Is the Federal Funds Rate?

Every six weeks or so the Federal Open Market Committee (FOMC), a committee consisting of the seven Federal Reserve Board members plus five presidents of the regional branches of the Fed, meets to set the interest rate. The interest rate it sets is the *federal funds rate*. This rate is the rate charged by one commercial bank to another for borrowing (usually overnight) some of its excess reserves at the Fed. Commercial banks that are unable to meet their legal reserve requirement borrow other banks' excess reserves, paying the federal funds rate, determined by the forces of supply and demand in this market. The Fed itself influences the supply of reserves in this market by undertaking open market operations, and so in this way can determine the federal funds rate. After each FOMC meeting the Fed does whatever is necessary with the money supply to cause the federal funds rate to closely match what the FOMC has announced. These announcements typically are no change, or a change up or down of 25 basis points. (The federal funds rate is traditionally set to a round quarter-percent, such as 3.5 or 3.25). But in tumultuous times, such as 2008 during the crises caused by the subprime mortgage disaster, large changes are undertaken. During 2008 two cuts of 75 basis points were made, as well as several 50 basis-point cuts. Figure 10.2 graphs the federal funds rate over time. Notice how it matches the broad movements of the interest rates graphed in figure 10.1; controlling the federal funds rate is how the Fed influences other interest rates in the economy. But notice that this Fed influence over the short-term rate (the 3-month T-bill rate) is much stronger than over the long-term rate (the 10-year Treasury note rate).

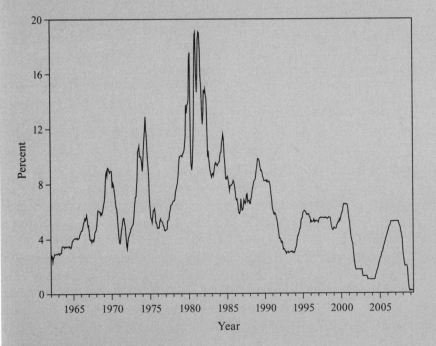

Figure 10.2 Federal Funds Rate
Monthly averages from 1962–01 to 2009–05. Source: www.federalreserve.gov.

The federal funds rate should not be confused with the *discount rate*, the rate charged by the Fed on loans to commercial banks. This is an administratively determined rate that is usually set at about a percentage point above the federal funds rate. These loans are typically short term, made to allow banks to meet temporary shortages of liquidity due to unusual disruptions. Banks are often reluctant to use the discount window because it may be interpreted as signal that the bank is in some kind of trouble.

no coupon (and so is sometimes called a zero-coupon bond); the return to holding such a bond comes entirely from buying it at a price below its face value.

The best way to think about how the yield (interest rate) on a bond is calculated is to view it as the annual return from owning the bond, expressed as a percentage of what was paid for the bond. The annual return takes two forms. First, there is the coupon, and second, any change in the price of the bond during the year. (Only the latter applies for a discount bond.) The sum of these is the annual return. This is easy to calculate for a bond that has one year to maturity; in this case the yield is given by

$$i = \frac{\text{Coupon} + (\text{Face value} - \text{Price})}{\text{Price}}$$

One-Year Bonds

How does the inverse relationship between interest rates and the price of bonds come about? Suppose that you own a coupon bond that is due to mature in one year, with face value $1,000 and coupon $100. If the interest rate is 10 percent, the current price of this bond should be $1,000 because the $100 interest coupon payment is 10 percent of the price of the bond. Now suppose that the interest rate rises to 12 percent. Seeing this increase, you decide to sell your bond and use the proceeds to buy a new bond that pays 12 percent. Unfortunately for you, however, nobody will be willing to pay $1,000 for your bond because everyone knows he or she can earn a 12 percent return elsewhere. To sell your bond, you will have to lower its price: as the interest rate rises, the price of bonds falls.

How far will the price fall? At first glance it could fall to $833.33 because at this price the $100 interest payment is a return of 12 percent. But it will not fall this far. Because the bond will pay off at $1,000 at the end of the year, the total return to investing in this bond (at the new lower price!) is the $100 coupon payment, plus a capital gain due to the rise in bond price from $833.33 to $1,000 over the year. This capital gain would make the return on this bond greater than 12 percent. To calculate the actual fall in the bond price, we can use the interest rate equation given above. Doing this, we get

$$0.12 = \frac{100 + (1,000 - \text{Price})}{\text{Price}}$$

Solving this for price, we find that the price will fall to $982.14.

An opposite result would occur if the interest rate were to fall to 8 percent. Everyone would want to buy your bond if it were priced at $1,000, because the 10 percent return on your bond would be higher than the 8 percent return available elsewhere. As a result potential buyers could bid up the price of your bond in their efforts to obtain it, at first glance to $1,250 because the $100 return is 8 percent of $1,250. Once again, this is not correct. At the end of the year this bond will pay off at $1,000, so holders will experience a capital loss if they buy it for $1,250, implying that the return would be lower than 8 percent. Using the interest rate equation above, we can calculate that the price will rise to only $1,018.52.

The bottom line here is that we can see where the inverse relationship between the interest rate and the price of bonds comes from—the natural forces of supply and demand in the bond market automatically (and very quickly, because of the efficiency of the bond market) bring this about. When the interest rate rises, people sell old bonds to buy new ones paying the higher interest rate, so the price of bonds falls; when the interest rate falls, people want to buy old bonds because these bonds are paying a higher interest rate, so the price of bonds rises. We told this story in terms of an initiating increase/decrease in the interest rate, but we could have told the story in terms of an initiating increase/decrease in the price of bonds. Suppose that in our story above the initial change was a rise in price of bonds from $1,000 to, say, $1,050. The interest rate automatically falls because the $100 coupon is a smaller percentage of the $1,050 price, and because purchasers will experience a capital loss of $50 over the year the bond is held. So, if someone decides to sell a bond, for whatever reason, and drops the bond price to sell it, the interest rate instantly rises. And if the interest rate rises, for whatever reason, the market reacts instantly to push down bond prices.

Curiosity 10.2: Why Are Bond Prices Never Equal to Their Face Values?

Bonds always have a face value that is a round number like $1,000 or $10,000, and coupons usually have reasonably round numbers such as $65.50 or $102.25.

When a bond is first issued, whoever is selling the bonds figures out a coupon that is approximately such that it matches the current interest rate. So, if the current interest rate is 6.55 percent, a $1,000 bond might have its coupon set at $65.50. But by the time the bonds are printed up for sale, a couple of days later, the interest rate has changed, and so the price of the bond needs to change.

After bonds have been sold by the issuer, the people who buy the bonds can sell them on the bond market. There is always a market for these "old" bonds, and buying and selling them takes place all the time. (The bond market is huge, about eight times the value of the stock market!) So the interest rate and the price of these bonds are continually changing.

We think of bonds as a conservative investment with low risk, and indeed some investors do buy bonds and hold them to maturity, knowing exactly what their long-run return will be. But the bond market is also a venue for speculators who are trying to make money in the short run. Huge amounts of money are made and lost in the bond market by speculators who are gambling on interest rate changes. If you think that interest rates will soon fall, you can make a lot of money by buying bonds now. If the interest rate does fall, the price of your bonds will increase, and you can sell them at a profit and go on to speculate on something else. Of course, if the interest rate rises, the price of your bonds will fall and you will lose money!

To make big money on anticipated interest rate changes you need to buy/sell long-term bonds, not short-term bonds. This is explained later when we get to long-term bonds.

Discount Bonds

This same inverse relationship between the interest rate and the price of bonds character-izes discount bonds. The most common example of a discount bond is a U.S. government Treasury bill, called a T-bill, sold originally at weekly auctions for maturity periods of three months, six months, and a year (and then, like all other bonds, available for resale on the regular money market, sometimes called the *secondary* market). If the interest rate is 10 percent, the price for a one-year $10,000 T-bill will be $9,090.91 since the return of $10,000 − $9,090.91 = $909.09 is 10 percent of the $9,090.91 price paid. The interest rate formula given earlier can still be used here; just set the coupon equal to zero.

If the interest rate were higher, say 12 percent, the price of the T-bill would be lower—in this case $8,928.57—to make the return of $10,000 − $8,928.57 = $1,071.43 be 12 percent of the $8,928.57 purchase price. If the interest rate were lower, say 8 percent, the price of the T-bill would be higher, in this case $9,259.26. Discount bonds also exhibit an inverse relationship between return and price.

But what if the T-bill were to mature in only three months? In this case in our interest rate equation the relevant interest rate is the three-month rate rather than the annual rate. To use this equation, we need to recognize this. If the annual rate were 8 percent, for example, the formula for determining the price of a T-bill with face value $1,000 due to mature in three months would be

$$0.02 = \frac{1,000 - \text{Price}}{\text{Price}}$$

because, when the annual interest rate is 8 percent, the interest over three months, a quarter of a year, should be 2 percent. As another example, suppose that the price of a T-bill with face value $1,000 is due to mature in one month, and is currently selling for $993.50. What is the current interest rate? Using the interest rate equation, we write

$$i = \frac{1,000 - 993.50}{993.50} = 0.00654$$

But interest rates should always be expressed as annual rates, so this one-month rate of 0.654 percent should be multiplied by 12 to get the appropriate annual rate, namely 7.85 percent.

As should now be evident, regardless of the type of bond, there is an inverse relation-ship between interest rates and bond prices. It should also be evident why this relationship between interest rates and bond prices is so important. A change in the interest rate, which happens on a daily basis, can create substantial capital gains or losses for those holding bonds, particularly for those holding long-term bonds. It is for this reason that the financial pages of newspapers provide so much commentary on the future course of the interest rate.

Long-Term Bonds

When a bond has several years before it matures, the interest rate is calculated as the *yield to maturity*—the annual interest rate that an owner of this bond would earn by holding the bond until it matured. Calculating this yield to maturity is complicated, as explained in appendix 10.1; what is explained here instead is a convenient approximation based on the logic of bond returns.

Suppose that you own a coupon bond that is due to mature in five years, with face value $1,000 and coupon $100. If the interest rate is 10 percent, the current price of this bond should be $1,000 because the $100 interest coupon payment is 10 percent of the price of the bond. Now suppose that the interest rate rises to 12 percent. Seeing this increase, you decide to sell your bond and use the proceeds to buy a new bond that pays 12 percent. Unfortunately for you, however, nobody will be willing to pay $1,000 for your bond because everyone knows that a 12 percent return can be earned elsewhere. To sell your bond, you will have to lower its price.

Because the bond will pay off at $1,000 in five years, the total return to investing in this bond (at the new, lower price!) is the stream of five $100 interest payments, plus a capital gain due to the rise in bond price from its new price to $1,000, spread over these five years. Calculating the price to which this bond will fall is complicated, as explained in appendix 10.1. (For this example it is $927.90.) But here is a good method for doing approximate calculations. Call the new lower price P. Over the five years the price will increase from P to $1,000, so on average the price will increase by $(1,000 - P)/5$ per year. A rough estimate of the *annual* return to buying this bond is the coupon of $100 plus this annual capital gain. Expressing this as a fraction of the purchase price P, we get the annual yield to be

$$i = \frac{100 + (1,000 - P)/5}{P}$$

Putting in 12 percent for the interest rate ($i = 0.12$) and solving for P, we get $937.50.

An opposite result would occur if the interest rate were to fall to 8 percent. Everyone will want to buy your bond if it were priced at $1,000, because the 10 percent return on your bond will be higher than the 8 percent return available elsewhere. As a result potential buyers will bid up the price of your bond in their efforts to obtain it. Using the accurate method described in appendix 10.1, this price will be bid up to $1,079.85; then, by the approximation method, the result is $1,071.43.

A very important lesson from all this is that capital gains and losses are much greater for longer maturity bonds than for short-term bonds. Let's look at the earlier example of a $1,000 face-value coupon bond with coupon $100 and time to maturity five years. A rise in the interest rate to 12 percent dropped the bond price to $927.90. Suppose that there had only been one year to maturity; then the price would have fallen to $982.14. Someone buying this bond would, during the remaining year of its life, receive the $100 coupon plus that year's capital gain, $17.86, generating a 12 percent return on outlay. If there had been five years to maturity, however, there would have to be five such annual capital gains as the bond price crawls up to its face value over the five years. Consequently the price must fall much further for a longer maturity bond. Capital losses and gains are much larger on long-term bonds than on short-term bonds.

Sample Exam Question 10.2:
Say you purchased a one-year bond with face value $10,000 and a coupon of $500, paying $9,950. Six months later, when the interest rate is 4 percent, you wish to sell this bond.
    What price do you expect to get?

10.3   Monetary Policy and Interest Rates

The central bank controls the money supply through open-market operations—buying and selling government bonds. If it wishes to increase the money supply, it buys government bonds on the open market, but to buy these bonds it must induce us to sell them by bidding up their price. This rise in the price of bonds means that the interest coupon on a bond is now a lower percentage payment—that is, the interest rate falls. (This just reflects the inverse relationship between interest rates and the price of bonds.) Similarly, if the central bank wishes to decrease the money supply, it sells government bonds on the open market (the central bank has a large portfolio of government bonds that it can draw on for this purpose). To sell bonds, it must make them attractive to potential buyers by offering a higher interest rate, accomplished by selling the bonds at a lower price.

The main result here is that by changing the money supply, the central bank also changes the interest rate by affecting the price of bonds: an increase in the money supply lowers the interest rate by bidding up the price of bonds, and a decrease in the money supply raises the interest rate by lowering the price of bonds. Because of this, central bank monetary policy can be formulated either in terms of setting the interest rate or in terms of setting the money supply: the one is a mirror image of the other. Currently monetary policy is formulated in terms of the interest rate: the Fed announces a change in the interest rate and then adjusts the money supply to achieve this announced rate.

Why does monetary policy target on the interest rate rather than the rate of growth of the money supply? One reason is that it is much easier for the public to understand the central bank's monetary stance if it is described in terms of an interest rate. A second reason is that using a monetary aggregate as a guide to policy can be problematic, for reasons we discussed earlier in the context of the rules-versus-discretion debate. It is not clear what definition of the money supply should be chosen for policy purposes, the connection between monetary aggregates and spending behaviour is not stable, and measuring the magnitude of any monetary aggregate is problematic. All these problems are avoided by using the interest rate as the target of monetary policy; the money supply is adjusted by whatever is necessary to achieve this interest rate. As we will see in chapter 11, this interest rate policy runs into trouble in an inflationary environment. But in periods of low inflation, such as we have been experiencing for several years, this is a sensible way to conduct monetary policy.

This explanation of the determination of the interest rate focuses on what is happening in the bond market. For convenience, economists often view the determination of the interest rate in another, equivalent way—by interpreting the interest rate as the "price" of money and by looking at what is happening to the supply of and demand for money. The rationale for this approach is that individuals are thought to hold wealth in one of only two forms, money and bonds, so an increase in the demand for one implies a decrease in the demand for the other.

Consequently, because buying bonds increases the supply of money, it should lower its "price," the interest rate. An increase in the demand for money, for example, caused by an increase in the level of income, should increase its "price," so the interest rate should rise. In terms of the bond market, the increased demand for money means people want to sell bonds to get cash. This selling lowers the price of bonds, raising the interest rate. This topic could be exposited by means of some graphical curve-shifting, but it is an instance in which the common sense of supply and demand forces is all that is necessary; the curves are superfluous. Don't confuse supply and demand for money with the "money market," which refers to the market for short-term bonds.

> **Sample Exam Question 10.3:**
> "Earlier in the week the Fed's traders intervened aggressively in the money market to push the yield on last week's bills sharply higher."
> Exactly what kind of intervention is being referred to?

10.4   The Transmission Mechanism

Introducing the interest rate means that we must change the story we had told earlier about how monetary policy affects economic activity. In our earlier story—the explanation of the modern quantity theory—an increase in the money supply caused people to find themselves holding more of their wealth in the form of money than they wished to hold in the form of money. We assumed that they spent these excess money holdings to try to get rid of them. Now we note that increasing the money supply causes the interest rate to fall, which (as described in our discussion of crowding out in chapter 5) stimulates spending

Curiosity 10.3: What Is Quantitative Easing?

The basic idea behind using monetary policy to stimulate the economy is that the central bank can lower the interest rate and thereby increase aggregate demand. But what if, as happened in Japan in the early 2000s and in the United States during the subprime mortgage crisis of 2008–9, the central bank interest rate (the Federal Funds rate in the United States), falls to zero without having the desired effect of stimulating spending?

Why would the fall in the interest rate to zero fail to stimulate spending? During a recession, when a policy action of lowering interest rates is undertaken, everyone has negative expectations regarding economic activity. Individuals are worried about their jobs and so for precautionary reasons save rather than borrow and spend. Businesses are reluctant to borrow to embark on investment projects because they believe that in the current economic climate, they will not be successful. The bottom line is that even with a very low interest rate nobody is willing to borrow to spend. On top of this, banks are reluctant to lend. Because of the uncertain economic climate, banks are fearful that individuals and businesses may not be able to repay loans. To deal with this increased risk, they either refuse to lend or refuse to lend at reasonable interest rates (despite having lots of money available to lend). So even though the Federal Funds rate is low, this low rate does not translate into low rates offered by the banks.

So what can a central bank do when faced with this situation? "Quantitative easing" refers to a central bank policy of printing money in this circumstance, in the hope that this extra money will somehow stimulate spending. During the "great recession" instigated by the subprime mortgage crisis, the Fed bought huge amounts of bonds on the open market, increasing the money base dramatically. Under ordinary circumstances the commercial banks would use the extra reserves created in this way to expand loans, the money supply would increase by the money multiplier times this increase in the money base, and aggregate demand would increase. But in the aftermath of the subprime mortgage crisis banks were not eager to lend. Look at the following numbers. In the last half of 2008, by buying bonds on the open market and loaning funds to banks, the Fed increased the money base from $832 billion to $1,651 billion, almost doubling it! But what did the banks do with all these extra reserves? They mostly kept them as excess reserves—during this same time period the banks' excess reserves increased from $2 billion to $767 billion! Far from doubling, during this period M1 increased by about 15 percent and M2 by about only 6 percent.

It is doubtful that quantitative easing increased spending much during the great recession. Its main purpose was to provide liquidity to the banks to ensure that the financial system survived the crisis intact. The most important element of this policy has yet to be played out, however—when the crisis subsides and the economy begins to recover, the Fed will have to shrink the money base back to a reasonable level. Otherwise, rejuvenated bank lending will increase the money supply by too much, creating inflation.

Open-market operations ⇒ Fed buys bonds to ↑ money supply
                       ⇒ ↑ price of bonds
                       ⇒ ↓ interest rate
                       ⇒ ↑ consumption, investment, and government spending
                       ⇒ ↑ aggregate demand for goods and services
                       ⇒ Keynesian multiplier process
                       ⇒ ↑ income

Figure 10.3 The Transmission Mechanism
Monetary policy lowers the interest rate, increasing aggregate demand for goods and services and setting the Keynesian multiplier process in motion.

by consumers, firms, and local governments. The increase in spending leads to the familiar Keynesian multiplier process, moving the economy to a higher level of income, as illustrated in figure 10.3.

In this new story the impact of monetary policy is transmitted to economic activity through the intermediary of the interest rate. (See curiosity 10.3 for discussion of what happens when the interest rate falls to zero!) Most economists feel that this new *transmission mechanism* is the way in which monetary policy operates to influence economic activity; consequently we adopt it henceforth in this book. The monetarist view of the transmission mechanism, described in chapter 9 as the modern quantity theory, can be seen to be consistent with this mechanism, but the explanation is too advanced for inclusion in this book. We will simply view the chapter 9 story, in which people lower excess cash balances by spending them, as supplementing this interest-rate transmission mechanism.

> **Sample Exam Question 10.4:**
> "The decline in both the number of payroll jobs and hours worked surprised many analysts, who said the report put new pressure on the Fed to. . . ."
>   Complete this clipping.

10.5 Monetary Policy versus Fiscal Policy

The view of discretionary monetary policy that has emerged from this chapter and the preceding two chapters is that through open-market operations the central bank can stimulate the economy by increasing the money supply, alternatively viewed as pushing down the interest rate. In a longer run context, an eye must be kept on the rate of growth of the money supply to ensure that inflation is not allowed to escalate, but in a noninflationary environment, discretionary use of monetary policy is a useful alternative or supplement to fiscal policy.

Both fiscal and monetary policy shift the *AD* curve in the aggregate-supply/aggregate-demand diagram. Fiscal policy changes aggregate demand directly; monetary policy changes aggregate demand by changing the interest rate. Two marked differences between monetary and fiscal policy, however, should be noted.

1. *Timing considerations.* Monetary policy can be implemented much more quickly than fiscal policy, since it does not require congressional approval. Once implemented, however, it affects the economy more slowly than fiscal policy because it takes time for decision makers to react to lower interest rates. It has been estimated, for example, that only about one-third of the impact of an interest rate change on aggregate demand occurs within one year, and only about one-half within two years. Furthermore these lags are variable as well as long, making it quite difficult for monetary authorities to deduce the correct timing for monetary policy. Therefore any temporary, discretionary, diversion from the monetarist rule must be undertaken with great care.

2. *Discrimination considerations.* Monetary policy affects the economy very broadly, allowing the impersonal forces of supply and demand to distribute its impact efficiently across the economy. Fiscal policy has this effect when it takes the form of tax changes, but not when it takes the form of government spending changes; the discriminatory effects of government spending could be either an advantage in that the spending could be directed at a depressed region or a disadvantage in that it may be directed by political whims. Despite the impersonality of monetary policy, however, it is discriminatory. The components of aggregate demand that are more sensitive to interest-rate changes bear the costs of adjustment. The sector most strongly affected in this regard is the housing sector, which is notoriously sensitive to interest-rate changes. A fall in the mortgage rate from 10 to 8 percent, for example, decreases the monthly payment on a thirty-year mortgage by more than 16 percent. This saving markedly increases the demand for residential construction. The export- and import-competing sectors are also strongly affected. Interest-rate changes cause foreigners to change their demand for our currency to invest in our financial assets, altering the exchange rate and affecting the profitability of business in the international sector.

Our discussion of monetary policy is not yet complete. The next chapter examines its role in an inflationary environment, providing further insight into the relationship between monetary policy and interest rates. Chapter 14 looks at how monetary policy is affected by forces coming from the international sector of the economy.

Sample Exam Question 10.5:
"Looking at the high correlation between recessions and housing slumps, some people have concluded that the Fed has been responsible for creating recessions."
  What is the logic of these people?

Media Illustrations

Example 1

The average yield at this week's auction of $17.8 billion of 91-day Treasury bills was 11.17 percent, up from 10.95 percent last week. Accepted bids for the bills ranged from a high of $97.300 for an 11.13 percent yield to a low of $97.288 for an 11.18 percent yield. The average bid price was $97.290.

Has the average bid price risen or fallen from what it was last week?
The yield, or interest rate, has risen from last week to this week. The price must have fallen to produce this rise in yield.

How would one calculate that a bid of $97.300 corresponds to a yield of 11.13 percent?
A 91-day T-bill bought now for $97.30 will be worth $100.00 in 91 days when it matures, so its return over 91 days is $(100 - 97.30)/97.30$. To find the corresponding annual yield, we must convert the return over 91 days to a return over 365 days by multiplying by 365/91, obtaining 11.13.

Example 2

Some economists criticized the central bank for not moving in the face of the waning recovery. One, who prefers anonymity, stated: "The failure to move today leaves us with low inflation, a weak economy, and climbing jobless claims; these are classic signs of an impending downturn. The Fed fiddles while the economy burns."

What kind of movement would this economist want to see?
This economist must feel that there is little danger of an expansionary monetary policy creating inflation and would argue that a discretionary increase in the money supply, or, equivalently, a fall in interest rates, is in order.

Why might the Fed not move?
The Fed may not yet feel that the economy is definitely entering a recession—often early numbers are revised, and often what appears to be the beginning of a recession is no more than a temporary downturn. If the Fed is too quick to react, it could overstimulate and spark inflationary forces.

Example 3

Several Treasury bond issues will raise $40 billion, with the Federal Reserve Board picking up at least $20 billion. The Fed can also be counted on to take down more of the bonds than the planned $20 billion it has announced if they seem to be selling badly.

What is the main implication of the Fed picking up $20 billion of these bonds?
The money supply will increase by $20 billion times the money multiplier.

What does the second sentence imply about the Fed's monetary policy?
If the bonds are selling badly, the interest rate is not high enough to attract buyers. If the Fed does not step in, the price of these bonds will fall and the interest rate will rise. The fact that the Fed can be counted on not to let this happen suggests that the Fed's monetary policy is targeting the interest rate, with little concern about money-supply growth.

Example 4

The eagerly awaited weekly money stock figures measure more than just the supply of money. The weekly number measures money demand as much as it does supply. The evidence now suggests the alarming growth rate of the money stock mainly reflects an upsurge in money demand, rather than an overly expansive money-supply policy.

What would happen to the interest rate if there were an upsurge in money demand with no corresponding increase in money supply?
There would be a rise in the interest rate. The higher demand for money would bid up its price, the interest rate. Alternatively, those wanting more cash balances would sell bonds to obtain money. This selling would lower the price of bonds, raising the interest rate.

What monetary policy does the central bank appear to be following here?
The central bank appears to be matching changes in the demand for money with changes in the supply of money, so as to keep the interest rate constant.

Comment on the conclusion that money supply policy is not "overly expansive."
This conclusion is erroneous. By targeting the interest rate, the central bank has lost control over the rate of growth of the money supply, so it can easily become overly expansive, as it has in the situation described in this clipping. For example, if inflation temporarily becomes higher, demand for money increases accordingly, and this policy produces a concomitant increase in the money supply. This rise in money-supply growth causes this temporary increase in inflation to be maintained. The economy moves permanently to a higher money-supply growth and inflation.

Example 5

On Friday the market withstood what bond investors ought to have viewed as a rather bearish jobless report. The number of employed U.S. workers rose by 125,000 in April, higher than the 75,000 expected. The unemployment rate dropped to 7.2 percent from 7.3 percent the previous month.

This jobless report looks bullish—job creation is up and unemployment is down. Why is it called bearish?
This is a bullish report for the economy, but not for the bond market. The upswing in economic activity should lead people to expect that the Fed will fear that the economy will overheat and so will act to raise interest rates, causing bond prices to fall.

Chapter Summary

- The inverse relationship between the interest rate and the price of bonds is important because interest rate changes can create sizable capital gains or losses for those holding bonds, particularly long-term bonds.

- Open-market operations affect the interest rate, thereby changing aggregate demand for goods and services and setting in motion the traditional Keynesian multiplier process. As a result monetary policy is often viewed as operating through interest rates.

- Expansionary monetary and fiscal policies both shift the *AD* curve to the right, but they differ in other respects, such as lag structures and discriminatory impacts.

Formula Definitions

- For one year to maturity $i = \dfrac{\text{Coupon} + (\text{Face value} - \text{Price})}{\text{Price}}$

- Approximation for n years to maturity $i = \dfrac{\text{Coupon} + (\text{Face value} - \text{Price})/n}{\text{Price}}$

Media Exercises

(Group B questions require more thought.)

A1. Falling interest rates have triggered a rally in the bond market that has many investors rejoicing.

Why would falling interest rates trigger a rally in the bond market?

A2. Lenders would be wise to move their short-term holdings into longer term assets to take advantage of the capital gains generated by declining interest rates.

a. What are the capital gains mentioned in this clip, and how do they come about?

b. Why aren't these capital gains associated with short-term as well as long-term assets?

A3. The proper lines of action for controlling inflation are not too difficult to envisage. First, we must stop relying on monetary policy to do the job. The monetary

tool has been easiest and most convenient for all governments to use because it requires no legislation. It's a matter of boards of directors speaking in well-modulated voices around a polished table with charts on the wall. It has been given a good trial. But it hasn't worked, and its economic impact has been discriminatory.

a. What would be the monetarists' "proper lines of action for controlling inflation"?

b. How has monetary policy been discriminatory?

A4. Basically investors profit in two ways from putting their money into bonds: through the coupon rate, or interest rate, that is attached to each bond and provides a steady income; and through potential. . . .

Complete this clip.

A5. Federal Reserve Chairman Alan Greenspan last week told Congress the economy is showing some signs of strain, notably tightness in the labor markets, and said Fed policy makers stood ready to raise or lower interest rates if necessary to maintain the nation's economic expansion.

Would the Federal Reserve likely raise or lower interest rates if the labor markets became tighter? Explain why.

A6. There are difficulties in having the central bank present growth rate targets in advance. Central banks find it much easier to explain events after the fact if they are allowed to operate from a position of secrecy, with little communication with the public. Politically unpopular increases in interest rates might also have to be tolerated at embarrassing times under a policy of published target growth rates.

a. What is a target growth rate policy, and how would this target rate be chosen?

b. Why would such a policy imply that increases in interest rates might have to be tolerated?

A7. Some portfolio managers were forced to buy securities in the ten-year to thirty-year sector to meet targeted returns for the month and to extend duration, traders said. Duration is a measure of the sensitivity of a bond portfolio to interest rate changes, and maintaining a chosen duration is a key consideration for fund managers.

Would extending the duration of a bond portfolio make it more or less sensitive to interest rate changes? Explain your reasoning.

A8. **The wiser course would be to avoid switching monetary policy and keep the money-supply growth stable. This will automatically bring interest rates down during the recession when demand for funds is weak.**

a. What kind of monetary policy would involve "switching"?

b. Explain the logic that lies behind the second sentence.

A9. **Monetary policy is a peculiar tool in that it does not seem to have an intermediate switch. Either it is completely ineffective or it is too effective. In the past few months it has been too effective, almost destroying our housing industry.**

How would monetary policy destroy the housing industry?

A10. **While the official unemployment rate stayed at 7.1 percent, other figures showed the jobless rate reaching its highest level in nine years, and analysts predicted the Federal Reserve would come under renewed pressure to cut interest rates once more in hopes of kindling a recovery.**

a. How could other figures show the jobless rate higher if the unemployment rate didn't change?

b. How would the Federal Reserve go about cutting the interest rate?

c. How would this kindle a recovery?

d. What technical economic term does the word "kindle" bring to mind in this context?

A11. **Thanks to a sharp cut in interest rates engineered by the Fed, many economists expect the economy to be growing again, albeit slowly, by spring, which is the soonest any of President Bush's legislative proposals are likely to be enacted.**

a. What major advantage of monetary policy over fiscal policy does this clipping underline?

b. How would the Fed have engineered the cut in interest rates?

c. If this policy is so good, why isn't it done more vigorously, more often?

A12. **At the heart of the inflation-versus-deflation argument is the massive stimulus that the U.S. Federal Reserve has injected into the economy by way of near-zero percent interest rates and quantitative easing.**

a. Do the Fed actions support the argument for inflation or for deflation? Explain.

b. What is the difference between lowering interest rates and quantitative easing?

A13. By raising and lowering short-term interest rates to keep inflation moving at a steady pace, many central bankers and academics thought they had finally found a monetary policy solution to conquer the booms and busts of the business cycle.

a. What is this monetary policy called?

b. When would interest rates be raised and when lowered?

A14. The government clearly sees some room for interest rates to drop. It should help cushion the short-term effects of the recession and help the economy pick up over the next eighteen months.

How would lower interest rates help the economy pick up?

A15. The issue is whether monetary policy can do the trick or not, and it would appear to many that it can't.

This clip comes from late 2008 when the economy was entering a recession.

a. What is meant by monetary policy "doing the trick"?

b. How would monetary policy attempt to do this?

c. Why might it not be successful?

A16. A combination of a significant upward revision to GDP growth, a downward revision of the output gap, and stronger-than-expected inflation data suggest that soon the central bank will. . . .

a. What is the output gap?

b. Complete this clipping.

A17. The Bank of England has switched from interest rate cuts to "quantitative easing." This policy involves buying bonds from commercial banks in the hope that these institutions will again lend in vast quantities to businesses and individuals after sitting tight since the credit crisis erupted in 2007.

a. What terminology would most economists use to describe "quantitative easing?"

b. How is this supposed to induce banks to begin lending?

c. Why would commercial banks be sitting tight since the 2007 crisis?

A18. With the backdrop of a still deteriorating international economy, the British and European central banks were also introducing quantitative easing. But there should be no illusions—cranking up the printing presses, which is basically

what they are doing, is not a good thing, but there aren't too many other options.

a. What is meant by "quantitative easing"?

b. Why is it "not a good thing"?

c. What would be the main alternative option?

A19. Lenders and borrowers are all so nervous that the huge planned increase in the money supply, referred to as "quantitative easing," may have a much smaller stimulating effect than it would have in normal circumstances. This strategy is not without risks in terms of future. . . .

a. This clip is from 2008. Why would lenders and borrowers both be nervous?

b. Why would the stimulating effect be smaller than normal?

c. What does this tell us about the income multiplier with respect to the money supply?

d. Complete the final sentence.

A20. Another criticism of deficit budgets is that they hamper the private sector's ability to raise capital.

a. How do budget deficits hamper the private sector's ability to raise capital?

b. How could the central bank avoid this problem, and at what cost?

A21. Bonds, however, turned up on news of strong tax revenue. It is now projected that there could be a budget surplus of as much as $39 billion, much higher than the $18 billion forecast.

Why would bonds "turn up" on this news?

A22. Over the past six years, the government's share of total borrowing in the U.S. credit markets has fallen to 6 percent from 60 percent. That decrease has played a major role in _____ interest rates.

Fill in the blank, and explain your reasoning.

B1. Yields on Treasury bills started to rise early in the week as dealers began to unload the bills because of higher than anticipated carrying costs.

How would dealers unloading bills cause their yields to rise?

B2. In the financial markets, red ink is flowing as some investment dealers continue to lose money on the Treasury bills they buy from the federal government. The

biggest buyers of the bills, the banks, have been reducing their holdings steadily since last September in order to meet rising loan demand.

a. Why are investment dealers losing money?

b. Is the information conveyed in the second sentence consistent with the fact that dealers are losing money? Explain your reasoning.

B3. **For example, a twenty-year government bond paying 10.25 percent was selling for $1,007.10, priced above its par value of $1,000 to yield 10.15 percent.**

The quoted yield of 10.15 percent is slightly lower than $102.50 expressed as a percentage of $1,007.10. Why?

B4. **It is now evident that loan demand has dropped sufficiently since the beginning of the year to allow the money supply to grow at a rate of less than 10 percent at current levels of interest rates.**

This clip suggests that the demand for money controls its supply. How can this be?

B5. **Bonds rallied sharply yesterday, cheered on by the news that the recession isn't over yet. Prices climbed by as much as $8.75 for each $1,000 face amount in the U.S. government securities market after the Commerce Department reported that GDP fell by 0.1 percent in the second quarter.**

Why would bad news rally bonds?

B6. **The Fed pumped more money into the nation's banking system to reduce the federal funds rate—the rate at which banks lend each other money overnight—to 3.75 percent from 4 percent.**

a. How would the Fed pump more money into the banking system?

b. Explain how doing so would lower the federal funds rate.

B7. **The economy surprised the bond market again Friday, with a report on explosive job growth in February sending prices plunging in volatile trading, a day after higher-than-expected jobless claims sparked an early rally Thursday.**

Explain why news on the job front affects bond prices this way.

B8. **However, with the sharp fall in interest rates, central bank officials expect a pickup in economic activity that will bring about an upsurge in monetary growth.**

a. Why would a sharp fall in interest rates be expected to cause a pickup in economic activity?

b. Why would a pickup in economic activity bring about an upsurge in monetary growth?

B9. The release of U.S. housing starts in April—down 17 percent to their lowest level in eight years—drove North American bond markets higher yesterday.

Why would this bad news drive bond prices higher?

B10. Stocks fell yesterday as the movement in rates rekindled concerns about stock market valuations. The Dow Jones industrial average closed down just 33 points but was off by as much as 166 points at one point because of rising rates.

Explain what's going on here and why.

B11. According to Ibbotson Associates, twenty-year government bonds are on track to post annual returns of 30 percent by the end of 1995. That would lag only the 40 percent returns of 1982 and the 31 percent returns of 1985.

In 1995 the interest rate was far, far below 30 percent. How could 1995 returns on bonds be as high as 30 percent?

B12. "The thrust of the central bank's policy has been to reduce demand for loans on the basis of price—not by limiting the amount of money that is available."

"It isn't the function of the commercial banks to be self-appointed rationers of credit. We are in a very competitive business. If my bank won't lend to you, another one will."

These two comments summarize the responses of senior bankers who were asked whether their present lending policies—particularly on consumer loans— are consistent with the central bank's objective of lowering the inflation rate by cutting back on credit demand.

a. What does "reduce demand for loans on the basis of price" mean?

b. In what way is this policy identical to a policy of "limiting the amount of money that is available," and in what way is it different?

c. Do the banks ration credit? Explain how or why not.

d. Explain how a policy of "cutting back on credit demand" is accomplished, and how it will lower inflation, as claimed in the last sentence.

B13. The rise in market rates, which analysts said has helped keep stock prices more or less flat since the beginning of the year, has cost bondholders dearly.

a. Why would rising market rates help keep stock prices from increasing?

b. Why would they cost bondholders dearly?

B14. Higher interest rates would outweigh upward revisions in earnings estimates resulting from stronger than expected economic growth, said Douglas Cliggotte, a market strategist at J.P. Morgan & Company.

Explain what is being said here.

B15. "The Federal Reserve must continue to evaluate, among other issues, whether the full extent of the policy easings undertaken last fall to address the seizing-up of financial markets remains appropriate as those disturbances abate." Analysts said the words caused some owners of Treasury securities to sell.

Explain why owners of Treasury securities sold.

B16. Meanwhile investors prepared for as much as $6 billion in corporate-bond sales this week by selling Treasuries, both to clear space in their portfolios and to hedge against a move in interest rates.

In the circumstances described in this clipping, why would selling Treasury bonds hedge against a move in interest rates? (Hedging means insuring against.)

B17. Bond prices slumped again on worries about a fast-moving economy, dragging down blue-chip stocks.

Why would slumping bond prices drag down blue-chip stocks?

B18. The Fed is expected to lower the federal funds rate tomorrow. But as far as the economy goes, the decision is basically irrelevant. The actual, or effective, Fed funds rate is already close to zero, 0.125 percent; the Fed funds rate is currently at 1 percent.

a. What is the difference between the Federal funds rate and the actual (or "effective") Fed funds rate?

b. What would cause this large difference to happen?

B19. Alan Greenspan, chairman of the Fed, was the leading proponent of the view that it is too difficult, and potentially too harmful, to pop a bubble by raising interest rates. If a bubble emerged, better to quickly lower interest rates to cushion the blow to the rest of the economy. The current financial crisis, which began with a spike in U.S. foreclosures after house prices surged, seriously challenged that line of thinking.

In retrospect, what policy should have been followed in light of the U.S. housing bubble? Explain your reasoning.

B20. As expected, the FOMC lowered the Fed funds rate today by 25 basis points to 2.0 percent. It was a relatively small cut compared to the previous three meetings where the FOMC cut the rate by 75, 50, and 75 bps respectively.

a. What is the FOMC?

b. What is the Fed funds rate?

c. What does bps mean?

d. What was the Fed funds rate before this action?

e. Is the Fed easing or tightening monetary policy here?

B21. On the face of it, market worries have some justification: If the economy is picking up and the Fed is printing money, is that not . . .?

a. What market worries are meant here?

b. Complete this clipping.

B22. The Fed has responded to the subprime mortgage crisis by easing the supply of liquidity. This does not necessarily mean that the federal funds rate will be cut.

Does easing the supply of liquidity imply a fall in the federal funds rate? Explain why or why not.

B23. While U.S. Treasuries are at record low yields, corporate bonds are at record highs. Corporations are paying an average interest rate of 10.8 percent on debt, compared with 2.6 percent on ten-year U.S. Treasuries.

This clip is from 2008. What must be causing this dramatic difference?

B24. According to the Maastricht Treaty, EU member states are not allowed to finance their public deficits by printing money. That is one reason why the Bank of England will buy government bonds from financial institutions, not directly from the government. The Bank believes this form of quantitative easing is different because they are "printing money" as part of monetary policy—to prevent deflation. They are not printing money to help the government finance its deficit. Also this is a temporary policy: the Bank expects to sell the government bonds back into the market when the economy recovers.

a. Is the effect on the money supply different when the central bank buys bonds from financial institutions rather than from the government itself? If yes, explain how the effect is different.

b. What is deflation? Why would a central bank want to prevent it?

    c. What would happen if the Bank did not "sell the government bonds back into the market" when the economy recovers?

B25. One reason for raising interest rates was the prospect of a refinancing issue: a $12 billion issue matures April 1, and the government is expected to seek some new money, in excess of its refinancing needs.

Why doesn't the government get the central bank to wait until after the refinancing before increasing interest rates, so as to minimize its interest costs?

B26. Economists call the process debt monetization. Without it, rising federal deficits tend merely to shuffle spending to the government sector from the private sector.

    a. What is the process called debt monetization?

    b. Without it, how would the spending merely get shuffled?

    c. With debt monetization, will the spending also merely get shuffled? Explain why or why not.

    d. Is there any disadvantage to debt monetization?

Numerical Exercises

AN1. Suppose that a discount bond with par value $10,000 will mature in exactly one year.

    a. If its current price is $9,500, what is its projected yield?

    b. If its current price is $9,000, what is its projected yield?

    c. Are your answers to the first two parts of this question consistent with the inverse relationship between interest rates and the price of bonds?

AN2. Consider a bond with face value $1,000, current price $958, and coupon $80, due to mature in six years. What yield to maturity does the approximation method produce for this bond?

AN3. A bond due to mature and pay $1,000 in one year's time has a coupon of $85 and a current price of $1,025. What is the interest rate?

AN4. Suppose that the interest rate is 8 percent, and a bond with an annual coupon of $75 matures in one year's time, paying its face value of $1,000. What is this bond's current price?

AN5. Consider a bond with a face value of $1,000, due to mature in one year's time. Its current price is $1,035, and the current interest rate is 5.8 percent. What must its coupon be?

AN6. Suppose that the current interest rate is 5 percent. Consider a bond with face value $1,000 and price $1,080, due to mature in four years. Using the approximation method for calculating yield to maturity, what is the approximate coupon on this bond?

BN1. Suppose that "the" multiplier is 3, the income multiplier with respect to the money supply is 4, the money multiplier is 5, and that when the central bank buys $4 billion bonds on the open market during a recession, the interest rate falls by one percentage point. Suppose that to fight a recession, monetary policy is undertaken to lower the interest rate by one half of a percentage point. What should happen to the income level?

BN2. Suppose that the impact on the interest rate of a $3 increase in government spending can be eliminated by a $2 increase in the money supply. If the income multiplier with respect to government spending is 4 and the income multiplier with respect to the money supply is 3, what mix of monetary and fiscal policy is required to increase income by $9,000 without changing the interest rate?

BN3. Suppose that the current interest rate is 6 percent.

    a. What price should one expect to pay for a new three-month Treasury bill with face value $10,000?

    b. What price should one expect to pay for a three-month Treasury bill with face value $10,000 that is one month old?

BN4. In appendix 10.1 information is listed on two notes and a bond that all mature at the same time. Explain why their prices are so different.

BN5. Suppose that the current interest rate is 6 percent. What price should one expect to pay for a $1,000 treasury bill, due to mature in six months, that had originally been sold when the interest rate was 7 percent?

Appendix 10.1   All about Bonds

A bond is a formal contract between the issuer of the bond (the borrower) and the owner of the bond (the lender). The issuer promises to pay the *face value*, or *par value*, of the bond at a specified future date, the *maturity date*, as well as make periodic *coupon* payments until that maturity date. Face values are typically in large round numbers such as $1,000 or $10,000, but by tradition bond prices are quoted in percentages.

An example can clarify all this. The terminology "ATT $7^{1}/_{8}$s of '02 at $103^{7}/_{8}$s" refers to bonds issued by AT&T that pay an annual coupon of $7^{1}/_{8}$ percent of face value, mature in year 2002, and have a current price of 103.875 percent of face value. If the bonds are only available in units of $1,000, such a unit would cost $1,038.75 and carry an annual coupon of $71.25. As described in the body of this chapter, the current price is usually different from the face value, depending on the prevailing interest rate.

There are many different interest rates, with rates on government bonds used as benchmarks. These bonds are called *Treasuries* because they are sold through the U.S. Department of the Treasury. Their benchmark status comes from the fact that the federal government is the largest borrower in the U.S. economy and is widely regarded as the best credit risk, with the chance of default effectively zero. Interest rates paid on private bonds are higher than on comparable Treasuries (an exception is tax-free municipal bonds issued by local governments), and move with the rate on Treasuries. There are three types of Treasuries—bonds, notes, and bills—differing according to the length of time from issue until they are due. T-bonds mature in over ten years, T-notes in one to ten years, and T-bills in one year or less. T-bills are discount bonds, as described in the body of this chapter. The longest Treasury bond issued is a thirty-year bond, often referred to as the *long bond*. The long bond is the most volatile and widely watched security in the Treasury market, frequently changing by more than 1 percent in price during a day. The average maturity on federal debt is about six years.

The interest rate on Treasuries is reported in the business section of major newspapers. For example, in *The Wall Street Journal* this information appears in the "Money & Investing" section under the general heading "Treasury Bonds, Notes & Bills." For T-bills it looks like this:

Maturity	Days to Mat.	Bid	Asked	Chg.	Ask Yld.
Aug 05 '99	87	4.48	4.47	−0.01	4.58

where yield is yield to maturity, calculated as described in curiosity 10.1. The 4.48 and 4.47 under Bid and Asked are the discount in percentages from face value. For a bill with face value $1,000, these figures would imply a bid price of $955.20 and an ask price of $955.30. The smallest price change on a T-bill is $^{1}/_{100}$th of one percent (0.01 percent), called a *basis point*.

For Treasury bonds and notes this information looks like this:

Rate	Maturity Mo/Yr	Bid	Asked	Chg.	Ask Yld.
$5^{5}/_{8}$	May 01n	100:24	100:26	. . .	5.19
8	May 01n	105:08	105:10	. . .	5.19
$13^{1}/_{8}$	May 01	114:29	115:01	−1	5.17

All three of these bonds mature in May of 2001. The first two have an *n* after the May 01, indicating that they are T-notes; the third is a T-bond. Because they are all maturing at the same time, they should all have virtually the same yield to maturity, in this case

5.19 percent. (Slight differences arise from technical matters, such as the fact that one bond may pay its coupon semiannually rather than annually.)

For some odd reason, prices in this market are quoted not in decimals of a percentage point, as in other markets, but rather in 32nds of a percentage point of the face value. In the preceding quotes, the number after the colon gives 32nds, so that 105:10 means that the price is $105^{10}/^{32}$ percent of the face value. A full percentage point, thirty-two 32nds, is called a *point;* one 32nd is called a *tick*. A tick is worth 31.25 cents for a $1,000 bond, and $312.50 for a million-dollar bond. Notice that the prices of the three bonds listed are quite different, despite their maturing at exactly the same time. Can you explain the marked difference in prices?

Calculation of yield to maturity for maturities longer than a year is more complicated than the calculation presented earlier for one year to maturity, involving the concept of a present value. If the interest rate were i, then $40 today would be worth $40(1 + i)$ next year, $40(1 + i)^2$ in two years and $40(1 + i)^n$ in n years. This logic can be worked in reverse to find out how much a future payment would be worth today, called its *present value*. Calculating a present value is done by *discounting* a future payment. If you were to receive $100 in one year's time, it would be worth $100/(1 + i)$ today because this sum today would be worth $100 in one year. Similarly the present value of $100 paid n years from now would be $100/(1 + i)^n$.

A yield to maturity of a coupon bond is calculated by discounting the stream of future payments to the bondholder to find their present value, which should be equal to the current price of the bond. Thus for a bond maturing in n years,

$$\text{Current bond price} = \frac{\text{Coupon}}{(1+i)} + \frac{\text{Coupon}}{(1+i)^2} + ... + \frac{\text{Coupon}}{(1+i)^n} + \frac{\text{Face value}}{(1+i)^n}$$

This equation can be used to solve for the interest rate i—the yield to maturity—if the price of the bond is known, or to solve for the price of the bond if i is known. Note that solving this equation to find yield to maturity is not easy without a computer. But it is possible to use an approximation based on the fact that the annual dollar yield is the coupon plus the annual capital gain. The annual capital gain (or loss) can be approximated by dividing the difference between the face value and the current bond price by the number of years to maturity, as described in the body of this chapter.

All yields on financial assets should be reported as yields to maturity, but curiously some are not, perhaps because of tradition attached to simpler calculations done before the advent of the computer. One alternative, called the *current yield,* expresses the coupon as a percentage of its current price, ignoring the capital gain/loss. By tradition, newspapers usually report current yields for corporate bonds, but yield to maturity for most other bonds. For example, information on corporate bonds looks like

Bonds	Cur. Yld.	Vol.	Close		Net Chg.
ATT $5^1/_8$ 01	5.2	120	$99^1/_8$	−	$^1/_4$
ATT $7^1/_8$ 02	6.9	2	$103^7/_8$	+	$^1/_2$

Firms can raise funds by borrowing from a bank, issuing bonds, or selling stock. Appendix 8.1 discussed the financial intermediation process. The interest rate paid by a firm on a bank loan should be roughly in line with the interest rate it must pay on bonds, but it is not immediately obvious how the interest rate enters into the third option, selling stock. The price of a firm's stock is determined on the stock market by a myriad of factors, but in the long run its primary determinant is the firm's expected earnings. Consequently expected earnings can serve as a proximate measure of the return to owning a stock. A rise in the interest rate with no change in expected earnings means that the price of the stock will be bid down to make the expected percentage return to owning stock adjust to the now-higher interest return on alternative financial assets. Similarly, if the interest rate is unchanged and there is a rise in expected earnings, the price of the stock will be bid up to make the higher expected earnings correspond in percentage terms to the interest return on alternative financial assets. This way interest rates, bond prices, and stock prices are roughly connected.

11   Real-versus-Nominal Interest Rates

Up to this point our analysis of interest rates has been in the context of a noninflationary economy. The interest rate that we read about in the newspaper, pay on our mortgages, and earn on our bank deposits, however, contains a premium for expected inflation. Consequently a major determinant of this interest rate is the expected rate of inflation, which in an inflationary economy usually swamps the effects of the factors discussed in the preceding chapter. Forecasting interest rates in an inflationary economy hinges on forecasting inflation. All other forces affecting interest rates are of secondary importance.

Economists draw a distinction between the interest rate with and without this premium for expected inflation; the former is called the *nominal interest rate*, and the latter the *real interest rate*. The most common error students make when analyzing the interest rate is to overlook the difference between the real and nominal interest rates. The purpose of this chapter is to spell out this difference and explain its application in a variety of contexts. This is the most important chapter in this book because real-versus-nominal interest rates is the macroeconomic concept most often used to interpret media commentary.

Upon completion of this chapter you should

- understand the difference between nominal and real interest rates;

- realize that monetary policy is much more complicated than the previous chapter would have us believe; and

- recognize that anything affecting the expected rate of inflation, such as money-supply growth, influences the bond market through its impact on the nominal interest rate.

11.1   Expected Inflation

Suppose that the interest rate is 5 percent and that suddenly everyone expects prices to rise by 3 percent (instead of 0 percent) during the next year. Those banks loaning money for a year at 5 percent will expect to receive, at the end of the year, dollars worth 3 percent less in terms of their purchasing power, so their expected net return in real terms is only 2 percent. To obtain a return of 5 percent, they will want to charge 8 percent. Those consumers willing to borrow earlier at 5 percent should now be willing to pay 8 percent because they expect to be able to save 3 percent by buying their car, for example, now rather than next year, and because they expect to pay back their loans with devalued dollars. Consequently the interest rate increases by 3 percent, the expected rate of inflation.

This example reflects a fundamental economic result: built into the interest rate is a premium for expected inflation. Lenders require this premium to prevent inflation from eroding the real value of their wealth, and borrowers pay this premium to be able to buy now before prices go up. We thus expect the interest rate to be affected by the expected rate of inflation, as illustrated in figure 11.1. Economists have captured this phenomenon by distinguishing between the real and the nominal interest rates.

The *nominal interest rate* includes the inflation premium; it is the interest rate observed on the markets, discussed in the media, paid on mortgages, and earned on savings accounts. The *real interest rate* is the nominal rate less the expected rate of inflation:

Real rate = Nominal rate − Expected inflation rate

> **Sample Exam Question 11.1:**
> Suppose that the real rate of interest is 3 percent, the real rate of growth is 2 percent, and the rate of growth of the money supply is 6 percent.
>   What is the nominal interest rate?

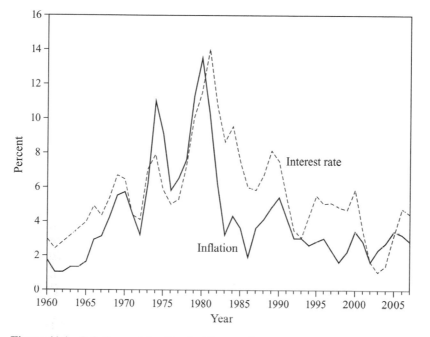

Figure 11.1   Inflation and the Nominal Interest Rate
Inflation movements appear to match up with movements in the nominal interest rate as we would
expect if inflation changes cause changes in inflation expectations. Source: Economic Report of the
President, 2009. www.gpoaccess.gov/eop/.

11.2   The Real Rate of Interest

Because the expected rate of inflation is not known, the real rate of interest cannot be
measured directly. Nevertheless, measurements of it appear in the media. Such measurements have two possible origins:

1. It could be an *ex post* measurement, calculating last year's real interest rate as last
   year's nominal rate less last year's actual rate of inflation. Note that this does not tell
   us what the current real interest rate is, nor does it tell us what the real rate of interest
   at the beginning of last year was. Such an ex post measurement is shown in figure 11.2,
   calculated by subtracting the two curves in figure 11.1.

2. It could be an *estimate* of the current real interest rate (the *ex ante* real interest rate),
   obtained by subtracting an estimate of the expected rate of inflation from the nominal
   rate of interest. A popular (but usually unjustified) estimate of the expected rate of
   inflation in this context is the previous period's actual rate of inflation. A more realistic
   estimate of the expected rate of inflation would incorporate knowledge of things known
   to affect inflation, such as the rate of growth of the money supply.

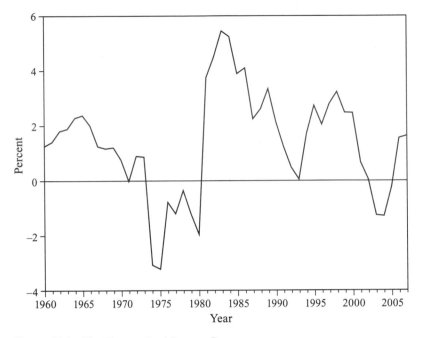

Figure 11.2   The Ex post Real Interest Rate
Subtracting actual inflation from the nominal interest rate yields the ex post real interest rate. In the mid-1970s, inflation exceeded the nominal interest rate, so the ex post real interest rate was negative, due probably to the unexpected nature of the inflation. In the 1980s, the nominal interest rate was quite a bit higher than inflation, making the ex post real interest rate very high, perhaps due to very high expectations of inflation or to the high real interest rate policies of the time. Source: Economic Report of the President. www.gpoaccess.gov/eop.

Despite these measurement difficulties, the real rate of interest is a useful concept because it is the real rather than the nominal interest rate that affects aggregate demand for goods and services. This point is best explained by means of an example.

Suppose that there is zero expected inflation, and a firm calculates that at an interest rate of 5 percent (in this case both the real and the nominal interest rate), it is profitable to build a new plant. Next suppose that the expected inflation soon jumps from 0 to 7 percent, raising the nominal interest rate to 12 percent. Because the firm must now pay 12 percent interest to borrow the funds to build the plant, it seems that the investment project is no longer profitable, but this assumption is not so. Paying the extra 7 percent to cover expected inflation should not affect the firm's decision. The firm's future costs should rise by 7 percent, but because also should its receipts, its profits should grow, in nominal terms, by 7 percent. This growth provides just enough extra return to pay for the extra 7 percent interest costs. The relevant interest rate is thus the real rate of interest, not the nominal rate of interest.

This example suggests that firms should use the real rate of interest to evaluate investment projects, and economists should use the real rate of interest to analyze the influence of the interest rate on aggregate demand in the economy. Chapter 10 assumed zero inflation and so was analyzing the role of the real interest rate. What role does the nominal interest rate play?

> **Sample Exam Question 11.2:**
> "The current high interest rate does not seem to be slowing spending as one would expect. Indeed, it seems as though people are spending even more."
> Why would the high interest rate not be lowering spending here?

11.3   The Nominal Rate of Interest

It would be a mistake to conclude from the preceding discussion that the nominal interest rate is unimportant either to individuals or to government. It is the nominal rate that makes headlines in newspapers, determines homeowners' monthly mortgage payments, and influences voters. But most important, because the nominal rate is determined in the bond market, changes in this rate create capital gains or losses in the bond market, and predictions of it can make or lose fortunes for speculators.

The influence of open-market operations on the interest rate become complicated and equivocal once one recognizes that it is the nominal interest rate that is determined on the bond market. Suppose that the central bank increases the money supply. It does so by buying bonds, in the process bidding up their price and thereby lowering the interest rate. This was a main point in the preceding chapter where there were no concerns about inflation.

The increase in the money supply, however, may be interpreted as an increase in the rate of growth of the money supply, causing the expected rate of inflation to increase, especially if the economy is at full employment. The increase in expected inflation pushes up the nominal rate of interest So there are pressures on the nominal interest rate both up and down, as illustrated in figure 11.3.

If in due course it becomes clear, however, that the increased money supply does not represent an increase in the rate of money-supply growth, expectations of higher inflation should disappear, leaving us with an unequivocal fall in the interest rate.

This analysis suggests that the central bank's short-run control over the interest rate is not so clear-cut as the previous chapter indicated. In particular, it suggests that in an inflationary environment, the most effective way for the central bank to decrease the interest rate is to lower the inflation rate. This action should lower *expected* inflation (perhaps

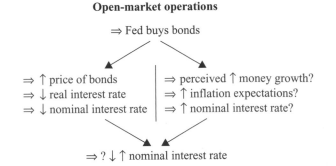

Figure 11.3   Impact of Monetary Policy on the Interest Rate in an Inflationary Environment
Expansionary monetary policy can raise or lower the nominal interest rate, depending on the policy's
impact on inflation expectations.

with a lag, depending on the credibility of the central bank), and the expectation of lower
inflation should lower the nominal interest rate directly. To accomplish this purpose, the
central bank will have to lower the money-supply growth rate, which in the short run will
raise, not lower, the interest rate. In other words, to lower the interest rate in an inflationary environment, the central bank must lower money-supply growth (the opposite of what
the previous chapter suggested!) in order to create a short-run increase in the interest rate
(the opposite of the ultimate goal). This action helps lower inflation, eventually resulting
in lower inflation expectations, thereby causing the interest rate to fall.

Another complication faced by the monetary authorities is that the interest rate is no
longer a reliable indicator of monetary policy. The preceding chapter suggested that a high
interest rate corresponded to a restrictive monetary policy and a low interest rate corresponded to an easy monetary policy. A high interest rate can nonetheless arise because of
high inflation, which can by no stretch of the imagination be due to a restrictive monetary
policy. This possibility creates problems for central banks wanting to use the interest rate
as a target of monetary policy.

> **Sample Exam Question 11.3:**
> "The Governor of the Bank of Canada promised us that his policy of reducing money
> growth would lower both inflation and interest rates. He has succeeded on the infla-
> tion front, but why haven't we had the promised lowering of interest rates?"
>   How would you answer this question?

Curiosity 11.1: What Is the Term Structure of Interest Rates?

Bonds with identical risk, liquidity, and tax characteristics usually have different interest rates because of different times remaining to maturity. A graph of interest rates against times to maturity for identical bonds is called a yield curve; it describes the term structure of interest rates. Figure 11.4 provides an illustration based on the Treasury yield curve reported regularly in the "Money & Investing" section of *The Wall Street Journal*. Yield curves almost always slope upward, showing that usually bonds with longer time to maturity pay higher interest rates (i.e., have higher yields to maturity). Why?

One reason may be that investors require a liquidity premium for taking on a longer maturity bond. A long-term bond involves more risk from interest-rate fluctuations that change its price much more than the price of a short-term bond. Another reason may be that people fear a resurgence of inflation at any time and require a premium for locking in their money at an interest rate that does not protect them from future unexpected inflation. A third reason may be that long-term interest rates embody expectations about what short-term interest rates will be between now and when the long-term bond matures. An upward-sloping curve therefore simply reflects expectations of higher short-term interest rates in the near future, perhaps because of higher expected inflation. Of course, people may expect that future inflation will be lower than current inflation, in which case the yield curve will be downward-sloping.

The yield curve is closely watched in financial sections of newspapers because of information it may provide regarding the direction in which the market expects short-term interest rates to move. A sharply upward-sloping curve, for example, often occurs after inflation has been brought down because people do not yet believe inflation's fall is permanent.

Another way of measuring this same phenomenon is the spread, the difference between the long- and short-term interest rates. For this purpose the benchmark long-term interest rate is the 30-year T-bond rate, and the benchmark short-term interest rate is the 90-day T-bill rate.

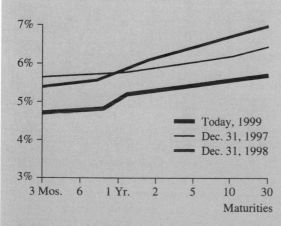

Figure 11.4 Yield Curves
The interest rate increases as time to maturity lengthens from 3 months to 30 years.

11.4   Policy Implications

Using the interest rate as a target of monetary policy is an important issue, mainly because the Fed has gotten into trouble in the past by doing so (e.g., its use of the federal funds rate as a target during the 1970s). There are two major problems with using an interest rate as a target:

1. *The Fed may lose control of the money supply.* Suppose that for some reason the inflation rate bumps up, and this higher rate soon raises expectations of inflation, thus increasing the nominal interest rate. If the Fed is targeting on an interest rate, it will increase the money supply to push the interest rate back down. This stimulus to the economy will worsen the inflation, and the increase in the money supply will reinforce people's expectations of a higher inflation. Expected inflation rises again, pushing up the nominal interest rate, this time by more than before. The Fed now needs a bigger increase in the money supply to push the interest rate back down, and the process is repeated. Targeting on an interest rate can create a vicious circle, leading the Fed to increase the money supply at an undesirably high rate and creating a high inflation.

2. *The approach may destabilize the economy.* Suppose that the economy is hit with an increase in aggregate demand—say, an increase in export demand. The multiplier begins to operate, and income increases. Higher income increases the demand for

---

Curiosity 11.2: Was the Fed Ever Monetarist?

For a variety of reasons, in the 1970s the Fed allowed the money supply growth rate to creep up, producing a much higher inflation (over 10 percent) than normal. Paul Volcker was brought in as chairman of the Fed in late 1979 and shortly thereafter the Fed announced that it was following a new policy—restricting M1 growth to fight inflation.

The predicted happened: low money growth resulting from Fed policy collided with high money-demand growth caused by inflation. Real interest rates shot up, causing a severe recession that, after a long adjustment period in the early 1980s, squeezed inflation out of the economy.

This period is often thought of as a monetarist period in the Fed's history because of its announced policy of targeting on a monetary aggregate. Some economists, however, claim that this characterization is inaccurate. They note that during this period the Fed did not appear to be serious about its alleged targets because it consistently missed its target range. A more reasonable explanation of Fed behavior, they argue, is that the Fed was focusing on interest rates, moving them high enough to create a severe recession needed to kill inflation but claiming, as a smokescreen, to be using monetary targets so that it would not be blamed directly for the high interest rates.

Currently the Fed is definitely not monetarist, having abandoned in frustration any use of monetary aggregates because of their erratic velocities.

money, so the interest rate increases, serving as an automatic stabilizer by somewhat decreasing aggregate demand. If the Fed is targeting on the interest rate, it will increase the money supply to prevent the interest rate from increasing, thus preventing this automatic stabilizer from operating.

Do these problems with an interest-rate target mean that the Fed should use a monetary-aggregate growth rate as a target? No. Using a monetary aggregate as a target also has its own serious problems:

1. *Measurement problems.* With the exception of the money base, monetary aggregates are not reliably measured. Both the M1 and M2 measures experience substantial revisions over time.

2. *Uncontrollability.* With the exception of the money base, monetary aggregates are not tightly enough under the control of the Fed. Both M1 and M2 are affected by bank borrowing from the Fed, public cash demands, banking innovations, and shifts among deposit types, for example.

3. *Velocity changes.* All monetary aggregates are not reliably linked to economic activity because of velocity fluctuations caused by financial innovations and deregulations.

4. *Money-demand shocks.* Shocks to money demand, such as failure of a large bank, a postal strike, or a stock market crash, destabilize the economy under a monetary-aggregate growth target because the central bank won't react by matching the demand for money shock with a money-supply change.

Problems with both types of policy targets create a dilemma: How should monetary policy be conducted? An alternative that has come to be very popular around the world is inflation targeting—dedicating monetary policy to achieving a specific numerical inflation rate. New Zealand and Chile were first to adopt this policy, in 1991; a popular target is about 2 percent for the core CPI. A crucial dimension of this policy is to create credibility, ensuring that the public believes that the monetary authority will achieve its stated inflation goal. (Independence of the central bank is a key prerequisite here.) If this is the case, the central bank can, when needed, undertake short-run stabilization policy (which without credibility would jeopardize the long-term goal of controlling inflation) without affecting people's expectations of inflation. One way of creating credibility is to adopt a hard-and-fast rule such as is advocated by the monetarists, but this would prevent the use of monetary policy for short-run stabilization. An alternative approach is to ensure that central bank actions are transparent and well understood. By explaining fully how short-term stabilization is embedded within a long-term policy of targeting on inflation, a central bank should be able to build and maintain its credibility. For example, as an economy enters a recession, the central bank could stimulate the economy but make clear that this stimulation is undertaken in the knowledge that because of the recession it should not affect the inflation goal.

More generally, Federal Reserve monetary policy appears to be based on the following principles:

1. Quickly adjust the money supply to meet shocks to money demand. When this shock has passed, readjust the money supply. Adopt stability of the financial system as a priority goal.

2. Never use an interest-rate target in an inflationary environment.

3. Use a monetary-aggregate target only in cases of strong inflation.

4. In a noninflationary environment be pragmatic and eclectic; use the deliberately vague concept "credit conditions" as a target that may or may not, depending on circumstances, involve what is happening to interest rates or to monetary aggregates.

Curiosity 11.3: What Is the Taylor Rule?

As should be evident from reading section 11.4, getting monetary policy right is a very challenging task, placing the Fed an awkward position. The Fed must decide policy in environments in which information is limited and knowledge about how the economy operates is incomplete. A consequence of this is that subjective judgment on the part of the Fed decision makers plays a prominent role in determining monetary policy reactions to macroeconomic events. This creates a major problem for economists developing models to use for forecasting and explanatory purposes—subjective reactions by the Fed cannot be put into equations and employed in economists' macroeconomic models. But perhaps Fed policy reaction, although subjective, can be approximated by a simple formula. The most prominent of these formulas is the *Taylor rule*, developed in 1993 by Stanford economist John Taylor to be used as a way of formalizing recommended Fed policy. Its prominence is due to its simplicity, its success in representing Fed reactions, and its common sense.

The essence of the Taylor rule is that the Fed is expected to adjust the nominal interest rate to increase the real interest rate to fight inflation when inflation rises above a target inflation rate, and to decrease the real interest rate to stimulate the economy when GDP falls below its potential. The following equation reflects this

$$\text{Nominal } i \text{ rate} = \text{Equilibrium nominal rate} + 1.5 * (\text{Inflation} - \text{Inflation target})$$
$$- 0.5 * (\text{Potential GDP} - \text{GDP})$$

The equilibrium nominal rate is the real rate of interest consistent with equilibrium in the economy plus the expected rate of inflation (the target rate of inflation). The 1.5 value is greater than one to ensure that if inflation increases above its target, the nominal interest rate increases by more than this difference to ensure that the real interest rate increases to fight inflation. The 0.5 value provides a means for policy makers to trade off higher inflation and lower growth.

Simple policy rules such as this are difficult to defend. Given the acknowledged lag in the impact of monetary policy, surely it would make a difference if the level of GDP relative to potential were going up or going down. If GDP were above potential and heading up, it would seem logical to increase the interest rate. But if GDP were above potential and heading down, it would seem logical to lower the interest rate.

5. Adopt low inflation as a priority goal, and only use discretionary policy to deal with other goals, such as smoothing the business cycle, if action is definitely warranted and if doing so will not jeopardize the inflation goal.

6. Any use of the interest rate as a policy tool—as opposed to a "target"—needs to be in terms of the real interest rate. For example, an increase in expected inflation of 1 percent should require a greater increase in the nominal interest rate (to imply a higher real interest rate) to fight the inflation. This appears to be the way the Fed is currently applying monetary policy.

These points summarize much of what the Fed has learned, often the hard way, since its creation in 1913:

- *Be pragmatic.* Do what works; use interest rates (or monetary aggregates) as an indicator of monetary policy only when circumstances warrant.

- *Be eclectic.* Do not pay undue attention to any one polar view of the economy, such as that of the monetarists, the Keynesians, or the supply-siders.

- *Be flexible.* Do not commit yourself publicly to a specific policy in case it becomes necessary to alter course; criticism is more easily deflected this way.

- *Be careful.* Move only when the right move is unequivocally clear; never try to "fine-tune" the economy.

- *Exploit strengths.* Because inflation is always and everywhere a monetary phenomenon, make inflation a top priority.

The Fed continues to learn. The subprime mortgage crisis and the recession that followed have taught the Fed some tough lessons. First, Fed responsibilities should extend beyond the banking system to the entire financial system, requiring a broader view of its regulatory function. Major players in the subprime mortgage crisis, the investment banks, were not subject to Fed regulation, a consequence of which was that the Fed was not fully aware of the potential for disruption to the financial system. Second, excessive money growth need not manifest itself in higher inflation; it could instead be creating a housing bubble. Housing costs enter the inflation measure via rents, not house prices, disguising this influence of money growth on inflation. Third, falling interest rates do not encourage spending in uncertain times, rendering monetary policy of questionable potency in just the circumstances in which it is needed to stimulate the economy.

Despite all these problems, Fed monetary policy continues to be seen by many as our main macroeconomic policy tool. Political bickering has rendered fiscal policy undependable, crowding out has lowered its multiplier value below unity, and the impact of big deficits on the national debt creates long-term problems.

> **Sample Exam Question 11.4:**
> "Sometimes using monetary policy for stimulus is like pushing on a string."
>   What does this mean?

Media Illustrations

Example 1

The bond markets were stunned by the shock of Thursday's flash second-quarter news that the economy has grown three whole percentage points. You and I would say that's good news. But the bond markets' terrified interpretation last Thursday was that it might encourage the private sector to borrow, nudging up interest rates. Add that discomforting prospect to the other horrifying disclosure—that, at last reading, our money supply had climbed by a mammoth $4.8 billion—and you'll know why people were heading for the bond market exits.

Why are people heading for the bond market exits?
Nominal interest rates are expected to rise because of higher private borrowing and because of higher expected inflation caused by the large growth in the money supply. People are selling bonds to avoid the capital loss that the rise in the interest rate will cause.

Example 2

And many borrowers fear that if American inflation can't be whipped, American bond markets may evolve into replicas of Europe's capital markets—surrendering their status as providers of long-term, fixed-cost funds to government and industry. Of course, some economists see long-term bonds returning to favor with a vengeance as inflation finally succumbs to slowing money-supply growth. Others, though, envisage inflation and interest rates peaking higher and higher each business cycle, as sound money management succumbs to electoral politics so that investors progressively shorten their commitments.

Why will long-term bond markets lose favor if inflation is not whipped?
If inflation continues to rise, the nominal interest rate will also rise, decreasing the price of long-term bonds. People will be reluctant to invest in long-term bonds if there is a high probability that they will suffer a fall in their value. Only a very high expected real rate of return would convince people to take on this risk of capital loss. This would make the long-term bond market a prohibitively expensive way to raise funds.

What does "sound money management succumbs to electoral politics" mean?

This phrase means that monetary authorities cave in to politicians' demands to increase the money supply prior to elections, to produce a temporary fall in the interest rate and a brief lowering of unemployment below the NRU.

How does this politically motivated action raise interest rates to higher and higher levels?

Before each election this action temporarily pushes interest rates down, but after a while, when higher inflation becomes expected, nominal interest rates rise.

Why would investors progressively shorten their commitments?

When the interest rate rises, capital losses on short-term bonds are much less than on long-term bonds.

Example 3

The Fed chairman added that the principal misunderstanding about the Fed's role in the present situation is that the Fed could achieve more or less immediately a low level of interest rates if it wanted to.

Doesn't the Fed control interest rates? Why can't it achieve immediately a low interest rate if it wants to?

The Fed's main control over interest rates comes from its control over inflation. To lower interest rates, it could decrease the rate of growth of the money supply, and this decrease would in time lower the rate of inflation, causing the interest rate to fall. In the short run this policy would involve a rise in the interest rate. An immediate fall in the interest rate could be achieved by an increase the money supply, but this would last only so long as expectations of inflation did not rise.

Example 4

Although interest rates were for many years the main policy indicator used by most central banks, the experience with severe inflation beginning in the 1970s made it clear that interest rates were fickle guides for ensuring that monetary policy was directed toward price stability.

How would interest rates be used to indicate whether monetary policy was restrictive or easy?

High interest rates may indicate that monetary policy is restrictive, since high interest rates may be created when the central bank decreases the money supply. Similarly low interest rates may indicate an easy monetary policy.

How would a central bank ensure that monetary policy was directed toward price stability?

For price stability the money supply should be increased at a rate approximately equal to the real rate of growth of the economy.

Why would severe inflation show interest rates to be fickle guides for monetary policy?
Severe inflation raises expectations of inflation, bumping up nominal interest rates, making it appear, using the interest rate indicator, that monetary policy is restrictive. This appearance would lead the monetary authorities to increase the money supply, exactly the wrong policy to deal with high inflation.

Example 5

The idea of investing in debt securities was a gamble on the government's good intentions to fight inflation. The budget makes it clear that the government has taken this task to heart. It stresses the fact that the deficit will be covered by sales of bonds to the general public and not to the central bank. It is a sign that the government has recognized the need to manage its cash requirements within the limitations of a capital market regulated by a well-determined monetary policy.

What is the nature of this gamble?
Buying debt securities, or bonds, would be a profitable move if the interest rate were to fall, increasing the price of these bonds. Interest rates will decline if the government is successful in reducing inflation.

Of what relevance to this gamble is the fact that security sales will be to the general public rather than the central bank?
If the bonds were sold to the central bank, the money supply would be increased, aggravating the inflation.

What is a well-determined monetary policy? What limitations does it impose in this context?
A well-determined monetary policy is one in which the central bank increases the money supply at a low, steady rate. This implies that there is a limit to the quantity of government bonds the central bank can buy each year.

Example 6

It had been feared that more good economic readings would trigger a selloff in the bond market, which typically responds negatively to such news because. . . .

Complete this clipping.
. . . good economic news means either that inflationary pressures are mounting, thereby raising the nominal interest rate and lowering the price of bonds, or that the Fed may put on the brakes, decreasing the money supply and raising interest rates, effects that would also lower bond prices.

Chapter Summary

- A premium for expected inflation is built into the interest rate. This phenomenon is formalized by distinguishing the *nominal* from the *real* interest rate. The former is what is observed, what is discussed in the media, and what affects bond prices. The latter is what influences spending behavior.

- Open-market operations designed to affect the interest rate may move the nominal interest rate in a direction opposite to that intended if inflation expectations are affected. One important policy lesson is that in an inflationary environment the most effective way to lower interest rates is to lower the rate of growth of the money supply, which in the short run will probably increase the interest rate.

- Targeting the interest rate as a policy goal can create major problems, such as an accelerating money-supply growth rate. Targeting a monetary aggregate growth rate can be difficult because of measurement problems, lack of full control, and velocity changes. Targeting on an inflation rate is a popular alternative. Several Fed guidelines for effective monetary policy have emerged from years of experience.

Formula Definition

Nominal interest rate = Real interest rate + Expected inflation rate

Media Exercises

(Group B questions require more thought.)

A1.   One view in the market has been that because the economy seemed weaker than it should be, the Federal Reserve Board would cut its discount rate from 7.5 percent. This reduction, of course, would be positive for bonds. On the other hand, there have been those thinking that rising money-supply growth would rule out such a discount rate reduction.

a. Why would a cut in the discount rate be positive for bonds?

b. Why might rising money-supply growth rule out a discount rate reduction?

A2.   Analysts say the three-month rally in bonds has been fueled by Washington's promise to balance its budget by 1991 and OPEC's decision to abandon support for world oil prices in the short run.

Explain the logic behind these two explanations for the bond rally.

A3.   Corporate treasurers should not be frightened by the recent rise in interest rates on bonds. Rates of even 13 percent will look like bargains if inflation

heats up over the next 18 months. Investors should continue to shun the market for long-term securities.

a. Why will rates of even 13 percent look like bargains?

b. Why should long-term securities be shunned?

A4. News of economic weakness last week cleared the way for higher bond prices. Traders went on a buying spree after Friday's announcement by the Labor Department of a lower-than-expected increase in nonfarm payrolls. The New York market moved quickly to capitalize on this good bad news: prices shot up more than a point ($10 on every $1,000 of face value) in minutes.

a. Why is this referred to as "good bad news"?

b. Explain why bond prices rose.

A5. Producer prices crept up a modest 0.2 percent in April, the government said yesterday in a report that could give the Federal Reserve room to cut interest rates again in a bid to boost the slowly recovering economy.

How does the modest rise in prices give the Fed room?

A6. As a result interest rates, which particularly affect certain sectors (capital spending, houses, and cars), are raised to levels that were previously viewed as impossible. But clearly they aren't out of line with what the central bank views as appropriate.

a. How might interest rates rise to such high levels?

b. Why might they nonetheless be viewed as appropriate?

A7. Moreover, contrary to the central bank's pronouncements, higher interest rates have not caused everyone to borrow less. Most people are borrowing as much as ever—or more—to buy goods now.

Why have higher interest rates not led to a fall in borrowing, as standard economic theory suggests should happen?

A8. When you look at real interest rates, they're way too high, probably because most people are still determining whether low inflation is a long-term reality.

Explain the logic of this explanation.

A9. In his eyes the battle is between the rate-lowering effect of the recession and the high rate of inflation. That sums up the problem now facing the interest rate forecasters.

Explain how these two effects operate on interest rates in different directions.

A10. In one camp are those who think interest rates will either stabilize or move up because the economic outlook is improving and will rebound from the paltry 0.7 percent real growth in the gross domestic product in the first quarter. Moreover, they argue, growth in money supply has been way above the Fed's target.

Explain the rationale behind the two reasons given for expecting a higher interest rate.

A11. In economic theory, money is a commodity that responds to the law of supply and demand. When the supply of money rises, the price—the interest rate—should drop. But the market for money is perverse. When lenders see the money supply increasing, they think. . . .

Complete the argument about to be developed here.

A12. Capacity utilization at 82.4 percent was unchanged in January for U.S. mines, factories, and utilities. Economists are worried that demand on industry may soon outstrip capacity, thereby encouraging producers to raise prices. Inflation, the undisputed Achilles heel of bonds, would result.

Why is inflation the "Achilles heel" (great weakness) of bonds?

A13. The principal power of the central bank to lower interest rates lies in its ability to contribute to a lower rate of inflation, and that takes time.

a. How would the central bank contribute to a lower rate of inflation?

b. How would this technique lower interest rates?

c. Why does all this take time?

A14. I think the bond market's got room on the upside. With real rates so high and inflation looking like its not coming back, there's room for further rally.

Explain the logic of this thinking.

A15. Bond prices soared and yields plunged after the Labor Department said the producer price index rose by 0.4 percent in March. Although Wall Street had been expecting a rise of only 0.3 percent, the core index, excluding the volatile food and energy sector, rose a slight 0.1 percent against expectations of a 0.3 percent rise.

Explain why bond prices would soar and yields would plunge on this news.

A16. **On Wall Street, inflation alarms are ringing. Higher inflation is on the way, warns one trader who expects inflation to rise to 5 percent next year. Judging from market action in recent days, many other bond traders seem to agree.**

What kind of market action must have been occurring?

A17. **The revision to inflation numbers indicating that inflation has actually been running a half-percentage point higher than the market had thought stirred things up for long-term bonds.**

What kind of stirring up happened on the bond market? Why?

A18. **A major revision to last year's inflation numbers yesterday indicated that U.S. inflation had actually been running a half percentage point higher than the market had previously assumed. This implies that in real terms the Fed's benchmark federal funds interest rate is considerably more accommodative than the Fed had thought. This foretells. . . .**

Complete this statement.

A19. **This brings us back to the fears of higher interest rates before the market break. These fears are still potent, especially if investors see through the temporary reduction in interest rates made possible by stepping up the rate of creation of the money supply.**

a. How does stepping up the rate of creation of the money supply reduce interest rates?

b. Why would it be only temporary?

A20. **The desire to see interest rates lower, or to avoid increases, is natural. But attempts to accomplish that desirable end by excessive monetary growth would soon be counterproductive. The implications for interest rates would in the end be perverse.**

Explain why interest rate movements would in the end be perverse.

B1. **A smaller-than-expected decrease in the U.S. money supply dealt the North American capital market a hard blow, as bond prices sagged across a broad front.**

Explain why bond prices sagged.

B2. **Swings in the price of bonds reflected a high degree of uncertainty about inflation and changing perceptions in the market. The release of figures that showed the economy to be stronger than expected tended to push prices _____ and yields _____.**

Fill in these two blanks and explain your reasoning.

B3. **The Fed is scrambling hard to keep interest rates from increasing in the face of renewed inflationary pressures, but the banking industry is a lot less interested in cooperating with the Fed because of the rising loan demand they are facing.**

a. Why would loan demand be rising?

b. What policy would you recommend to the Fed?

B4. **The Franklin Savings bonds will carry a 3 percentage point premium over inflation. The yield of every fixed-income instrument is determined by two things, expectations of the inflation rate and expectations of real return. This deal takes the uncertainty out of the inflation component.**

a. What real rate of return will an investor get if he or she buys this inflation-indexed bond? (Australia, Canada, Great Britain, New Zealand, and the United States all issue small quantities of indexed bonds.)

b. Will one be better off buying this bond (rather than a regular bond) if the current market expectation of inflation is too high or too low? Explain your reasoning.

B5. **A decline in the rate of inflation is the one sure route to lower interest rates, the central bank told us two years ago. Inflation is now only about one-third of what it was two years ago, but interest rates are higher. How come? We've paid the price, a fearsome price in slow growth and high unemployment for this one sure route to lower interest rates. Why haven't we had the promised results?**

a. What is the rationale behind this one sure route to lower interest rates?

b. What could have prevented the promised results from materializing?

B6. **Amid all the evidence of a budding recovery, however, there lurks a spoiler: long-term interest rates. Bond traders, worried about inflation and a massive supply of Treasury debt, have bid long rates up above 8 percent, raising real interest rates to about 5 percent.**

a. How would bond traders go about bidding rates up?

b. Why would worries about inflation cause them to do so?

c. Why would a massive supply of Treasury debt cause them to do so?

d. How do you suppose the author obtained the 5 percent real interest rate figure?

B7. **The past few years have been, in effect, a crash course in basic economics for investors and others with a hand in the game. They're much harder to fool now with actions that seem to improve the situation in the short run but make it worse in the long run.**

Give an example of a policy action that improves the situation for investors in the short run but makes it worse in the long run.

B8. **This Canadian bond is structured so that the coupon payments are low, in this case 4.25 percent, and the principal is adjusted as inflation changes over the life of the bond. The issue met stiff opposition, mainly because of the size of the coupon.**

a. What name would you give to this bond? (Take a guess!)

b. From this information, what can you say about the current Canadian real interest rate? Explain your reasoning.

B9. **This 30-year Treasury bond, usually called the long bond on Wall Street, is far more volatile than other fixed-income securities. But, although the Fed has been successful in pushing down short-term interest rates to 4 percent, the long bond yield has fallen very little and is still up at 7.5 percent.**

a. Why would the price of the long bond be so volatile relative to other bonds?

b. Why would the yield on the long bond be so much higher than on short-term bonds?

B10. **For some months now, the central bank has reduced the attention it pays to the levels of interest rates and has kept a close eye on expansion of the money supply. This policy change has made market interest rates more responsive to the high rate of inflation.**

a. Why would this policy change have caused interest rates to become more responsive to the high rate of inflation?

b. Is this a good or a bad thing?

B11. **Continued relief that the slowly growing economy is not producing significant levels of inflation moved the 30-year benchmark treasury bond 19/32 for the week to $103.28 to yield 7.30 percent versus 7.35 percent a week earlier.**

a. Are these numbers consistent with the fact that the economy is not producing significant levels of inflation? Explain why or why not.

b. What was the price of this bond last week?

B12. He claims that if the real interest rate is expected to remain unchanged, the upward-sloping term structure suggests that the market expects inflation to. . . .

Complete this clipping, and explain your rationale.

B13. By raising short-term rates now, the central bank has succeeded in reassuring the markets that it will not allow _____. That, in turn, convinces investors to accept lower long-term yields.

a. Fill in the blank.

b. Explain the logic of how higher short-term rates can lead to lower long-term rates.

B14. Indexed bonds—also known as real-return bonds—pay investors an annual rate of interest plus the inflation rate from that year. If the government really believes that its inflation targets will be met, it should issue more indexed bonds. This would minimize its interest costs because. . . .

Complete this clipping and explain your reasoning.

B15. In addition some economists argue that there is useful information contained in the yields of nonindexed and indexed government bonds. The difference in the two yields is a market-based signal of _____.

Complete this clipping and explain your reasoning.

B16. For one thing, the current economy doesn't look the way it generally has in the past when the Fed has embarked on a series of rate increases. Real interest rates, for example, already are high, not low. That's because inflation has been falling _____ than interest rates.

Fill in the blank and explain your reasoning.

B17. The U.S. bond market is betting that inflation is about to pick up, shortening the odds that the Federal Reserve will soon _____.

a. Fill in the blank.

b. What is happening to bond prices?

B18. Analysts said there is little reason for Treasuries to break out of recent ranges until there are clearer signs that either growth is slowing or inflation is picking up.

Explain in what way these two phenomena could affect Treasuries.

B19. Currently the spread between long-term rates and inflation is above average, implying that investors believe that. . . .

Complete this statement.

B20. There's nothing wrong with any level of interest rates produced by the natural forces in the economy. But artificially lowered rates are dangerous because they are produced by artificial increases in the money supply. And the extra money sluicing around in the system at a time when production is close to capacity is more likely to go into higher prices than anywhere else.

a. What is meant here by artificial increases in the money supply?

b. Explain how such artificially lowered rates may end up creating higher interest rates.

Numerical Exercises

AN1. The current price of a Treasury bill due to pay $1,000 in one year's time is $930. Say it suddenly becomes apparent that the money supply growth rate has jumped from 6 to 8 percent.

a. What should the interest rate become?

b. What should the price of this T-bill become?

AN2. Suppose that the economy is at full employment with expected inflation rate 7 percent and nominal interest rate 11 percent. Say the expected inflation rate now rises to 9 percent. After this change,

a. What is the nominal interest rate?

b. What is the real interest rate?

AN3. If the money supply is growing at 7 percent, the real interest rate is 3 percent, and the real rate of growth of GDP is 2 percent, what should the nominal interest rate be?

AN4. Suppose that the real interest rate is 3 percent and the real growth rate is 2 percent, the money multiplier is 4, and the money supply is growing at 10 percent per year. What should be the price of a T-bill due to mature in one year at its face value of $1,000?

BN1. If the money supply is growing at 9 percent, the real interest rate is 3 percent, the real rate of growth of GDP is 2 percent, and velocity is increasing by 1 percent per year, what should the nominal interest rate be?

BN2. Suppose that the real interest rate and the real growth rate are both 3 percent, the money multiplier is 4, banking innovations are decreasing the demand for money by 1 percent per year, and the money supply is growing at 10 percent per year. What should be the price of a T-bill due to mature in one year at its face value of $1,000?

Appendix 11.1   Eight Applications of Real-versus-Nominal Interest Rates

Because it is a key ingredient in explaining such a wide variety of media commentary, the distinction between real and nominal interest rates is the most important macroeconomic concept introduced in this book. There are eight general types of applications to note.

1. *Definitional interpretation.* Some applications merely require knowledge of the difference between real and nominal interest rates and the fact that it is the real interest rate that affects spending:

   Moreover, contrary to the central bank's pronouncements, higher interest rates have not caused everyone to borrow less. Most people are borrowing as much as ever—or more—to buy goods now.

   In this case, the higher interest rate must be a higher nominal interest rate but a lower real interest rate because of high inflation expectations.

2. *Forecasting interest rates.* Substantive changes in the nominal interest rate are usually due more to changes in expected inflation than to changes in the real interest rate:

   Corporate treasurers should not be frightened by the recent rise in interest rates on bonds. Rates of even 13 percent will look like bargains if inflation heats up over the next 18 months.

   A corporate treasurer deciding when is the best time to issue his or her corporation's bonds must pay close attention to inflation expectations.

3. *The interest rate as a monetary policy indicator.* Equating high interest rates with tight monetary policy is a recipe for disaster in an inflationary environment. The high interest rate could be a high nominal rate but a low real rate, and so be a misleading guide to the true stance of monetary policy. An example was discussed earlier as example 4 in the media illustrations section of this chapter:

   Although interest rates were for many years the main policy indicator used by most central banks, the experience with severe inflation beginning in the 1970s made it clear they were fickle guides for the task of ensuring that monetary policy was directed toward price stability.

4. *The influence of expected inflation on the bond market.* Millions of dollars are made and lost on the bond market daily, due to fluctuating nominal interest rates:

   A smaller than-expected decrease in the U.S. money supply dealt the North American capital market a hard blow, as bond prices sagged across a broad front.

This is a typical news report emphasizing that inflation expectations are strongly influenced by money growth figures. In this case, because the decrease was smaller than expected, inflation expectations were revised upward, raising the nominal interest rate and lowering bond prices.

5. *How economic news affects the bond market.* An apparent oddity in the real world is the fact that bad economic news (e.g., higher unemployment) is interpreted as *good* news for bond markets, causing the bond market to surge, and good economic news causes the bond market to fall. This phenomenon can be explained by analyzing the influence of this news on the nominal interest rate, either by appealing to the impact of this information on expected inflation, or by introducing expectations of a central bank reaction to influence the real interest rate. Consider the following example:

Bonds rallied sharply yesterday, cheered on by the news that the recession isn't over yet. Prices climbed by as much as $8.75 for each $1,000 face amount in the U.S. government securities market after the Commerce Department reported that GDP fell by 0.1 percent in the second quarter.

This news clip reports a typical reaction to information released monthly regarding employment or quarterly regarding GDP. Continued recession reduces fears of inflation. This reduced concern lowers inflation expectations, thereby lowering the nominal interest rates and raising bond prices. Alternatively, continued recession may cause people to believe that the Fed will stimulate the economy by lowering interest rates.

6. *Central bank control of the interest rate.* The Fed's ability to manipulate the interest rate is limited. Although it may have considerable control in the short run, in the longer run inflation expectations play a prominent role. An example was discussed as example 3 in the media illustrations section of this chapter:

The Fed chairman added that the principal misunderstanding about the Fed's role in the present situation is that it could achieve more or less immediately a low level of interest rates if it wanted to.

7. *Equivocal impact of monetary policy.* In the absence of changes in inflation expectations, an increase in the money supply lowers the interest rate. But an increase in the money supply when the economy is near full employment could be interpreted as creating inflation, increasing inflation expectations, reversing this fall in the nominal interest rate. Higher inflation expectations could also be triggered by fears that an unexpected increase in the money supply reflects a higher money growth rate. Consider the following example:

This brings us back to the fears of higher interest rates before the market break. These fears are still potent, especially if investors see through the temporary reduction in interest rates made possible by stepping up the rate of creation of the money supply.

This clip shows how changes in inflation expectations can offset the usual downward impact on the interest rate of a higher money supply, rendering it only temporary.

8. *Explaining international interest-rate differences.* As will be seen in chapter 16, real interest rates are roughly equal across countries. Nominal interest rates, however, can differ substantially:

Prior to 1989 it was widely believed that New Zealand ten-year government bond interest rates could not fall below those of Australia. Once NZ rates fell below those of Australia, the view on relative rates changed to one where NZ rates could not fall below those of the United States due to the high liquidity of the U.S. bond market. But this also has been proved wrong.

This clip is particularly interesting because it points to a phenomenon that is easily explained by macroeconomic theory but apparently not well understood by observers. In this case New Zealand inflation (and so expected inflation) has fallen relative to Australian and U.S. inflation by enough to cause its nominal interest rate to fall below Australian and U.S. interest rates. This phenomenon is explained at greater length in chapter 16.

12   Stagflation

Stagflation is the simultaneous occurrence of high or rising levels of both inflation and unemployment, a phenomenon that for many years economic theory claimed could not exist. For a decade, ending in the late 1960s, economists believed a trade-off existed between inflation and unemployment. This trade-off was represented graphically by the Phillips curve (shown in figure 12.1), a part of economic folklore so prominent that it has actually appeared on the front pages of newspapers. This curve was thought to be downward-sloping because a rise in unemployment should dampen forces that influence inflation, and a fall in unemployment should strengthen these forces.

The existence of this trade-off implied that the economy could "buy" a reduction in unemployment with an increase in inflation or "buy" a reduction in inflation with an increase in unemployment. All a policy maker needed to do was determine the character of the economy's Phillips curve, choose the point on that curve that was considered the least undesirable, and then adopt monetary or fiscal policy to move the economy to that chosen position. Throughout the 1960s this theory was regarded with some respect. Policy makers subscribed to it and undertook policies accordingly.

These policies did not lead to the expected results, however; if anything, the economic situation seemed to become worse—the economy began to experience stagflation, which the Phillips-curve theory implied could not exist. The 1975 to 1985 data points shown in figure 12.1 illustrate this stagflation and hint that perhaps the Phillips curve shifted upward during this period of high inflation. In response to this problem, economists considerably modified their conception of the Phillips curve—developing a distinction between the long and short runs, incorporating the economy's natural rate of unemployment, and recognizing the role of expectations in determining economic activity.

The purpose of this chapter is to explain the modern interpretation of the Phillips curve and, in doing so, offer an explanation for stagflation and a look at several related policy problems. Although, at first glance, explaining these things appears to involve learning a different curve-shifting apparatus, it turns out that the Phillips curve is merely a convenient way to express and analyze aggregate supply. The Phillips curve and the story it helps us tell about macroeconomic reactions are remarkably similar to the aggregate-supply curve and to the discussion in chapter 6.

Upon completion of this chapter you should

- know the distinction between the short- and long-run Phillips curves, as well as the implication this distinction has for a trade-off between inflation and unemployment;

- understand the rationale behind wage–price controls as a policy to deal with stagflation; and

- be able to explain how stagflation can come about.

12.1   The Phillips Curve

The modern interpretation of the Phillips curve rests heavily on the concept of the natural rate of unemployment (the NRU), described in chapter 4. Before the great recession began in 2008 the U.S. natural rate was thought to be about 5 percent, determined by the amount of frictional and structural unemployment, as well as by institutional phenomena such as minimum-wage legislation and unemployment insurance programs. With unemployment

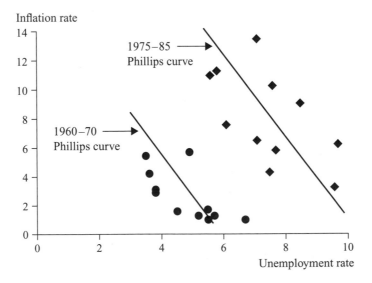

Figure 12.1   The Phillips Curve
The Phillips curve shifted upward from the 1960–70 period to the 1975–85 period. Source: Economic Report of the President, 1990. www.access.gpo.gov/eop/.

above 10 percent in 2009, however, this figure probably should be revised upward slightly—a high level of unemployment means that those not working fail to gain working experience and so become less employable. When the economy recovers, they have more difficulty finding a job: frictional and structural unemployment increase. Regardless of the exact level of the NRU, in this chapter it serves as a measure of the "full-employment" rate of unemployment to which the forces of supply and demand push the economy in the long run.

In the long run the rate of inflation is determined by the rate of growth of the money supply, so once the economy adjusts to this money-supply growth, it should settle at its natural rate of unemployment. Consequently in the long run the natural rate of unemployment can coexist with any rate of inflation: there is no trade-off between inflation and unemployment. Reflecting this fact, the long-run Phillips curve is a vertical line located at the natural rate of unemployment NRU, as shown by *LRPC* in figure 12.2.

A trade-off is thought to exist in the short run, however—represented by a traditional downward-sloping Phillips curve, shown by *SRPC* in figure 12.2. Let us begin with the

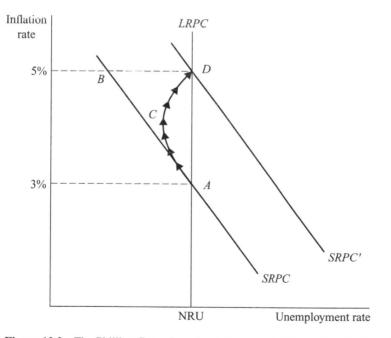

Figure 12.2 The Phillips-Curve Reaction to Increase in Money-Supply Growth
The higher rate of money-supply growth stimulates the economy creating an unexpectedly higher inflation rate and consequently a lower unemployment rate: the economy moves toward point *C*. Once this inflation becomes expected, however, *SRPC* shifts upward and unemployment returns to the NRU: the economy moves to point *D*.

economy in equilibrium at position *A*, at the NRU, and with an inflation of 3 percent. Suppose that the central bank increases the rate of growth of the money supply by two percentage points, with the idea of moving the economy to position *B*, where inflation is 5 percent and unemployment is lower. The reaction of the economy to this shock can be explained in a fashion virtually identical to our explanation of a movement along the short-run aggregate supply curve as exposited in chapter 6. There are two main differences: (1) now we measure unemployment instead of GDP on the horizontal axis, so that the upward-sloping, short-run aggregate supply curve is represented by a downward-sloping short-run Phillips curve, and (2) we measure inflation instead of the price level on the vertical axis. The following paragraphs present a shortened version of the chapter 6 explanation, with only a slight modification changing "price increases" to "price increases in excess of the 3 percent expected inflation."

The jump in money-supply growth creates an excess supply of money and stimulates aggregate demand. Inventories fall, and business in the service industry is turned away, indicating to firms that demand for their good or service has risen. How are firms likely to react to this rise? Near the NRU, firms are operating at a high capacity level, implying that extra output will involve higher per unit cost. Consequently firms are likely to increase prices beyond the expected 3 percent annual increase—say, by 4 percent. This extra-large price increase makes it profitable for firms to increase output, and it may entice new firms to appear. As a result the demand for workers increases.

When firms try to hire these extra workers, however, they discover to their surprise that workers are hard to come by. Because the economy is at its natural rate of unemployment, a pool of unemployed eager to work at the going wage does not exist. To solve this problem, firms bid up the wage rate slightly more than the 3 percent that everyone expects, by perhaps 3.5 percent, which induces some students to quit school, some homemakers to leave home, and some job searchers to find more quickly a job with the wage they feel they deserve. This way firms are able to hire more workers and increase output. This combined increase in inflation and decrease in unemployment is shown in figure 12.2 by a movement out toward point *B*.

In essence, firms are willing to employ the extra workers because it is profitable for them to do so. The extra rise in price (4 percent) has more than compensated firms for the extra wage (3.5 percent) that they are now paying. The real wage has fallen. Ordinarily workers would not put up with a lower wage. At a lower real wage some workers would withdraw their services, choosing instead to become students or homemakers or to search the job market for a better job. Consequently, for the movement out toward point *B* in figure 12.2 to be maintained, workers must for some reason be willing to supply more labor at a lower real wage. Economists offer two main explanations for this willingness:

1. *Information problems.* Workers may not realize what is happening, genuinely mistaking a 3.5 percent increase in the money wage for a 0.5 percent rise in the real wage. They know exactly what is happening with the money wage, but are slow to recognize what has happened to the overall price/inflation level.

Curiosity 12.1: What Are New Classicals and New Keynesians?

Several schools of macroeconomic thought have appeared in this book at one stage or another: the Keynesian school, which supplanted the classical school; monetarists, who critiqued the Keynesians; and supply-siders and real business-cycle theorists who focused on the supply side of the economy. Two recent schools are the New Classical school and the New Keynesian school. Both schools place great emphasis on generating explanations based on individuals acting rationally in their self-interest, which collectively causes macroeconomic phenomena such as excessive unemployment and business cycles. Like the Keynesian school, the New Keynesian school favors government intervention in the economy, whereas the New Classicals—like the classicals and the monetarists—do not.

Oversimplifying somewhat, the difference between them is most sharply drawn on the issue of what gives the short-run aggregate supply curve its upward slope, or equivalently, what causes the short-run Phillips curve to be downward-sloping. New Classicals believe that wages and prices are flexible, that markets always clear, and that it is information problems that cause short-run deviations from the NRU, thereby explaining business cycles.

In contrast, New Keynesians believe that wages and prices are not flexible, that markets do not always clear, and that information problems must be supplemented by the concept of sticky wages and prices. They have devoted their research energies to finding intellectually respectable ways of explaining wage and price rigidities as arising from efficient, rational microeconomic behavior on the part of labor and firms. They would note, for example, that firms find it easier in the short run to meet demand changes by adjusting quantity rather than price. Contractual labor markets and, in particular, implicit contracts play a major role in their explanations, causing some to distinguish between New Classicals and New Keynesians on the basis of their belief in the invisible hand versus the invisible handshake.

Dynamic stochastic general equilibrium (DSGE) models, mentioned briefly in curiosity 6.2, can be viewed as a modern variant of New Classical models. One of its hallmarks is consistency in modeling—aggregate behavior is consistent with the behavior of economic actors (individuals and businesses), short-run behavior is consistent with long-run behavior, and expectations are consistent with the environment created by the behavior of all the actors. This consistency is where the "general equilibrium" terminology in DSGE comes from. These models are the foundation of modern advanced macroeconomic theorizing, but they lie beyond the scope of this book.

2. *Contract obligations.* Workers may be obliged by a formal or informal contract to supply labor at a money wage increasing at a 3 percent annual rate until the expiration of that contract. Some contracts are renegotiated sooner than others, implying that overall wages do not keep up with overall price increases beyond 3 percent.

What is notable about both of these explanations is that they explain only a temporary fall in real wages. Workers eventually realize that their real wage has fallen and demand a rise in the money wage to compensate them fully for unexpected higher prices. Eventually all contracts are renegotiated, bringing the real wage back to its original level and *building into new contracts the higher expected inflation.* Consequently the economy's movement toward point B is only temporary. People's expectations of inflation increase; in time, money wages rise to restore the original real wage and thereafter rise at a rate matching the new, higher inflation rate.

In figure 12.2 higher expected inflation shifts the *SRPC* curve upward. The economy moves along the curved arrowed line from A out toward B, perhaps as far as point C, but eventually back to the NRU at point D, and the *SRPC* curve ends up eventually at *SRPC'*. Why does *SRPC* shift upward with higher inflation expectations? If everyone expects inflation to be two percentage points higher, then—regardless of the unemployment rate— workers demand and firms grant wage increases two percentage points higher than usual, thus shifting the *SRPC* up by two percentage points.

A clear implication of this analysis is that in the long run the economy moves along the long-run Phillips curve rather than the traditional downward-sloping, short-run Phillips curve, with no trade-off between inflation and unemployment. Persistent government action to move the economy to a lower level of unemployment only serves to push it to higher levels of inflation, with no long-run improvement in unemployment, thus contradicting the opinions of those who advocate the use of government policy action to influence the level of unemployment in an inflationary environment.

> **Sample Exam Question 12.1:**
> "As actual inflation increased, workers and businesses began to incorporate expectations of higher and higher inflation into their behavior. The Phillips curve consequently . . .".
>
> Complete this clipping.

12.2   Policy Implications

Several interesting policy considerations stem from the theory that there is no long-run trade-off between inflation and unemployment:

1. *Reducing the NRU.* In the long run, unemployment can be reduced only by lowering the NRU. Government policy in this regard takes the form of alleviating imperfections in the labor market: labor retraining programs, programs to increase labor market information or reduce the cost of obtaining such information, programs to increase labor mobility, elimination of minimum-wage legislation, restructuring of welfare and unemployment insurance programs, and fiscal policy to reduce demand in geographic or industry bottlenecks.

2. *The accelerationist hypothesis.* By accelerating the inflation rate, the government may continually fool labor and outstrip contracts, lowering unemployment permanently

below its natural rate. This possibility reflects the *accelerationist hypothesis* that the relevant trade-off is between unemployment and accelerating inflation rather than between unemployment and inflation. In this context the natural rate of unemployment is sometimes called the nonaccelerating-inflation rate of unemployment (NAIRU). This terminology suggests that if a central bank tried to reduce the unemployment rate below the NRU (e.g., because it underestimated the NRU), it could be led to increase the money supply at an excessive rate.

3. *Policy ineffectiveness debate.* In our modern society information is communicated rapidly and interpreted with sophistication. An increase in the rate of growth of the money supply soon becomes widely known, and the new, higher rate of inflation it implies quickly becomes anticipated. If people form their expectations of future values of economic variables by working through the appropriate economic theory in conjunction with the best available information, they are said to produce *rational expectations.* Such expectations should be much more accurate than expectations formed by ignoring current information on relevant economic variables and simply extrapolating past values of the variable to be forecast.

In the example of figure 12.2, if people form their expectations of inflation rationally, when the higher money-supply growth rate becomes known the inflation of position *D* is expected. This analysis suggests that *SRPC* shifts immediately up to *SRPC'* and the economy moves directly to *D*, without taking the path through *C*. It thus appears that if expectations are formed rationally, even the short-run trade-off disappears. According to this thinking, once we are at the NRU, any systematic policy is completely ineffective. Only erratic, unpredictable policies can have any effect, and even then only in the short run.

This remarkable conclusion has sparked what is known as the *policy ineffectiveness debate.* Opponents of such a view make two arguments:

a. *Policy credibility.* If a policy change is not thought to be credible—for example, if people do not believe that the Fed will maintain a change in the rate of growth of the money supply—then short-run reactions can be quite different from long-run reactions.

b. *Wage and price inflexibility.* Even if expectations are formed rationally, the conclusions about policy ineffectiveness do not follow because prices and wages are not perfectly flexible (e.g., existing wage contracts may prevent wages from adjusting immediately).

4. *Reducing inflation quickly.* Although the policy ineffectiveness conclusion does not hold exactly, it does suggest that movement up the long-run Phillips curve may occur much more rapidly than the exposition of figure 12.2 suggested. If people form their expectations in a sophisticated fashion, and if their past experience has led them to believe that increases in the inflation rate can occur quickly, inflation expectations adjust quickly in the upward direction when the money-supply growth rate rises. In

figure 12.2 this process is reflected by a relatively steep short-run Phillips curve. The short-run reduction in unemployment due to an increase in the inflation rate is small and of short duration.

Inflation can thus rise quickly. If so, shouldn't this process operate in reverse equally quickly? If expectations are formed rationally, a decrease in the rate of growth of money supply from 5 to 3 percent should cause the economy to move down quickly from point *D* to point *A* in figure 12.2, so that the cost of lowering inflation is only a modest increase in unemployment for a short period of time. Unfortunately, this assumption is not valid. An effort to decrease the rate of inflation by decreasing money-supply growth involves a prolonged period of high unemployment.

> **Sample Exam Question 12.2:**
> Suppose that the economy has an NRU of 6 percent, an inflation rate of 4 percent, and its short-run Phillips curve is such that a 2 percent increase in inflation brings a decrease in unemployment of 1 percent.
>   If the central bank increases the money growth rate from 6 to 9 percent, what is the rational expectation of inflation?

12.3   Fighting Inflation with Recession

The reasons why lowering inflation requires a major recession highlight the two arguments of those who oppose the policy ineffectiveness conclusion:

1. *Is the policy credible?* When the Fed announces that it is decreasing the rate of growth of the money supply, people have reason not to believe that the central bank will stick to this policy; they accordingly do not revise inflation expectations downward. In the past there have been too many instances in which such a policy was announced and then abandoned later when the resulting unemployment became politically too uncomfortable. This *credibility effect* inhibits the success of the policy.

2. *Are wages and prices inflexible?* Contract obligations slow down wage adjustments in the downward direction just as in the upward direction, but a more important factor affects wage stickiness in this context. In contrast to the case of increasing prices and wages, people are quite reluctant to lower their customary annual wage and price increases, for reasons expounded at some length in chapter 6. Money wages do not fall quickly because of implicit contracts, concern about relative wages, worker belief that recessions are temporary, and the payment of efficiency wages.

The upshot of all this is that when the central bank decreases the rate of money-supply growth from 5 to 3 percent, there is little immediate decrease in the rate of inflation.

Because prices continue to increase at 5 percent while the money supply increases at 3 percent, the demand for money grows by more than the supply of money. The resulting excess demand for money increases interest rates and in general decreases aggregate demand for goods and services, creating a major recession. (Recall our baby-sitting co-op example of this phenomenon in curiosity 9.1.) In figure 12.3 the economy begins at position *D* and moves out toward point *E*. The *SRPC* is drawn relatively flat to the right of the natural rate of unemployment to reflect this stagflation phenomenon. The economy remains at point *E* until the natural economic pressures of the recession force firms and labor to moderate price and wage increases and to lower inflation expectations, eventually allowing the economy to move along the arrowed path toward position *A*.

A classic real-world counterpart to figure 12.3 is shown in figure 12.4, which traces the reaction of the economy to the severe monetary policy imposed by the Fed to lower inflation when Paul Volcker was chairman. Figure 12.5 carries on from where figure 12.4 leaves off, showing how cyclical behavior of the economy is reflected in a Phillips-curve diagram. But beware! If we had continued to plot data in figure 12.5 for the years after 1994, they would not fit the pattern because the NRU began to fall, as explained in curiosity 12.2.

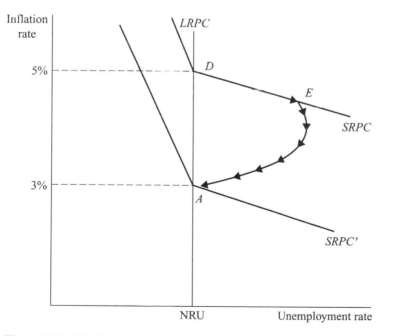

Figure 12.3 The Phillips-Curve Reaction to Decrease in Money-Supply Growth
The lower rate of money-supply growth, with inflation remaining at about 5 percent, decreases the real money supply creating a recession. The economy moves to *E* and remains there until expectation of inflation fall, shifting *SRPC* downward, taking the economy to *A*.

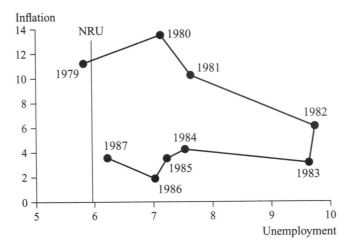

Figure 12.4 Fighting Inflation with Recession
At the end of the 1970s inflation had risen to double-digit levels. Paul Volcker, the new chairman of the fed, engineered an extremely tight monetary policy that created a major recession, lowering inflation to a more moderate level. Unemployment eventually returned to its natural rate.

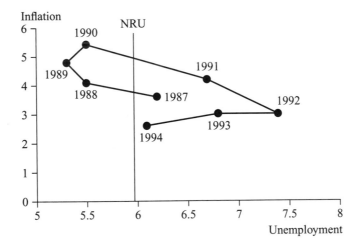

Figure 12.5 Illustrating Business Cycle Behavior on a Phillips-Curve Diagram
This figure carries on from figure 12.4. The movement from 1987 to 1990 reflects the pattern drawn in figure 12.2; the movement from 1990 to 1994 reflects the pattern drawn in figure 12.3.

Curiosity 12.2: Why Did the NRU Fall in the Late 1990s?

Because the NRU, the natural unemployment rate, corresponds to the NAIRU, the nonaccelerating inflation rate of unemployment, inflation should be decreasing for unemployment levels above the NRU and increasing for unemployment levels below the NRU. A graph of inflation changes against unemployment could therefore be used to find the unemployment rate corresponding to zero change in inflation and thus produce an estimate of the NRU. Such a graph for the years 1970 to 1994 was provided in the first edition of this book, suggesting an NRU of about 6.5 percent. This method of estimating the NRU works well if the NRU has remained constant for an extended period of time. But in the late 1990s it became quite clear that the NRU had fallen dramatically—the economy had moved down to an unemployment rate of 4.3 percent without any rise in inflation. In chapter 4 we learned that the natural rate of unemployment was not a fixed, immutable figure but rather one that could change as the character of an economy changed.

Economists have put forward several reasons explaining why the U.S. NRU fell during the late 1990s:

1. The prolonged boom of the late 1990s caused a lot of people who might otherwise have been unemployed to gain job experience. This improved their labor skills, allowing them more easily to find and hold a job. As a result both search and structural unemployment fell. Check curiosity 4.4 on hysteresis in chapter 4.

2. The Internet has lowered the cost of job search, lowering search unemployment. Thousands of companies post help-wanted ads on the Internet, and there are more than 200 sites at which job seekers can check job listings or post their resumes. It is estimated that more than 3 million people use the Internet to look for work on any given day.

3. Advances in computer technology have increased job opportunities for the disabled. For example, physically challenged people can work at home in the software industry, and mentally challenged workers in the fast food industry can take orders without knowing how to add or read—by touching pictures of items on a computer register. These advances have lowered structural unemployment.

4. A welfare reform bill has imposed a five-year lifetime limit on welfare recipiency and a requirement that after two years people on welfare must attend training classes or participate in government-run jobs programs. These changes may lower institutionally induced unemployment.

5. The demographics have changed—groups that historically have had below-average unemployment rates are today a larger share of the workforce.

Supplementing this fall in the NRU are several reasons why the move to lower unemployment did not prompt businesses to raise prices during the 1990s boom:

1. There was strong competition from abroad, because of free-trade agreements and the Asian slowdown.

2. Costs fell as a result of lower oil, commodity, and computer prices, as well as a strong U.S. dollar.

(continued)

The path down toward position A in figure 12.3 contrasts sharply with the path up toward position D in figure 12.2, implying that the *SRPC* has a kink, being steeper below the NRU and flatter above the NRU. The movement from A up to D occurs quickly and has only a small short-term reduction in unemployment, whereas moving from D down to A involves a prolonged period of high unemployment. This asymmetry explains why inflation is fought so fiercely. Inflation can rise quickly, with little benefit, but is pushed back down only at high cost.

It should by now be obvious why the Fed is so reluctant to intervene to stimulate the economy during a recession. If the recession is a figment of measurement problems, or if the economy has already begun to climb out of recession but that fact is not yet evident, action by the Fed could inadvertently trigger higher inflation, which would be costly to eradicate. The main problem, it seems, is that the only way the Fed knows how to lower inflation is to create a recession. Wage-price controls are allegedly a means of avoiding this high cost.

Sample Exam Question 12.3:
"Undoubtedly, the amazing drop in the unemployment rate adds to pressure on Mr. Greenspan, the chairman of the Fed, to. . . ."
Complete this clipping.

12.4   Wage-Price Controls

A major reason why lowering inflation requires a prolonged recession is the *coordination problem:* people will not moderate wage and price increases until everyone else does. A wage-price control policy, such as that imposed by President Nixon in 1971, puts legal constraints on wage and price increases. Controls policies and their variants, such as wage-price guidelines with no formal legal penalties, or guidelines with a tax on excessive wage or price increases, are called *incomes policies*. An incomes policy imposes the missing coordination and, by doing so, allows the economy to move quickly down the long-run Phillips curve, thus avoiding the high cost of a prolonged recession. This is the benefit of a policy of wage-price controls.

Curiosity 12.3: What Is the Sacrifice Ratio?

What is the cost of reducing inflation by a percentage point? According to the 1995 Economic Report of the President, the cost at that time was thought to be a cumulative total of two percentage points of lost output. For example, to decrease inflation by three percentage points, we must sacrifice a total of 6 percent of GDP. This could take the form of 2 percent of GDP for three years or 1 percent of GDP for six years, or some other combination of number of years and loss of annual output. This relationship is formalized through the concept of the sacrifice ratio, defined as

$$\text{Sacrifice ratio} = \frac{\text{Cumulative cost as \% of GDP}}{\text{Percentage point decrease in inflation}}$$

This cost can be translated into unemployment using Okun's law. As described in chapter 4, Okun's law says that two percentage points of annual potential output are lost by each percentage point in unemployment above the NRU. This implies that a sacrifice ratio of 2 corresponds to a cost of one percentage point of annual extra unemployment required to reduce inflation by one percentage point.

The sacrifice ratio can vary across countries and over time depending on the flexibility of wage-setting systems and the credibility of central bank policies. Estimates suggest that during the late 1970s it was about 5 or 6 and that during the later years of the Volcker era at the Fed it had fallen to 3 because Volcker had built up such high credibility. This description of the sacrifice ratio suggests that the total cost in terms of lost output is the same whether the central bank adopts the "cold turkey" approach to lowering inflation, in which there is an immediate large reduction in the rate of growth of the money supply, or the "gradualism" approach in which the rate of growth of the money supply is lowered gradually over an extended time period. Realistically, however, it would be advisable to use the cold turkey approach only if the central bank has high credibility and the nation's wage- and price-setting systems are quite flexible. Otherwise, inflation would not fall quickly to match the lower growth in the money supply, the demand for money would increase by much more than the supply of money, aggregate demand would then fall, and the economy would enter a severe recession.

Most economists do not look upon wage-price controls with favor, for two reasons:

1. *Complementary monetary and fiscal policy are required.* Most empirical evidence suggests that control policies do not work, even if, as was done by Diocletian during the Roman empire, the death penalty is imposed for violation. This evidence, however, comes from situations in which the control policies could not have been expected to be successful. In figure 12.4, if the rate of growth of the money supply were not reduced from 5 to 3 percent, it would be impossible for a policy of wage-price controls to be successful. Some evidence, such as the 1975 to 1978 Canadian experience, suggests that control policies can be of benefit if they are complemented by appropriate monetary and fiscal policies—a crucial proviso to the adoption of wage-price control policies.

2. *Costs and benefits should be compared.* There are high costs associated with controls. The most important costs result from the constraints that controls place upon the operation of the price system, hindering its job of allocating and distributing goods and services in an efficient fashion. These costs could be considerable but can be alleviated somewhat by designing some flexibilities into the controls program. For example, the controls rules could permit extra wage or price increases in markets experiencing obvious shortages. In any event, a decision to adopt or reject a guidelines or controls program should be made by comparing its costs and benefits.

> **Sample Exam Question 12.4:**
> "Price controls have historically never worked. What could possibly make the President think they will work now?"
>   How would you answer this question?

12.5   Explaining Stagflation

The Phillips curve can be used to create some explanations for stagflation, which can be defined as high inflation combined with high unemployment, or as rising inflation in conjunction with rising unemployment. In the world of the original Phillips curve, both such phenomena were impossible.

Consider first stagflation defined as high inflation combined with high unemployment. High inflation can be created by a high money-supply growth rate. There are three basic ways in which high unemployment can accompany this high inflation:

1. *High NRU.* The natural rate of unemployment may itself be high, owing to factors affecting frictional or structural unemployment, or for institutional reasons such as generous unemployment insurance benefits.

2. *A current fight against inflation:* The government may be in the process of fighting an inflation by creating a recession, so that the economy is temporarily lodged near a point like *E* in figure 12.3.

3. *Real wage overhang.* Following a permanent negative supply shock, workers may refuse to allow their real wage to fall. If they have sufficient power or a wage indexation policy to hold up their real wage, unemployment beyond the natural rate will develop.

Consider now stagflation defined as rising inflation in conjunction with rising unemployment. There are several ways in which these things can happen at the same time:

1. *An increase in money growth.* The dynamic reaction of the economy to an increase in the rate of money-supply growth is such that, in its later stages, inflation and unemployment increase together, as illustrated by the path from point *C* to *D* in figure 12.2.

2. *A supply shock.* A negative supply shock raises costs, causing producers to raise prices. The higher prices lower aggregate demand, so output and employment fall.

3. *Labor hoarding.* As an economy moves into recession and unemployment rises, firms tend to keep on some redundant employees (in order to keep trained labor available for the end of the recession). This policy raises per unit costs, requiring higher markups to maintain profitability. The lower output level also implies a loss of economies of scale, also raising per unit costs.

4. *Participation rate changes.* A rise in inflation often occurs when employment is rising. It is possible that discouraged workers rejoin the labor force if they see employment rising, and the measured level of unemployment rises as a result.

5. *Inflation variability.* When inflation is higher, its rate is more variable, increasing uncertainty in economic markets. Firms react by investing less, thus decreasing economic growth.

Sample Exam Question 12.5:

"In some countries there is a national wage bargaining process whereby the annual percentage wage increase for all workers is determined by a central wage-determination committee. The danger with this is that this committee may choose an easy way out—increase the real wage each year by an amount equal to historical annual productivity increases."

What is the danger here?

Media Illustrations

Example 1

Just as in the '30s when government intervened to save capitalism from itself, so again must it intervene massively now to save government capitalism from itself. Since government now protects individuals and corporations from the consequences of excessive wage and price increases, government must now prevent those excessive increases by permanent wage and price controls.

How did government intervene in the '30s to save capitalism from itself?
The Great Depression is viewed by the author of this clipping as a product of the capitalist system. The government intervened in the Depression by using fiscal policy to increase government spending.

What are the consequences of excessive wage and price increases, and how does the government protect individuals and corporations from these consequences?
Excessive wage and price increases, if not accommodated by money-supply increases, decrease sales and lead to unemployment. The government protection takes the form of monetary accommodation designed to maintain full employment.

Under what circumstances would wage and price controls succeed in preventing these excessive increases?
Controls would succeed only if complemented by a decrease in money-supply growth.

Example 2

The central bank was presumably trying to maintain very high interest rates and, I assume in the face of political reality and pressure from the economy, released the interest rate a few weeks ago. The monetarists will allow you to go ahead and ruin people and countries. But when eventually in good and common sense you say, "Enough is enough," the monetarists say, "Well, you spoiled the experiment."

How and why was the central bank maintaining high interest rates.
The central bank was fighting inflation by employing a tight monetary policy, cutting back on the rate of money-supply growth. This would push up interest rates.

What does releasing the interest rate imply about the central bank's monetary policy?
Releasing the interest rate means that the money supply has been allowed to grow at a faster rate.

What does ruining people and countries mean in this context?
Ruining people and countries means that the economy is forced to endure a very high rate of unemployment for a prolonged period of time.

What was the experiment, and how and why was it spoiled?
The experiment was the maintenance of a low rate of money supply growth to see whether it would lower inflation and how long it would take to do so. The experiment was spoiled

by the central bank allowing money-supply growth to rise before inflation had been lowered. This change in policy was prompted by the political unacceptability of the prolonged high rate of unemployment this policy produced.

Example 3

This suggests that wages play a game of catch-up, then fall behind for a while. But on the average, they advance about 3 percent a year, in real terms. We are still not far off this pace. The only trouble is that the economy is no longer productive enough to yield 3 percent average wage gains in real terms. If the cycle now goes into the catch-up phase, the demands for real gains to make up for the real losses of the past three years will collide with an economy going into at least a temporary stall.

Describe a scenario in which wages in real terms fall behind for a while and then go through a catch-up stage.

An unexpected increase in inflation will cause the real wage to fall. Once labor realizes that real wages have fallen, catch-up wage increases will be demanded.

Explain how catch-up wages in conjunction with a productivity slowdown could create a "stall" in the economy.

Catch-up wages would restore the real wage to its original level, plus the traditional annual 3 percent for productivity gains. If actual productivity gains were less than 3 percent, this rise in the real wage would put it higher than what is consistent with the natural rate of unemployment. Firms could not afford as much labor and would lay workers off, creating a "stall."

Why would this stall be temporary?

Eventually the higher unemployment would dampen real wages, restoring the real wage to a level consistent with the natural rate of unemployment.

Example 4

He favors a slow recovery, for example, because the natural rate of unemployment may turn out to be higher than anyone thinks.

Explain why underestimation of the natural rate would imply that a recovery should be slow.

Policy makers would feel free to engineer a recovery if inflation had fallen to an acceptable level. A stimulating policy would be undertaken to move the economy back to the natural rate of unemployment from its present inflation-fighting rate. In doing so, however, it is important that the natural rate of unemployment be known. If it is underestimated, the recovery policy may push the economy below this rate and quickly accelerate the inflation, destroying the hard-won results of the fight against inflation. If a slow recovery is engineered, an underestimation may be noticed before too much damage is done.

Chapter Summary

■ The Phillips curve cannot be interpreted, as it once was, as a menu of choice offering policy makers an exploitable trade-off between inflation and unemployment. Instead, this relationship reflects supply forces, analyzed earlier in the short-run aggregate supply curve. An unexpected increase in inflation causes a temporary increase in aggregate supply because of worker misperceptions and contracts. In the long run, however, workers become fully aware of the new inflation rate, and contracts are renegotiated accordingly, causing unemployment to return to the NRU. Higher inflation expectations cause the Phillips curve to shift upward, explaining why the Phillips-curve relationship had appeared to break down after the 1960s.

■ Although movements up the long-run Phillips curve occur quite quickly, movements down this curve require a prolonged period of high unemployment to squeeze down high inflation expectations, mainly because people do not at first find a Fed policy of fighting inflation fully credible, and because wages and prices are downward-sticky. These different reactions create an asymmetry in the Phillips curve, implying that benefits from accelerating inflation are small and short-lived, whereas costs associated with lowering inflation are substantial and long-lived—explaining why governments have become so paranoid about inflation.

■ Wage-price control policies are designed to force coordination of deceleration of wage and price increases, thereby facilitating a movement down the long-run Phillips curve. Although this policy inhibits the operation of the price system, it has the benefit of avoiding the prolonged high unemployment that would otherwise characterize moving to a lower inflation rate. Such a policy would only succeed if accompanied by complementary monetary and fiscal policies.

■ Several explanations were offered for *stagflation*, defined either as high unemployment in conjunction with high inflation or as unemployment and inflation increasing simultaneously.

Definitional Formula

$$\text{Sacrifice ratio} = \frac{\text{Cumulative cost as \% of GDP}}{\text{Percentage point decrease inflation}}$$

Media Exercises

(Group B questions require more thought.)

A1. **The central bank warned about a possible "collision" in the future between rising wages and prices and its hold-the-line monetary policy.**

What is the nature of this collision, and what results will it produce?

A2. **The damnable paradox is that we are also at "full employment," or at least at the "natural rate" of unemployment. This means only that we are at or near the lowest rate to which unemployment can be pushed by expanding demand without. . . .**

Complete this clipping.

A3. **Unemployment rates in Canada and the United States are sufficiently low that employers are having difficulty filling many jobs. The point at which red flags go up, economists say, is 9 percent in Canada and 6 percent in the United States.**

a. What two names are given to the unemployment rates described in this clipping?

b. What danger do the red flags signal?

A4. **The response of the monetary authorities to any hint of inflation is to dampen demand by raising interest rates and slowing economic activity—that is, *by causing a recession*. It always seems to me that one of the great failures of the economic profession is that the only thing it seems to be able to recommend to eliminate inflation is a recession, but that's the way it is.**

a. What diagram is usually used to illustrate this phenomenon?

b. What role does the recession play in the economy's movement to a lower inflation rate?

c. What alternative policy could be recommended, and how would it work?

A5. **In the 1980s America has succeeded in lowering unemployment and inflation at the same time, and the council believes this can continue even though industry is now running at more than 80 percent of capacity.**

Explain how inflation and unemployment could have been lowered at the same time. Illustrate this movement on a Phillips curve diagram.

A6. **He warned yesterday that economic recovery in the Western world could be short-lived if governments injected too much financial stimulus into their economies in an attempt to boost employment and output.**

a. What is too much financial stimulus in this context?

b. Why would too much stimulus make the recovery short-lived?

A7. Those policies were predicated on 1930s Keynesian assumptions that economic recoveries always run out of steam and at certain points need artificial stimulation of demand and fine-tuning to keep them running at acceptable levels. The evidence of the 1970s and beyond is that whenever governments stepped in to administer stimulative medicine, they triggered runaway inflation which finally had to be stopped with strong, painful doses of recession.

    a. What do Keynesians recommend for artificial stimulation of demand?

    b. Describe how such stimulation could trigger runaway inflation.

    c. Explain why stopping this inflation requires a recession.

    d. What alternative policy might be possible?

A8. What it does mean is that overall financial policy must be, and must be seen by a skeptical public to be, consistent with a continuing movement toward cost and price stability.

    a. What kind of monetary policy would be consistent with a continuing movement toward price stability?

    b. Why is it important that the public see this consistency?

A9. We cannot afford to take any major risks with inflation. If we let inflation get away on us again, even for just a while, the path back to price stability will be even more painful than it has been during the last few years.

    a. What is meant by a painful path?

    b. Why would letting inflation get away for only a while require a painful return?

A10. On the other hand, there was a singular economic success in the past decade: a rampant inflation was curbed, albeit at the cost of _____, and Federal Reserve actions to keep the flow of money into the economy at moderate levels have kept the lid on since.

    a. How do you think the inflation was curbed?

    b. Fill in the blank.

    c. Explain how keeping the flow of money into the economy at moderate levels keeps the lid on inflation.

    d. What would you guess this moderate level to be?

A11. Stockman told the U.S. Chamber of Commerce that "high interest rates, unacceptable levels of current unemployment, lost output, financial strains, and the

rising bankruptcies in the economy are all unpleasant facts of life but are all part of the cure, not the problem."

Explain how these things could be part of the cure, not the problem.

A12. The civilian unemployment rate has declined nearly two percentage points in the past two years and now stands at 5.25 percent, the lowest rate in ten years. Many worry that because this rate is below the sustainable "natural" rate of unemployment. . . .

Complete this clipping.

A13. Many economists applaud increased unemployment and lower growth as a necessary evil.

Explain what is meant here by a necessary evil.

A14. Despite the inflationary pressures that remained when he took office, President Jimmy Carter was reluctant to mount a strong anti-inflation program lest it interfere with his commitment to. . . .

Complete this clipping.

A15. Most estimates suggest that America's natural rate of unemployment is around 6 percent, only slightly higher than it was in the 1960s. Since the current jobless rate is 6.1 percent, this suggests that the Fed was right to push up interest rates this spring—and may even have acted a bit too late.

Explain the rationale behind why the Fed was right to push up interest rates.

A16. Are too many Americans at work these days for the economy's own good? Absolutely, says Martin Feldstein, former head of the Council of Economic Advisors. By his calculations, unemployment has already fallen way below the level he believes is sure to trigger _____.

a. Fill in the blank.

b. What do economists call this level of unemployment?

A17. Inflation expectations are quite well anchored, giving the Federal Reserve Board breathing room for further possible rate cuts.

What is the rationale behind this statement?

A18. Core prices, as measured by the Fed's preferred index based on personal consumption expenditures, are up 2.5 percent over the past year, above the Bernanke comfort zone of 1 to 2 percent.

What are the implications for monetary policy of going above this comfort zone?

A19. Policy makers are performing a balancing act, trying to bring inflation down without. . . .

Complete this clipping.

A20. Unless the economy slows more than the Fed now expects, the central bank might need to _____ sooner rather than later to control inflation.

Fill in the missing part of this statement.

A21. Canada's unemployment rate fell to its lowest level in thirty years in October, fueling fear of _____ and adding to the pressure for _____ from the Bank of Canada.

Fill in the blanks in this clipping.

A22. Federal Reserve chairman Ben Bernanke said inflation should ease later this year and in 2009, while warning that policy makers will act if price increases don't slow over the "medium term."

What action would the Fed take if price increases did not slow?

A23. U.S. consumer price inflation is receding, a development that gives the Federal Reserve additional leeway to _____ in the weeks ahead should it be needed, a likely scenario.

Fill in the blank and explain what role inflation is playing.

A24. But one bright spot was a sign that U.S. inflation is in check, and economists said that trend, combined with a soft job market, will give the Fed room to. . . .

a. Complete this statement.

b. Explain what inflation and a soft job market have to do with this.

A25. The Fed took a somewhat more hawkish view of inflation than it did in the March statement. Today's statement made specific reference to inflationary pressures, saying that energy and other commodity prices have increased, an acknowledgment absent from the March statement.

a. What does a "more hawkish view" of inflation mean?

b. What implication does this have for the monetary policy we can expect to see from the Fed?

A26. As the election draws nearer, the prospect of an economy awash in money becomes likely. It is therefore reassuring that the central bank remains vigilant about the dangers of inflation.

Why would the proximity of an election affect money creation?

A27. America's Fed, though one of the world's most independent central banks, also faces the dilemma of potentially conflicting objectives of low inflation and low unemployment. Having such dual objectives almost guarantees that inflation will be higher.

Why would dual objectives make more difficult the task of controlling inflation?

A28. Beset by low productivity growth, spiraling oil prices, and declining international competitiveness, Jimmy Carter adopted a policy of low interest rates, economic expansion, and dollar depreciation. Its problem was that this policy generated. . . .

Complete this clipping.

A29. Many politicians say they favor low interest rates but believe in their hearts that higher rates are necessary to control. . . .

Complete this clipping.

A30. The government made the biggest blunder. Between 1985 and 1989 the Bank of Japan (Japan's Fed) kept interest rates too low.

How could keeping interest rates too low be a mistake?

A31. Even some Fed critics are reluctant to change its structure. Mr. Feldstein warns that "substituting political judgments for economic judgments brings a built-in bias toward _____."

Fill in the blank and explain your reasoning.

A32. The truth is that recessions are almost always policy-induced. They are the product not of time or chance but of government action. They are almost always policy-induced because they almost always follow hard upon an outbreak of inflation. And inflation is always the result of government policy, namely _____. Why did governments in the modern era pursue inflationary policies?

a. Fill in the blank.

b. Why might governments pursue inflationary policies?

c. Exactly what is meant here by a policy-induced recession? How is it brought about, and why?

A33. **There is little doubt that the key reason for this slide toward ever more inflation was an effort by public policy in most countries to achieve and maintain more output and employment from their economies than was consistent with price stability.**

    a. What level of output and employment would be consistent with price stability?

    b. How would public policy be used to achieve more output and employment?

    c. Explain how doing so would create a "slide toward ever more inflation."

B1. **Nor will decrees of one percent cuts in interest rates bring anything but more inflation. Nor yet do grand spending programs "create" more jobs: they only redistribute them, from industry to industry, from region to region, from private sector to public sector.**

Explain how the contents of this clipping fit with modern macroeconomic theorizing.

B2. **We're not likely to see a really tight monetary policy. The governor of the central bank made clear that the central bank is following an "intentionally moderate" monetary policy in order to "minimize the strains involved in adjusting to a less inflationary economy." He points to the "awkward economic fact that in the short run anti-inflationary policies tend to restrain output more than prices."**

This is a good example of the way in which bureaucrats disguise harsh facts in flowery language. What is being said here, in blunt terms?

B3. **Moreover, if a policy is to be credible enough for workers, consumers, and investors to build their expectations upon it, then at the least it must appear feasible to them. Since the central bank has not achieved zero inflation in the postwar era, why should individuals believe in such a policy now? If a zero-inflation goal lacks credibility, then an attempt by the central bank to achieve it will. . . .**

Complete this clipping, and explain the rationale behind your thinking.

B4. **The traditional macroeconomic approach, flooding the whole economy with demand in the hope of floating any unemployed little boats, no longer applies. Unemployment today is more a matter of defective labor markets. So make labor markets work better.**

    a. With whose name is the traditional macroeconomic approach usually associated?

    b. Why is this traditional approach no longer applicable?

c. How does the policy prescribed in this clipping fit into modern macroeconomic theory?

B5. But he defended the slow, steady decline in interest rates beginning in the spring of 1989 as the best that could have been done, given the fear of future inflation—a fear that has until recently kept long-term interest rates high despite repeated cuts in short-term rates by the Fed.

a. Explain why a faster fall in interest rates was not advisable.

b. How does fear of inflation prevent long-term interest rates from following short-term rates?

B6. "Walk, don't run" is the message from the monetary authorities. Clearly, their thinking is that what the economy needs now is not a speedy recovery from recession, but one that is slow, drawn out, and, in many respects, painful.

What rationale could lie behind this thinking?

B7. For example, price control policies have been tried on several occasions and in a number of countries, including Canada and the United States. The U.S. program, which was adopted in the second half of 1971, partly suspended the market system, producing distortion and shortages while suppressing inflation instead of resolving it.

a. What is the difference between suppressing inflation and resolving it?

b. What is it about the U.S. policy that probably caused the suppression phenomenon?

B8. The Fed has always acknowledged openly that disinflation involved employment costs. A key message in its officials' speeches during disinflation was that the employment consequences would be reduced once wage and price setters realized that it was absolutely committed to lowering inflation.

a. Explain why disinflation (a reduction in inflation) involves employment costs.

b. Explain the role of wage and price setters in reducing these costs.

B9. As well, the chairman of the Fed had come to represent what many liberals regard as a policy-induced recession.

What is a policy-induced recession?

B10. Some economists said the declining unemployment rate partly explains why the central bank has been pursuing a restrictive monetary policy for more than a year.

Explain the logic behind this thinking.

B11. For example, the upward shift in the Phillips curve that occurred in the early 1970s followed several years in which policy makers allowed money growth to accelerate in an (ultimately vain) attempt to keep _____. The downward shift in the mid 1980s occurred only after policy makers demonstrated that they were willing to _____ to move the inflation rate lower.

Fill in the blanks.

B12. But increasingly there does seem to be agreement on one point, namely that the advancing share of governments in the economy has been strongly inflationary. This is mainly because individuals and companies have not been prepared to pay (through taxes) for extra public services or income redistribution and have instead demanded bigger and bigger income increases to offset the tax and keep real incomes growing.

a. The argument presented here is not the usual argument claiming government deficits are inflationary. What is the usual argument?

b. How would you exposit the argument in this clipping on a Phillips-curve diagram?

B13. The employment numbers were a bit of a shocker, but the market isn't that concerned about inflation because of the potential for Asian weakness to slow the U.S. economy.

a. What must the unemployment numbers have shown?

b. How would Asian weakness alleviate fears of U.S. inflation?

B14. A striking feature of the economy's performance over the past four years is how well behaved inflation has been despite tight labor markets. This experience has led some analysts to declare the Phillips curve dead! One response is to argue that the Phillips curve is not dead, merely. . . .

Complete this clipping.

B15. American businesses created 262,000 new jobs last month, and unemployment fell to an astoundingly low 4.3 percent, a level not seen since February 1970. And still, remarkably, no sign of _____. All this good news is worrying, even befuddling, many economists.

a. Fill in the blank.

b. Why would this good news worry and befuddle economists?

B16. It is economists who repeat their own mistakes because their calculations are looking at the world through a rearview mirror. Business leaders describe the

change in two words: productivity and competition. Both, they say, wring out inflation and enable them to increase production and hire more people without raising wages, and without putting pressure on their own prices.

What economist mistake during the late 1990s is this clipping talking about?

B17. **Just 21,000 new jobs were created in February, compared with forecasts for 125,000, marking another month in which economic growth failed to translate into strong hiring. _____ allows companies to lift output without boosting payrolls, leaving slack in the economy to keep wages in check and allowing the Fed to view inflation as a distant risk despite powerful growth.**

a. Fill in the blank.

b. Exactly what policy implications does this have for Fed monetary policy?

B18. **The main reason the U.S. experienced very little inflation in the late 90s, despite full employment and low interest rates, was because. . . .**

Complete this clipping.

B19. **The governor of the central bank responded by saying that there is nothing in the experience of any country that would suggest that monetary policy can produce sustainable decreases in unemployment beyond those that can be achieved by maintaining stable prices.**

Explain the rationale behind this view.

B20. **The message from the central bank to the private sector is: Do not give in to inflationary psychology, Do not assume that you can easily accommodate cost pressures, and Do not expect monetary accommodation of accelerating energy price increases.**

a. What is meant by "assume that you can easily accommodate cost pressures"?

b. What is meant by "monetary accommodation of accelerating energy price increases"?

B21. **Mr. Blair gave the unfortunate impression of swallowing without too much demur a new consensus that central banks should concern themselves with jobs as well as _____ and that governments should create new jobs by means of large infrastructure investments.**

a. What kind of policy is referred to at the end of this clip?

b. Fill in the blank.

c. The author of this clip uses the word "unfortunate" to indicate that she does not agree with the new consensus among European leaders. What would be her rationale?

B22. What is important for inflationary expectations is how the bank has responded to such shocks in the past. A central bank that has shown it will not accommodate inflationary shocks will find it much easier to maintain a stable inflation rate—whatever its level—than one with a reputation for accommodation.

a. What does "accommodate inflationary shocks" mean?

b. Explain why a central bank with a reputation for not accommodating inflationary shocks will find it easier to maintain a stable inflation rate.

B23. By tying the pay of the governor of the central bank to his success in keeping inflation below 2 percent, New Zealand has succeeded in keeping inflation low. Now there are calls to tie the pay of the minister of employment to his success in keeping unemployment below 2 percent.

Comment on the wisdom of this proposal.

B24. According to one theory, the U.S. recession–inflation debate boils down to whether the natural unemployment rate is higher or lower than the current 5.7 percent level.

a. What is the theory being referred to?

b. The debate is about what policy is appropriate. Explain the role in this debate of the natural rate.

Numerical Exercises

AN1. Suppose that the short-run Phillips curve is such that a two percentage point increase in inflation decreases unemployment by one percentage point. Say the economy is in equilibrium with a real growth rate of 2 percent and an unemployment rate of 7 percent and the central bank increases the rate of growth of the money supply from 5 to 8 percent. When the economy has reached its new equilibrium, what will be the levels of inflation and unemployment?

AN2. The Bank of Canada's battle to cut inflation to 2.0 percent from 5.0 percent cost the Canadian economy $105 billion in lost production, says a new study. If Canada's full-employment level of output is $700 billion, what is its sacrifice ratio?

BN1. Suppose that the economy is at its natural rate of unemployment of 6 percent, but policy makers plan to reduce inflation from 7 percent to 4 percent gradually over a period of three years by creating a recession. If the sacrifice ratio is 5,

    a. Relative to maintaining full employment, what is the cumulative loss in output this recession will entail?

    b. What steady level of unemployment over these three years should accomplish this goal? Hint: Use Okun's law.

BN2. Suppose that person A forms his inflation expectations as the average of this period's inflation and last period's inflation, whereas person B forms her expectations rationally (i.e., by using all information plus knowledge of how the macroeconomy operates). Say the economy is in equilibrium at its NRU and the Fed surreptitiously increases the money growth rate from 6 to 7.5 percent, increasing inflation during the year from 4 to 4.5 percent and lowering unemployment slightly. At the end of this year it becomes clear what the Fed has done; at this point,

    a. What is A's expected inflation?

    b. What is B's expected inflation?

Appendix 12.1   The Real Cause of Inflation

At one time economists classified inflation into two types: (1) *demand-pull inflation* is generated by excess demand for goods and services pulling up prices, and (2) *cost-push inflation* is generated by higher costs—such as energy price increases imposed by an oil cartel or wage increases demanded by powerful labor unions—being passed on in higher prices by monopoly firms. Currently this classification is seldom used, except in classifying short-run forces affecting prices. In the long run neither type of inflation can be sustained without an accommodating growth in the money supply.

If the central bank does not accommodate demand-pull and cost-push price increases with accompanying increases in the money supply, the demand for money grows faster than the supply of money. The resulting excess demand for money pushes up the interest rate and decreases aggregate demand for goods and services, killing the inflationary forces. Consequently economists have come to view the cause of inflation as excessive money-supply growth, agreeing with the monetarist view that in the long run inflation is always and everywhere a monetary phenomenon.

Surely, though, the real cause of inflation is what is causing the central bank to increase the money supply at an excessive rate! The purpose of this appendix is to consolidate material from earlier chapters that lend insight to this issue. A common theme is that central banks pursued a policy that at first appeared not to involve a loss of control of the money supply, but in retrospect clearly did.

Underestimating the NRU

Suppose that the central bank has chosen to target monetary policy on the NRU so that, whenever unemployment departs from its natural rate, monetary policy reacts by pushing it back. A problem with this approach is that the NRU is never known. It must be estimated, and it can easily be underestimated. One reason for underestimation is that many politicians find it difficult to believe that the natural rate can be so high and, consequently, continually bring pressure to bear on the central bank to lower unemployment.

Suppose that the economy is at the NRU, but the central bank does not realize this and thinks that the NRU is lower. An expansionary monetary policy will be undertaken to push down unemployment, creating some unexpected inflation. The unexpected inflation causes the real wage to fall, either because workers are slow to realize what has happened or because of contract obligations that prevent immediate adjustment of wages. The fall in the real wage induces firms to increase output. After a time, however, inflation expectations increase and contracts are renegotiated, restoring the real wage to its original level and moving the economy back to the true natural rate. This situation prompts the central bank to increase its stimulation in order to keep the economy below the NRU, thereby accelerating the inflationary forces and causing this process to be repeated. The economy is prevented from moving back to its actual NRU, but at a cost of an accelerating inflation. By targeting on an underestimate of the NRU, the central bank could lose control of the money supply.

Reaction to a Negative Supply Shock

There are two ways in which a negative supply shock can lead to an inappropriate central bank policy:

1. A negative supply shock makes the economy less productive, causing the level of national output/income to fall, even if the level of unemployment does not change. If the government does not recognize this fact and thinks instead that the decrease in income reflects a cyclical downturn, it may use monetary policy to stimulate the economy. The policy of targeting on the income level would then create a situation very similar to that described earlier for targeting on the unemployment rate. Stimulation will be successful in the short run but not in the longer run because the situation will require further stimulation and an acceleration of inflation will take place. By targeting on the pre–supply-shock level of output, the central bank could lose control of the money supply.

2. A negative supply shock decreases the productivity of labor. Firms cannot afford to hire as many workers at the prevailing real wage, so unemployment develops unless the real wage falls to reflect the lower productivity of labor. If the real wage is prevented from falling—by strong labor unions, for example, or a national labor contract expressed in real terms—the economy will become stuck at a level of unemployment above the natural rate. The central bank could misread this unemployment level as a cyclical phenomenon and adopt a stimulating dose of monetary policy. The result is similar to that given earlier for targeting on an underestimate of the NRU. As long as the real wage is artificially held too high, this policy will accelerate the inflation. By targeting on the pre–supply-shock unemployment rate, the central bank could lose control of the money supply.

Fixing the Nominal Interest Rate

It has been common for central banks to adopt a policy of targeting on or fixing the nominal interest rate. Under this policy a shock to the monetary sector that causes a rise in the interest rate would prompt the central bank to push the interest rate back down by increasing the money supply. The increase in the money supply may cause people to revise expected inflation upward, a revision reinforced by any actual price increases created by the extra money, which are likely to occur if the economy is near full employment. Higher expected inflation increases the nominal interest rate. Any success the central bank has in pushing down the nominal interest rate will be temporary and likely to be more than offset by a rise in expected inflation. This rise in the interest rate prompts the central bank to increase again the money supply to meet its target interest rate, thus leading to a vicious circle. By targeting on the interest rate, the central bank loses control of the money supply.

Financing Government Spending

Countries with military dictatorships or with central banks that lack independence from politicians sometimes finance a large portion of government spending by printing money. This is a tempting option for any government faced with a budget deficit because printing money reduces interest costs and achieves the political end of avoiding higher taxes. Too much of this financing, however, creates inflation. A central bank that promises to finance government budget deficits loses control of the money supply.

Repeating the Political Business Cycle

When the central bank is not independent, politicians can and do pump up the money supply shortly before an election to buy votes with lower interest rates and a lower unemployment rate. After the election, however, these short-run effects wear off, returning the economy to its natural rate of unemployment but at a higher inflation rate and a higher nominal interest rate. Because of the asymmetry of the Phillips curve, it is often the case that by the time the next election rolls around the economy has not been squeezed back to its original inflation rate, so the next round of politically induced money-supply increases start from a higher base. As this cycle repeats itself, the central bank loses control of the money supply.

Fixing the Exchange Rate

As explained more fully in chapter 14, fixing the exchange rate causes an economy's money supply to grow at the money-supply growth rate that characterizes its major trading partners. In effect monetary policy must be devoted to fixing the exchange rate, so control over money growth is lost. Suppose, for example, that our rate of inflation is 5 percent and that of our trading partners is 15 percent. If we fix the exchange rate, each year our goods become 10 percent less expensive to foreigners, and foreign goods become 10 percent more expensive to us. We soon experience a dramatic increase in our exports and a decrease in our imports, producing a surplus of foreign currency in the hands of our citizens. When the central bank exchanges the foreign currency for dollars at the fixed rate, these dollars increase the domestic money supply. By targeting on the exchange rate the central bank loses control over the money supply.

Media Illustrations

Example 1

The Federal Reserve Bank Act of 1978 requires the Fed to pursue full employment as well as low inflation, but Mr. Greenspan has said that he favors legislation to make price stability the Fed's sole objective.

Why might the chairman of the Fed prefer to have price stability as his sole objective? Using monetary policy to achieve a specific unemployment rate could cause the Fed to lose control over the money supply, with consequent disaster for the inflation goal. The Fed would argue that that monetary policy is capable of achieving only one objective, and since money growth is so strongly related to inflation, it seems reasonable to make inflation the primary goal of the monetary authority.

Example 2

But monetary policy cannot be tuned to real economic variables like growth or employment, not only because policy takes effect with long and uncertain lags but because any commitment to real growth targets simply invites workers and business to increase wages and prices at will, in the knowledge that the central bank will "ratify" their demands via the money supply.

What is meant by commitment to a real growth target?

The government has promised to maintain the economy at a specified level of unemployment. This implies a steady real growth as the labor force grows.

What is meant by the central bank ratifying demands for higher wages and prices?

Higher prices and wages cause the demand for money to exceed the supply of money. This excess demand for money causes demand for goods and services to fall, decreasing the level of economic activity. This decline cuts into business profits and causes layoffs. So, in general, firms and workers will think twice about raising wages and prices. But if the central bank increases the money supply to prevent this unemployment, it has effectively said okay to the price and wage hikes, "ratifying" them.

Example 3

The realistic alternative to high interest rates is not lower interest rates (except temporarily) but even higher interest rates and a monetary inflation that would make our heads spin.

What monetary policy scenario does the author of this clip have in mind?

Suppose that the monetary authorities decide to target on a lower nominal rate of interest and increase the money supply to attain that rate. This increase in the money supply could raise inflation expectations, increasing the nominal rate. This causes the monetary authorities to renew their efforts to lower the interest rate to the target level. Accordingly they increase the money supply by even more, accelerating the inflation and continuing this vicious circle.

How does the "except temporarily" fit in?

Each increase in the money supply will decrease the interest rate in the short run. It is not until expectations of inflation increase that the interest rate rises.

What policy would you recommend to achieve a lower interest rate?

What is needed is a policy of cutting down on the rate of growth of the money supply to cut inflation and thereby to lower the nominal rate of interest. In the short run this causes a rise in the real (and nominal) interest rate, slowing economic activity. After a while inflation should fall to a lower level, lowering inflation expectations and allowing the nominal interest rate to fall.

Example 4

We at the Fed are frequently pressed by people to do things that would involve giving up control over money creation without any apparent recognition on their part that this is what they are asking. We, of course, have to refuse.

Give three examples of such requests.

A common request is for an immediate lowering of the interest rate. To do so would require increasing the money supply in ever-increasing quantities to outstrip people's expectations.

A second common request is to produce a rate of unemployment lower than the NRU. Doing so would require an accelerating inflation.

A third common request is to use monetary policy to fight a negative supply-side shock. Monetary policy is not able to undo the negative consequences of such a shock, so its use in this circumstance serves only to disrupt money-supply growth.

A fourth common request is to finance government deficits to avoid the higher interest rates they produce. Doing so would mean that the government deficit would determine the money growth rate.

13   The Balance of Payments

Economies in which foreign trade plays a prominent role are said to be "open." Macroeconomic analysis of such economies requires that considerable attention be paid to economic forces generated by the interaction of this economy with its major trading partners—for convenience, usually referred to collectively as "the rest of the world." Individuals voluntarily engage in international trade because doing so allows them to enjoy a higher standard of living. How this comes about is explained in appendix 13.1 at the end of this chapter where the *principle of comparative advantage* is discussed. The rest of this chapter, and the following three chapters, examine the macroeconomic implications of international economic interactions.

Thirty years ago U.S. imports and exports were each only about 5 percent of GDP, so the United States was for many years considered a closed economy, the macro-economic analysis of which could safely ignore forces arising from the international dimension. Now both imports and exports are almost 15 percent of GDP, and although the United States is not nearly so strongly affected by international forces as is a small open economy such as Canada (in which imports and exports each comprise more than 25 percent of GDP), U.S. worries about the value of the U.S. dollar and a persistent trade deficit are persuasive testimonies to the need to include the role of international forces in our macroeconomic analysis. The advent of the global economy, the rise of multinational corporations, and the growth of speculative trading in international currencies underline this need. The most convincing factor from our perspective, however, is that it is currently impossible to analyze media commentary on the U.S. economy without a good understanding of the role played by international forces.

Integrating the international sector into macroeconomic analysis all at once can be overwhelming. To avoid this problem, our discussion of the international sector is divided into four short chapters. This chapter looks at the balance of payments, a summary measure of the foreign exchange market, which unifies analysis of the international sector of the economy.

Upon completion of this chapter you should

- ▪ view a country's balance of payments as a measure of disequilibrium in its international sector;
- ▪ know how the balance of payments, the balance of trade, the current account, and the capital account are interrelated; and
- ▪ understand a main reason for persistent trade deficits.

13.1   The Balance of Payments

An economy has two basic kinds of economic interactions with the rest of the world: buying and selling goods and services, and buying and selling assets, mainly financial assets. In the former category are imports and exports of physical goods, such as lumber and automobiles; imports and exports of services, such as transportation and tourism; and payments for capital services, such as interest and dividend payments. The main components of the latter category are purchases or sales of bonds and common stock, and direct investment through purchase of businesses or real estate.

Each of these activities gives rise to a situation in which either foreigners wish to obtain our dollars or we wish to obtain foreign currency. The former is viewed as a demand for our dollars on the *foreign exchange market*, and the latter is viewed as a supply of our dollars on this market (because we bring our dollars to this market to get foreign currency).

For example, exports of either goods or services creates a demand for our dollars as those buying the exports seek dollars to pay for them (or, if they pay with foreign currency, as we seek to convert that currency into our dollars). Imports, on the other hand, cause us to supply dollars to the foreign exchange market as we seek foreign currency to pay for these imports. If foreigners wish to buy our bonds, a demand for our dollar is created. If we wish to buy foreign bonds, we supply dollars to the foreign exchange market to obtain the foreign currency to pay for the bonds.

The balance of payments is the difference between the sum of all the demands for and all the supplies of our dollar on the foreign exchange market. Any purchases or sales of dollars on this market by a government, typically undertaken by its central bank, are not counted because they are thought to be artificial, rather than reflecting the true forces of supply and demand. If the total number of dollars supplied is equal to the total number of dollars demanded, the result is a zero balance of payments. In this case the international sector of the economy is said to be in balance or in "equilibrium," and no economic forces for change arise from the international sector.

A *balance of payments surplus* occurs when the demand for our dollars on the foreign exchange market exceeds the supply. A *balance of payments deficit* is the opposite—a situation where the supply of dollars exceeds its demand. Be careful here! In most supply and demand diagrams a surplus occurs when supply exceeds demand. If you wish, think of a balance of payments surplus as a surplus of foreign currency flowing into our country.

> **Sample Exam Question 13.1:**
> Suppose that during the year the government bought $6 billion of U.S. dollars on the foreign exchange market. What must the balance of payments have been?

13.2   Determinants of Foreign Exchange Market Activity

Balance of payments surpluses and deficits arise from changes in the supply of and demand for our dollar on the foreign exchange market. Several variables affect supply and demand activity in this market:

1. *Exchange rate.* The price or value of our dollar in terms of foreign exchange, called the *exchange rate*, is determined in the foreign exchange market. If, for example, a dollar can buy thirteen Mexican pesos, the exchange rate is thirteen pesos per dollar. A balance of payments surplus means that demand for our dollar on the foreign exchange market exceeds its supply, so the price of the dollar (the exchange rate) will be bid up, say to fourteen pesos per dollar. The dollar is now more valuable; it buys fourteen instead of thirteen pesos. This stronger dollar makes imports cheaper for U. S. citizens, so imports increase—thus increasing the supply of dollars on the foreign

> **Curiosity 13.1: Where Is the Foreign Exchange Market?**
>
> The foreign exchange market is the largest financial market in the world, with a trading volume of about 4 trillion dollars per day. The vast majority of these trades are undertaken for speculative purposes (only about 5 percent of trades are to finance exports and imports), with the average size of a trade in the millions of dollars. About 86 percent of these trades involve the U.S. dollar, about 37 percent involve the euro, 16 percent the yen, 15 percent the pound, 7 percent the swiss franc, 7 percent the Australian dollar, and 4 percent the Canadian dollar. This market does not have any single location—trades are made by phone or electronically in several markets around the world at all hours of the day. About 34 percent of the trading takes place in the United Kingdom, about 17 percent takes place in the United States, and about 6 percent in Japan.

exchange market. Similarly our exports are more expensive to foreigners so exports fall, decreasing the demand for dollars on the foreign exchange market. This way the rise in the exchange rate eliminates the balance of payments surplus. The opposite occurs when we have a balance of payments deficit: the exchange rate falls to eliminate the deficit.

2. *Income.* At a higher level of income, we import more. As a result our supply of dollars on the foreign exchange market increases, creating a balance of payments deficit and downward pressure on the exchange rate. Note that this result assumes that our rise in income is unique to us; it is not part of a worldwide boom. If other countries' incomes are increasing at the same time, then our exports should also increase, making uncertain the net effect on our balance of payments and exchange rate.

   Another impact of income on the balance of payments is somewhat speculative in nature but, remarkably, usually strong enough to more than offset the effect of higher imports, in part because any change in imports takes time to appear. A rise in our income indicates that we are enjoying prosperity, leading everyone to believe that business here will be more profitable. This causes foreigners to buy stock in our corporations, anticipating that our stock prices will rise to reflect our expected higher profitability. To buy more of our stock foreigners must obtain more of our dollars—the demand for our dollars on the foreign exchange market increases.

3. *Interest rate.* When our interest rate is higher, foreigners are more interested in buying our financial assets, so they demand more of our dollars on the foreign exchange market. This demand creates *capital inflows*, a balance of payments surplus, and upward pressure on the exchange rate. Two caveats concerning capital inflows are important. First, the result depends on the interest rate increase not being part of a worldwide pattern. If interest rates throughout the world rise, the fact that our interest rate is higher should not entice foreigners to switch to our bonds. Second, the relevant difference in interest rates is the difference in real interest rates, not nominal interest rates; investors are concerned with real returns. For more on this topic, see chapter 16.

4. *Price level.* A rise in our price level increases the price of our exports and the price of import-competing goods and services, so our exports fall and our imports rise. As a result the demand for our dollars decreases, and the supply of our dollars increases, creating a balance of payments deficit and downward pressure on the exchange rate. Again, such effects occur only if there is no equivalent price increase in the rest of the world.

5. *Relative prices.* Changes in the prices of things we export relative to the prices of things we import can have a big impact on the supply and demand for our dollar on the foreign exchange market. Suppose that the world price of things we export increases markedly. Then even if the total quantity of our physical exports remains unchanged, the value of our exports increases, increasing the demand for our dollar on the foreign exchange market. A change of this nature is called a change in our "terms of trade." For Canada, a country that exports a lot of commodities like oil, gas, lumber, wheat, and minerals,

Curiosity 13.2: Why Is There More Than One Exchange Rate?

There are two ways of measuring the exchange rate between U.S. dollars and Mexican pesos. Earlier we defined it as the number of pesos per dollar, 13 pesos per dollar. Alternatively, we could have defined it as the number of dollars per peso, or 0.077 dollars per peso (i.e., a peso is worth about 8 U.S. cents). These are equivalent ways of expressing the exchange rate: one is just the inverse of the other. Both measures appear in the media. This book uses the former because when that measure of the exchange rate increases—to 14 pesos per dollar, for example—the dollar becomes more valuable. With the latter measure, however, an increase in the exchange rate corresponds to a fall in the value of the dollar.

If the exchange rate is 13 pesos per dollar and also 104 Japanese yen per dollar, it may appear that there is more than one exchange rate, but the exchange rate between pesos and yen should be 13 pesos per 104 yen (i.e., 8 yen per peso), implying that both measures of the value of the dollar are equivalent. Suppose that this were not the case, and the peso/yen exchange rate was 9 yen per peso. People could make easy money by using 100 dollars to buy 1,300 pesos, using the 1,300 pesos to buy 9 * 1,300 = 11,700 yen, and then using the 11,700 yen to buy 11,700/104 = 112.50 dollars. This "arbitrage" activity serves to make all exchange rates consistent with one another.

whose prices are determined on world markets, an increase in commodity prices will have a big impact on the value of Canada's exports and so on demand for her dollar. (Of course, if commodity prices fell because the world entered a worldwide recession, the opposite would occur—the demand for Canada's dollar would fall.)

6. *Expectations.* If foreigners expect the value of the dollar to rise, they can reap a capital gain by buying our bonds and then selling them again after the exchange rate has risen. This speculation creates an inflow of capital, a balance of payments surplus, and upward pressure on the exchange rate. Such speculative funds are available in large amounts and can be moved very quickly from one currency to another. Speculative activity is indeed the primary determinant of exchange rates in the short run. Daily volume on the foreign exchange market is about $1 trillion, the bulk of which is speculative.

To summarize, several factors influence activity in the foreign exchange market. The balance of payments summarizes this activity, telling us whether the market is in disequilibrium, in what direction, and by how much, allowing us to predict economic forces for change (see chapter 14).

Sample Exam Question 13.2:

"Now it's the once-mighty German mark's turn to come under attack. Following Thursday's cuts in the Bundesbank's trend-setting interest rates, the mark slipped further against the pound and the U.S. dollar."

Explain why the mark is falling here. (Note: The German mark is no more, having been displaced by the euro in 1999.)

13.3   The International Economic Accounts

Knowledge of the balance of payments is all that is needed for analysis of the economic forces that automatically are set in motion whenever there is a disequilibrium in the international sector of the economy. Often, however, analysts are interested in the source of any disequilibrium in the international sector, that is, the relative contributions to an equilibrium position of the various components of the demand for and supply of dollars on the foreign exchange market. Consequently the balance of payments is broken down into several subsidiary measures, which together are referred to as the *international accounts* or the *balance of payments accounts*.

At the most general level, the balance of payments is broken into two accounts, the current and capital accounts, as shown in table 13.1.

Table 13.1   Balance of Payments, 2007 ($ billions)

	Demand for U.S. dollars	Supply of U.S. dollars	Balance
Current account			
Merchandise exports	1148		
Merchandise imports		−1968	
Merchandise trade balance			−820
Service exports	497		
Service imports		−378	
Services balance			119
Balance of trade			−701
Income receipts	818		
Income payments		−736	
Net transfer payments		−113	
Current account balance			−732
Capital account			
Capital inflows	2063		
Capital outflows		−1290	
Statistical discrepancy		−41	
Capital account balance			732
Current account plus capital account (balance of payments)			0.122
Official settlements balance (negative of the balance of payments)		−0.122	

Source: Economic Report of the President 2009. www.gpoaccess.gov/eop/.

The *current account* measures the difference between the demand for and the supply of dollars arising from transactions that affect the current level of income here and abroad. It has three components:

1. The *trade balance,* or *balance on goods and services,* which is the sum of the following:

   a. The *merchandise trade balance,* the difference between exports and imports of goods (e.g., wheat and automobiles).

   b. The *services trade balance,* the difference between exports and imports of services (e.g., insurance, transportation, banking, and tourism).

2. *Net investment income from abroad*, such as interest and dividend payments.

3. *Net transfers from abroad*, such as gifts, pension payments, and foreign aid.

Typically the United States has a deficit on merchandise trade—it imports more goods than it exports—but a surplus on service trade—it exports more services than it imports. (This surplus reflects U.S. comparative advantage in services, see appendix 13.1.) Overall, the U.S. balance of trade is usually in deficit.

In the late 1980s the United States became an international debtor and began sending substantial interest payments abroad each year. Consequently recent annual U.S. net investment payments have typically been in deficit. Net transfer payments also are typically in deficit because the United States sends more humanitarian and military aid abroad than it receives. An exception occurred in 1991 when other countries transferred funds to the United States to pay their share of the U.S. military operation against Iraq.

Curiosity 13.3: How Do We Know the Statistical Discrepancy?

In table 13.1 the statistical discrepancy entry is quite small, but in most years it is actually quite large. Big discrepancies are in fact quite common because the government is unable to monitor closely the movement of dollars across its borders. Cross-border shopping, for example, is not tracked accurately, and illegal cross-border activities can be of significant magnitude.

An interesting question here is how the international accounts statistician could possibly provide a measure of this statistical discrepancy. The reason is that the final figure for the balance of payments is known. The final figure is accurately measured by the net amount of buying or selling of foreign currency by the Fed, plus changes in foreign central bank dollar holdings in the United States. Thus, in order to measure the statistical discrepancy, all that needs be done is to subtract the sum of the current and capital accounts from total official transactions.

An unresolvable problem is that it cannot be known how much of the statistical discrepancy belongs to the current account and how much to the capital account. By tradition, it is included in the capital account on the belief that most hidden transactions take the form of capital flows.

Because the trade balance is large and volatile relative to net factor payments and net transfers, the trade balance is the prime determinant of the current account and for this reason is the focus of attention in the popular press. In recent years the trade balance and the current account have been in deficit. A deficit on the current account is typically offset by a surplus on the capital account.

The *capital account* measures the difference between the demand for and the supply of dollars arising from sales or purchases of assets to or from foreigners. When a Canadian buys a U.S. bond, for example, a demand for U.S. dollars is created. The capital account measures *capital flows* between a country and the rest of the world. A capital account surplus measures a net capital inflow, and a capital account deficit measures a net capital outflow.

When added together, the current and capital accounts produce the balance of payments. In an accounting sense, because the demand for and supply of dollars on the foreign exchange market must balance, a nonzero balance of payments must be matched by changes in government holdings of foreign exchange reserves. In table 13.1 there is a $0.122 billion balance of payments surplus (for expositional purposes not rounded to zero in table 13.1)—that is, an excess demand of $0.122 billion dollars on the foreign exchange market. This is matched by a $0.122 million supply of dollars by the U.S. central bank on the foreign exchange market; the Fed should accumulate $0.122 billion in foreign exchange reserves in meeting this excess demand for dollars. The *official settlements account* measures the accumulation of domestic dollars in the foreign exchange reserve account of the Fed. Central banks' demands for dollars are not included in the balance of payments because they do not represent free-market forces. The economist's concept of the balance of payments can be measured by the negative of the official settlements balance.

Warning! Some textbook treatments of the balance of payments present the accounting view—the balance of payments always balances. This is unfortunate because it hides the fact that the balance of payments measures disequilibrium in the international sector— the difference between the free-market forces of demand for and supply of dollars on the foreign exchange market.

Sample Exam Question 13.3:
"Everyone loves the U.S. dollar these days, and the fall in the current account deficit just added to its popularity."
    Why would a fall in the current account deficit make the dollar more popular?

$\uparrow$ G or $\downarrow$ taxes $\Rightarrow$ budget deficit
$\Rightarrow$ government sells bonds
$\Rightarrow$ $\uparrow$ interest rate
$\Rightarrow$ $\uparrow$ capital inflows
$\Rightarrow$ $\uparrow$ exchange rate
$\Rightarrow$ $\downarrow$ exports and $\uparrow$ imports
$\Rightarrow$ balance of trade deficit

Figure 13.1   How Budget Deficits Cause Trade Deficits

13.4   The Twin Deficits

An interesting aspect of the balance of payments accounts is that it is quite possible to have an economy in international equilibrium while simultaneously its subsidiary accounts are unbalanced, as long as they offset each other. The U.S. economy, for example, for several years had a current account deficit that was offset by a surplus in its capital account. (This is not necessarily a bad thing—all that is happening is that we are borrowing from foreigners to finance some current spending. The key thing, as in the case of budget deficits discussed in an earlier chapter, is what is this extra spending, consumption or investment?)

How might this situation come about? A prominent explanation is that it is a side effect of large government budget deficits—hence termed the *twin deficit* problem. A large government deficit increases the interest rate as the government sells bonds to finance its deficit. This rise in the interest rate makes U.S. bonds look very attractive to overseas investors, so capital flows into the United States, creating a balance of payments surplus. This bids up the value of the dollar, which in turn decreases exports and increases imports, creating a balance of trade deficit. This process is illustrated in figure 13.1.

Readers with good memories might recall from chapter 7 that foreign financing can be used to supplement national saving. That is exactly what is happening here.

> **Sample Exam Question 13.4:**
> "The U.S. trade deficit is not permanent. When the United States ceases to be a major importer of capital . . .".
> Complete this argument explaining why the U.S. trade deficit will disappear.

Media Illustrations

Example 1

Looking at the data, some people might say the balance of payments has "improved" radically, from a $7 billion current account deficit three years ago to surpluses of $4

billion and $2 billion in the last two years. It is this ongoing current account surplus that led the optimists to predict that the dollar should appreciate.

What is the logic of this thinking?

The logic is that the improvement in the current account causes a balance of payments surplus (an excess demand for the dollar on the foreign exchange market), which under a flexible exchange rate system should lead to a rise in the value of the dollar.

What problem is there with this logic?

It is careless to identify a change in any subsidiary account of the balance of payments with a change in the balance of payments itself. It could be, for example, that there has been a fall in the capital account offsetting the impact on the balance of payments of the improvement in the current account.

Example 2

The link between the current and capital accounts is often misunderstood. Leaving aside the relatively small influence of central bank intervention in foreign exchange markets, any deficit or surplus on capital account must be matched by an equal and opposite surplus or deficit on current account. It follows that as long as the United States is to be a capital importer, it must have. . . .

To what does the central bank intervention refer?

It refers to net purchases or sales of foreign currency by the central bank.

What is the implication for the balance of payments of this central bank intervention being very small?

The implication is that the balance of payments is essentially zero. The magnitude of the balance of payments is measured by the net government sales or purchases of foreign currency.

What is the logic behind why any deficit or surplus on capital account must be matched by an equal and opposite surplus or deficit on current account?

If the balance of payments is zero, then the sum of the current and capital accounts, which yields the balance of payments, must be zero.

How would you complete the final sentence?

. . . a current account deficit.

Example 3

While some in the United States put the trade deficit down to failing U.S. competitiveness or protectionist policies abroad, some economists claim that its genesis lies in the budget deficit, and the consequent shortfall in U.S. domestic savings relative to investment.

How would failing competitiveness or protectionist policies abroad lead to a trade deficit?

Failing competitiveness means that foreign competitors are underpricing U.S. businesses both abroad and at home, decreasing U.S. exports and increasing U.S. imports, both of which create a trade deficit. Protectionist policies abroad means that foreign tariffs or quotas inhibit or prevent U.S. exports, creating a trade deficit.

How would a budget deficit lead to a shortfall in domestic savings relative to investment?

To finance the deficit, the government would sell bonds, diverting domestic savings from financing private investment.

How could the budget deficit be responsible for the trade deficit?

The budget deficit causes the interest rate to rise, making U.S. bonds attractive to foreign investors. To get U.S. dollars to buy U.S. bonds, foreigners bid up the value of the U.S. dollar. A higher dollar value causes U.S. exports to become more expensive to foreigners and imports to become cheaper to Americans. In turn exports fall and imports rise, creating the trade deficit.

What connection is there between this example and the preceding example?

In this example the budget deficit induces capital inflows, creating a surplus on the capital account that must be offset by a deficit on the current account. This process reflects the result illustrated in the preceding example that a deficit or surplus on capital account must be matched by an equal and opposite surplus or deficit on current account.

What conclusion can be drawn about U.S. competitiveness?

The existence of the balance of trade deficit in this context does not point to unproductive U.S. business. All it says is that the exchange rate is too high to allow U.S. business to sell abroad at historical levels.

Chapter Summary

- The *balance of payments* is the difference between the demand for and supply of dollars on the foreign exchange market, so it measures disequilibrium in the international sector of the economy. Demand for dollars on the foreign exchange market arises from demand by foreigners for our exports or for our assets, particularly financial assets. Supply arises from our demand for imports or foreign assets.

- The *exchange rate* measures the price of our dollar in terms of foreign currency, determined by the forces of supply and demand in the *foreign exchange market*. The major variables influencing supply and demand in this market are income, the interest rate, the price level, relative prices of imports and exports, and expectations of the future exchange rate.

- The balance of payments account is broken into two halves, the *current account* measuring transactions affecting our current income and the *capital account* measuring purchases and sales of assets. The *balance of goods and services*, sometimes called the *balance of trade*, is a component of the current account measuring the difference between exports and imports of goods and services.

■ A popular explanation for past U.S. twin deficits is that the government budget deficit was responsible for the trade deficit. To finance a government deficit, the interest rate must rise. A higher interest rate creates capital inflows, bidding up the value of the dollar, thereby discouraging exports and encouraging imports, thus producing the trade deficit.

Media Exercises

(Group B questions require more thought.)

A1. **A strong dollar is a mixed blessing. It _____ the price of imports, thus inflation, and it makes trips to foreign countries for Americans. But it makes our exports _____.**

Fill in the blanks.

A2. **According to the trade report, the U.S. trade surplus with Western Europe more than quadrupled in 1991 to $16.13 billion from $4 billion in 1990. This partly reflected strong demand in Europe, combined with a _____ in the value of the dollar.**

Fill in the blank.

A3. **Analysts have warned for months that the trade gap would widen once consumer demand picks up.**

Explain why the gap would widen. Will it become a bigger surplus or a bigger deficit?

A4. **The report concludes that the recent strength in U.S. investment has been financed by domestic investors redirecting funds from foreign capital markets to U.S. capital markets. Thus increased demand for U.S. dollars isn't the reason for the strength of the U.S. dollar, but rather a decreased U.S. demand for foreign currencies.**

What could have caused U.S. investors to redirect their funds?

A5. **Also, through the mid-1980s the policies followed by the Reagan administration, particularly tight monetary policy combined with large government deficits, made the value of the dollar very high.**

How would these policies increase the value of the dollar?

A6. **He says an overvalued dollar would be just another blow to an already fragile economy.**

Explain how an overvalued dollar would be a blow to the economy.

A7. **The rise of the dollar could batter the profits of some U.S. companies this year and slice into capital spending.**

a. Which companies may have their profits battered, and why?

b. Why would this slice into capital spending?

A8. **The large and persistent trade deficit has provoked concern among the general public and in the financial markets. The deficit resulted from the high-dollar policies of the Reagan administration in the early 1980s.**

What is a high-dollar policy, how does it work, and how would it create a trade deficit?

A9. **With our unemployment rate so close to the natural rate, there is no room for interest-rate cuts, but if unemployment should start to rise, Alan Blinder, vice-chairman of the Federal Reserve Board, may want an early cut in rates. If he succeeds, bond yields and the dollar could both be in for a mauling.**

Why would the dollar fall in this circumstance? Would this outcome be desirable?

A10. **They conclude that in many Canadian export sectors the devaluation of the Canadian dollar will not greatly aid sales. Progress will be slow, they stated, because any U.S. slowdown would overshadow the price effects of the devalued dollar.**

a. How would the devaluation of the Canadian dollar normally aid Canadian sales?

b. What is meant by the U.S. slowdown overshadowing the price effects of the devalued Canadian dollar?

A11. **"The stronger yen is the best single thing that could have happened to the trade deficit," a senior Administration official said last week.**

Explain the logic behind this statement.

A12. **The U.S. current account deficit is close to 5% of GDP but has not caused a fall in the U.S. dollar because. . . ."**

Complete this statement.

A13. **The quarterly GDP figures released earlier today pointed to a strong recovery in our economy, causing our dollar to rise sharply.**

Why would an increase in our income level cause our dollar to rise? Wouldn't the higher income increase our imports and so increase the supply or our dollar on the foreign exchange marked?

A14. The dramatic increase in the price of oil has caused the Canadian dollar to rise markedly.

   a. Why would an increase in the price of oil affect the Canadian dollar?

   b. What terminology do economists use to refer to this price increase?

B1.   Normally, a weak trade figure would send the dollar into a tailspin. But market players could be judging that signs indicate a still strong U.S. economy, implying continued upward pressure on interest rates. Currency traders may be working on the expectation that the Fed is going to have to push up short-term rates to choke off some domestic demand.

   a. Why would a weak trade figure normally send the dollar into a tailspin?

   b. Explain why a strong economy suggests high interest rates.

   c. Why would the tailspin be avoided here?

B2.   He argued that one by-product of the ballooning federal deficits of the early 1980s was a large rise in _____ and a concomitant loss of American competitiveness on world markets. The resulting rise in the U.S. _____ was the counterpart of the _____ that kept domestic investment from falling as much as did national saving.

   Fill in the blanks.

B3.   These reports suggest that the United States is heading for a recession. Activity on the futures market for the U.S. dollar suggests that the market thinks the dollar will soon depreciate.

   What logic lies behind the market's thinking?

B4.   Historically the winners on the foreign exchange market are the big banks. Citicorp, for example, typically earns about $600 million a year from its currency trading operation. The losers? Central banks, for one. Recently the Bank of England bought pounds to _____, but the pound kept _____ and huge losses developed. Many small speculators are also losers. Of the 1,287 seats on the Chicago Mercantile's International Monetary Mart, about 25 percent change hands every year, most because unsustainable losses have been incurred.

   a. Fill in the blanks.

   b. What would a bank like Citicorp do to make money at the expense of the Bank of England in the scenario described in this clipping?

B5. **The survey found that 28 percent of U.S. dollar trading in North America is in the mark, 23 percent in the yen, 13 percent in the British pound, and 9 percent in the Swiss franc. Rounding out the list of major trading currencies, at 3 to 7 percent each, are the Canadian and Australian dollars and the French franc.**

The U.S. trades more with Canada than with any other country. Why is the Canadian dollar so low in this survey?

B6. **The statistical evidence is that there is a strong correlation between increases in current account surpluses and declines in the value of the dollar. This is just the opposite of the conventional wisdom.**

a. What is the conventional wisdom, and what logic lies behind it?

b. How can this statistical evidence be explained?

B7. **Trade in services is harder to understand because you can't see it, and indeed it is sometimes called invisibles trade. For example, if a company uses a consultant based in another country, the payment made to the foreign consultant is considered _____ in the services account.**

Fill in the blank.

B8. **A major negative influence on the U.S. economy has been the strong dollar. Its strength causes excessive imports. The excess of imports over exports— more than $120 billion (U.S.) a year—must be subtracted when calculating GDP.**

a. How would a strong dollar be a negative influence on the economy?

b. GDP measures the amount produced domestically. Imports are produced by foreigners and so should be irrelevant for measuring GDP. Explain why this clipping suggests that they be subtracted when calculating GDP.

B9. **Last year Argentina experienced robust growth and fiscal restraint, but some analysts continue to worry about its current account deficit, which today is 4 percent of GDP. But this worry is wrongheaded because this deficit is the result of the confidence of foreign investors in Argentina's new economic system.**

Explain how this deficit could be a result of the confidence of foreign investors in Argentina.

B10. The April U.S. trade deficit narrowed by 41 percent from March. Investors greeted the news with gusto, driving bonds more than a point higher in minutes. It was a classic suckers' rally. Traders soon realized the trade improvement

was due to a 23 percent climb in exports. Fears of surging demand in an environment of near-full employment and capacity constraints were rekindled. Prices turned on a dime and wound up nearly two points off their highs by the end of the day.

a. Explain why the narrowing of the trade deficit would cause the price of bonds to rise.

b. Explain in your own words why prices then fell, as reported in the second half of the clipping.

B11. A trade deficit, he said, is not an indication that a country has low productivity or low-quality products. It is an indication that the domestic investment rate is high relative to the rate of _____.

Fill in the blank and explain your reasoning.

B12. It comes as a surprise to many people that the great advantage of engaging in free trade is not the resulting increase in employment in export industries. In fact, in the long haul free trade has nothing to do with unemployment because. . . .

a. If higher employment is not the great advantage of engaging in free trade, what is?

b. Complete this clipping.

B13. At the moment the market is completely ignoring things like record U.S. trade deficits and the widening current account deficit. It is also largely ignoring the possibility of Federal Reserve rate cuts. Traders and investors are instead focusing only on the fiscal and monetary easing in Japan and monetary easing in Germany.

a. In what way is fiscal easing in Japan relevant here?

b. In what way is monetary easing in Germany relevant here?

B14. The degree of openness of the economy is sometimes measured by imports or exports expressed as a fraction of GDP. By this measure, Singapore probably wins the prize since both exports and imports are about 150 percent of GDP.

How can imports or exports be more than 100 percent of GDP? Hint: Imports can be inputs to the production of goods.

B15. For many years the driving force behind the global economy has been a tacit agreement between the United States and China. The United States provides a

ready market for cheap Chinese goods and keeps mostly silent about the way China manages its currency and despoils its environment to sustain growth. In return China helps finance. . . .

Complete this clipping and explain your reasoning.

Numerical Exercises

AN1. Suppose that a U.S. Toyota dealer imports 100 cars worth $10,000 each and the Japanese manufacturer buys a U.S. bond with the $1 million proceeds. What happens to the U.S. balance of trade? The current account? The balance of payments?

AN2. If the exchange rate is 0.7 euros per dollar and 12 pesos per dollar, what should be the exchange rate between euros and pesos?

AN3. In the example of appendix 13.1, how much extra total output would result if Ecuador chose to forgo five instead of two tons of wheat?

AN4. Suppose that to produce two bolts of cloth, England must forgo 15 bottles of wine, and that to produce 3 bolts of cloth, Portugal must forgo 40 bottles of wine. Which country has a comparative advantage in which good?

AN5. In question AN4, if the world price of cloth were $60 per bolt and the world price of wine $6 per bottle, how should England and Portugal specialize?

BN1. Suppose that the central bank has intervened in the foreign exchange market to fix the exchange rate by selling $4 billion. If the current account deficit is $10 billion, what is the capital account balance?

BN2. In question AN4, if the world price of cloth were $30 per bolt and the world price of wine $5 per bottle, how should England and Portugal specialize?

Appendix 13.1   The Principle of Comparative Advantage

Economists believe that countries are better off specializing at what they do best and trading, rather than forbidding trade, and meeting all their needs through domestic production. It would be very expensive for the United States to grow its own supply of bananas, for example; it is much cheaper to grow extra wheat and trade it for bananas.

This banana example is easy to understand because banana-producing countries such as Ecuador are much more efficient at producing bananas than is the United States, and the United States is much more efficient at producing wheat than is Ecuador. In such a case specializing and trading is obviously to the advantage of both countries. But what if, say, the United States were more productive than Ecuador in the production of both bananas and wheat? In this case the United States is said to have an *absolute advantage* in the production of both commodities, and it is tempting to conclude that because of this the United States will be better off producing both items and ignoring Ecuador. That this is not the case is an important contribution of economic theory known as the *principle of comparative advantage.*

This principle is best explained in terms of opportunity cost, or how much of one good must be forgone to produce a unit of the other good. Suppose that to produce an extra ton of bananas the United States must forgo five tons of wheat, but Ecuador must forgo only two tons of wheat: Ecuador's comparative advantage lies in bananas. To produce an extra ton of wheat Ecuador must forgo one-half of a ton of bananas, but the United States must forgo only one-fifth of a ton of bananas; the United States' comparative advantage lies in wheat. When compared to Ecuador, the United States is relatively (or comparatively) more productive in growing wheat than bananas; Ecuador, compared to the United States, is comparatively more productive in producing bananas. Notice that reaching this conclusion regarding comparative advantage took no notice of these countries' absolute advantages. In general, relative to country B, country A has a comparative advantage in a product when it can produce that product at a lower opportunity cost than can country B.

The essence of the law of comparative advantage can now easily be explained in terms of this example. Suppose that both economies are producing both goods. The United States could forgo a ton of bananas and produce five extra tons of wheat, while Ecuador could forgo two tons of wheat and get an extra ton of bananas. If they both do so (i.e., produce more of the good in which they have a comparative advantage), what is the outcome? U.S. wheat production is up by five and banana production down by one; Ecuador wheat production is down by two and banana production is up by one. The net change is three extra tons of wheat and no change in bananas. (Check your understanding by computing how much extra total output would result if Ecuador chose to forgo five instead of two tons of wheat.)

This result is referred to as the principle of comparative advantage: total output is maximized if countries specialize in the production of commodities in which they have a comparative advantage. A classic example used to illustrate this phenomenon is the case of a lawyer who can earn $100 per hour lawyering and $20 per hour typing, whereas her secretary's skills are such that she can earn only $5 per hour either lawyering or typing. Should the lawyer do her own typing? She would be foolish to do so. By doing her own typing she would be forgoing lucrative lawyering. More work in total would be accomplished if the lawyer specialized in lawyering and the secretary specialized in typing, despite the lawyer being more productive at both.

How is this extra output divided between the two countries? In the example, the United States could replace its lost ton of bananas by trading two tons of wheat to Ecuador for the extra ton of bananas that Ecuador has produced. This exchange would leave the United States with the same quantity of bananas as before, but more wheat; Ecuador would end up with the same quantities of bananas and wheat as when it started. Clearly, Ecuador would have no motivation to specialize under this arrangement, so the United States will have to be willing to share some of the extra wheat. To get a share of the extra wheat, Ecuador will demand a higher price for its bananas. The forces of supply and demand for bananas versus wheat will determine the relative price of bananas and wheat, in turn determining the share of the extra output going to each country.

This price will have to be more than two tons of wheat for one ton of bananas to motivate Ecuador to trade bananas for wheat; otherwise, it could obtain wheat more cheaply by switching production from bananas to wheat. Similarly the price will have to be less than five tons of wheat per ton of bananas to motivate the United States to trade wheat for bananas. (If the price were six tons of wheat per ton of bananas, the United States would be motivated to grow bananas and trade for wheat!) The relative price determined by the market forces of supply and demand is called the *terms of trade*—the quantity of imported goods a country can obtain in exchange for a unit of exported goods. For the macroeconomy it is measured as the ratio of export prices to import prices.

14   Policy in an Open Economy

Balance of payments surpluses and deficits mean the international sector of our economy is in disequilibrium. The importance of the balance of payments is that it measures imbalance in our international sector, thereby pointing to economic forces for change. One purpose of this chapter is to identify these forces and how they bring about change.

Monetary and fiscal policies are shocks to the economy that affect many economic variables, such as income, interest rates, and prices. Changes in these variables create imbalances in the international sector, which in turn set in motion forces that modify the impact of these policies on the economy. A second purpose of this chapter is to examine how our earlier discussions of monetary and fiscal policies must be adjusted to recognize the influence of forces generated through the international sector of the economy. The recent increase in the openness of the U.S. economy requires that its macroeconomic analysis pay more attention to these forces.

Upon completion of this chapter you should

- be able to explain how a nonzero balance of payments affects the economy when the exchange rate is flexible and when it is fixed;

- understand how international forces affect the strength of monetary and fiscal policy, including the dramatic result that monetary policy is completely ineffective under fixed exchange rates; and

- know how the government can influence the foreign exchange market and thus the exchange rate.

14.1   International Imbalance with a Flexible Exchange Rate

Exactly what are the forces for change that an imbalance in the balance of payments engenders? This is a crucial question, the answer to which depends on whether the economy is operating on a flexible or a fixed exchange rate system. Let us first examine a flexible exchange rate system.

Under a flexible exchange rate system, the government allows the forces of supply and demand to determine the exchange rate. If there is a balance of payments surplus, demand for our dollar on the foreign exchange market exceeds its supply. So market forces cause a rise in the value of our dollar. Those who want the extra, unavailable dollars try to obtain them by offering extra foreign currency for them, so our dollar becomes more valuable in terms of foreign currency. This *appreciation* of our dollar is often described by the statement "The exchange rate has risen."

This process operates in reverse if there is a balance of payments deficit. In this case the demand for our dollar on the foreign exchange market is less than its supply, so market forces cause a fall in its value. This *depreciation* of our dollar is often described by the statement "The exchange rate has fallen."

Note that under a flexible exchange rate system, any tendency toward a balance of payments surplus or deficit is automatically and instantaneously eliminated by a flexing of the exchange rate so that our measure of the imbalance (the balance of payments) is always zero. The balance of payments measure is nonzero only if the government engages in some net buying or selling of foreign currency. In the context of a flexible exchange rate, the terminology "balance of payments surplus or deficit" must be interpreted as reflecting a surplus or deficit that would appear if the exchange rate were not permitted to adjust instantaneously.

Curiosity 14.1: What Is the Effective Exchange Rate?

Looking at the value of the U.S. dollar in terms of any other single currency can be misleading. It is possible, for example, for the value of the U.S. dollar to rise relative to one currency but at the same time fall relative to another currency. The impact on the balance of payments is not clear. It would depend on how much trade was conducted with each of these countries. A better measure of the U.S. dollar exchange rate is the trade-weighted or effective exchange rate—an index calculated as a weighted average of U.S. dollar exchange rates with all other countries, where the weights reflect the proportion of total U.S. trade done with each of these countries. These weights are approximately European Union 19 percent, Canada 17 percent, Japan 11 percent, Mexico 11 percent, China 10 percent, United Kingdom 5 percent, Korea 4 percent, Taiwan 3 percent, and all other countries less than 2 percent each. Figure 15.2 in chapter 15 shows the recent history of the U.S. effective exchange rate.

Under a flexible exchange rate, the initial reaction of the economy to an imbalance in the balance of payments is therefore a change in the exchange rate, which in turn creates additional forces for change in the economy. If, with other variables constant, the exchange rate rises, demand for our exports falls because foreigners find our exports more expensive in terms of their currency. Furthermore imports become cheaper to us (because our dollar now buys more foreign exchange), so there is a fall in demand for domestically produced goods and services that compete with imports. Both phenomena imply that aggregate demand for domestically produced goods and services falls.

Similarly, if the exchange rate falls, demand for exports and import-competing goods and services should be stimulated, implying a rise in demand for domestically produced goods and services.

To summarize, *if the economy has a flexible exchange rate, an imbalance in the international sector of the economy, measured by the balance of payments, automatically causes the exchange rate to change*; this change in turn causes the import-competing and export sectors of the economy to adjust, thus affecting aggregate demand for goods and services.

Sample Exam Question 14.1:
"Fortunately for us, currency flexibility has cushioned the impact of this year's sharp declines in exports."
    What must have been happening to the exchange rate here?

14.2   International Imbalance with a Fixed Exchange Rate

Under a fixed exchange rate system, the government does not allow the forces of supply and demand to determine the exchange rate. The government instead fixes the exchange rate at what it believes is the "right" rate, and the central bank, armed with a stockpile of *foreign exchange reserves*, stands ready to buy or sell foreign currency at that rate. If there is a balance of payments surplus, the demand for our dollar by foreigners is greater than the supply, so some of these foreigners will seek extra, unavailable dollars. Under a flexible exchange rate, they would have to get dollars by offering more foreign exchange, but under a fixed exchange rate, this higher cost can be avoided because the Fed will exchange their foreign currency for dollars at the fixed rate. When the Fed does so, it takes the extra foreign exchange (currency) and in return provides dollars. The most important implication of this process is that *the domestic money supply increases* by the increase in dollars times the money multiplier. The increase in the money supply in turn affects economic activity as described in earlier chapters.

When there is a balance of payments deficit, the opposite occurs. We are supplying more dollars on the foreign exchange market (e.g., seeking foreign currency to take vacations abroad) than there is foreign demand for dollars, so those of us unable to obtain foreign currency from foreigners go to the Fed to buy foreign exchange at the fixed rate. To buy the foreign currency, we give the Fed dollars, removing them from public circulation and thereby decreasing the domestic money supply.

To summarize, *if the economy has a fixed exchange rate, an imbalance in the international sector of the economy, measured by the balance of payments, automatically causes the money supply to change*, in turn affecting economic activity.

Armed with these two general results—that international imbalance causes exchange-rate changes under a flexible exchange rate system and money-supply changes under a fixed exchange rate system—we can examine how monetary and fiscal policy are affected by repercussions from the international sector. To maintain simplicity, all analysis ignores price-level changes and inflation. Incorporating them would not change the general results, only the breakdown of nominal income changes into real changes and price changes.

Sample Exam Question 14.2:
"Unfortunately, our lack of currency flexibility has exacerbated the impact of this year's sharp declines in exports."

What must have been happening here?

14.3   International Influence on Fiscal Policy

Under Flexible Exchange Rates

An increase in government spending leads to an increase in income and an accompanying increase in the interest rate, causing some crowding out. The increase in income increases imports, creating a balance of payments deficit, but the increase in the interest rate causes capital inflows, creating a balance of payments surplus. Which will dominate? The consensus among economists on this empirical question is that the latter will outweigh the former. Because of the high mobility of international capital, a slight increase in our interest rate causes a substantial capital inflow, outweighing the impact on the balance of payments of the accompanying rise in imports. Strengthening this phenomenon is the impact of our higher income on foreigners' view of the profitability of investing in our stock market, discussed earlier in chapter 13. This creates extra demand for our dollar on the foreign exchange market, enhancing the movement to a balance of payments surplus.

Once this empirical question is settled, it is easy to see how international forces modify the impact of fiscal policy. Under a flexible exchange rate system, the balance of payments surplus created by a stimulating dose of fiscal policy causes the exchange rate to appreciate. This increase decreases exports—directly decreasing demand for domestically produced goods and services. It also increases imports, thereby decreasing demand for domestically produced goods and services that compete against imports. The decrease in aggregate demand for domestically produced goods and services partially offsets the impact on the economy of the stimulating dose of fiscal policy, decreasing the strength of fiscal policy in affecting the income level. All this is summarized in figure 14.1, where the terminology—such as "B of P" stands for "balance of payments" and "agg D for g&s" stands for "aggregate demand for domestically produced goods and services"—should be obvious.

Under Fixed Exchange Rates

When the exchange rate is fixed, the balance of payments surplus created by a stimulating dose of fiscal policy does not cause the exchange rate to rise. It causes instead an increase in the money supply as the Fed buys foreign currency (the balance of payments surplus) with dollars. This increase in the money supply augments the stimulating effect of the policy dose, making fiscal policy stronger in affecting the income level. This process too is shown in figure 14.1.

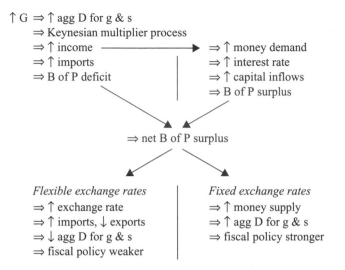

Figure 14.1   Reaction to Fiscal Policy
The flowchart shows the reaction of the economy to an increase in government spending under both flexible and exchange rate systems.

Sample Exam Question 14.3:
"Economics students are taught about crowding out. But what about crowding in? Couldn't forces from the international sector strengthen fiscal policy?"

Is this possible? If so, explain how it could come about. If not, explain why not.

14.4   International Influence on Monetary Policy

Under Flexible Exchange Rates

An increase in the money supply lowers the interest rate, and the lower interest rate stimulates aggregate demand and moves the economy to a higher level of income. This rise in income increases imports, creating a balance of payments deficit, and the fall in the interest rate reduces capital inflows, thus augmenting this balance of payments deficit. Higher income may cause foreigners to invest more in our stock market, but this is not viewed as being strong enough to offset this balance of payments deficit.

Under a flexible exchange rate system, the balance of payments deficit causes the exchange rate to depreciate. This lower exchange rate increases exports—directly increasing demand for domestically produced goods and services. It also decreases imports—

increasing demand for domestically produced goods and services that compete against imports. The rise in aggregate demand for domestically produced goods and services augments the impact on the economy of the stimulating dose of monetary policy, thus giving greater strength to monetary policy in affecting the income level. This process is shown in figure 14.2.

Under Fixed Exchange Rates

When the exchange rate is fixed, the balance of payments deficit created by a stimulating dose of monetary policy does not cause the exchange rate to fall. Instead, it causes a decrease in the money supply as the Fed buys dollars with foreign exchange to prevent the balance of payments deficit from lowering the exchange rate. The decrease in the money supply diminishes the stimulating effect of the policy dose, making monetary policy weaker in affecting the income level. This sequence of events is also shown in figure 14.2.

There is more to this story, however. An increase in the money supply created the balance of payments deficit, and an automatic decrease in the money supply is decreasing the deficit. So long as there is a net increase in the money supply, there will be a balance

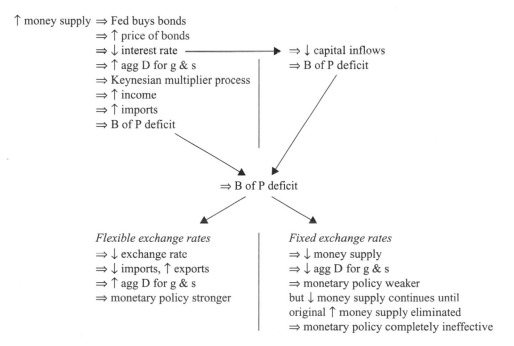

Figure 14.2 Reaction to Monetary Policy
This flowchart shows the reaction of the economy to an increase in money supply under both flexible and fixed exchange rate systems.

of payments deficit. But so long as there is a balance of payments deficit, there will be a decreasing money supply. Consequently only when the original money supply increase has been completely wiped out will the deficit be eliminated. The economy will regain equilibrium back where it started, so the end result of this monetary policy is no change. This reflects an extremely important general result: *under a fixed exchange rate, monetary policy is completely ineffective as a policy tool.* Monetary policy implicitly is being used to fix the exchange rate, so is not available for other purposes.

Sample Exam Question 14.4:
"But adopting fixed exchange rates entails a steep price, namely that the government is prohibited from _____ to fight slumps. The upshot is a neat illustration of the "no-free-lunch" maxim so beloved by economists."
Fill in the blank.

14.5   Sterilization Policy

Monetary policy in the context of a fixed exchange rate is ineffective because an expansionary monetary policy creates a balance of payments deficit, which automatically decreases the money supply, offsetting and eventually eliminating the original increase in the money supply. What if, however, the monetary authorities take monetary action to counteract the automatic change in the money supply, allowing the original monetary dose to be maintained? As the money supply decreases automatically in the preceding example, the monetary authorities could annually increase the money supply by exactly the same amount.

This policy is called a *sterilization* policy because it "sterilizes" the automatic money-supply change that results from an imbalance in international payments under fixed exchange rates. Pursuing this policy maintains the original monetary policy dose and allows monetary policy to retain its effectiveness.

Unfortunately, there is a catch: the sterilization policy maintains the imbalance in international payments. In the example, the balance of payments deficit, which would normally disappear as it automatically decreased the money supply, now persists as this automatic mechanism is "sterilized." What are the implications of a continuing balance of payments deficit?

Consider how the government, through its agent the central bank, deals with the balance of payments deficit. The deficit means that the supply of dollars on the foreign exchange market exceeds the demand, so those unable to obtain foreign exchange for their dollars go to the government to exchange them at the fixed rate. The government sells foreign currency to them at the fixed rate, as it has promised to do, and in return obtains domestic dollars, which normally would thereby be removed from public circulation, thus decreasing the money supply. (Under a policy of sterilization, of course, the central bank arranges to have these dollars put back into circulation.) The key point here is that during this process the government is selling off its holdings of foreign exchange. As long as the balance of payments deficit continues, the government's stock of foreign exchange—its foreign exchange reserves—steadily falls, year after year.

The major problem with sterilization policy should now be evident. By maintaining the balance of payments deficit, the sterilization policy causes the government's foreign exchange reserves to run low, threatening its ability to continue this policy, and worse, alerting foreign exchange speculators that the dollar may soon have to be allowed to fall. The resulting foreign exchange crisis usually results in a devaluation (a substantive fall in the fixed exchange rate value), creating embarrassment for the government and profits for speculators.

If a balance of payments surplus is being maintained by a sterilization policy, however, opposite results are obtained. Foreign exchange reserves accumulate to embarrassingly high levels, ultimately causing an upward revaluation of the currency and, once again, profits for speculators. But these automatic forces are not so powerful in this instance. For many years China has been running a balance of payments surplus and has been "sterilizing" this by buying U.S. government bonds so that there is no upward pressure on the Chinese yuan. There appear to be no automatic forces preventing China from following this policy indefinitely. But there is a major caveat. Should China stop buying U.S. bonds, the value of the U.S. dollar will fall markedly, reducing markedly the value of the Chinese holdings of U.S. bonds. By following this "sterilization" policy China has in effect put itself in a very awkward position.

> **Sample Exam Question 14.5:**
> "A continuing balance of payments deficit leads to a corrective force—our international reserves run out and we are forced to devalue. But a continuing balance of payments surplus doesn't have an effective corrective force—China, for example, is simply allowing her international reserves to accumulate, much to the annoyance of the Americans who think that the Chinese should. . . ."
>
> Complete this clipping.

14.6   Government Influence on the Exchange Rate

It is rare to find an exchange rate system that is fully flexible. Usually government intervenes in the operation of the foreign exchange market to "modify" the natural forces of supply and demand. Sometimes intervention is intended to prop up an exchange rate for

Curiosity 14.2: What Is the J Curve?

Demand is always less sensitive to price changes in the short run than in the long run, when there is sufficient time for people to acquire information, change habits, and renegotiate contracts. Consequently, when the exchange rate falls, although imports are more expensive and exports less expensive, in the short run (six months to a year) the volume of imports and exports won't change much. If the volume of imports doesn't change much, but they are more expensive, the value of imports increases. And if the volume of exports doesn't change much, but they are less expensive, the value of exports falls. These effects push the economy to a balance of trade deficit, not the surplus we had claimed. In the short run, instead of improving the balance of payments, a devaluation worsens it.

Fortunately, in the long run volumes do change by enough to improve the balance of trade. A graph of the balance of trade over time would show an initial fall toward a deficit, but eventually a rise toward a surplus. These values trace out a path that looks like the letter J and is accordingly called the J curve. This short-run reaction captured by the J curve is very frustrating for policy makers because the economy initially goes in the wrong direction, creating great uncertainty.

reasons of prestige, and at other times it is intended to push down the exchange rate in order to produce jobs through stimulation of demand for exports and import-competing goods and services. Neither of these interventions can be viewed with favor because they attempt to set the exchange rate at an unnatural level. A more convincing rationale for government interference in this market is that without such interference the exchange rate may be volatile, so volatile that it is disruptive to international business activity. Government action designed to cushion temporary shocks to the exchange rate, rather than to influence its long-run level, is thought to be a legitimate policy.

The government employs two main mechanisms to influence the exchange rate. First, it can intervene directly in the foreign exchange market, buying or selling dollars. This intervention is viable as long as the government's stock of foreign exchange reserves is not threatened, as it would be, for example, if it tried to keep the exchange rate above its long-run level through continual purchases of dollars with its foreign exchange reserves. Second, government can influence the exchange rate by using monetary policy to change the real interest rate; changes in the interest rate in turn affect capital inflows and outflows and thus the exchange rate. Most governments, through their central banks, adopt a combination of these two policies.

Sample Exam Question 14.6:
"When the government wants to strengthen the dollar it _____ foreign reserves and _____ domestic dollars. It does the opposite when it wants to keep the dollar from rising too sharply."
Fill in these blanks.

14.7   Fixed-versus-Flexible Exchange Rates

Which exchange rate system—fixed or flexible—is better? Both exchange rate systems have advantages and disadvantages, so an answer to this question depends on the particular situation.

If every city in the United States had its own currency, economic activity and productivity in the United States would be severely curtailed. Commercial transactions involving firms in different cities would have currency–exchange-rate risks to contend with, people would have to bear costs of changing currencies every time they visited a different city, and long-term investment would be inhibited by exchange-rate uncertainty, for example. The same would be so, but to a lesser degree, if every state had its own currency, so there are tremendous benefits associated with having a common currency (a fixed exchange rate) among all U.S. cities and all U.S. states. The advantages of fixed exchange rates constitute the rationale behind the creation of a common currency in Europe.

Suppose, however, that a fall in oil prices caused a major recession in Texas. Adjustment in Texas might take the form of an eventual fall in the wage of Texans, but primarily it would take the form of labor and capital moving out of Texas to other states. If Texas had its own currency, the adjustment could be facilitated by a fall in the value of the Texas currency, plus adoption of an appropriate Texas monetary policy. This is the advantage of flexible exchange rates: flexing of the exchange rate and adoption of suitable monetary policy—neither possible under a fixed exchange rate (recall that under a fixed exchange rate an independent monetary policy is not possible)—can facilitate adjustment to recessions and booms.

There is a major difference between the Texas example and a world consisting of different countries, however. With different countries, labor and capital are usually not allowed to move across borders freely, suggesting that the main mechanism by which Texas adjusts to its recession does not work across countries. This difference markedly increases the importance of having a flexible exchange rate across separate countries, and explains why within a single country it is advantageous to have a fixed exchange rate (a common currency), but across countries it is better to have a flexible exchange rate.

Unfortunately, exchange rates can flex for reasons other than the need to facilitate adjustment to recession or boom. History has shown exchange rates to be much more volatile than experts had predicted in 1971 when the world moved away from a predominantly fixed exchange rate system. As activity in financial assets markets has come to dominate the short-run determination of exchange rates, we have discovered that speculators can affect exchange rates dramatically, turning them from a stabilizing force into a destabilizing force. This possibility has caused central banks to modify the flexible exchange rate system by using monetary policy or direct intervention to stabilize exchange rates. In doing so, they must be careful to allow exchange rates to change to reflect fundamental forces—such as inflation-rate differences, productivity–growth-rate differences, and natural-resource discoveries.

It must be noted that the volatility of flexible exchange rates has a counterpart in fixed exchange rate systems. Even if the exchange rate is fixed at its appropriate long-run level, speculative forces and capital flight can cause a huge drain on a country's foreign exchange reserves, as happened during the Asian crisis in the late 1990s. Only if a country has an equally huge stock of foreign exchange reserves can such foreign exchange crises be overcome without a currency devaluation.

Here is an instructive list of preconditions for country A fixing its exchange rate with country B.

1. Country A has a poor reputation for controlling inflation, while country B has a good reputation.
2. Country A has a high level of trade with country B.
3. Country A has flexible labor markets to cushion export price shocks.
4. Shocks to country A's economy are highly correlated with shocks to country B's economy.
5. Country A has little involvement in global capital markets, so the risk of speculative attack is low.
6. Country A has a high level of foreign exchange reserves to beat off speculative attacks

---

Sample Exam Question 14.7:
"A key feature of the European union adopting the euro as their currency is their policy of free movement of people across countries."

What does free movement of people across countries have to do with the euro?

Media Illustrations

Example 1

Then there's the state of the dollar, which has been bleeding steadily despite transfusions from borrowings and foreign reserves. Will the higher interest rates stop the hemorrhage?

What does "bleeding steadily" mean in this context?
It means that the value of the dollar has been falling.

What does "transfusions from borrowings" mean, and how do borrowings tend to stop the bleeding?
The borrowings are bond sales to foreigners. Such sales mean that either foreigners buy dollars to buy the bonds or we convert the foreign currency proceeds of these sales into

dollars, both of which increase the demand for dollars on the foreign exchange market, putting upward pressure on the dollar.

What does "transfusions from foreign reserves" mean, and how do foreign reserves tend to stop the bleeding?
This phrase refers to the government using some of its foreign exchange reserves to buy dollars on the foreign exchange market. The extra demand for the dollar puts upward pressure on its price.

What will happen if the "transfusions from foreign reserves" method is employed over a long period of time?
The government will run out of foreign reserves, a currency crisis will develop, and the dollar will be devalued.

What logic lies behind the idea that higher interest rates might "stop the hemorrhage"?
The higher interest rates should induce capital inflows, increasing the demand for U.S. dollars and putting upward pressure on its price.

Example 2

Furthermore current monetary policy appears to be conducted as if we were on a fixed exchange rate. Policy is effectively geared to maintaining the exchange rate at the expense of a domestic recovery.

How would monetary policy be conducted if we were on a fixed exchange rate?
Any change in the exchange rate would call forth a change in the money supply to push the exchange rate back to its original level. For example, should a balance of payments surplus develop; the exchange rate will rise. To offset this rise, the monetary authorities could increase the money supply, decreasing the interest rate and thereby reducing capital inflows and eliminating the balance of payments surplus. Note that this example is in essence just another way of telling our earlier story, in which the increase in the money supply happens automatically.

How could maintaining the exchange rate be at the expense of a domestic recovery?
A domestic recovery involves an increase in income, increasing imports and creating a balance of payments deficit. This deficit would put downward pressure on the dollar. To prevent any change in the exchange rate, the monetary authorities would decrease the money supply, increasing interest rates to attract capital inflows that would eliminate the balance of payments deficit. This action dampens the domestic recovery in two ways. First, it prevents a fall in the exchange rate that would stimulate the economy by increasing exports and demand for import-competing goods and services. Second, it involves a contractionary monetary policy, which works against any stimulus to recovery the economy is experiencing.

Example 3

The government may be tempted to increase official currency reserves in order to reduce the pressure on the dollar and the consequent threat to manufacturing industries. But such a move would be difficult. The government would need to borrow large sums on the market because its cash balances are not strong, especially considering its large cash requirements for the coming year.

What kind of pressure is the dollar under, and why would it be a threat to manufacturing industries?

The dollar is experiencing upward pressure. An increase in the value of the dollar makes it more difficult for manufacturing industries to sell abroad and to compete against imports in its domestic market. This threat may be alleviated to some extent by reductions in the cost of imported inputs.

How would increasing official currency reserves reduce this pressure on the dollar?

To increase official currency reserves, the government would have to buy foreign currency on the foreign exchange market by selling domestic dollars. This puts downward pressure on the price of domestic dollars.

Why would this move be difficult? Can't the government have its central bank accomplish it by writing checks for the foreign currency?

If the central bank wrote checks to buy the foreign currency, it would be creating new money. Because of other cash needs, the prudent (i.e., noninflationary) annual increase in the money supply may already have been reached. Thus the extra dollars to pay for these purchases of foreign currency may have to come from bond sales. Other cash needs may already be requiring large bond sales, so to sell even more bonds, the government might have to raise the interest rate.

Example 4

The response has been to search out the middle ground. The central bank has a simple operating formula: Some of the adjustment will be taken through the exchange rate, some through interest rates, and the rest through a loss of international reserves.

To what is the central bank adjusting here?

Since the economy is experiencing a loss of international reserves, it must be adjusting to a balance of payments deficit.

In what direction will the exchange rate be adjusting?

The balance of payments deficit will cause the exchange rate to fall.

How will interest rates be adjusting?

The central bank will be selling bonds to push up interest rates, thus to increase capital inflows or decrease capital outflows, and help eliminate the balance of payments eficit.

Chapter Summary

- In a flexible exchange rate system, a nonzero balance of payments causes the exchange rate to change automatically, but in a fixed exchange rate system, it causes the money supply to change automatically.

- Recognizing the international sector of the economy modifies the impact of fiscal and monetary policy by an amount that depends on the exchange rate system. The most dramatic result is the complete ineffectiveness of monetary policy under a fixed exchange rate. By fixing the exchange rate, an economy has in effect opted to employ monetary policy to fix the exchange rate, rendering it unavailable for any other purpose.

- Sterilization policy can be used to regain the use of monetary policy, but at the cost of continuing the disequilibrium in the international sector. Sterilization causes foreign exchange reserves to rise continually if there is a balance of payments surplus or to fall continually if there is a balance of payments deficit.

- Governments may wish to influence the foreign exchange market to make it less volatile. They can do so either by buying or selling in this market, or by using monetary policy to influence the interest rate and thereby change capital inflows.

Media Exercises

(Group B questions require more thought.)

A1. **The central bank, which handles the reserve fund for the government, sells reserves and buys dollars when it wants to. . . .**

Complete this clipping, explaining your rationale.

A2. **By keeping interest rates _____, the bank has attracted offshore investment and created a demand for dollars. In turn this has pushed _____ the dollar, taking millions of dollars off the bottom lines of exporting companies. To curb the dollar's _____, the bank must periodically enter the foreign exchange market. . . .**

a. Fill in the blanks, and explain your reasoning.

b. Explain why the bottom lines of exporting companies were affected.

c. Complete the final sentence, explaining your reasoning.

A3. **The U.S. government launched a major effort yesterday to rescue the value of the dollar, after the greenback took a beating in foreign exchange trading to fall to a new post–Second World War low against the Japanese yen. The**

_____ intervened repeatedly in currency markets, _____ more than one billion dollars in an unusually aggressive and successful attempt to stave off speculators.

Fill in the blanks.

A4. **The central bank turned to _____ to stop the Canadian dollar's _____ when it became apparent it was using up reserves to little avail.**

Fill in the blanks.

A5. **The central bank, fearing inflation, has kept interest rates up. However, to offset the upward pressure those rates are putting on the currency, it has also been. . . .**

a. Why would fear of inflation cause the central bank to keep interest rates up?

b. How do high interest rates put upward pressure on the currency?

c. Complete this clipping to describe what other activity the central bank has been pursuing.

A6. **Our international reserves fell by $330 million to $3.2 billion last month—not much ammunition if the going gets tough.**

a. What must have been happening to cause the reserves to fall?

b. What is meant by "not much ammunition if the going gets tough"?

A7. **Reagan's own Council of Economic Advisors put the case for a muscular dollar with surprising force: the strong dollar has stimulated production and investment in sectors less involved in international trade. In other industries competition from imports has prompted more expenditure in plant and equipment as well as greater attention to controlling wages and other costs. Prices of traded goods and close substitutes have been kept lower than they would have been otherwise, thereby benefiting both U.S. consumers and U.S. producers who use imported inputs.**

a. What is the basic argument against a muscular dollar?

b. In a half dozen words, summarize the case for a muscular dollar.

A8. **The floating exchange rate system has served us well. In recent years currency flexibility has facilitated adjustment, first to higher inflation, and then to sharp declines in export prices and volumes.**

a. Explain how currency flexibility would facilitate adjustment to higher inflation. Would the exchange rate flex up or down?

b. Explain how currency flexibility would facilitate adjustment to declines in export prices and volumes. Would the exchange rate flex up or down?

A9. Official intervention in the foreign exchange market does appear to be a useful policy when overshoots take place in fragile circumstances.

a. What is an overshoot?

b. Explain the exact form of this official intervention to counteract a specific overshoot.

c. What does official intervention do that makes it useful?

A10. The dollar has been falling largely because it was overvalued during the first half of the 1980s. The Fed's tight monetary policy drove up interest rates in an attempt to smother inflation and hold wages down. The Reagan administration now sings the praises of the lower dollar.

a. Explain how the dollar was overvalued.

b. How does tight money smother inflation?

c. What are the praises of a lower dollar?

A11. Canada's official international reserves rose to an all-time high in October as the Bank of Canada acquired close to U.S.$600 million trying to. . . .

Complete this clipping.

A12. Aggravating the perils of an expansionary fiscal policy is its effect on our trade deficit, which has reached unprecedented heights in recent years. Expansion worsens the trade deficit in two ways.

What are these two ways?

A13. The Fed has shared in all of the Clinton administration's interventions so far. Through last June, the most recent period for which Fed disclosures are available, its biggest single intervention came on June 24, 1994, spending yen and marks to buy $1.56 billion when the dollar _____ to 101 yen for the first time.

Fill in the blank and explain your reasoning.

A14. The deal won't hold together if, say, recession-bound Spaniards are screaming for easy money while inflation-wary Germans want to keep money tight.

What deal is being talked about here?

A15. "One has to be very careful in talking about exchange rate stability to recognize that goals trade off," Lawrence H. Summers, the deputy treasury secretary, told a Senate panel last month, "and that to pursue exchange rate stability as a goal, one inevitably gives something else up."

What is given up by pursuing exchange rate stability?

A16. The greenback fell against currencies around the world on the stunning decision by the Fed to buy up to $300 billion of long-term U.S. Treasury bonds to help jolt the economy out of its deep depression.

a. How would buying these bonds help move the economy out of recession?

b. Why would the greenback fall on this news?

A17. The New Zealand dollar pushed toward U.S.55c yesterday as the greenback was dumped on a surprise U.S. Federal Reserve initiative to pump more money into a still-choked financial system.

a. Prior to this move, was the NZ dollar trading at U.S.56c or U.S.54c? Explain your reasoning.

b. Why would the U.S. dollar fall on this news?

c. Why would the Fed have been pumping so much money into the financial system in 2008?

A18. The New Zealand dollar has lost more than 10 percent this year against the U.S. dollar on speculation that an economic slowdown would prompt New Zealand's central bank to cut rates from 7.25 percent, one of the highest interest rates in the developed world.

Explain the logic behind this statement.

A19. In Europe, the weaker dollar has raised fears that a moderate recovery will be dampened.

Why would a weaker U.S. dollar affect Europe?

A20. Many countries peg their own currencies to the greenback, meaning that they are subcontracting their own monetary policies to the Fed. These countries import U.S. inflation when the Fed makes a mistake.

Explain how these countries would "import" inflation.

A21. Exporters want the central bank to lower interest rates.

Why would exporters want lower interest rates?

B1. **The two-pronged attack—raising interest rates to attract liquid capital into the country and using foreign currency holdings to sop up unwanted dollars—has been designed to cushion the fall of the dollar.**

    a. Explain how these two actions cushion the fall of the dollar.

    b. Which is only of short-run validity? Why?

B2. **The minutes also reveal that stemming the rise of the dollar forced the government to borrow heavily on domestic financial markets.**

    a. What is the government doing to stem the rise of the dollar?

    b. Why does this action imply that the government needs to borrow on domestic financial markets? (That is, what alternative to borrowing is possible, and what are its implications?)

B3. **These are the extreme positions. The Bank of Canada's actual path is somewhere in the middle. Some of the brunt of higher U.S. interest rates is taken in higher domestic rates, some through a lower valued Canadian dollar, and some through a loss of international reserves.**

    a. What are the extreme positions to which the first sentence refers?

    b. What are the long-run implications of this middle-of-the-road policy?

B4. **As interest rates rose by record leaps this week, the dollar continued its slide.**

What is going on here? Isn't the dollar supposed to rise when interest rates increase?

B5. **It is surprising that with the dollar trading so high, the central bank has not allowed some easing of interest rates at the expense of a weaker dollar. Since North America has entered into recession and exports are falling off, clearly the capacity constraints argument with respect to export industries carries less weight.**

    a. Explain the rationale for easing interest rates.

    b. What is the "capacity constraints argument," and why is it relevant here?

B6. **Bennett is on a high horse about economists ignoring the supply-side effects of exchange rate changes. He thinks the supply-side effects make the impact of a devaluation much less palatable.**

    a. How would exchange-rate changes affect the supply side?

    b. Why might these effects make a devaluation less palatable?

B7. By avoiding policies to slow the growth of domestic demand and instead forcing the U.S. dollar to serve as the adjustment vehicle in narrowing the trade deficit, the United States will ensure that the global economic landscape during the next five years will be turned upside down.

a. How would slowing the growth of domestic demand narrow the trade deficit?

b. What is meant by "forcing the U.S. dollar to serve as the adjustment vehicle"?

B8. The problem is that it has taken longer than usual for the exchange rate to affect trade. It generally takes six months to a year before the J curve effect takes hold, but this time it has taken a year and a half.

a. What is meant by the J curve effect taking hold?

b. What point on the J curve does this phrase probably refer to?

B9. When the Bank of Canada's foreign exchange traders go into the market to support the Canadian dollar, they trade U.S. dollars from Canada's reserves for Canadian dollars that other people are trying to sell. The Canadian cash resulting from this transaction goes into the government's ordinary account, reducing the finance minister's need to borrow from other sources to cover the deficit. Since the beginning of the fiscal year, about $2 billion in Canadian funds has appeared from this source.

a. In the absence of the intervention, was the Canadian dollar trying to rise or fall during the period referred to in this clipping?

b. What are the "other sources" from which the finance minister would ordinarily borrow?

c. If this is such a good way of supplementing tax revenues, why not do more of it, more often?

B10. Speculators are clearly betting that a French franc will soon buy fewer German marks. While France and Germany apparently have had the financial muscle to fend off the speculators so far, it is not clear whether they are prepared to pay the price of a disrupted economy for a prolonged period.

a. What are the French and German central banks doing during this speculative attack?

b. What is the disruption to the French economy?

c. What is the disruption to the German economy?

B11. Japanese officials and many private economists say the stronger yen will initially cause Japan's trade surplus to rise because it inflates the U.S. dollar value of Japanese exports even though volume may be falling.

What technical terminology do economists use to refer to this phenomenon?

B12. Indeed the yen may have to stay strong for two years or more, many experts say, to have much impact on American–Japanese trade.

a. What is the rationale behind this statement?

b. What technical terminology do economists use to describe this phenomenon?

B13. During the past two years, the Clinton Treasury, which calls the shots on intervention in consultation with the Federal Reserve, has bought dollars on only 18 days. Through June, it had spent $12.5 billion. In contrast, the Bush Treasury intervened on 97 of 260 business days and sold a record $19.5 billion of dollars in 1989 alone, in an attempt to restrain the dollar's _____ against the yen and mark.

a. Was the Clinton Treasury trying to push the exchange rate up or down?

b. Fill in the blank and explain your reasoning.

B14. Last week, as arguments over the Bank's latest move rattled around the financial community, the majority view was that the Bank of Canada had blundered. The dollar's decline was what many economists call an external shock—the Asian financial crisis has sent commodity prices tumbling—and the Bank should have let it go, so that . . . .

a. What action must the Bank of Canada have taken to prevent the dollar's decline?

b. Complete this clipping.

B15. Pressures from a household spending spree and the buoyant building sector won the battle to determine interest rates yesterday, but the central bank hinted that the strong currency could win the war.

What is the logic behind this statement?

B16. The flow of foreign money into China is what is really causing its inflationary problems.

Explain how this flow is causing inflation in China. How could this be prevented?

B17. The Czech central bank is trying to stop the government issuing the country's maiden sovereign international bond i.e., the first bond issued by the Czech government in a foreign currency, these (Euro) next year because it fears it could create another exchange rate bubble.

Why would this bond issue create a rise in the value of the Czech currency?

B18. The fund also said Russia should focus on cutting inflation by allowing a more flexible exchange ruble rate.

How would this cut inflation? What must currently be happening with regard to the exchange rate?

B19. Speculation that Japan would not intervene ahead of the meeting helped yen bulls weaken the dollar to ¥113.58, a level not seen since January 2001.

a. Before the exchange rate moved to ¥113.58, what would have been a more likely exchange rate, ¥110.00 or ¥116.00? Explain.

b. How would Japan have intervened had they wanted to? Why would it want to do this?

B20. Our nation's national saving rate is now running below 3 percent. In 1960 it was close to 13 percent. Our incredibly low saving rate has lead to an incredibly high current account deficit, which has led to an incredibly low value of the dollar.

a. Why would our low saving rate lead to a current account deficit?

b. Will this necessarily lead to a low value of the dollar?

B21. Cheng said that China should shift part of its $U.S.1.4 trillion in foreign exchange reserves out of U.S. dollars and into other, stronger currencies. But Gilmore replied that this would cause a run on the dollar and China will not drive a run on the dollar, not now and not ever.

What is the reasoning behind the view that China will never drive a run on the dollar?

B22. The strength of the GDP data only highlighted the diverging views between the dollar bulls, who predict that strong growth will support the currency, and the bears who warn that stronger growth will only serve to widen the current account deficit and thus undermine the greenback. Those forces seem to be coming together to keep us right where we are for the time being.

Explain the nature of these two forces.

15   Purchasing Power Parity

Earlier discussions of the international sector were conducted in the context of a noninflationary environment, both in the United States and in the rest of the world. Although relaxing this simplifying assumption does not undo the lessons we learned earlier, it does allow us to modify them to explain some anomalies. The purpose of this chapter is to explain a general rule of thumb, called purchasing power parity, that can provide a guide to the behavior of an economy's exchange rate over the long run in an inflationary environment.

Upon completion of this chapter you should

- understand why in the long run under a fixed exchange-rate system a country's monetary policy and thus inflation rate are forced to be the same as that of the rest of the world;

- know how to use the purchasing power parity rule of thumb to predict what will be happening to the exchange rate in the long run in an inflationary environment under a flexible exchange-rate system; and

- be able to calculate the purchasing power parity exchange rate and explain why it is used to calculate standard-of-living comparisons between countries.

15.1   Inflation with a Fixed Exchange Rate

In chapter 13 we saw that a rise in our price level, with no corresponding rise in foreign prices, leads to a balance of payments deficit, which under a fixed exchange-rate system in turn leads to an automatic contraction of our money supply. The same will happen if the rate of inflation in our economy is greater than the rate of inflation in the rest of the world.

Suppose that U.S. inflation is 8 percent, but it is only 5 percent in the rest of the world, due to differing money-supply growth rates. With a fixed exchange rate, during the first year U.S. prices rise by 3 percent more than foreign prices. If nothing changes, during the following year the gap between U.S. and foreign prices widens by another 3 percent, and so on, year after year. It is not true, however, that nothing changes.

Prices in the United States are rising relative to foreign prices, so U.S. exports should fall and imports should rise. As a result the United States should develop a balance of payments deficit, and the rest of the world should develop a balance of payments surplus. Under fixed exchange rates these developments should automatically decrease the U.S. money supply and automatically increase the foreign money supply. The fall in money-supply growth in the United States lowers its rate of inflation over the long run, and the increase in money-supply growth in the rest of the world increases foreign inflation over the long run. The pressure on both inflation rates continues as long as the U.S. inflation rate exceeds that of the rest of the world. Eventually inflation and money-supply growth in the rest of the world should match those of the United States. This is described in the left-hand side of figure 15.1, assuming that inflation in the rest of the world will rise to match U.S. inflation.

U.S. inflation 8% and foreign inflation 5%
⇒ each year U.S. g & s become 3% relatively more expensive
⇒ ↓ U.S. exports and ↑ U.S. imports
⇒ U.S. B of P deficit and foreign B of P surplus

Fixed exchange rate
⇒ automatic ↑ foreign money supply
⇒ ↑ foreign inflation
⇒ elimination of disequilibrium if ↑ foreign inflation to 8%
⇒ new equilibrium with original imports and exports because back to original relative prices

Flexible exchange rate
⇒ ↓ U.S. exchange rate (↑ foreign exchange rate)
⇒ elimination of disequilibrium if ↓ U.S. exchange rate by 3% per year; speculators automatically make this happen
⇒ new equilibrium with original imports and exports because no change in real exchange rate

Figure 15.1   Resolving Inflation Differences
Under a fixed exchange rate a small foreign country is forced to experience the monetary policy and inflation of the United States, and under a flexible exchange rate the exchange rate adjusts continually to offset the inflation differential; miraculously, this happens without any changes in imports and exports because speculators, seeing the inflation differential, buy and sell currencies accordingly!

Does inflation in the rest of the world rise to match American inflation? Does American inflation fall to match foreign inflation? Or do they both move to an intermediate rate? From 1945 to 1971, when most countries were on a fixed exchange-rate system, the Bretton Woods system, all countries fixed their exchange rates relative to the U.S. dollar so that in essence everything was measured in U.S. dollars. As a result the United States could simply print U.S. dollars to cover its balance of payments deficit, eliminating any automatic contraction of the money supply. Consequently the rest of the world was forced to experience U.S. monetary policy and inflation rate.

The bottom line here is that under a fixed exchange rate, a small open economy loses control of its monetary policy, which is forced to be identical to that of the larger country to whose currency its exchange rate is fixed. Note that this analysis corroborates the result of the preceding chapter: monetary policy is ineffective under a fixed exchange rate.

Sample Exam Question 15.1:
Suppose that the United States and Canada, on a fixed exchange rate, are both experiencing real growth of 2 percent, and money growth of 5 percent.
    If the United States increases its money growth to 9 percent, what should happen to Canada's inflation rate?

Curiosity 15.1: What Was the Bretton Woods System?

In 1944, when an Allied victory was certain, the Allies held a conference at Bretton Woods, New Hampshire, to discuss what kind of currency exchange rate system the world should adopt after the war. Influenced heavily by its most prominent participant, John Maynard Keynes, countries decided to have all central banks buy and sell their own currencies so as to fix their currency in terms of U.S. dollars, with gold or U.S. dollars serving as reserves. Any country experiencing high inflation, and thus a balance of payments deficit, would under this system be subjected to an automatic harsh discipline: it would be forced to shrink its money supply, which would lower its inflation and thereby restore equilibrium in its international sector. The only exception was the United States, which could ignore its balance of payments deficits because it, and it alone, could print reserves—U.S. dollars.

The conference also established the International Monetary Fund (IMF) to achieve stability in the international monetary and financial system, typically by providing loans to countries having temporary difficulties dealing with balance of payments problems. It also created the International Bank for Reconstruction and Development, commonly called the World Bank, focused on poverty, primarily by making long-term loans to assist developing countries building infrastructure such as dams and roads. Finally, it led in 1947 to the General Agreement on Tariffs and Trade (GATT), supplanted in 1995 by the World Trade Organization (WTO), to provide a forum for trade negotiations, to deal with trade disputes, and to advocate free and fair trade. The World Bank has about 10,000 employees, the IMF about 2,700, and the WTO about 600.

15.2   Inflation with a Flexible Exchange Rate

The fixed exchange-rate system described in curiosity 15.1 was attractive to the United States because it could do what it wanted and other countries had to adjust. Of course, if the United States created a big inflation, other countries could decide to abandon the fixed exchange-rate system and no longer tie their currency to the U.S. dollar, thereby escaping the high American inflation. This sequence of events is exactly what happened during the Vietnam war, causing the world to move to a flexible exchange-rate system.

Consider the same example: 8 percent inflation in America and 5 percent inflation in the rest of the world, but with a flexible exchange rate. Now the balance of payments deficit in the United States automatically causes the dollar to depreciate rather than causing money supplies to change. If the depreciation is 3 percent per year, then the 3 percent inflation difference causing U.S. goods and services annually to become 3 percent more expensive is exactly offset, and the international sector remains in balance. The *real* exchange rate is unchanged.

Curiosity 15.2: What Is the Real Exchange Rate?

In the example in which U.S. inflation is 8 percent and foreign inflation 5 percent, we saw that under a flexible exchange-rate system the U.S. dollar would depreciate by 3 percent per year. This 3 percent annual depreciation just offsets the annual relative increase in U.S. prices of 3 percent, so there should be no incentive for anyone to change demand for imports or exports. Although there has been a change in the nominal exchange rate, there has been no change in the real exchange rate.

The nominal exchange rate is the one we read about in the newspaper. It tells us the rate at which our currency exchanges for foreign currencies. The real exchange rate, sometimes called the terms of trade, tells us the rate at which our goods and services exchange for foreign goods and services; it is therefore the exchange rate that influences imports and exports. The real exchange rate can be calculated from the nominal exchange rate as follows:

$$\text{Real exchange rate} = \text{Nominal exchange rate} \times \frac{\text{Domestic price level}}{\text{Foreign price level}}$$

The domestic to foreign price ratio in this formula is calculated as the cost of a typical basket of traded goods and services in the United States in U.S. dollars divided by the cost of that same basket in the foreign country in its currency.

From this formula, if U.S. prices increase by 8 percent per year and foreign prices increase by 5 percent per year, then each year the ratio of their price levels increases by about 3 percent, canceled out by the 3 percent fall in the nominal exchange rate. The real exchange rate is unchanged, as it should be in this example. A crucial assumption in the PPP rule of thumb is that the real exchange rate is constant, something we know is not true. Figure 15.2 shows how the real exchange rate has changed dramatically in response to factors such as resource discoveries and real interest-rate differentials.

Warning! Students tend to forget that it is the real exchange rate that affects demand for imports and exports. Read curiosity 15.2 with extra care. If our prices rise by x percent more than our trading partner's prices, a depreciation of our currency by x percent leaves the real exchange rate unchanged; there should be no impact on exports and imports because of this nominal exchange rate depreciation.

Speculators foresee all this and buy/sell currencies accordingly, causing the rate of change of the exchange rate to equal the difference between foreign and U.S. inflation rates. Notice that the change in the exchange rate is ongoing. Each year the exchange rate must change by an amount equal to the difference in inflation rates. This result is often referred to as *purchasing power parity*, or PPP:

Rate of change of exchange rate = Foreign inflation rate − Domestic inflation rate

In the example, the rate of change of the U.S. dollar value should be 5 percent less 8 percent equals −3 percent, a depreciation of 3 percent per year. This example is summarized in figure 15.1 for both the fixed and the flexible exchange-rate systems.

Sample Exam Question 15.2:
Suppose that the United States and Canada, on a flexible exchange rate, are both experiencing real growth of 2 percent, and money growth of 5 percent. If the United States increases its money growth to 9 percent, what should happen to Canada's inflation rate?

15.3   Purchasing Power Parity

Like the formula for inflation from chapter 9, the PPP relationship is best described as a rule of thumb for predicting long-run behavior. In the short run, exchange rate changes are very volatile, affected by political events, business cycles, speculator activity, monetary policies, and rumors affecting financial markets, among many other things. Consequently PPP is unlikely in the short run to be a good guide to exchange rate behavior.

Even in the long run, PPP can be a poor guide because it assumes that the real exchange rate is constant, whereas in fact a variety of factors can permanently influence our ability to compete on international markets:

1. Natural resource discoveries such as Alaska or North Sea oil.

2. A change in our "terms of trade"—the world price of things we export changes relative to the world price of things we import.

3. Invention of new products such as iPods.

4. Changes in barriers to trade such as tariff reductions associated with free trade agreements.

5. Changes in consumers' tastes for imported versus domestic goods.

6. Permanent changes in countries' relative real interest rates.

7. Differing rates of productivity growth across countries.

8. Overall inflation rates not accurately reflecting price changes in traded goods and services.

All the factors listed above can permanently affect the exchange rate in the long run in the absence of inflation, thus invalidating the PPP result; in short, they change the real exchange rate, causing the nominal exchange rate to change without any need for an inflation difference. This is illustrated in figure 15.2. A large swing in the real U.S. exchange rate occurred during the 1980s as the result of a high relative U.S. real interest rate. Despite

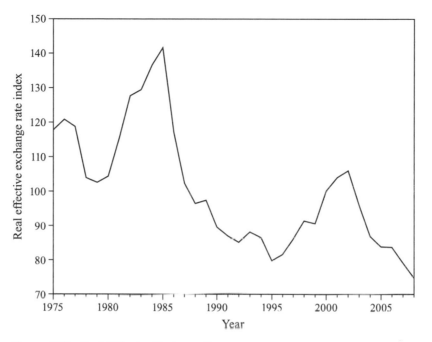

Figure 15.2   Real Effective Exchange Rate
This graph shows how dramatically the real exchange rate can change. The high interest rate policies of the 1980s caused capital inflows, pushing up the real value of the U.S. dollar. Source: International Monetary Fund.

the failures of the PPP theorem, it is still of value, mainly because predicting inflation differentials is sometimes easier than predicting changes in other factors that affect the exchange rate, so PPP can be a useful guide to predicting future exchange rates. The PPP is particularly useful when looking at countries with markedly different inflation rates—the impact on their nominal exchange rate of changes in their real exchange rate is swamped by the influence of their inflation difference. Figure 15.3 illustrates this.

Warning! The PPP rule of thumb can lead to very erroneous predictions. In the early 1970s it looked as though the British pound would depreciate steadily against the U.S. dollar because its inflation rate was so high. But for two reasons it did not. First, Margaret Thatcher became prime minister in Britain and invoked a monetarist policy of reducing the money growth rate, lowering British inflation. And second, the British discovered oil in the North Sea. For the PPP rule of thumb to provide accurate forecasts of exchange rates, the inflation differences must be maintained, and there must not be any change in the real exchange rate.

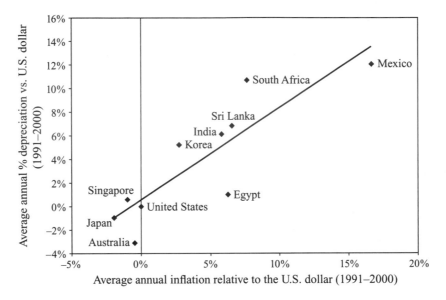

Figure 15.3   Illustrating PPP
Source: International Financial Statistics.

The PPP rule of thumb is often described as stating that the cost of a tradable good must be the same in dollars whether purchased abroad (after exchanging the dollars for local currency) or at home. If this were not the case, arbitragers would buy the product in the cheaper country and send it to the expensive country for sale. On a grand scale, such practices would cause a balance of payments deficit in the expensive country—causing its exchange rate to fall and thereby eliminating the cost advantage of the cheaper country. Exactly the same logic was used earlier to derive the PPP result in terms of inflation differentials.

Anyone who has traveled to foreign countries can confirm that many tradable goods do not cost the same in dollars at home as abroad. Transportation costs, taxes, lack of perfect substitutability between products, and interest rate differences affecting exchange rates are some of the reasons for the differences, but whatever the reasons, PPP does not work well when defined in terms of absolute price levels.

Defining PPP in terms of inflation differentials circumvents this problem. Suppose that because of things such as taxes or transportation costs, the absolute dollar price of a particular tradable good tends to be 10 percent higher in one country than another. Defined in terms of absolute prices, PPP says something should change, but there are no forces to cause a change. If there are inflation differentials, however, the 10 percent difference grows or shrinks, eventually by enough to cause forces for change to arise. Thus, looking at inflation differences enables more confidence to be placed in the PPP prediction, at least insofar as the long-run picture is concerned.

Sample Exam Question 15.3:
Suppose that the current exchange rate is $1.20 Canadian to $1 United States.

If the inflation rate in Canada is 8 percent and in the United States is 5 percent, if these countries have a flexible exchange rate, what would you expect the exchange rate to be two years from now?

15.4   The PPP Exchange Rate

A traveler also might notice that prices of nontradables— such as haircuts and hotel rooms—can differ markedly from country to country, at times by amounts dramatically different from what PPP would imply. Because PPP only applies to tradables, this phenomenon is not anomalous, but it does suggest that the exchange rate can be misleading if used to calculate cost-of-living comparisons.

Say you are offered a job in Mexico paying 500,000 pesos a year. You check the newspaper, find that the exchange rate is 12 pesos to a U.S. dollar, and quickly calculate that this amount is equal to about U.S.$42,000. It would be a mistake to compare this figure to your current salary in the United States because it may be that the cost of living in Mexico differs markedly from the cost of living in the United States. To make a fair comparison, you have to find out how much it would cost you to live your current lifestyle in Mexico.

The real problem here is that the exchange rate does not reflect cost-of-living differences between countries. It reflects instead the forces of supply and demand for the dollar in the foreign exchange market, determined by the relative costs of tradables and by a variety of other factors (e.g., interest-rate differences). To make cross-country cost-of-living comparisons, we need a different exchange rate, one explicitly designed to tell us the purchasing power of a peso in Mexico compared to the purchasing power of a dollar in the United States.

The *PPP exchange rate* does just that. It is calculated by taking the ratio of the cost of a typical bundle of goods and services in pesos in Mexico to the cost of that same bundle in dollars in the United States. Formally, it is calculated as follows:

$$\text{PPP exchange rate} = \frac{\text{Foreign cost of typical bundle in foreign currency}}{\text{Domestic cost of typical bundle in domestic currency}}$$

If the ratio is 11, then the PPP exchange rate is 11 pesos per dollar, so the 500,000 peso salary, in terms of its purchasing power in Mexico, is equivalent to about U.S.$45,000. An innovative, albeit extreme, way of measuring the PPP exchange rate was developed by *The Economist* magazine through checking the cost of a Big Mac in different countries.

If, for example, a Big Mac costs 16 pesos in Mexico and 2 dollars in the United States, the PPP exchange rate is 8 pesos per dollar.

Using this alternative exchange rate to make cross-country comparisons can make a big difference. Recently the International Monetary Fund calculated world income shares using purchasing power parity exchange rates instead of current exchange rates. The result vastly boosts developing countries' share of the world's GDP—to 34.4 percent from 17.7 percent. The explanation for this result is that the PPP exchange-rate accounts for the fact that many nontradable goods and services in developing countries are much cheaper than in developed countries.

In 2006, for example, U.S. per capita GDP was $43,801. Switzerland's per capita GDP was $52,544 using the market exchange rate, but only $37,747 using the PPP exchange rate. The market exchange rate for Swiss francs was about 1.25 francs per dollar but the PPP exchange rate was about 1.7 francs per dollar because the cost of living was higher in Switzerland—in Switzerland 1.7 francs were needed to buy what in the United States would cost a dollar, but a tourist exchanging dollars for francs received only 1.24 francs for a dollar. For countries with a high cost of living, such as Switzerland and Norway, using PPP exchange rates lowers per capita GDP figures for international comparison purposes. For countries with a lower cost of living, such as Mexico and Turkey, using the PPP exchange rate raises their per capita GDP figure for international comparison purposes. Mexican per capita GDP in 2006 was $7,915 when calculated using the market exchange rate (about 10.9 pesos per dollar) but was $12,104 using the PPP exchange rate (about 7.2 pesos per dollar). PPP exchange rates can be found at www.oecd.org.

> **Sample Exam Question 15.4:**
> Suppose that the current exchange rate between the United States and Mexico is 13 pesos to a dollar.
> If you are about to vacation in Mexico, would you prefer the PPP exchange rate to be 10 pesos per dollar or 16 pesos per dollar? Give your reasoning.

Media Illustrations

Example 1
This is the reason why the fixed exchange-rate system was scrapped in 1971. The United States had been pursuing an inflationary monetary policy to help pay for the Vietnam war and new social programs, and its trading partners did not all want to participate in it.

What is an inflationary monetary policy?
Inflation results from increasing the money supply at a rate greater than the real rate of growth of the economy.

What are the three basic ways of paying for the Vietnam war and new social programs? To which does the "inflationary monetary policy" refer?

This government spending must be financed by raising taxes, selling bonds to the public, or printing money (selling bonds to the central bank). The last of these is most directly tied to inflation.

What is forcing U.S. trading partners to participate in this inflationary monetary policy?

Under a fixed exchange rate a small open country is forced to experience the same monetary policy as the country to which its exchange rate is fixed. In this example the trading partners had fixed their exchange rates to the U.S. dollar.

If the fixed exchange rate system were scrapped, what exactly would these trading partners have to do to opt out of participating in this inflationary monetary policy?

They would have to reduce their money-supply growth rate to produce the long-run inflation rate they desire, and allow their exchange rate with the U.S. dollar to rise continually, at a rate equal to the difference between the U.S. rate of inflation and their own.

Example 2

While critics have suggested that the central bank could lower rates and, in so doing, let the dollar fall on international exchange markets, the report said that the dollar has already fallen in the last half-dozen years and raises the question of why things have not gone better if exchange-rate depreciation is so good for the economy.

What rate is it suggested be lowered, and why would it cause the dollar to fall?

If the interest rate is lowered, capital inflows will fall, decreasing the demand for our dollar, causing its price in terms of foreign currency to fall.

What is the rationale behind the belief that exchange rate depreciation is good for the economy?

A fall in our exchange rate makes our exports cheaper to foreigners and our imports more expensive to us, so demand for domestic production, in the form of exports and import-competing goods and services, should increase, stimulating our economy.

How would you explain why the fall in the dollar over the last half dozen years has not caused things to go better?

It could be that the reason why the dollar has fallen over the past half dozen years is that during this time our inflation was greater than that of our trading partners, so that the fall in the exchange rate served merely to keep the real exchange rate steady.

Example 3

In three to five years, the U.S. dollar will presumably resume its long-term slide unless Washington reverses its economic policies of the post–Second World War period and takes a tough stand against inflation. Observers believe a Reagan administration may take that tougher stand.

What would an administration need to do to take a tough stand against inflation?
To cut inflation in the long run, the rate of growth of the money supply would have to be cut back to a level more in line with the real rate of growth of the economy.

What is the logic of the first sentence of this clipping?
According to purchasing power parity, if the rate of inflation in the United States is higher than that of its trading partners, in the long run the exchange rate will fall (the dollar will continue to slide) at a rate equal to the difference between U.S. inflation and that of its trading partners.

Example 4

News that U.S. job creation in January was more robust than anticipated sent a signal to currency markets to expect a stepped-up fight against inflation, unleashing a bout of buying fervor for the U.S. dollar.

Why would this news cause people to expect a stepped-up fight against inflation?
Unexpected job creation might signal that the economy is moving into a boom, pushing unemployment below the NRU, threatening inflation.

Why would a bout of buying fervor for the U.S. dollar result?
A stepped-up fight against inflation would involve a rise in the real interest rate to dampen aggregate demand. This rise in the interest rate would increase capital inflows, bidding up the value of the U.S. dollar. In addition, if the stepped-up fight against inflation were to succeed, inflation in the United States would fall below foreign inflation, which by PPP also leads to a rise in the U.S. dollar. Currency speculators anticipate this and buy U.S. dollars to reap the resulting capital gain.

Chapter Summary

- With a fixed exchange rate, a small open economy is forced to experience the money-supply growth and inflation of its major trading partners. A lower inflation rate, for example, causes exports to become cheap and imports expensive, inducing a balance of payments surplus that automatically increases the money supply and pushes up inflation.

- With a flexible exchange rate, a country with a lower inflation rate will experience a rise in its exchange rate, offsetting any price difference created by differing inflation rates. Its real exchange rate remains unchanged, reflecting *purchasing power parity:* the rate of change of a country's exchange rate equals the difference between foreign and domestic inflation.

- Purchasing power parity is a rule of thumb for predicting long-run nominal exchange-rate behavior. There are many reasons why PPP is unlikely to hold in the short run, and even in the long run several factors can cause the real exchange rate to change and thus cause purchasing power parity not to hold.

- The purchasing power parity exchange rate measures cost-of-living differences across countries.

Definitional Formulas

$$\text{Real exchange rate} = \text{Nominal exchange rate} \times \frac{\text{Domestic price level}}{\text{Foreign price level}}$$

$$\text{PPP exchange rate} = \frac{\text{Foreign cost of typical bundle in foreign currency}}{\text{Domestic cost of typical bundle in domestic currency}}$$

Rule of Thumb

PPP: rate of change of exchange rate = Foreign inflation − Domestic inflation

---

Media Exercises

(Group B questions require more thought.)

A1.   American tourists who are pleased to get $1.35 or so Canadian dollars for their U.S. dollars only to find that most purchases cost _____ are learning a simple lesson in the _____ theory of exchange rates.

Fill in the blanks.

A2.   If Ukrainian prices hadn't risen in line with Russian prices, market forces would have sucked Ukraine dry of food and consumer goods as Russians sought cheaper goods than they could get at home.

How would this result have been different if both areas had their own currencies?

A3.   All countries that consistently run lower inflation rates than their trading partners over a long period of time have an upward trend in. . . .

Complete this statement.

A4.   How does the average Chinese survive on just enough money each month for 17 Big Macs—which is what official Chinese per capita income implies? The answer is, of course, that he doesn't, because converting incomes at current exchange rates doesn't reflect _____.

Fill in the blank.

A5. **A second issue concerns how long the fixed exchange rate could be maintained. The exchange rate, of course, depends on an uncertain future, but if the initial value chosen was appropriate and if domestic costs remained in line with foreign costs, then the rate may be sustainable for some time.**

a. What is meant by domestic costs remaining in line with foreign costs?

b. What would happen if domestic costs exceeded foreign costs?

A6. **To be sure, the central bank said the broad money aggregates have merely been upgraded to "indicative policy guides," rather than formal targets, but it did make plain its rejection of the former unspoken policy of targeting the exchange rate.**

Why would adoption of this new policy require rejection of the old?

A7. **While the table shows that there are more countries against which the U.S. dollar has appreciated over the past 12 months rather than depreciated, the extra local currency that a fixed U.S. dollar outlay will buy is not necessarily a great windfall to the U.S. traveler.**

Explain why the U.S. traveler may not find this to be a windfall.

A8. **Word that growth in the cost of living was slower in the United States than in Germany last year attracted buyers for the U.S. dollar.**

Explain why this report on cost of living should attract buyers for the U.S. dollar.

A9. **Tying the Canadian dollar to the U.S. dollar may eliminate some worries, but it will create others, among them concern that the United States might not be as dedicated as Canada is to fighting inflation.**

Explain why this concern is created by adopting a fixed exchange rate.

A10. **The cheapest Big Mac, at $1.03, is in China, and the most expensive, at $3.96, is in Switzerland. These figures imply that the yuan is the most undervalued currency and the Swiss franc the most overvalued.**

What economic theory gives rise to this conclusion? What is its logic?

A11. **But economic theory and our own experience tell us that using monetary policy to drive down the exchange rate will be successful only until. . . .**

Complete this statement.

A12. **In 1993, for example, the peso declined 0.6 percent, whereas consumer prices rose 9.8 percent in Mexico versus just 2.5 percent in the United States. This**

led to an _____ of the peso, contributing to the forces causing the Mexican financial crisis of December 1994.

Fill in the blank and explain your reasoning.

B1. **The conventional wisdom has been that inflation is bad for the economy. If our inflation is running higher than our trading partners' inflation, according to this argument, our growth slows and jobs are lost.**

a. Explain how the mechanism described here works.

b. How could this problem be avoided without curbing our inflation?

B2. **Monday's trade figures—twice as bad as analysts were generally expecting them to be—reinforced fears that the economy was overheating, with imports outstripping exports and inflationary pressures surging. The government is now expected to raise interest rates almost immediately.**

a. Would you expect imports to outstrip exports in the presence of surging inflation? Explain why or why not.

b. Why would the government be expected to raise interest rates?

B3. **Foreign countries are now free to pursue an independent course of monetary policy, and old conflicts about the U.S. role in exporting inflation and about the adjustment responsibilities of surplus (or deficit) nations suddenly seem to have lost their relevance.**

a. What major change do you think has led to the remarks in this clipping?

b. How could the U.S. export inflation?

c. What are the adjustment responsibilities mentioned in this clipping?

B4. **The record has not been good. Our past experience with exchange rate depreciation has been that all too often it has led, not to a sustained improvement in our competitiveness, but to. . . .**

Complete this statement, and explain your reasoning.

B5. **Why has he argued for a stable dollar and a zero inflation? Aren't these inconsistent goals?**

Explain how these goals could be inconsistent.

B6. **While acknowledging that a weaker dollar initially favors exports, he said this advantage will only last as long as. . . .**

Complete this statement, and explain your reasoning.

B7. **Finally, there is the question of monetary policy and imported inflation. Under a fixed exchange rate, Canada's inflation would be more closely tied to that of the United States Given the experience of the past few years, that may not be a bad thing.**

   a. Explain how Canada's inflation would be more closely tied to that of the United States under a fixed exchange rate.

   b. In light of the final sentence, what change in monetary policy would come about in Canada if the exchange rate were fixed? Explain why.

B8. **Big Mac watchers rely on the theory of purchasing power parity (PPP) for currencies. This argues that an exchange rate between two currencies is in equilibrium (at PPP) when it leaves hamburgers costing the same in each country. Comparing actual exchange rates with PPPs is one indication of whether a currency is under- or overvalued.**

   a. What meaning would be attached to a statement that a currency is undervalued by a PPP measure?

   b. By means of an explicit example, explain how you would use the price of hamburgers to find the PPP exchange rate.

   c. How would you use this calculation to claim a currency is under- or overvalued?

   d. What objection do you have to using this method to calculate the PPP rate?

B9. **The surest way to sustain the exchange value of our currency is to maintain its purchasing power at home.**

   Explain the rationale for this statement.

B10. **An even better case study is Singapore. The Singapore Monetary Authority deliberately targets a trend appreciation in the Singapore dollar versus the U. S. dollar in order to maintain price stability.**

   a. Why would this policy achieve price stability?

   b. What trend rate would be appropriate?

B11. **Switzerland used to boast one of the lowest inflation rates in the world and one of the strongest currencies, thanks to sound monetary policies and prudent public finances.**

   a. What kind of monetary policy is being referred to here?

   b. After achieving a low inflation, what more would the policy authorities need to do to ensure a strong currency?

B12. Exporters and some economists have argued that the central bank should drive down the value of the dollar to boost economic activity. The Fed claims, however, that its ability to influence the real exchange rate is severely limited.

    a. How would the central bank drive down the value of the dollar?

    b. Why does the second sentence refer to the "real" exchange rate? What alternative exchange rate might be in mind here?

    c. Explain why the central bank's ability to influence the real exchange rate is limited.

B13. If inflation exists in the rest of the world, but not in Canada, our merchandise trade surplus should soar with exports becoming cheap and imports expensive. Of course, that would stimulate economic activity in Canada, and pretty soon the inflation rate would begin to rise. How would the authorities counter that undesirable development? By keeping money growth low and interest rates much higher than U.S. interest rates—the same way that the Bank of Canada has fought inflation in the past and still does today.

    a. What exchange-rate system must this author be assuming? How can you tell?

    b. Comment on the suitability of the monetary policy that this author claims the Bank of Canada would employ to fight this inflation.

B14. Our leaders have convinced themselves that the falling dollar will improve the economy by eliminating the trade deficit, reducing inflation, and improving our GDP.

Are these conclusions correct? If not, or if only under certain circumstances, explain why not.

Numerical Exercises

    AN1. Suppose that the real rates of growth in the United States and Canada are both 2 percent, inflation in Canada is 9 percent, and the U.S. dollar is appreciating against the Canadian dollar by 4 percent per year. What is the U.S. money growth rate?

    AN2. In 1975 the U.S./Canada exchange rate was 1.02 (i.e., 1 U.S. dollar bought 1.02 Canadian dollars). The Canadian price level rose by 52 percent between 1975 and 1980, while the U.S. price level rose by 41 percent. From this information what do you predict the 1980 exchange rate to be?

AN3. Suppose that a typical basket of goods and services consists of 4 units of housing and 7 units of food. In the United States a unit of housing costs 2 U.S. dollars and a unit of food costs 1 U.S. dollar; in Canada these prices are 3 Canadian dollars and 2 Canadian dollars, respectively. If the current exchange rate is 1.5 Canadian dollars per U.S. dollar, what is the purchasing power parity exchange rate?

BN1. Suppose that the U.S. and Canadian economies, on a flexible exchange rate, are both experiencing a real growth rate of 3 percent, but that the Canadian money supply growth rate is 10 percent compared to only 6 percent in the United States. Currently 1 U.S. dollar buys 1.2 Canadian dollars. How many Canadian dollars would you guess 1 U.S. dollar will buy two years from now?

BN2. Suppose that in mid-1990 one U.S. dollar bought 1.1 Canadian dollars and in mid-1992 it bought 1.2 Canadian dollars. During this period the annual rate of inflation was 5 percent in the United States and 8 percent in Canada.

   a. By how much does PPP predict the U.S. dollar nominal exchange rate should change during this period?

   b. Has the U.S. dollar real exchange rate risen or fallen during this period? By how much?

BN3. Suppose that the American and Canadian economies are in equilibrium with an exchange rate of 1 U.S. dollar per 1.3 Canadian dollars and a common inflation rate of 5 percent. If the United States increases the rate of growth of its money supply by two percentage points, what do you expect to happen to the real exchange rate,

   a. Under a fixed exchange rate?

   b. Under a flexible exchange rate?

BN4. In 1997 per capita GDP in U.S. dollars in Korea was $9,620. If the market exchange rate was 1,100 won/dollar and the PPP exchange rate was 730 won/dollar, what was Korea per capita GDP in U.S. dollars using the PPP exchange rate?

BN5. In 1997 Canadian per capita income in U.S. dollars was $20,064 when calculated using the market exchange rate, but $23,761 when calculated using the PPP exchange rate. If the market rate of exchange was 1.4 Canadian dollars per U.S. dollar, what was the PPP exchange rate?

16   Interest-Rate Parity

The central theme of this chapter is that real interest rates are approximately the same across countries, a result known as the *interest-rate parity theorem.* Three questions should immediately come to mind: What causes interest-rate parity? Why is it only approximate? Why does it relate to the real interest rate rather than to the nominal interest rate?

The previous chapter explained how differing rates of inflation in trading countries affected the international balance between those countries and thereby influenced the exchange rate between their currencies. However, an important dimension of this international relationship was not addressed. One might expect differing inflation rates to give rise to different nominal interest rates, which could in turn influence the balance of payments and thus the exchange rate. The foregoing statement is misleading, however, because the exchange rate is affected by real, not nominal, interest-rate differences; the purpose of this chapter is to explain why this statement is true.

Upon completion of this chapter you should

- understand why real interest rates should be approximately the same in all countries, a result known as interest-rate parity; and

- be able to explain why a nominal interest-rate difference between countries should have no impact on the exchange rate except insofar as it reflects a real interest-rate difference.

16.1   Why Are Real Interest Rates Similar in Different Countries?

In chapter 13 we saw that a rise in a country's real interest rate, with no change in other countries' real interest rates, causes a net capital inflow. We discussed how this would affect the balance of payments and consequently influence other economic variables of interest. One impact of the net capital inflow that we did not discuss was its effect on the real interest rate itself.

Suppose, for example, that the real interest rate in a small country such as Canada rises, creating a net capital inflow into Canada. This puts downward pressure on the Canadian real interest rate. This result occurs for two reasons. First, foreigners will want to invest in Canadian bonds to obtain the higher return, so the demand for Canadian bonds increases, bidding up Canadian bond prices and thereby lowering the Canadian real interest rate. Second, Canadian firms selling bonds will find it cheaper to raise capital in other countries, so they will remove their bonds from the Canadian market and take them to foreign bond markets. The fall in the supply of bonds on the Canadian market also causes the price of Canadian bonds to rise, thus lowering the Canadian real interest rate.

The bottom line here is that a rise in the Canadian real interest rate sets in motion forces that push this interest rate back toward the "world" real rate of interest. In general, however, these forces will not succeed in pushing the Canadian interest rate all the way to the "world" real rate because the relationship between the "world" real rate and a specific country's real rate is only approximate.

> **Sample Exam Question 16.1:**
> "Before the advent of modern international financial markets in the mid-1970s, domestic financial markets placed a serious constraint on the ability of governments to borrow their way to popularity or prosperity. Historically, domestic financial markets were largely closed systems where excessive borrowing by governments led quickly to . . ."
>
> Complete this clipping, and explain how the advent of modern international financial markets has changed this situation.

Curiosity 16.1: Can Monetary Policy Change Real Interest Rates?

Interest rate parity suggests that the world real interest rate is determined by major countries like the United States and that smaller countries such as Canada are forced to have a real interest rate equal to this world real interest rate plus a risk premium. An implication of this statement is that Canadian monetary policy should not be able to affect the gap between the Canadian and U.S. real rates and thus unilaterally change the Canadian real interest rate. However, central banks do raise and lower their real interest rates to affect their exchange rate, at least temporarily—once again confirming the maxim that interest rate parity should be interpreted as an approximate relationship holding over the long run.

Suppose that the real interest rate in Canada rises to make the difference between Canadian and U.S. real interest rates greater than the Canada/U.S. risk premium. Investors hold diversified wealth portfolios consisting of optimal fractions of assets with different risk/yield combinations. When the Canadian yield moves higher, the optimal fraction of Canadian bonds in investor portfolios rises slightly, so investors adjust their portfolios to hold more Canadian bonds. The operative word here is "slightly": they are not willing to buy massive quantities of the Canadian bonds because doing so would raise the overall risk of their portfolio beyond what the higher yield on Canadian bonds warrants. Consequently, although the rise in the Canadian real interest rate is curtailed by extra foreign purchases of Canadian bonds, it is not eliminated.

The activity of buying these bonds creates, in addition, a demand for Canadian dollars that bids up the value of the Canadian dollar beyond the level that many would consider to be normal. As a result investors may think that the Canadian dollar is more likely to fall in the future and thus may consider Canadian bonds as being riskier than before the interest rate rose. The rise in the value of the Canadian dollar also limits the quantity of extra bonds bought by foreigners, preventing the Canadian real rate from falling back to its original level.

A determined central bank can modestly increase its real interest rate above that of the "world" real rate, beyond the risk premium, thereby creating a continuing capital inflow. The capital inflow will initially be quite large, as investors readjust their portfolios, but then will fall off to a modest level that reflects a higher fraction of the flow of new saving. A policy of keeping the real interest rate above the world rate, such as that followed by the United States during the 1980s because of budget deficits and a low saving rate, causes foreign debt (U.S. bonds owned by foreigners) to increase, something that cannot go on forever. Interest-rate parity is consequently a better guide to long-run than short-run behavior.

16.2   Why Approximately?

The "world" real rate is a fictitious rate, thought to be determined by activity in a few large, stable financial markets such as those in the United States, Germany, Great Britain, and Japan. For expositional convenience, however, we consider the world real rate to be the rate prevailing in the United States, keeping in mind that the U.S. real rate can in reality be affected by financial activity in these other large countries. The forces described in our Canadian example come about because the Canadian financial market is quite small relative to the U.S. market. If the Canadian and other small markets were microcosms of the U.S. market, the rate prevailing in the U.S. market would undoubtedly also prevail in these smaller markets. They are not exactly the same as the U.S. market, however, if for no other reason than that they are located in another country, with bonds denominated in another currency. The U.S. market sets a standard, not just in terms of a numerical rate but also in terms of the institutional structure associated with its financial transactions. Investing in a U.S. bond carries with it an implicit degree of riskiness, associated with the political stability, market liquidity, degree of business risk, and legal system characterizing the United States. The implicit degree of riskiness associated with, say, Canadian bonds, may be greater than with U.S. bonds (e.g., because of uncertainty caused by the possibility of Quebec separation), implying that the real rate in Canada must incorporate a *risk premium* and therefore be higher than in the United States to compensate for the difference in risk.

A major dimension of the risk factor is the possibility of changes in currency values, and for this reason the risk premium is sometimes called a *currency premium*. A U.S. investor buying Canadian bonds, for example, will be paid Canadian dollars when the bond matures, so the investor is running the risk that the value of the Canadian dollar may be lower at maturity than it was when he or she bought the bonds. Offsetting this danger is the possibility that the value of the Canadian dollar may be higher, but the point is that there is a risk. An investor will accept this risk only if a higher real rate of return is offered. An investor can purchase insurance to protect against this type of risk (this is called *hedging*), but at a cost that is of course higher, the higher is the risk. To cover this cost, the real interest rate on the Canadian bond must be higher to make it comparable to U.S. bonds in the eyes of U.S. investors.

> **Sample Exam Question 16.2:**
> "West Germany's decision to spend 85 billion dollars on reunification probably pushed up interest rates in the United States by half a percentage point."
> How would what happens in Germany push up U.S. interest rates? (This clip is from before the European Union adopted the euro as its common currency.)

16.3   Why Not Nominal Interest Rates?

The best way to explain why nominal interest rate differences are not relevant, except insofar as they reflect differences in real interest rates, is to look at a specific example.

Suppose that the United States and Canada are in equilibrium with a flexible exchange rate, that both countries have a real growth rate of 2 percent per year, that their money supplies are both growing at 7 percent per year, and that their real rates of interest are 3 percent and 4 percent, respectively, implying a risk premium of one percentage point in favor of the United States.

What are the inflation rates in the United States and Canada? Using our rule of thumb from chapter 9, the rate of inflation in both countries should be 5 percent, calculated in each case as 7 percent − 2 percent.

What are the nominal interest rates in the United States and Canada? Using the relationship between the real and nominal interest rates, the nominal interest rate in the United States should be 3 percent + 5 percent = 8 percent, and in Canada it should be 4 percent + 5 percent = 9 percent.

What is happening to the exchange rate? Because the rates of inflation in these two economies are the same, the purchasing power parity theorem implies that the exchange rate is constant.

Will there be capital flows? Since the one-percentage-point higher real interest rate in Canada just compensates U.S. lenders for the higher risk of investing in Canadian bonds, there should be no capital flows.

Now suppose that the rate of growth of the money supply in Canada jumps to 13 percent per year. When a new equilibrium is eventually attained, what should have happened to Canada's inflation rate, nominal interest rate, and the exchange rate? Inflation should jump to 11 percent, calculated as 13 percent − 2 percent. The nominal interest rate should jump to 11 percent + 4 percent = 15 percent. Because the difference between the Canadian and U.S. inflation rates is now six percentage points, the PPP theorem tells us that the exchange rate—from Canada's point of view—should be depreciating at a rate of 6 percent per year. All these numbers are summarized in figure 16.1. To check your understanding, cover up the last three rows and then, using the information in the first three rows, fill in the last three rows.

Suppose that you are a U.S. investor who, before the change in the Canadian money-supply growth rate, was indifferent between buying bonds in Canada versus in the United

	Original situation		New situation	
	United States	Canada	United States	Canada
Real growth	2	2	2	2
Real *i* rate	3	4	3	4
Money growth	7	7	7	13
Inflation	5	5	5	11
Nominal *i* rate	8	9	8	15
Rate of change of exchange rate	0	0	+6	−6
Capital flows	None	None	None	None

Figure 16.1 Nominal Interest Rates and Capital Flows
The example illustrates why nominal interest rate differences due to expected inflation differences do not affect capital flows. In moving from the original situation to the new situation, Canada's money growth rate increased from 7 percent to 13 percent.

States. There has been no change in the difference between the U.S. and Canadian real interest rates, so the interest rate parity theorem implies that there should be no change in the rate of capital flows. But there has been a dramatic change in the difference between the U.S. and Canadian nominal interest rates, with the Canadian rate now much higher. Why won't U.S. investors rush to buy Canadian bonds to reap the higher nominal return?

The Canadian nominal interest rate has jumped by six percentage points relative to its U.S. counterpart, but a U.S. investor will discover that this extra 6 percent is illusory. While his or her funds are invested in the Canadian bond, the value of the Canadian dollar should fall by 6 percent, so when he or she cashes in the bond and repatriates the proceeds, the extra 6 percent return is offset by the loss on the currency exchange.

Can't the investor buy insurance against such a currency devaluation and thereby avoid this loss? Buying such insurance is possible (doing so is called *hedging*), but how much do you think the insurance premium will cost? It should be more than 6 percent. The insurance agent will go through the same arithmetic, concluding that the Canadian dollar should depreciate by 6 percent, and so will charge a premium of 6 percent plus a commission.

This example can be summarized as follows: a difference in nominal interest rates that reflects only a difference in inflation rates (and thus does not correspond to a difference in real rates) generates no capital flows because the difference in nominal rates is offset by anticipated changes in currency values. Consequently the *interest rate parity* result must be written in terms of real interest rates:

Foreign real *i* rate = U.S. real *i* rate + Risk premium

The risk premium could be positive if the foreign country is thought to be riskier than the United States, as is the case with Canada. It could be negative if the foreign country is thought to be less risky than the United States, as may be the case with Switzerland. Because the risk premium is never known, and because monetary policy can cause a country's real interest rate in the short run to depart slightly from this formula, as explained in curiosity 16.1, this formula is best viewed as a rule of thumb useful for predicting long-run behavior and for analyzing differences between countries' nominal interest rates.

Sample Exam Question 16.3:
Suppose that the Canadian risk premium is 1 percent, the Canadian interest rate is 10 percent, the U.S. interest rate is 7 percent, and the two economies are in mutual equilibrium.

What should be happening to the U.S. exchange rate?

Curiosity 16.2: What Is a Forward Exchange Rate?

A U.S. firm closes a big deal with a Mexican buyer who will pay 5 million pesos when the product is delivered in three months' time. This firm is not in the business of speculating on the future value of pesos, so may understandably be nervous about how many U.S. dollars this foreign currency will buy in three months. To avoid this problem, the firm can "hedge" the transaction by entering a contract to sell 5 million pesos in three months at the three-month forward exchange rate. This way the firm guarantees how many U.S. dollars the 5 million pesos will buy in three months.

If the current or spot Mexican peso exchange rate is 4 U.S. cents per peso, then the 5 million pesos would today be worth U.S.$200,000. The person agreeing to buy these 5 million pesos from this firm in three months will want some reward for taking on the risk of an unexpected change in the value of the peso during this three-month period. This reward, which could be called an insurance premium paid by the firm, takes the form of a percentage "discount" of the spot rate to produce the forward rate.

The spot rate of 4.0 cents per peso could, for example, be discounted to produce a forward rate of 3.95 cents per peso. This implies that the 5 million pesos will in three months provide the firm with U.S.$197,500 instead of the U.S.$200,000 the firm would have received if the forward contract had not been signed and the exchange rate had not changed. The magnitude of the discount depends on what the Mexican peso is expected to do during these three months. If inflation in Mexico exceeds inflation in the United States, everyone would expect the Mexican peso to fall (because of the PPP theorem), so the forces of supply and demand in this market should cause the discount to be greater.

The "Currency Trading" column in the "Money & Investing" section of *The Wall Street Journal* reports daily the 30-, 90-, and 180-day forward rates for the British, Canadian, French, German, Japanese, and Swiss currencies. The discounts embodied in these forward rates are sometimes used to measure the market's expectations of future relative inflations across countries. As an example, consider the following entry for the Japanese yen, reporting the midrange of buying and selling rates among banks for transactions of a million dollars or more:

	Currency	
Country	U.S.$ equivalent	Per U.S.$
Japan (yen)	0.008405	118.98
1-Month forward	0.008431	118.50
3-Months forward	0.008514	117.46
6-Months forward	0.008628	115.90

Media Illustrations

Example 1

At the same time that Secretary Blumenthal was testifying to Congress, the Treasury borrowed $1.6 billion in Germany in the form of securities denominated in marks. It offered to pay an interest rate of roughly 6 percent per year on mark-denominated three- and four-year securities. On comparable securities denominated in dollars, the Treasury is currently paying about 9 percent—or 3 percentage points per year more. [This clip appeared before the birth of the euro.]

Why is the rate of interest offered on mark-denominated securities less than that offered on dollar-denominated securities?
The value of the U.S. dollar, relative to the German mark, must be expected to decline during the next three or four years.

Assuming that mark- and dollar-denominated securities are risk-equivalent, what would you guess is the difference between U.S. and German inflation?
If these securities are risk equivalent, the difference in nominal interest rates should be due mainly to expected inflation differences, so a good guess would be 3 percent.

What does the U.S. Treasury believe about the future value of the U.S. dollar in terms of marks? What do German investors buying these securities believe?
If the value of the U.S. dollar fell by 3 percent per year over the life of these bonds, the cost to the U.S. Treasury would be the 6 percent interest plus the 3 percent fall in the exchange rate, for a total cost of 9 percent, equivalent to the cost of selling bonds denominated in dollars. Consequently the U.S. Treasury must believe that over the life of these bonds the value of the U.S. dollar will fall by less than 3 percent per year. The German investors could have bought bonds denominated in dollars and earned 9 percent less the exchange loss, but instead opted for the guaranteed 6 percent. Consequently they must believe that the U.S. dollar will fall by more than 3 percent per year over the life of these bonds.

Example 2

The Fed has made occasional attempts to lower interest rates and accept some lowering of the dollar as a trade-off. Sometimes it works, and sometimes, like last summer, we end up with the worst of all possible worlds—higher interest rates and a lower dollar.

What causes the trade-off mentioned at the end of the first sentence?
If interest rates are lowered, foreigners will decrease their purchases of U.S. bonds. This decrease in capital inflows creates a balance of payments deficit, leading to a fall in the value of the U.S. dollar.

How would the Fed lower interest rates?
The Fed could buy bonds, bidding up their price, thereby lowering the interest rate.

What implication would this action have for the money supply and expected inflation?
This action involves an increase in the money supply, which could create an increase in expected inflation.

Explain how the "worst of all possible worlds" could occur.
The Fed's efforts to reduce the interest rate could increase inflation expectations causing the nominal interest rate actually to increase. This higher expected inflation rate would cause foreign exchange speculators, through the logic of purchasing power parity, to expect a fall in the U.S. dollar. To exploit this, they sell dollars, causing its value to fall.

Example 3

This does not mean there is a massive flow of U.S. funds into Canada, because the differentials are mitigated by other factors. The discount on the forward Canadian dollar has kept step with the interest-rate differential, and it is only on an unhedged basis that the full advantage of the differential can be gained.

What terminology do economists usually employ to describe a "flow of U.S. funds into Canada"?
It would usually be referred to as capital flows from the United States to Canada.

What must have happened to raise the possibility of a massive flow of U.S. funds into Canada?
The difference between the Canadian and U.S. nominal interest rates must have widened considerably.

What is the "discount on the forward Canadian dollar"?
This discount is the difference between the Canadian spot and forward exchange rates. It reflects an anticipated fall in the Canadian dollar over the time horizon in question, plus a return for taking on the risk of holding Canadian dollars over this period.

Why would the discount keep step with the interest-rate differential?
Suppose that the interest-rate differential increased by two percentage points. This increase probably occurred because of an increase in expected inflation in Canada of 2 percent (or a decrease in expected inflation in the United States of 2 percent, or some combination thereof). Purchasing power parity then predicts a 2 percent increase in the rate at which the Canadian dollar is depreciating. Since everyone can figure this out, the natural forces of supply and demand increase the discount by two percentage points.

What is an "unhedged basis," and why does it imply gaining the full advantage of the differential?
Contracting on the forward exchange market to avoid the risk of currency fluctuations is called "hedging." If this is not done, the full difference between the Canadian and U.S. interest rates is pocketed (but not necessarily kept, since losses from an unfavorable movement in the exchange rate may be incurred).

Chapter Summary

- Real interest rates are equal across countries except for a risk premium—a result known as *interest rate parity.*

- A nominal interest rate difference that only reflects a difference in expected inflation causes no capital flows because the purchasing power parity theorem causes people to expect an exchange rate change that will exactly offset the nominal interest rate difference.

Rule of Thumb

IRP: Foreign real *i* rate = U.S. real *i* rate + risk premium

Media Exercises

(Group B questions require more thought.)

A1. **He can't understand why we would put our money in domestic bonds at 9 percent, when we could get double-A rated New Zealand bonds at 19 percent.**

Offer an explanation for this choice.

A2. **Although they may think they have little in common, the conservative corporate treasurer and the brash, high-flying currency trader are alike in one important respect—they both speculate on the value of the dollar.**

a. How could a corporate treasurer be a speculator on the value of the dollar?

b. How can he or she avoid undertaking such speculation?

A3. **Higher inflation in both Germany and Japan has pushed up their interest rates. What he doesn't understand is why the U.S. interest rate hasn't followed suit. He claims that international financial markets are so closely integrated these days that the U.S. interest rate reaction should have been apparent by now.**

Comment on this observation.

A4. **Last week's movement was largely triggered by Bank of Canada concerns about the drop in the Canadian dollar in the face of higher U.S. interest rates.**

What is the "movement" referred to in this clip? Explain your reasoning.

A5. Prior to 1989 it was widely believed that New Zealand ten-year government bond interest rates could not fall below those of Australia. Once New Zealand rates fell below those of Australia, the view on relative rates changed to one where New Zealand rates could not fall below those of the United States, due to the high liquidity of the U.S. bond market. But this also has been proved wrong.

What must be happening to cause New Zealand rates to fall below those of Australia and the United States?

A6. A recent study claims that Japanese households are likely to decrease their saving rate in the 1990s but doesn't say what implication this will have for interest rates in the United States.

What do you think this decrease in Japanese savings will do to U.S. interest rates? Why?

A7. While the chartered banks have so far refrained from raising their rates, the finance minister warned reporters that this situation cannot last. The Canadian and U.S. economies are so interrelated, he said, that it will be impossible for Canadian interest rates to remain much lower than U.S. rates for an extended period of time.

Contradict this Canadian politician's comment by constructing a scenario in which Canadian rates are persistently lower than U.S. rates.

A8. But economists predict most countries will conclude that their best course is to make floating rates more tolerable, for example, by increasing opportunities for companies and banks to hedge themselves against currency swings.

What is meant by "to hedge themselves against currency swings"?

A9. Argentina's _____ is measured by the spread between yields on Argentine dollar-denominated bonds and U.S. Treasuries.

Fill in the blank.

A10. But that still leaves an enormous five percentage point spread between the world's two most powerful central banks—8 percent in Germany and 3 percent in the United States. The question raised when the German–American spread began to widen last year was: Who is following the right policy? A possible answer is that both central bank leaders were following the right policy.

How could both central banks be following the right policy here?

A11. **Annual inflation is at 35 percent and expected to rise to 45 percent by the end of the year. Interest rates are already well above 40 percent. The Zimbabwe dollar has dropped in value by more than 65 percent this year.**

Shouldn't the high interest rate cause people to buy Zimbabwe dollars to earn the high interest return, and so cause the Zimbabwe dollar to rise rather than fall in value? Explain what is going on here.

B1. **The global trend toward higher short-term interest rates is a reflection of world-wide increases in _____. The 4.8 percent yield on Japanese short-term securities is due to a strong yen; Australia's 16.1 percent yield is a product of its weak dollar.**

a. Fill in the blank.

b. Why is the low interest rate associated here with the strong currency and the high interest rate associated with the weak currency?

B2. **An investor can sidestep the risk of _____ by obtaining a forward contract. In a forward contract, the bank guarantees the exchange rate for the investor when the issue is bought, so the investor is protected against _____. But there's a catch: _____. This usually renders the actual yield on the foreign bonds _____ the yield on domestic bonds.**

Fill in the blanks.

B3. **The governor of the Bank of Canada urged Canadians today to continue the fight against inflation but warned that they cannot expect any significant drop in interest rates until the United States takes convincing action to reduce its budget deficit.**

a. Explain the connection between the U.S. budget deficit and the Canadian interest rate.

b. Under what circumstances is it true that Canadians cannot expect a drop in interest rates until the United States reduces its budget?

c. Are these circumstances such that Canadians should be urged to fight against inflation, as the governor does?

d. Under what circumstances could Canadians expect a fall in interest rates, in contradiction to the governor's claim?

B4. **What are the factors behind the recent decline in the value of the dollar? A speculative blip can be ruled out as the reason because the currency was selling at a forward premium for most of the period.**

   a. What is a forward premium?

   b. Why would it rule out a speculative blip?

B5. **He believes that Canada's lower inflation rate could lead to tighter spreads between the Canadian and U.S. interest rates.**

What logic lies behind this thinking?

B6. **Canadians must convince investors and speculators that the Canadian dollar will hold its value. For the moment, that means Canada must decisively match U.S. interest rates. Paradoxically, in the past Canada has usually ended up with the worst of both worlds: higher interest rates and a devalued dollar.**

   a. Construct a scenario in which this recommended policy of matching U.S. interest rates could lead to exactly the paradox cited.

   b. Why would the author have called it a paradox?

B7. **By narrowing the spread between short-term interest rates in Canada and the United States in line with the Canadian dollar forward rate, the Bank of Canada stopped the arbitrage activity that was pushing up the Canadian dollar.**

   a. What is the Canadian dollar forward rate, and why is it relevant here?

   b. Explain the arbitrage activity and how it works in this case to push up the Canadian dollar.

B8. **Few people are recommending a devaluation of the dollar. Rather, they are saying, "Lower interest rates, and accept the falling dollar that follows." Some might claim that this isn't possible because the interest rate is set by the market. But the central bank can certainly add money to the system (e.g., through purchasing bonds) and that should drive rates down.**

   a. Explain why lowering interest rates should cause the dollar to fall.

   b. How does the central bank purchasing bonds add money to the market?

   c. Will this drive interest rates down? Explain why or why not.

B9. **When interest rates abroad are rising rapidly as they have risen in recent months, the scope for Canadian interest rates to lag behind foreign rates is necessarily limited unless we want to invite yet further substantial depreciation of the currency.**

Under what circumstances is this claim valid?

B10. **Some bankers say Turkey's lax approach to state finances could end in disaster. Inflation last year was 96 percent, and the state is now servicing its debts at a compound interest rate of 123 percent, a real rate of 27 percent.**

This real interest rate is way above the "world" real interest rate and so violates the IRP theorem. How would you explain this?

B11. **Since the forward rate is currently higher than the spot rate, the market must be anticipating that the dollar will _____.**

Fill in the blank, and explain your reasoning.

B12. **Eastern Europeans were borrowing unhedged in "cheap" Swiss francs to "invest" in local property markets. The 2008–9 meltdown, in which property values fell and so did their currency, was for them a disaster.**

a. What is meant here by "cheap" Swiss francs? Isn't the Swiss franc a strong currency?

b. What does "unhedged" mean, and why is it relevant to this clipping?

B13. **Normally an overheating economy would demand higher interest rates to keep inflation in check, but the Bank of Canada said the Canadian dollar and the situation in the U.S. have allowed it to hold its key interest rate steady yesterday.**

a. How would higher interest rates keep inflation in check?

b. Why would the Canadian dollar be of relevance here?

c. What must be the "situation" in the United States? Explain.

Numerical Exercises

AN1. Suppose that the current exchange rate is 200 yen per dollar, the U.S. interest rate is 6 percent, the Japanese interest rate is 4 percent, and there is no risk premium. What do you expect the exchange rate to be a year from now?

AN2. Suppose that the current exchange rate is 4 pesos per dollar but is expected during the next year to rise to 4.4 pesos per dollar. If the current U.S. interest rate is 6 percent, what should be the Argentine interest rate on a comparable security, assuming a zero risk premium?

AN3. Suppose that the Canadian economy, on a fixed exchange rate, has a real growth rate of 2 percent and is in equilibrium with an inflation rate of 10 percent and a risk premium of 1 percent. Suppose that changes in the United States cause its real rate of interest to increase from 3 percent to 4 percent and its inflation rate to increase by two percentage points. When the Canadian economy has settled to a new equilibrium after this change, what is its nominal interest rate?

AN4. Suppose that inflation in the United States is 8 percent, its real interest rate is 3 percent, and the real interest rate in Canada is 4 percent. Assuming a fixed exchange rate, what is the Canadian nominal interest rate?

AN5. Suppose that the U.S. and Canadian economies are in mutual equilibrium with a flexible exchange rate, both with long-run real growth of 2 percent. The U.S. money-supply growth rate is 8 percent, and its real interest rate is 3 percent. If the risk premium (Canada is riskier) is 1 percent, and the value of the U.S. dollar is appreciating by 4 percent per year, what is Canada's nominal interest rate?

AN6. If the Canadian risk premium is 1 percent, the Canadian interest rate is 10 percent, the U.S. rate is 15 percent, and the two economies are in mutual equilibrium, what should be happening to the U.S. exchange rate?

AN7. Under a fixed exchange rate U.S. real growth is 2 percent and money supply growth is 8 percent. Then if Canada's real interest rate is 4 percent, what should Canada's nominal interest rate be?

BN1. Suppose that Canada and the United States are in equilibrium with a flexible exchange rate and a risk premium (Canada is riskier) of 1 percent. The real rates of growth in Canada and in the United States are both 3 percent, but the U.S. interest rate is 10 percent and the Canadian interest rate is only 7 percent. What is happening to the U.S.–Canada exchange rate?

BN2. Suppose that firm A signs a contract to buy some hardware from a Japanese company for 600 million yen, delivery and payment to take place one year hence. The current exchange rate is 200 yen per dollar, the U.S. interest rate is 6 percent, the Japanese interest rate is 4 percent, and there is no currency risk premium. Which of the following strategies would you recommend that the firm adopt?

a. Firm A trades dollars for yen today and invests in Japanese bonds for a year; or

b. Firm A invests in U.S. bonds for a year and enters a futures contract, agreeing to buy 600 million yen in one year at an exchange rate of 195 yen per dollar.

BN3. Suppose that the Canadian economy, on a flexible exchange rate, has a real growth rate of 3 percent and is increasing its money supply by 10 percent per year. Suppose that changes in the United States cause its real interest rate to rise from 4 percent to 5 percent and its inflation rate to increase by 2 percentage points. Assuming a risk differential premium of one percentage point, after the Canadian economy has settled to a new equilibrium, what is its nominal interest rate?

BN4. Suppose that under a flexible exchange rate system the current exchange rate is 4 pesos per dollar, inflation in Argentina is 5 percent, and inflation in the United States is 8 percent. Suppose that you are an American expecting to pay 10,000 pesos in a year's time and wish to hedge against an unfavorable exchange rate movement. Approximately what forward exchange rate do you expect to pay?

BN5. Your company expects to sell a thousand printers in Argentina in one year's time, at a price of 900 pesos each.

a. How would you eliminate the exchange rate risk?

b. If today's exchange rate is 4 pesos per dollar and the exchange rate one year from now turns out to be 5 pesos per dollar, what can you say about the wisdom of having eliminated the exchange-rate risk?

Appendix A   Answers to Sample Exam Questions

Chapter 3:   Measuring GDP and Inflation

3.1 Items b and c are transfer payments that do not reflect productive activity, so GDP is not affected. But item a, despite not corresponding to productive activity, does increase GDP because government services, even if useless (!), are valued at their cost.

3.2 Welfare payments are transfer payments that do not represent output, so this information is irrelevant. Output must have increased by $10 billion to meet the higher consumption demand, by $3 billion to build up inventories and by $4 billion to offset the fall in imports, so in total GDP increases by $17 billion. Remember, consumption includes imports. If consumption increases by 10 and imports decrease by 4, then consumption of domestically produced goods and services must have increased by 14.

3.3 Yes, the oil spill increased GDP because the clean up provided for a service valued at $2 billion. It could be argued, though, that this service simply offset a negative output (the pollution) associated with the oil production/delivery process. Because this negative output is ignored when measuring GDP, we should ignore the cost of rectifying it. This thinking, associated with the Green movement, does not mean we should subtract this spending when calculating GDP, just that we should not count it.

3.4 Real 2003 GDP is $11/1.065 = 10.3$ trillion 2000 dollars. Notice that this answer is careful to state that the figure is in year 2000 dollars!

3.5 The change in the CPI was 6.4, so inflation was $6.4/195.3 = 3.3$ percent.

3.6 If inflation is anticipated, lenders and borrowers can agree on an interest rate that accommodates this anticipated fall in the purchasing power of the money borrowed/loaned. But if inflation turns out to be a lot higher than anticipated, the lenders will be repaid in dollars that are worth far less than they had expected, and the borrowers are repaying in dollars worth far less than expected. The lenders have lost; the borrowers have gained.

Chapter 4:   Unemployment

4.1 The number employed is all those with full- or part-time jobs, in this case 95 million. Since the labor force is 100 million, this means that there are 5 million unemployed. The unemployment rate, the unemployed as a percentage of the labor force, is $5/100 = 5$ percent.

4.2 The number employed plus the number unemployed is the labor force, in this case 110 million. The participation rate is this number as a fraction of the adult population, $110/150 = 73$ percent. For this question the number of discouraged workers is irrelevant information—they are just potential workers who are not counted as being in the labor force.

4.3 These measures increase the NRU.

4.4 Potential output defined as the output produced by an economy operating at its NRU.

Chapter 5:   The Role of Aggregate Demand

5.1 The MPC is the change in consumption per change in disposable income. Here the change in consumption is $347 billion, and the associated change in disposable income is $475. So the MPC is $347/475 = 0.73$.

5.2 . . . the economy has fallen so far into recession that firms will react to increased demand by increasing output, not prices.

5.3 In the first round of the multiplier process income increases by $10 billion. This increases spending by $10*0.6 = \$6$ billion, so during the second round of the multiplier process income increases by $6 billion. This increases spending by $6*0.6 = \$3.6$ billion, so during the third round of the multiplier process income increases by $3.6 billion. All this implies that after three rounds of the multiplier process income has risen by $10 + 6 + 3.6 = \$19.6$ billion.

5.4 (a) The federal government needs to sell bonds to obtain cash to finance its budget deficit.

(b) Washington's activity in the bond market has pushed up interest rates, making it expensive for state governments and corporations to borrow.

5.5 (a) An inventory correction is a move by producers to adjust inventories to their desired level. If inventories are too low, producers will take steps to build them up; if inventories are too high, they will take steps to reduce them.

(b) Inventories are currently too high. So firms will cut back on production to lower inventories, causing GDP to fall. The blank should be filled with "lower."

5.6 "Filling in holes" refers to increasing aggregate demand when the economy is in recession; "shaving off peaks" refers to decreasing aggregate demand when the economy is in a boom.

5.7 Income increases by the change in government spending times the multiplier, $10*3 = \$30$ billion. This increases tax receipts by $30*0.2 = \$6$ billion. So the deficit increases by $10 - 6 = \$4$ billion.

5.8 . . . infrastructure that will make future generations more productive.

Chapter 6:   The Supply Side

6.1 (a) Yes, by definition, hoarded workers are superfluous.

(b) Hoarding workers is not short-run profit-maximizing behavior. But from a longer run perspective it is profit-maximizing because laying off these workers would mean that many of them would not be available when the economy recovers and more workers are needed, necessitating hiring inexperienced (and so less productive workers) requiring high training costs.

6.2 "excess supply" (at the current income the price is too high, making demand less than income/supply ; "excess demand" (at the current income price is too low, making demand more than income/supply.

6.3 (a) When the economy is operating near full capacity, an increase in aggregate demand will elicit price increases rather than output increases.

(b) Stimulating fiscal policy in this context will increase inflation pressures.

6.4 "excess demand" (firms are producing more output than they could produce at the NRU, so they must be demanding extra labor); "excess supply" (firms are producing less output than a labor market at the NRU would produce)

6.5 (a) The natural rate of unemployment.

(b) Any policy that reduces the NRU, such as labor retraining programs, geographic mobility subsidies, enhanced dissemination of information about job opportunities, and reducing regulations that increase the cost of hiring workers.

6.6 (a) Insiders have pleasant, well-paying jobs that are secure. When recession comes around, they feel no need to reduce their wages. Adjustment falls on the shoulders of outsiders, those who do not have secure jobs, with adjustment invariably taking the form of layoffs.

(b) Keynes claimed that the labor market is such that wages do not fall in a timely fashion in the face of high unemployment, implying a need for stimulative policy action. The insider–outsider story is one of several reasons for why wages are slow to fall.

6.7 (a) By keeping the real wage higher than productivity, workers created and maintained a situation in which the demand for labor was less than the supply of labor. On the *AS/AD* diagram we would be located to the left of the *LRAS* curve, and stuck there until the real wage falls to a level consistent with long-run equilibrium in the labor market.

(b) Efficiency wages.

6.8 If the economy were located to the left of the maximum point on the Laffer curve, an increase in taxes should move the economy up toward the maximum. Since this did not happen, the economy must have been at the maximum point or to its right.

Chapter 7:   Growth and Productivity

7.1 Productivity is measured by output per hour worked, not by output per worker.

7.2 By protecting jobs America has been inhibiting productivity increases and frustrating the economy's efforts to change to produce what people want.

7.3 . . . foreign financing supplemented national saving.

7.4 Increasing taxes and decreasing government spending may be used to shift the *AD* curve to the left to reduce upward pressure on prices, cutting inflation. But higher taxes may have supply-side effects, such as reducing investment, and decreasing government spending may lower investment in infrastructure. Reducing investment causes the capital stock and thus potential output to grow by less than it would other-wise. A later demand expansion will more quickly exceed potential output and create price increases.

Chapter 8:   The Money Supply

8.1 M1 falls by \$1,000 because demand deposits have fallen by \$1,000. M2 remains unchanged because the decrease in demand deposits is offset by an equal increase in term deposits, both of which are measured in M2 (but only the former in M1).

8.2 By extending a $10,000 loan to someone, the bank simply opens a checking account in that persons name, with a balance of $10,000. Because balances in checking accounts are part of the economy's money supply, the bank has in essence "printed" money.

8.3 The current climate in the economy may be such that banks are reluctant to extend loans, perhaps for fear they will not be repaid.

8.4 If the money multiplier is 6, then 6 times the amount of bond purchase is $300 billion. Consequently the bond purchase was 300/6 = $50 billion.

8.5 (a) The money multiplier should fall. When the Fed increases reserves in the banking system the multiplied increase in the money supply relies on commercial banks increasing their loans. If they do not increase loans and instead hold these reserves as excess reserves, the money supply increases very little.

(b) The multiplier should fall. When people increase saving, an increase in income through a fiscal stimulus will increase aggregate demand for goods and services by much less. So the multiplier process slows down.

Chapter 9:   The Monetarist Rule

9.1 Velocity is the ratio of nominal income to the money supply, in this case 15,000/6,000 = 2.5

9.2 The $8 billion purchase of bonds increases the money supply by $8 \times 5 = \$40$ billion. This increases income by $40 \times 4 = \$160$ billion.

9.3 (a) Money supply growth is 5 percent. This should equal money demand growth. Money demand is increasing by the inflation rate plus long-run real growth of 2 percent. So inflation should be 3 percent.

(b) The money growth of 5 percent could move the economy to a higher real income, increasing the demand for money beyond the 2 percent increase due to long-run growth. This would lower the inflation, but only until the economy reaches full employment.

9.5 Inflation is money growth rate less real growth (5 = money growth − 2), so the desired money growth rate is 5 + 2 = 7 percent. So the desired growth in the money supply is $0.07 * 200 = \$14$ billion. So we want central bank bond purchases times the money multiplier (seigniorage $*$ 6) to equal 14 billion. So seigniorage is 14/6 = $2.33 billion.

9.6 The Fed increases the money supply by supplying reserves to the banking system; the commercial banks then increase loans to make the money multiplier work to increase the money supply. If the commercial banks do not increase loans, the money supply increase is far, far lower than what the Fed had anticipated. After the subprime mortgage crisis, banks were very reluctant to make loans for fear that they would not be repaid

Chapter 10:   Monetary Policy and Interest Rates

10.1 T-bills are short-term bonds with very little risk—the government is not going to go bankrupt. So a lower interest rate will attract buyers who wish to avoid risk.

10.2 In essence you own a six-month bond with face value 10,000 and coupon $500; what you paid for it originally is irrelevant. Six months is half a year, so the relevant interest rate for six months is 2 percent, one-half of the 4 percent annual rate. So we have 0.02 = [500 + (10,000 − price)]/price. Solving, we get price = $10,294.12.

10.3 Open-market operations by the Fed, in this case selling bonds to lower their price and raise the interest rate.

10.4 . . . stimulate the economy by increasing the money supply, lowering interest rates.

10.5 The Fed typically raises interest rates to cool off a boom. High interest rates have a very negative impact on the housing industry, pushing the economy towards recession. A slight error in this contractionary monetary policy could do more than just cool the boom, forcing the economy into a recession.

Chapter 11:   Real-versus-Nominal Interest Rates

11.1 Inflation, and so expected inflation should be 6 − 2 = 4 percent. Then the nominal interest rate should be 3 + 4 = 7 percent.

11.2 The high interest rate is a high nominal rate. The real interest rate must have fallen (because expected inflation has increased even more than the nominal interest rate), explaining why spending has increased.

11.3 To lower interest rates, expected inflation must fall. What must be happening here is that although inflation has fallen, people are not convinced that it has fallen permanently and so have not yet reduced their inflation expectations.

11.4 Pulling on a string will pull an object, but pushing on a string will have no effect. If an economy is in recession, nobody wants to spend anything—individuals want to save in case they lose their job, and corporations do not want to invest because business is stagnant. So even if monetary policy lowers the interest rate, it will have little or no effect on aggregate demand.

Chapter 12:   Stagflation

12.1 Shifted upward. Regardless of the level of unemployment, if everyone expects prices to increase by more workers will want bigger increases and firms will grant them because they believe they will be able to pass them on.

12.2 Rational expectations in this case are formulated by combining information about the money growth rate and theory about the macroeconomy. In this case theory tells us that changes in inflation should match changes in the money supply growth rate (because inflation equals money growth rate less real growth rate, the latter constant in the long run). Because money supply growth has increased by 3 percentage points, we should expect long-run inflation to increase by 3 percentage points, from 4 to 7 percent.

12.3 . . . increase interest rates to ward off inflationary pressures.

12.4 The historic failure of price controls is due mainly to the failure to complement them with appropriate monetary policy. If the rate of growth of the money supply is lowered to a level consistent with the controls, they may be successful.

12.5 The danger with this is that the real wage determined this way could easily be inconsistent with the NRU, leading to an undesirably high level of unemployment.

Chapter 13:   The Balance of Payments

13.1 The demand for U.S. dollars on the foreign exchange market must have been $6 billion less than the supply of U.S. dollars to this market, so the balance of payments must have been a deficit of $6 billion.

13.2 The German central bank, the Bundesbank, lowered interest rates. This decreased the demand for German marks on the foreign exchange market (and increased the supply of marks on the foreign exchange market as Germans sought to invest in foreign bonds paying higher interest), resulting in a balance of payments deficit— more supply of than demand for marks on the foreign exchange market, resulting in a fall in the price of the German mark.

13.3 Other things equal, a fall in the current account means a movement toward a balance of payments deficit—more supply of the U.S. dollar versus demand for the U.S. dollar on the foreign exchange market. In this circumstance one would expect the exchange rate to increase, so speculators would buy the U.S. dollar.

13.4 Importing capital means there is a capital account surplus. This pushes up the value of the dollar to create a current account deficit to make the balance of payments balance. When the capital account is in balance (so that the United States is no longer an importer of capital), the current account, as measured by the trade deficit, will be in balance.

Chapter 14:   Policy in an Open Economy

14.1 The exchange rate must have fallen. The fall in exports decreased the demand for our dollar on the foreign exchange market and so created a balance of payments deficit. This lowered the exchange rate.

14.2 The fall in exports decreased the demand for our dollar on the foreign exchange market and so created a balance of payments deficit. With a fixed exchange rate (lack of currency flexibility) this automatically decreased the money supply, further slowing economic activity.

14.3 It is possible under a fixed exchange rate. A stimulating dose of fiscal policy will create a balance of payments surplus, which under a fixed exchange rate automatically increases the money supply. This stimulates the economy, strengthening the fiscal policy.

14.4 Adopting a fixed exchange rate means that monetary policy must be devoted to fixing the exchange rate and so cannot be used for other purposes; the blank should be filled with "using monetary policy."

14.5 . . . allow China's currency to appreciate. The Americans believe that China is deliberately holding its currency at an artificially low level to enhance exports.

14.6 To strengthen the dollar, the central bank can create extra demand for the dollar on the foreign exchange market. It does this by using some of its foreign reserves to buy dollars. So the blanks should be filled with "sells" and "buys."

14.7 Adopting the euro means fixing the exchange rate across the member countries of the European Union. A flexing exchange rate can cushion recession in a country; in its absence movement of people from a recession country to a booming country serves as an alternative cushioning mechanism.

Chapter 15:   Purchasing Power Parity

15.1 The U.S. inflation rate should move from 3 to 7 percent. Under a fixed exchange rate Canada should experience the U.S. monetary policy, so Canadian inflation should also move to 7 percent.

15.2 Before the U.S. money growth increase both countries should be experiencing 3 percent inflation. The increase in the U.S. money growth should increase U.S. inflation rate to 7 percent. Under a flexible exchange rate Canada should experience a rise in its exchange rate of 4 percent per year, but no change in its inflation rate if it permits this rise in its exchange rate.

15.3 The Canadian exchange rate should be falling (the U.S. rate rising) by 3 percent per year, the difference between the two inflation rates. Over two years this means that the Canadian dollar should fall by 6 percent. (Technically it should be 3 percent compounded for two years, but 6 percent is close enough.) So we should expect the exchange rate two years from now to be 1.20 * (1.06) = \$1.27 Canadian per U.S. dollar.

15.4 If the PPP exchange rate were 10 pesos per dollar, I would need 10 pesos to buy a typical bundle of goods and services that in the United States cost one dollar. If the actual exchange rate is 13 pesos per dollar, then I get 13 pesos for one dollar but only need 10 of them to buy what one dollar can buy in the United States. I have three pesos extra. If the PPP exchange rate were 16 pesos per dollar, I would be 3 pesos short. I would prefer the PPP exchange rate to be 10 pesos per dollar.

Chapter 16:   Interest Rate Parity

16.1 In a closed financial market there is no possibility of borrowing funds from foreigners. This means that excessive government borrowing must markedly increase the domestic interest rate to be successful in selling its bonds, so the clip is best completed with ". . . an increase in the interest rate."

16.2 West Germany was one of the big players on the world financial scene, big enough to have an influence on the world real interest rate. (Now, of course, the German mark is gone; it is the euro and the EU interest rate that is of consequence for the world real interest rate.)

16.3 If the two inflation rates were the same, the Canadian nominal interest rate should be 1 percent higher than the U.S. rate. Because it is 3 percent higher, the Canadian inflation must be two percentage points higher than the U.S. inflation. From PPP we know that the value of the U.S. dollar relative to the Canadian dollar should be increasing by 2 percent per year.

Appendix B Answers to Even-Numbered Exercises

Chapter 3: Measuring GDP and Inflation

A2. The work of homemakers is not included in the GDP measure unless it is explicitly paid for, such as the salary of a butler, maid, or housecleaner.

A4a. Consumer price index.

A4b. . . . the prices of all domestically produced goods and services, not just those paid by consumers.

A6. Ecological damage is not deducted from GDP, and expenditures to clean up damage are added to GDP.

A8a. The cost of living reflects the cost of buying what one buys. The CPI reflects the cost of buying a fixed bundle of goods and services; it ignores the fact that individuals change this bundle as relative prices change, buying more of the relatively cheaper items and less of the relatively expensive items.

A8b. The CPI increases by more because it neglects the fact that people switch expenditures to cheaper items.

A10. Residential construction is a consumer purchase. Because residential construction yields a flow of housing services over a long period of time and is often financed by borrowing, it is thought to be more like an investment good than a consumption good. Check table 3.1.

A12. Productivity is measured by looking at real changes in output. If the CPI increases by less, a given nominal change in output corresponds to a larger increase in real output.

B2. Correct. Government spending on this person is considered a final output and is valued at its cost. General Motors' spending is an intermediate output and so is not counted; this wage income is offset by a fall in General Motors' profit.

B4.   Subtract from GDP the pollution costs of production, unless they are cleaned up, and do not add into GDP cleanup costs.

B6a.   Unadjusted GDP normally decreases markedly (by about 8 percent) moving from the fourth to the first quarter. The seasonal adjustment procedure removes this seasonal factor, and when doing so produces a smoother change in GDP from quarter to quarter.

B6b.   The marked increase in economic activity associated with the Christmas season.

B8.   Changes in computer prices are misleading because the quality of computers is changing so much. We need to correct for this before including computer prices in the CPI calculation. To account for increased computer quality, a rise in computer prices would have to be shrunk and a fall in computer prices would have to be increased.

B10.   Tax revenue would increase because each year the breaks determining movement into a higher tax bracket are adjusted upward by the CPI so as to keep these breaks constant in real terms. If the CPI increases by less, these break points increase by less, shifting some people to higher tax brackets. Remember, when calculating one's income tax, a standard deduction is available to everyone and increases with the CPI. If the CPI increases by less, the standard deduction is less, so most people will pay more taxes. Social security payments are increased each year using the CPI to keep them constant in real terms. If the CPI increases by less, social security payments increase by less.

AN2a.   No, this steel is an intermediate product.

AN2b.   Yes, government services are valued at the cost of their production.

AN2c.   If the value of the cars sold by GM is not affected (i.e., if GM does not increase prices by enough to increase sales by $200), then there is no increase in GDP. The service of the paper shuffler is an intermediate product, not a final product, so his productivity is not counted in GDP. In terms of income payments, the $200 salary increase is offset by a $200 profit decrease.

AN2d.   The antique dealer's $200 commission is a currently rendered final service, so it is included in GDP.

AN2e.   No, transfer payments are not included in GDP.

AN2f.   No, this would mean that part of this year's demand bought items produced last year, not this year. Then $200 would have to be subtracted, not added when calculating GDP.

AN2g.   No, capital gains are not included in GDP.

AN4.   (180/150) * 100 = 120. Alternatively, the typical bundle increased in price by 20 percent (i.e., 30/150), so the price index should increase by 20 percent, from base year 100 to 120.

AN6.   Real GDP = Nominal GDP/Price index, so 500 = (600/P) * 100, implying that the GDP deflator P = 120.

AN8.   Inflation = rate of change of CPI = 10/110 = 9.1 percent.

AN10. The 1972 $15 fee was 15/.261 = $57.47 in 1992 (base year) dollars, and 57.47 * 1.109 = $63.74 in 1999 dollars.

AN12. 21/118 = 18 percent.

BN2.   Real GDP in 1992 is the same as nominal GDP, namely $566 billion. Real GDP in 1993 is nominal GDP divided by the 1993 price index, namely 600/105 = $571.4 billion. Real GDP in 1994 is 1993 real GDP plus 3 percent, namely 571.4 * 1.03 = $588.5. The price index in 1994 is nominal GDP divided by real GDP, namely 642/588.5 times 100 = 109.1.

BN4.   Overstate. The CPI calculation does not account for consumers shifting expenditure from the relatively more expensive items to the relatively cheaper items. There's no need to do any calculations to deduce this answer!

BN6a. (950/123) * 100 = $772.4 billion.

BN6b. (123 − 119)/119 = 3.36 percent.

BN6c. Real income this year is $772.4 billion; real income last year was (900/119) * 100 = $756.3 billion. Growth is (772.4 − 756.3)/756.3 = 2.1 percent.

Chapter 4:   Unemployment

A2a.   As the labor force grows, the extra people seeking employment who do not find jobs like up the unemployment rate.

A2b.   If people don't bother looking for a job, they are not considered as being in the labor force and are not counted as unemployed—the unemployment rate is then lower than otherwise. If people look harder for jobs, the opposite occurs.

A4a.   Recent increases in employment may bring people not in the labor force to feel that their chances of obtaining a job are good, so they begin job hunting.

A4b.   This will increase the unemployment rate because now these people are counted as unemployed.

A4c.   The encouraged worker effect.

A6.   Higher. A higher participation rate means more people looking for jobs, and thus more are unemployed.

A8.   . . . fall. If the labor force fell by an amount equal to the number of job losses, the number of newly unemployed is offset by unemployed leaving the labor force. So the unemployment rate should not change.

A10.   . . . people leaving the labor force.

A12.   Rising employment may cause discouraged workers to become encouraged workers, increasing the unemployment rate.

A14.   A high natural rate of unemployment.

A16.   . . . the labor force will grow just as quickly.

A18.   The labor force grew by more than the number of new jobs.

B2a.   Fraction of females 16 years of age and over who are in the labor force.

B2b.   The number of males over age 15 grew by so much that, although the participation rate fell, the number of males in the labor force grew.

B2c.   Unable to determine what has happened to relative unemployment rates because we don't know male and female job growth magnitudes.

B4a.   Some people may deliberately become unemployed to live a temporary life of leisure until their unemployment insurance benefits expire.

B4b.   Those looking for jobs may take longer to accept a job because with unemployment insurance to support them they can be fussier about what job they take.

B6a.   Without unemployment insurance, firms prone to laying off employees would have to pay a higher wage to entice workers to take such a job; with unemployment insurance, workers should find such a job more palatable and so would accept it without as high a wage.

B6b.   Less sensitive because firms would think twice before laying off employees—doing so would increase their future unemployment insurance premiums.

B8.   Because the labor force is continually growing due to population growth.

B10.   . . . higher. The falling participation rate means people were leaving the labor force, decreasing unemployment.

B12.   . . . cause many of these jobs to disappear, raising unemployment.

B14.   Unemployment. With more generous social programs more people will delay finding a job to enjoy social assistance.

B16.   . . . workers to be laid off with very little cost. Consequently, when output declines during the recession, worker hours decline as well, offsetting the impact on productivity.

AN2.   Labor force is 70 percent of 150 million = 105 million. Unemployed is 10 percent of 105 = 10.5 million.

AN4.   If the unemployment rate is 10 percent, then the 90 million employed must be 90 percent of the labor force. Thus the labor force is 100 million, and the participation rate is 100/150 = 66.7 percent.

AN6.   Labor force is 80 percent of 25 million = 20 million. Employment is 16 + 2 = 18 million, so unemployment is 20 − 18 = 2 million. Unemployment rate = 2/20 = 10 percent.

AN8.   The participation rate is the number of people in the labor force expressed as a fraction of the total number of noninstitutionalized people aged 16 and over. For females this is 6/10 = 60 percent.

BN2.   Labor force is 60 percent of 150 million = 90 million. Number of unemployed is 10 percent of 90 million = 9 million, so number of employed is 81 million. Labor force grows by 3 percent of 90 million = 2.7 million to 92.7 million. Employment grows by 2 percent of 81 million − 1.62 million to 82.62 million. Unemployed is thus 92.7 − 82.62 = 10.08 million, so unemployment rate = 10.08/92.7 = 10.9 percent.

Chapter 5: The Role of Aggregate Demand

A2a.   A fiscal policy, either an increase in government spending or a decrease in taxes, would increase aggregate demand and through the multiplier process stimulate the economy. A large deficit could inhibit politicians from voting for a policy that would make the deficit even larger.

A2b.   A decrease in the savings rate means higher consumption, which increases aggregate demand, and so stimulates the economy.

A4.   This implies higher consumption spending, increasing aggregate demand and stimulating the economy.

A6a.   Keynesians believe that the economy's automatic back-to-full-employment forces often do not work fast enough, so government discretionary policy actions are needed to keep the economy at full employment.

A6b.   Fiscal policy is the government policy most identified with Keynesians.

A8a.   An increase in consumer spending increases aggregate demand, stimulating the economy.

A8b.   The reduced rate of inventory liquidation occurs because higher production meets some of the demand. The higher income that results leads to higher consumer spending, stimulating the economy.

A10a.   The fiscal stimulus could be an increase in government spending or a decrease in the tax rate.

A10b.   . . . inflation.

A12a.   An inventory correction is an addition to or a reduction of inventories to change inventories to their desired level.

A12b.   GDP will fall because inventories are being reduced by the cutback in production.

A14.   The multiplier process.

A16.   Reducing the deficit means a reduction in government spending or an increase in taxes, both of which decrease aggregate demand.

A18.   Firms are liquidating inventories by decreasing production. This decrease lowers income and sets a negative multiplier process in motion.

A20.   First blank: recession. Second blank: boom.

A22.   Fiscal policy.

A24.   Higher interest rates.

A26.   The Keynesian view rests heavily on the multiplier effect—an increase in government spending can have a greater impact on income. If the effect of higher government spending is crowded out, higher government spending cannot push the economy out of recession.

A28a.   Financing by printing money means that the government does not have to bid up the interest rate to sell its bonds. So spending that is sensitive to the interest rate is not crowded out.

A28b.   Printing too much money can cause inflation.

A30.   Government borrowing raises the interest rate. As a result many private borrowers may decide to abandon or postpone their spending.

A32.   Interest rates.

A34. Lower growth means lower tax revenues, directly affecting the deficit.

A36. The lower growth means a lower growth in tax revenues. If spending growth continues unchanged, a larger budget deficit will result.

A38a. The tax credits would increase disposable income, and consumer demand would increase by this amount times the MPC.

A38b. Not working because in this recession those employed save for fear that they may lose their jobs.

A40. . . . continues/worsens. The government is using fiscal policy to combat the recession; this involves running deficits.

A42a. Cutting inventory levels happens by decreasing output, so this pushes the economy toward recession.

A42b. . . . an eventual recovery. When inventory levels fall to their desired level, production will have to increase to maintain this level.

A44. The tax cuts increased disposable income, which increased consumption demand and, by the multiplier process, operated to increase income and jobs.

B2a. The buildup of inventories says that despite the 4 percent fall in output, aggregate demand has fallen even farther. The decline is being measured by the fall in demand.

B2b. Because it is unplanned, it can be interpreted as a fall in aggregate demand.

B4a. The folly is deficit spending—spending more than your income.

B4b. Deficit spending may be a wise policy for a government because it can keep an economy at full employment.

B6a. Consistent. Weak spending means that spending falls short of production, so inventories will rise.

B6b. It does matter. Inventory buildup cannot be continued—eventually inventory levels will become too high, prompting a cutback in production.

B8a. Demand exceeds income/output.

B8b. Firms may want to rebuild inventories that fall too low, which increases production and stimulates the economy.

B8c. The cumulative impact is the total fall in inventory levels. It is a potent force for recovery because firms may not want their inventories to fall much lower and will increase output to prevent further falls.

B10a. Severe straining implies that to find financing for its bonds, the government must raise interest rates sharply.

B10b. The clip says that private investment spending is exceptionally buoyant even though it is being crowded out. So probably the main type of demand crowded out is consumption demand, as the higher interest rates discourage consumers from borrowing.

B12. A dollar increase in government spending increases aggregate demand by a dollar. But a dollar reduction in taxes increases aggregate demand by less than a dollar because some fraction of the resulting increase in disposable income will be saved.

B14a. raising interest rates.

B14b. . . . foreign financing.

B16a. Investment in education.

B16b. . . . private investment in capital stock.

B18. Higher mortgage rates means that after you have paid your monthly mortgage you have less left over for spending on consumer items.

B20. The huge debt incurred by the government as it uses expansionary fiscal policy to combat the recession will require higher taxes in future. To prepare to pay these higher taxes without a big change in their lifestyle, people will cut back on their spending, slowing the recovery.

B22. If China does not experience a recession, its demand for American exports will stimulate the American economy.

B24a. Stashing cash in savings and paying off debt does not increase aggregate demand and so does not provide the needed stimulus to the economy.

B24b. Human behavior lies behind the Keynesian consumption function—people will increase their spending by the MPC times an increase in disposable income. This has proved to be too simple—the nature of the increase in disposable income and the state of the economy affect how consumers react to an increase in disposable income. In this case the government is trying to see if increasing disposable income by a small monthly amount has a different effect than increasing it by a large annual lump sum.

B26a. Decreasing spending/increasing saving.

B26b. This decreases aggregate demand for goods and services and so sets in motion a downward multiplier process, worsening the recession.

B26c. The paradox of thrift.

B28.   The high debt means that people will foresee high future taxes. To prevent these taxes from having a big effect on their lifestyle, people will increase saving. This lowers the MPC and so weakens the multiplier process.

AN2.   Multiplier = 35/14 = 2.5.

AN4. $\Delta G * 4 = 60$, so $\Delta G = 60/4 = 15$.

AN6.   The $8 billion increase in government spending increases income by $2.5 * 8 = \$20$ billion. This increases tax receipts by $20 * 0.25 = \$5$ billion. So the budget deficit increases by $8 - 5 = \$3$ billion.

AN8.   It should rise because the rise in taxes does not decrease aggregate demand by as much as the increase is government spending. This happens because some of the higher taxes are met by lowering saving.

BN2.   The increase in government spending increases aggregate demand for goods and services by $200. The decrease in taxes and the increase in transfer payments increase aggregate demand by the MPC times $200, so have less impact on income. (Transfer payments are usually directed at those with very low incomes who have a higher than average MPC, so the transfer payment option should increase income by more than the tax reduction option.) Increasing government spending by $200 and increasing taxes by the same amount will result in a much smaller impact on income because the higher taxes will decrease consumer spending and so offset the higher government spending.

BN4.   Equilibrium income is 250, since at that level of income aggregate demand is also 250.

BN6. $14.85 billion. If this amount is maturing, and only $13 billion are being sold, it must be the case that the difference, $1.85 billion is not being refinanced—it must be being paid off.

Chapter 6:   The Supply Side

A2a.   He must believe the economy is to the right of the peak of the Laffer curve.

A2b.   The tax cut could stimulate work effort, increasing aggregate supply by enough to meet the extra aggregate demand that is bidding up prices.

A4.   . . . natural rate of unemployment.

A6.   Tax revenues will be overestimated because higher tax rates create incentives to work less, move to the underground economy, and evade taxes.

A8.   The reaction to the supply shock moves the economy simultaneously to a higher price level and a lower output level (higher unemployment), from *A* to *C* in figure 6.5.

A10.   Incentives, in particular incentives to work, save, and invest.

A12a. Low unemployment creates inflation pressures.

A12b. The natural rate of unemployment (NRU) or the non-accelerating inflation rate of unemployment (NAIRU).

B2a.   Increase government spending and the ensuing multiplier process will increase employment and income.

B2b.   . . . the explanation for the high European unemployment is that the NRU is high, so a stimulating fiscal policy would be inappropriate.

B4a.   The trade-off between a higher national income and a more equitably distributed national income, sometimes called the trade-off between efficiency and equity.

B4b.   A supply-side economist.

B6a.   A policy of taxing firms on the basis of their employment or wage payment levels.

B6b.   Higher unemployment.

B8a.   Less output being produced than the economy would produce if it were operating at its NRU.

B8b.   . . . a continuing or even bigger negative output gap.

Chapter 7:   Growth and Productivity

A2.   . . . saving. Lower saving leads to lower investment, which slows growth of the capital stock, replaces obsolete capital stock with modern capital stock more slowly, and lowers the rate at which we come up with productivity-enhancing inventions through research and development.

A4a.   Slowdown in productivity growth.

A4b.   Higher saving promotes higher investment, which increases the capital stock, hastens the replacement of obsolete capital stock with modern capital stock, and raises the rate at which research and development produces new inventions, all contributing to raise productivity.

A6.   First blank: productivity growth. Second blank: keeping the economy at full employment.

A8.   . . . the short run.

A10.   productivity

A12.   Government spending on building infrastructure that can make the economy more productive.

A14.   Bad argument. We want the economy to adopt labor-saving technology because it frees up labor to produce other things, increasing our standard of living.

A16.   . . . productive investment.

A18.   He wants high consumption in the short term to help pull the economy our of recession. He wants high saving in the long term because that will enhance growth and productivity.

B2.   . . . the return to private business.

B4.   . . . financing investment in research and development and in the installation of new capital equipment.

B6.   With higher productivity, businesses can grant wage increases without needing to raise prices; consequently inflation pressures from the cost side are alleviated.

B8a.   The higher employment increases output, but this output is just replacing the output that used to be produced by energy. Because producing this output is now more expensive, less in total will be produced, so growth falls.

B8b.   Firms always try to be efficient, Maximizing efficiency when the price of energy is high is not as successful as maximizing efficiency when the price of energy is low. Consequently in the former case productivity is lower than in the latter case.

B8c.   Costs are increasing, although not by as much as if the firms made no effort to reallocate resources to minimize the increase in costs.

B10.   Increases in the labor-force participation rate, increases in hours worked per employee, and decreases in the unemployment rate.

B12a.   Productivity is measured by output per hour worked, not per dollar paid. The higher cost of labor forces French businesses only to hire workers if they are productive enough to be profitable. As a result French firms must invest heavily in capital equipment to make their workers more productive.

B12b.   Overall employment is low, particularly in industries (e.g., the service industry) in which capital cannot make workers more productive.

B14.   India's institutions are more conducive to rewarding entrepreneurship and enhancing growth than are China's.

B16.   . . . this creates incentives for people to work harder and longer, and undertake entrepreneurial activities.

B18a.   Higher investment would increase the economy's capital stock, enhancing growth and productivity.

B18b.   This favorable supply-side impact may raise income enough to generate extra taxes sufficient to decrease the deficit.

B18c.   Lower income taxes would increase consumer spending rather than investment spending.

AN2.   If national saving is $150 billion and investment is $170 billion, the extra $20 billion financing must have come from foreigners.

AN4.   With growth 1.8 percent, doubling will take $72/1.8 = 40$ years. With growth 1.4 percent, doubling will take $72/1.4 = 51.5$ years.

Chapter 8:   The Money Supply

A2.   People may be putting their money holdings into savings accounts to benefit from a high interest rate. These deposits add to M2 but are not included in M1.

A4.   Higher interest rates mean that people will want to take extra care to have their funds in savings accounts (not included in M1), which earn this higher interest rate, rather than in checking accounts (included in M1), which do not. Daily interest savings accounts allow people to earn interest on daily balances rather than on minimum monthly balances, so it is worthwhile making an extra effort to hold money balances in savings accounts for short periods, reducing holdings in checking accounts on average.

A6.   Financial innovation opens up many alternative means of holding cash balances that are just as liquid and just as quickly accessed as traditional checking accounts but bear a higher interest return. But these alternatives are not included in M1, so looking at growth in M1 no longer gives a good picture of what is happening to the quantity of easily accessed spending funds.

A8.   Bond sales to the central bank increase the money supply.

B2.   If interest rates on M2 holdings have fallen, people may move those holdings elsewhere, decreasing the rate of growth of M2. At a lower interest rate less income is forgone by holding more wealth in non–interest-earning assets such as cash and checking deposits (i.e., in M1). So people hold more M1 for the convenience it provides.

B4.   Blank: buying these bonds itself. Completion: . . . printing money.

B6.   By loaning money to the institutions in question, or buying bonds from them and simultaneously selling bonds on the open market to offset the impact this has on the money base.

AN2.   Buying $3 billion of bonds increases the money base by $3 billion. So the money supply increases by $3 * 6 = \$18$ billion.

AN4.   The money multiplier is the ultimate change in the money supply per originating change in the money base, in this case $20/5 = 4$.

AN6.   The money multiplier is the ultimate change in the money supply per originating change in the money base (ΔMB), so in this case $5 = 30/\Delta MB$. Solving, we get the required change in the money base is $6 billion—the Fed should buy $6 billion bonds on the open market.

BN2.   Both M1 and M2 increase further as the banks use their higher reserves to extend loans.

BN4.   In the United States the required reserve ratio on term deposits is less than on demand deposits. So this action will reduce required reserves, allowing banks to increase loans. The loan increases will increase both M1 and M2.

Chapter 9:   The Monetarist Rule

A2a.   Program the computer to increase the money supply at a low, fixed rate.

A2b.   The rules-versus-discretion debate.

A4a.   Noninflationary growth requires a money supply growth equal to the real rate of growth of the economy.

A4b.   They wish it to be rigid because they believe that discretionary changes in money supply are likely to do more harm than good (e.g., owing to long and variable lags).

A4c.   Others believe that situations in which the appropriate monetary policy is obvious (e.g., the savings and loan crisis of the late 1980s) do arise. So by refusing to allow discretionary use of monetary policy, we are forgoing benefits.

A6a.   Monetary policy is not useful for fine-tuning the business cycle because the money supply is too difficult to control precisely, its connection with aggregate spending is too fickle, and the lags associated with its impact on the economy are too long and variable.

A6b.   By setting the rate of growth of the money supply at a low fixed rate, in the long run inflation will be controlled.

A8a.   M1 was increasing at a modest rate, but inflation was proceeding at a much higher rate.

A8b.   Velocity.

A10.   . . . the rate of growth of the money supply at a low fixed rate, approximately equal to the real rate of growth of the economy.

A12a. Financial deregulation caused financial instruments that previously were not closely connected with spending to become easily used as media of exchange.

A12b. Set the rate of growth of the money supply equal to a low fixed rate, approximately equal to the real rate of growth of the economy.

A12c. Confusion and uncertainty regarding the appropriate definition of money makes it impossible to use this rule.

A14.   . . . independent, so that they cannot be influenced by politicians.

A16a. Discretion.

A16b. In anticipation of inflationary pressures (the bend in the river), the Fed is increasing interest rates now (begin the turn well before the bend is reached); if it waits for the inflation to be upon us, it will be too late for the policy to prevent the inflation (navigate the bend).

A18.   Monetary policy should tighten—rather than keeping interest rates low to stimulate investment spending and so promote growth, interest rates should rise to contract spending to alleviate inflationary forces.

A20.   . . . reducing interest rates.

A22.   . . . printing money to finance government spending.

A24a. . . . unreliable as indicators of the influence of monetary policy on the economy.

A24b. Rather than targeting on a monetary aggregate, monetary policy should target on inflation.

A26. Do not base monetary policy on a rule focused on a monetary aggregate.

B2a. Velocity shifts could be caused by financial innovations that allow people to conduct their financial transactions more efficiently.

B2b. The target is the fixed rate of growth of the money supply specified by the policy rule being followed.

B2c. Suppose that velocity increases by 2 percent per year. If the economy's real growth rate is 3 percent per year, then instead of the money supply being increased by 3 percent per year to create zero inflation, it should be increased by only 1 percent per year.

B4. Inflation; contractionary monetary policy.

B6a. Discretion.

B6b. If the recent inflation was low because of temporary phenomena such as a fall in import prices, then demand pressures may activate inflation soon.

B8. Using a policy rule rather than discretion.

B10a. Target monetary policy on the inflation rate.

B10b. An increase in the price of an asset such as a house. This is not consistent with economic reality when the price of the asset increases beyond its fundamental value.

B10c. When the bubble bursts, prices fall to their proper levels, and those owning the asset suffer a sudden fall in their wealth. This sharp fall in wealth decreases spending, setting in motion a multiplier process toward recession. In addition, if people had borrowed money backed by this asset, they suddenly find themselves owing more money than the asset is worth, leading to personal bankruptcies.

B12a. Budget deficits cause inflation if they are financed by printing money.

B12b. No contradiction, because we are not told what is happening to the money supply during these periods.

AN2a. Real income = $(800/120) * 100 = \$667$ billion.

AN2b. Velocity = $800/200 = 4$.

AN2c. Money growth rate needs to be 12 percent to create an inflation of 10 percent ($10 = 12 - 2$).

AN4.   Nominal income is $400 * 120/100 = 480$, so velocity is $480/40 = 12$.

AN6.   Higher government spending increases income by $3 * 10 = \$30$ billion. Selling \$2 billion in bonds decreases the money supply by $2 * 4 = \$8$ billion, decreasing income by $8 * 5 = \$40$ billion. The net change in income is a fall of \$10 billion.

AN8.   (a) Zero change in real income (because the supply curve is vertical), (b) 3 percent change in prices, and (c) 3 percent change in nominal income.

AN10.   The money supply increased by $8 * 15 = \$120$ billion. So 120 times the income multiplier with respect to the money supply equals 360. Solving, we get this multiplier equal to 3.

AN12.   Nominal growth is $8 + 2 = 10\%$, so money demand increases by 10 percent of $200 = \$20$ billion. To increase money supply by \$20 billion, the central bank must buy $20/5 = \$4$ billion bonds, so seigniorage is \$4 billion.

BN2.   Inflation = money growth rate − real growth rate + velocity growth, so 4 = money growth rate − 3 + 1, which implies that money growth rate = 6 percent.

BN4.   The fiscal policy increases income by $5 * 4 = \$20$ billion. Since we want only \$8 billion income growth, monetary policy must decrease income by \$12 billion. Suppose that \$1 billion bonds are sold. This decreases the money supply by $1 * 3 = \$3$ billion, which decreases income by $3 * 2 = \$6$ billion. We want twice this decrease, so we must sell \$2 billion bonds.

BN6.   In the derivation of the inflation equation, when real income increased by x percent, money demand also increased by x percent, and the resulting gap between this annual money-demand increase and the annual money-supply increase created inflation. If the income elasticity is less than one, then real growth does not increase money demand by as much, making this gap bigger and thus inflation greater. Clearly, the original inflation equation underestimates inflation in this circumstance.

BN8.   Money demand is growing by 2 percent because of real growth, 8 percent because of inflation, and zero percent because of velocity changes. So the money supply must be growing by 10 percent, which in this case is $0.1 * 500 = \$50$ billion. Seigniorage is \$5 billion. Because the central bank bought \$5 billion bonds, 5 times the money multiplier equals 50. From this the money multiplier is 10.

Chapter 10:   Monetary Policy and Interest Rates

A2a.   When interest rates fall, the prices of bonds rise, creating capital gains.

A2b. Short-term financial assets pay off at their face value shortly, so their price will not depart much from their face value.

A4. . . . capital gains.

A6a. A target growth rate policy is a policy of increasing the money supply at some fixed target rate of growth, usually chosen to be a low rate approximately equal to the real rate of growth of the economy.

A6b. If you target on the money supply, changes in interest rates cannot be offset by manipulating the money supply.

A8a. Switching would involve increasing or decreasing the money supply as economic conditions demand, as opposed to fixing the rate of growth of the money supply.

A8b. During a recession the growth of income slows. This lower growth in income implies a lower growth in money demand, causing it to fall short of the annual growth in money supply. The resulting excess money supply lowers the interest rate.

A10a. Probably there was an increase in discouraged workers.

A10b. The interest rate would be cut by the Fed buying bonds on the open market.

A10c. The lower interest rate would increase aggregate demand, moving the economy to a higher level of income.

A10d. The multiplier process; kindling a fire means doing something to start it going.

A12a. The Fed actions are stimulative, supporting the argument for inflation.

A12b. Quantitative easing is increasing reserves in the banking system (money base) in a situation where the interest rate has fallen to zero and so cannot fall any further.

A14. Lower interest rates should stimulate consumer, investor, and local government spending. This increase in aggregate demand for goods and services will set the multiplier in motion and push us out of the recession.

A16a. The output gap is the difference between actual GDP and the GDP that would be produced if the economy were operating at its NRU. A positive output gap means we are producing more than if the economy were at its NRU.

A16b. . . . raise interest rates.

A18a. Central bank bond purchases and loans to banks (i.e., printing money base) in a situation where interest rates are so low they cannot fall further.

A18b. It runs the risk of inflation.

A18c. Fiscal policy.

A20a. Bond sales by the government to finance its deficit compete with private bond sales, raising the interest rate and thereby hampering the private sector's ability to sell its bonds.

A20b. This could be avoided if the central bank were to buy the government bonds. The cost of this is higher inflation.

A22. Decreasing; by not competing for financing, the government does not bid up the interest rate.

B2a. The interest rate must be rising, causing the price of these bonds to fall.

B2b. Yes, rising loan demand is probably what is pushing up interest rates.

B4. The central bank must be targeting on the interest rate, keeping it constant by matching money-demand changes with money-supply changes.

B6a. By buying bonds on the open market.

B6b. Buying bonds would increase reserves in the banking system. Because of this banks would more easily be able to meet their legal reserve requirement and so would have less need to borrow reserves from other banks. Since the demand for such borrowed reserves is lower, their price, the federal funds rate, should be lower.

B8a. A fall in interest rates increases aggregate demand, stimulating the economy.

B8b. A higher growth rate for the economy means that the Fed will probably increase money growth to sustain this higher growth. Only when the economy grows out of the recession, returning to full employment, will the Fed cut back on this money growth.

B10. An increasing interest rate has caused returns on bonds to exceed expected returns on stocks (expected dividends on stocks are unchanged, so expected returns on stocks are lower if the price of the stock does not change). Stockholders consequently sell their stocks (lowering stock prices) to buy bonds.

B12a. Lowering demand on the basis of price means raising the interest rate (the "price" of money) to discourage some borrowers.

B12b. This is identical to a policy of limiting the amount of money that is available and letting the forces of supply and demand allocate the funds. It is different from a policy of rationing a limited quantity of money on the basis of criteria other than price.

B12c. The banks ration credit by not making loans to people or firms that are not credit-worthy. They also ration credit by setting interest rates. They do not ration credit in the sense that they extend loans at interest rates below the market rate of interest.

B12d. Credit is cut back by raising interest rates, squeezing some borrowers out of the market. The higher interest rate dampens aggregate demand, slowing inflation.

B14. Higher interest rates increase the return from buying bonds; higher expected earnings increase the returns from buying stocks. Stock prices should increase if the latter outweighs the former.

B16. With so many new bond sales on the horizon, it is reasonable to expect that interest rates will rise as sellers try to entice people to buy their bonds. A rise in interest rates will lower bond prices. To avoid losses due to these low prices, people will sell bonds now.

B18a. The Federal Funds rate is the rate paid by a commercial bank when it borrows excess reserves from another bank, usually overnight to meet its reserve requirement. The rate actually paid is the effective or actual rate. The official Federal Funds rate is what is announced by the FOMC following its rate-setting meeting held about every six weeks.

B18b. Almost all the banks are holding excess reserves, so the supply of excess reserves is very high relative to demand, lowering the rate below what the Fed had indicated was its target. That target would have been set a few weeks ago and so has become outdated.

B20a. Federal Open Market Committee

B20b. The Federal Funds rate is the rate paid by one commercial bank to another, usually overnight to meet reserve requirements.

B20c. Basis points, one one-hundredth of a percentage point.

B20d. 2.25 percent.

B20e. easing.

B22. Liquidity can be achieved by buying bonds held by banks or by loaning money directly to banks. This way reserves are created for those banks, and they do not need to borrow reserves from other banks. So the actual Federal Funds rate should fall. But the official Federal Funds rate, as announced by the FMOC, may not necessarily change.

B24a. No different.

B24b. Deflation is when prices fall, the opposite of inflation. When prices fall people hold off spending because they think that prices will fall further. This reduction in spending sets in motion a downward multiplier process, aggravating the deflation pressures.

B24c. The increase in the money base would lead to the money multiplier operating to increase the money supply, pushing us toward inflation.

B26a. Financing government deficits by selling bonds to the central bank (printing money).

B26b. Government bond sales would be at the expense of private bond sales, decreasing spending on private investment goods and services.

B26c. If the economy is at full employment, financing by printing money must in the long run also crowd out private spending because in the long run the economy will return to the NRU.

B26d. The disadvantage of debt monetization is that it creates inflation.

AN2. The annual return is the $80 coupon plus an approximate capital gain of $42/6 = $7. So the approximate yield is (80 + 7)/958 = 9.1 percent.

AN4. The current interest rate should be given by

$$i = \frac{\text{Coupon} + \text{Capital gain}}{p},$$

which for this case becomes

$$0.08 = \frac{75 + 1,000 - p}{p},$$

This gives p = $995.37.

AN6. The annual return is the coupon plus an approximate capital loss of $80/4 = $20. So the approximate yield is 0.05 = (coupon − 20)/1,080. Solving, we get the coupon to be approximately $74.

BN2. If we increase government spending by $3 and increase the money supply by $2, the interest rate does not change. Income increases by $3*4 = $12 plus $2*3 = $6 equals $18. But we need an income increase of $9,000. If this package is applied 500 times, income will increase by $500*18 = $9,000. This implies an increase in government spending of $3*500 = $1,500 and an increase in the money supply of $2*500 = $1,000.

    An alternative way of finding this solution is to set up two equations in the two unknowns ΔG and ΔMs. To keep the interest rate constant, we must have

$$\frac{\Delta G}{\Delta Ms} = \frac{3}{2},$$

and to increase income by \$9,000, we must have

$$4\Delta G + 3 * Ms = 9,000.$$

BN4.   These bonds were all originally issued at different times when interest rates were very different, and so have very different coupons. If the coupons were all the same, their prices would be the same.

Chapter 11:   Real-versus-Nominal Interest Rates

A2.   A balanced federal budget means the government has less need for financing, lowering the interest rate. The OPEC action means less fear of oil price increases, lowering expected inflation and therefore lowering the interest rate. Lower interest rates means higher bond prices.

A4a.   It is bad news on the employment front, but good news for those invested in bonds because they experience a capital gain.

A4b.   Economic weakness means (i) less demand for money so interest rates should fall; (ii) less fear of inflation, so interest rates fall; and (iii) the possibility of Fed action to decrease the interest rate to stimulate the economy. Falling interest rates mean rising bond prices.

A6a.   A high inflation may have raised inflation expectations to a high level, raising the nominal interest rate.

A6b.   In light of the existing inflation, these high interest rates correspond to a normal real interest rate and so are appropriate.

A8.   Actual inflation is low. When it is subtracted from the high nominal interest rate, we see a very high real interest rate. But what determines the nominal interest rate is expected, not actual inflation; inflation expectations are still high, despite the low actual inflation, keeping nominal interest rates high.

A10.   Higher growth should increase the demand for money, causing interest rates to rise. Further, if growth rebounds, the Fed may raise interest rates to guard against inflation. The very high rate of money-supply growth means inflation in the long run, according to our inflation equation. This raises expected inflation, which increases interest rates. This high money growth may also imply that the Fed may cut back sharply on money supply to contain this long-run money supply growth. Such a cutback on money supply should increase interest rates in the short run.

A12.   Higher inflation causes expected inflation to rise, increasing interest rates and thus lowering bond prices. So those holding bonds will suffer a capital loss.

A14.   Expectations of inflation should fall, implying that interest rates should fall and bond prices rise.

A16.   If people believe that higher inflation is coming, they should expect interest rates to rise and bond prices to fall. They will sell bonds to avoid capital losses.

A18.   . . . a tightening of monetary policy—an increase in the federal funds rate.

A20.   The excessive monetary growth would soon be recognized and inflation expectations would increase, raising the nominal interest rate.

B2.   . . . prices lower and yields higher. The unexpected strength in the economy may increase demand for money, raising interest rates; it may raise expectations of future inflation, likewise raising interest rates; and it may prompt the Fed to raise interest rates to cool off the economy.

B4a.   3 percent.

B4b.   Suppose that the current market expectation of inflation is 6 percent, so the premium built into the interest rate to cover inflation is 6 percent. With a real interest rate of about 3 percent, this implies a nominal interest rate of about 9 percent. Suppose that actual inflation turns out to be 8 percent so that the 6 percent figure is an underestimate. The actual real return to an investor is $9 - 8 = 1$ percent, less than the Franklin-guaranteed return of 3 percent.

B6a.   Bond yields would be bid up by traders selling bonds, causing their price to fall and consequently their yields to rise.

B6b.   If traders believe inflation will rise, they will want to get rid of bonds to avoid the capital loss caused by a fall in the price of bonds when people begin to expect higher inflation.

B6c.   To obtain financing for the massive supply of Treasury debt, the government will have to offer a high interest rate. Higher interest rates will lower bond prices. So, to avoid a capital loss, bond holders should sell their bonds.

B6d.   She or he probably subtracted the current inflation from 8 percent.

B8a.   A real-interest-rate bond or a real-return bond are good guesses for a name here. In reality it is probably called an indexed bond.

B8b.   The current Canadian real interest rate must be greater than 4.25 percent, which explains why investors are not keen on buying this bond.

B10a.   Higher inflation should increase the interest rate. If the Fed is targeting on the interest rate, it will try to prevent this rise, but if it is targeting on money-supply growth, it cannot act to prevent higher interest rates.

B10b.   This is a good thing. By trying to prevent a rise in the interest rate caused by higher inflation, a short-sighted Fed might increase the money supply to lower the interest rate. This action could create higher inflation, raising inflation expectations, and that would push the interest rate even higher.

B12.   . . . increase. If inflation is expected to increase, future interest rates should be higher, and so those buying long-term bonds need to be protected from such increases.

B14.   People probably do not believe that the government will meet its inflation target, so the market will have a higher expected inflation than inflation turns out actually to be. Without indexed bonds the government will have to pay an interest rate with an inflation premium equal to inflation expectations, higher than the inflation premium it would pay if it sold indexed bonds (and inflation was indeed lower than expected!).

B16.   Faster.

B18.   If growth slows, we might expect interest rates to fall (a lower demand for money, a lower expected inflation, and a possible reaction by the Fed to lower interest rates to stimulate the economy). This would push up bond prices. A higher inflation would increase inflation expectations and so raise the nominal interest rate. This would push down bond prices.

B20a.   Artificial increases in the money supply are increases produced solely for the purpose of pushing down the interest rate, as opposed to increases needed to match the economy's annual increase in money demand.

B20b.   This extra money supply increase may increase inflation expectations, raising the nominal interest rate.

AN2a.   The nominal interest rate becomes 13 percent.

AN2b.   The real interest rate remains unchanged at 4 percent.

AN4.   Inflation should be $10 - 2 = 8$ percent, so the nominal interest rate should be $8 + 3 = 11$ percent. The T-bill price T_p can be deduced from $0.11 = (1,000 - T_p)/T_p$. So $T_p = 1,000/1.11 = \$900.90$.

BN2.   Inflation should be $9 - 2 + 1 = 8$ percent, so the nominal interest rate should be $8 + 3 = 11$ percent. The T-bill price T_p can be deduced from $0.11 = (1,000 - T_p)/T_p$. So $T_p = 1,000/1.11 = \$900.90$.

Chapter 12:   Stagflation

A2.   . . . accelerating inflation.

A4a.   The Phillips-curve diagram.

A4b.   Unemployment serves to decrease aggregate demand and thereby slow inflation, eventually killing inflation expectations.

A4c.   Wage/price controls could be used to circumvent the prolonged period of high unemployment. If supplemented with appropriate monetary and fiscal policy, they can lower inflation expectations quickly and force coordination of wage- and price-increase slowdowns.

A6a.   Too much financial stimulus would be enough to activate inflationary forces.

A6b.   If inflation were reactivated, governments would have to kill it off by pushing the economy back into recession.

A8a.   A policy of holding the rate of growth of money supply to a low level, approximately equal to the real rate of growth of the economy, would be consistent with a continuing movement toward price stability. An alternative here might be a credible policy of steadily reducing the money growth rate to this rate.

A8b.   A decrease in the public's expectations of inflation is a key ingredient in reducing inflation without a prolonged period of high unemployment.

A10a.   The inflation was probably cured by reducing the rate of growth of the money supply and creating a major recession until inflation fell.

A10b.   High unemployment or a major recession.

A10c.   In the long run inflation is equal to the rate of growth of the money supply less the real rate of growth of the economy.

A10d.   Approximately equal to the real rate of growth of the economy.

A12.   . . . inflation will accelerate.

A14.   . . . lower unemployment.

A16a.   Rising inflation.

A16b. The NRU or NAIRU.

A18. Going above the comfort zone means that the Fed would feel the need to raise interest rates to fight the higher inflation.

A20. Raise interest rates.

A22. The Fed would raise interest rates to fight the inflation.

A24a. . . . lower interest rates.

A24b. The lower inflation and the soft job market suggest that the economy is in a recession, implying that stimulative policy from the Fed should not aggravate inflation.

A26. If politicians have some control over the central bank, they are likely to buy votes by pumping up the money supply before an election, which will lower interest rates and stimulate the economy.

A28. . . . inflation.

A30. It would lead to an excessive increase in the money supply and so inflation.

A32a. Printing too much money.

A32b. Section 13.1 provides several examples of how a government can lose control of the money supply.

A32c. A policy-induced recession is one created deliberately, by lowering the money growth rate, to reduce inflation.

B2. Fighting inflation by decreasing aggregate demand causes firms to cut back on production rather than lower price increases, causing a recession. He believes that by lowering the rate of growth of money supply gradually, firms will be more likely to adjust by lowering price increases than by cutting output.

B4a. Keynes.

B4b. It is now recognized that there is a natural rate of unemployment below which the economy cannot be pushed without accelerating inflation.

B4c. This policy is designed to decrease the natural rate of unemployment.

B6. A slow recovery avoids running the risk of activating inflation expectations. Furthermore it avoids the danger of inadvertently stimulating the economy too much, moving it below the natural rate of unemployment, and accelerating inflation.

B8a. To lower inflation, the rate of growth of the money supply must be lowered. Furthermore people must change their expectations of inflation because this is what will induce them to reduce the rate at which prices and wages are rising. Because expectations change slowly, and because contracts continue wage and price increases in the short term, inflation usually continues, despite lower money-supply growth. This trend causes money demand to exceed money supply, decreasing aggregate demand for goods and services and pushing the economy into recession.

B8b.   If wage and price setters lower their expectations of inflation quickly and as a result settle for lower wage and price increases, the time spent in recession will be shorter.

B10.   As the unemployment rate declines, it increases the danger of falling below the unknown NRU and creating inflationary forces. To ensure that these inflationary forces do not get started, the monetary authorities are adopting a restrictive monetary policy.

B12a.   The usual argument is that the government will resort to the printing press to finance its deficit, increasing the money supply and causing inflation.

B12b.   If the real wage is prevented from falling, the economy will be stuck at an unemployment level to the right of the long-run Phillips curve.

B14.   . . . shifting. The NRU must be falling, so the long-run Phillips curve is shifting to the left.

B16.   Economists thought that a fall in the rate of unemployment below their measure of the NRU, as happened in the late 1990s, would increase inflation.

B18.   . . . of increasing productivity.

B20a.   Accommodating cost pressures means passing higher costs on in higher prices.

B20b.   Monetary accommodation of accelerating energy price increases means increasing the money supply to prevent overall price increases caused by higher energy prices from creating unemployment. Without monetary accommodation, these higher prices increase the demand for money by more than current money-supply growth. The resulting excess demand for money decreases aggregate demand for goods and services, pushing the economy into a recession.

B22a.   Accommodating inflationary shocks means increasing the money supply to prevent those shocks from decreasing economic activity.

B22b.   If a central bank has a reputation of not accommodating inflationary shocks, business and labor will try not to increase prices and wages during these shocks; to do so will risk losing sales and jobs. Price and wage increases without corresponding money-supply increases would create excess money demand, decreasing aggregate demand for goods and services.

B24a. The Phillips-curve theory, or the accelerationist theory.

B24b. If the NRU is lower than 5.7 percent, there is some room for expansionary policy. If it is higher than 5.7 percent, expansionary policy would be a serious mistake because it would make worse an inflation that is sure to develop.

AN2. Dropping inflation by three percentage points costs $105 billion, which is a cost of $35 billion per percentage point. The sacrifice ratio is the cumulative cost of reducing inflation by one percentage point expressed as a percent of GDP. Thirty-five billion dollars is 5 percent of $700 billion, so the sacrifice ratio is 5.

BN2a. A's expected inflation is the average of this and last year's inflations, 4.25 percent.

BN2b. B's expected inflation is the rational expectation, the inflation rate implied by the money growth rate of 7.5 percent. Raising the money growth rate by 1.5 percentage points increases inflation by 1.5 percentage points, to 5.5 percent.

Chapter 13:   The Balance of Payments

A2. Fall.

A4. A rise in U.S. interest rates relative to foreign interest rates could have caused investors to buy U.S. bonds.

A6. A high value for the dollar would make our exports very expensive to foreigner. Demand for our exports falls, beginning a multiplier process that decreases our income level.

A8. A high-dollar policy is one creating a high interest rate that induces capital inflows, bidding up the value of the dollar. This increases imports and decreases exports and so creates a balance of trade deficit.

A10a. A devaluation of the Canadian dollar makes Canadian exports cheaper to Americans because Americans can buy more units of Canadian currency with a U.S. dollar.

A10b. The devalued dollar makes Canadian goods and services cheaper, and so Canadian sales to the United States should improve, but the U.S. recession decreases U.S. income and decreases U.S. imports by far more.

A12.   . . . capital inflows have offset its influence on the dollar.

A14a.   Canada exports oil, so an increase in its price increases the demand for Canadian dollars on the foreign exchange market.

A14b.   An increase in Canada's terms of trade.

B2.   First blank: the value of the U.S. dollar; second blank: balance of trade deficit; third blank: capital account surplus or capital inflows.

B4a.   First blank: push up the value of the British pound, or cushion its fall; second blank: falling.

B4b.   Citicorp would sell British pounds for future delivery, buying these pounds when the value of the pound fell.

B6a.   The conventional wisdom is that a current account surplus corresponds to a balance of payments surplus, which should lead to a rise in the value of the dollar.

B6b.   What is happening here is that a capital account surplus creates a balance of payments surplus, pushing up the value of the dollar, creating a current account deficit. Alternatively, a capital account deficit creates a balance of payments deficit, decreasing the value of the dollar and creating a current account surplus.

B8a.   The strong dollar makes our exports expensive to foreigners, so exports fall. This fall in demand for domestically produced goods and services sets a negative multiplier effect in motion.

B8b.   GDP is calculated by adding up all sales of final products, some of which are imports and some of which have imported components. To calculate only what has been produced domestically, imports must be subtracted out.

B10a.   The narrowing of the trade deficit suggests that the dollar should rise in value. If so, investors should not require as high an interest rate to entice them to buy U. S. bonds. As a result the U.S. interest rate should fall. This fall in the interest rates should increase the price of bonds.

B10b.   Fear of inflation raises inflation expectations, making people anticipate a rise in the nominal interest rate and thus a fall in the price of bonds. To escape the capital losses this would entail, people sell bonds, which causes their price to fall.

B12a.   The resulting increase in our standard of living.

B12b.   . . . in the long run the level of unemployment moves to the economy's natural rate.

B14.   Singapore could import goods, modify them, and then export them. The modification reflects the income generated by Singaporeans, but it may be a modest fraction of the imports and exports.

AN2.   If 0.7 euros buy one dollar and 12 pesos buy one dollar, then 0.7 euros should buy 12 pesos. Consequently 1 euro should buy 12/0.7 = 17.14 pesos, or 1 peso should buy 0.7/12 = 0.058 euros.

AN4.   To produce one bolt of cloth, England must give up 7.5 bottles of wine, whereas Portugal must give up 13.3 bottles of wine. Because England gives up fewer wine bottles per bolt of cloth, it has a comparative advantage in cloth; Portugal has a comparative advantage in wine.

AN2.   England can make 2 * 30 = $60 producing cloth or 15 * 5 = $75 producing wine—it will specialize in wine. Portugal can make 3 * 30 = $90 producing cloth or 5 * 40 = $200 producing wine—it will also specialize in wine.

Chapter 14:   Policy in an Open Economy

A2a.   First blank: high (high interest rates create capital inflows such as those described); second blank: up the value of (the capital inflows increase demand for the dollar, pushing up its value); third blank: rise.

A2b.   Exporters discover that foreign currency received from sales abroad translates into fewer domestic dollars.

A2c.   . . . to sell dollars. By selling dollars, the central bank decreases the excess demand for dollars that is pushing up the price of the dollar.

A4.   First blank: high interest rates; second blank: fall.

A6a.   The central bank must have been using reserves to buy dollars on the foreign exchange market to prevent the value of the dollar from falling.

A6b.   If the international financial community is convinced that the dollar is overvalued, the central bank will need a huge amount of foreign exchange reserves to fight off speculators and prevent the dollar from falling.

A8a.   Under a fixed exchange rate higher domestic inflation would cause our export prices to rise relative to foreign competition, so our exports would fall. Because imports become relatively cheaper, our imports would rise. These changes were prevented by a fall in the exchange rate.

A8b. Sharp declines in the value of exports would create a balance of payments deficit that would decrease the value of the dollar, allowing exporters to be more competitive.

A10a. The high interest rates caused capital inflows that bid up the value of the dollar.

A10b. Tight money causes the real interest rate to rise, decreasing aggregate demand and inhibiting price increases.

A10c. A lower dollar increases demand for our exports.

A12. Expansion increases our income, thereby increasing our imports and creating a balance of trade deficit. The rise in our income increases our demand for money. Our interest rate rises as a result, and so do capital inflows. These mechanisms bid up the value of our dollar, decreasing exports and increasing imports, both of which create a balance of trade deficit.

A14. The adoption of the euro as a common currency in Europe, implying fixed exchange rates and a common monetary policy for all.

A16a. It would increase the money supply and lower the interest rate, both of which should stimulate aggregate demand.

A16b. A fall in the interest rate would make U.S. bonds less attractive to foreigners, so capital inflows would slow or fall. Further, if this increases expectations of future inflation, then by PPP people would expect the dollar to depreciate.

A18. A fall in the NZ interest rate would reduce capital inflows and so lower the demand for the NZ dollar.

A20. If your currency is fixed to the U.S. dollar, you must experience the monetary policy of the United States. So, if the United States has inflation, you will too.

B2a. The government, through its agent the central bank, is selling dollars on the foreign exchange market.

B2b. To get the dollars to sell, the government is selling bonds. The alternative is to print dollars, increasing the money supply and risking inflation.

B4. The central bank must be creating the rise in the interest rate as a reaction to the fall in the dollar.

B6a. A fall in the exchange rate makes imported intermediate goods more expensive, raising production costs of domestic goods and services.

B6b. The devaluation will cause inflationary forces.

B8a.   The J curve taking hold usually means that the balance of trade is changing direction.

B8b.   It probably refers to the bottom of the J curve.

B10a. The French and German governments are both buying French francs.

B10b. The disruption to the French economy is that the money supply is being decreased and the economy is being pushed into recession.

B10c. The disruption to the German economy is that the German money supply is being increased, creating inflationary forces.

B12a. The rationale is the rationale of the J curve.

B12b. The J curve.

B14a. The bank must have increased interest rates.

B14b. . . . so that the economy would not be hurt by the higher interest rates, and so that the fall in the exchange rate could cushion some of the impact on Canada of the Asian financial crisis.

B16.   China could allow its exchange rate to rise, or it could sterilize this inflow of money (by decreasing the Chinese money supply at the same rate that the balance of payments surplus is increasing it).

B18.   Currently the exchange rate must be fixed to a currency of a country that is experiencing inflation and so the Russian economy is importing this inflation because with a fixed exchange rate it must experience the other country's monetary policy. It can avoid this by allowing its exchange rate to flex.

B20a. A low saving rate means that consumption and thus imports are high, pushing us toward a current account deficit.

B20b. A low saving rate also means that our interest rates are high, as those borrowing find that funds are in short supply. The high interest rate brings in capital inflows, which hold up the value of the currency. So a high current account deficit can be balanced by a high capital inflow, implying no fall in the value of the currency.

B22.   Strong growth will entice foreign investors to invest in U.S. businesses, increasing the demand for the U.S. dollar on the foreign exchange market. But strong growth also increases demand for imports, increasing the supply of U.S. dollars on the foreign exchange market.

Chapter 15:   Purchasing Power Parity

A2.   The value of the Ukrainian currency would have risen relative to the value of the Russian currency as the Russians demanded Ukrainian currency on the foreign exchange market to buy the cheaper Ukrainian goods. This rise would have dampened the Russian demand for Ukrainian goods and led to more modest price increases of the goods themselves.

A4.   Relative costs of living.

A6.   Fixing the exchange rate means the rate of money-supply growth is determined by the country to which your exchange rate is fixed, so a policy of targeting on a money-supply growth rate requires that the exchange rate not be fixed.

A8.   If inflation is lower in the United States than in Germany, PPP predicts that the value of the U.S. dollar should rise. People will buy U.S. dollars in anticipation of this increase.

A10.   The PPP theory claims that tradable goods should cost the same in all countries; otherwise, people would buy from the cheaper country, pushing up its exchange rate until cost equality is obtained. It is stretching things to apply PPP to hamburgers—these cannot be considered tradable goods because of the service component of their preparation and serving.

A12.   an increase in the real value of the peso.

B2a.   Yes. If the exchange rate is fixed, inflation higher than that of our trading partners should make our goods more expensive relative to those of foreigners, so our imports should rise. Our exports will become more expensive to foreigners, so our exports should fall.

B2b.   By raising interest rates, the government would be raising the nominal interest rate up to what the inflation warrants and beyond to raise the real interest rate to slow aggregate demand, fighting inflation.

B4.   . . . inflation. Lowering the exchange rate can be accomplished by selling dollars on the foreign exchange market, which increases the money supply, or by lowering the interest rate, which is done by increasing the money supply. This increase in the money supply, in conjunction with the higher cost of imported intermediate goods and services because of the lower exchange rate, promotes inflation.

B6.   . . . our prices do not rise to offset this advantage.

B8a.   Tradable goods and services in a country with an undervalued currency would be cheap to foreigners.

B8b.   Suppose that a hamburger costs 2 dollars in the United States and 7 francs in France. The PPP exchange rate would be 2 dollars for 7 francs, or 3.5 francs per dollar.

B8c.   If the actual exchange rate is, say, 4 francs per dollar, then the dollar would be overvalued.

B8d.   Hamburgers and the associated service of preparing and serving them are not tradable goods and services. This is only one of many relevant goods and services.

B10a.   If inflation in Singapore is less than inflation in the United States, the value of the Singapore dollar must continually rise, according to PPP.

B10b.   If the value of the Singapore dollar trends upward at a rate equal to the U.S. rate of inflation, inflation in Singapore should be kept around zero.

B12a.   The central bank could drive down the dollar's value by lowering interest rates to cut down on capital inflows, or by selling dollars on the foreign exchange market.

B12b.   These policies would drive down the nominal exchange rate. But they also engender higher money supply, which could increase prices. Higher prices wipe out any advantage of the lower dollar, leaving the real exchange rate unchanged.

B12c.   Actions by the central bank to influence the exchange rate are limited by inflation changes created by those actions.

B14.   A fall in the real exchange rate should increase demand for our exports and for domestically produced goods that compete against imports. This should reduce the trade deficit and increase GDP as the statement claims. But the fall in the value of our currency will make imports more expensive (and the extra demand noted above may create inflationary pressures), so it is doubtful that inflation will be reduced. But, if the fall in the exchange rate is a fall in the nominal exchange rate without a corresponding fall in the real exchange rate, the statement is completely wrong.

BN2.   The PPP theorem says that the exchange rate should have changed by the difference between their two inflation rates. In this case the U.S. dollar should have appreciated by $52 - 41 = 11$ percent to become $1.02 * 1.11 = 1.13$ Canadian dollars. A slightly more accurate answer is possible here, but it is beyond the scope of this book. Because Canadian prices have risen relative to U.S. prices by $1.52/1.41$, the exchange rate should become $1.02 * (1.52/1.41) = 1.10$ Canadian dollars.

BN2a.   PPP predicts the U.S. dollar should appreciate by 3 percent in each of these two years, from one U.S. dollar buys 1.1 Canadian dollars to one U.S. dollar buys

1.1 ∗ 1.06 = 1.166 Canadian dollars. A slightly more accurate answer is possible here, but it lies beyond the scope of this book. Rather than increasing by 6 percent over the two years, it actually should increase by 3 percent in the first year and another 3 percent in the second year, so compounding is relevant. This implies that instead of 1.1 ∗ 1.06 we have 1.1 ∗ 1.03 ∗ 1.03 = 1.170 Canadian dollars.

BN2b. Since the exchange rate has appreciated slightly more than this (by 1.2 − 1.17 = 0.03), the real exchange rate of the U.S. dollar in terms of Canadian dollars has risen by 0.03/1.17 = 2.6 percent.

BN4. Korean GDP in won can be calculated as 1,100 ∗ 9,620 or as 730 ∗ *PPPGDP*, where *PPPGDP* is the U.S. dollar value of Korean GDP calculated using the PPP exchange rate. Equating these two and solving, we get $14,496 for *PPPGDP.*

Chapter 16:   Interest Rate Parity

A2a. The corporate treasurer may have accounts payable or receivable that are due at some future date in a foreign currency.

A2b. By hedging.

A4. The movement was an upward movement in the Canadian interest rate as the Bank of Canada sought to prevent the Canadian dollar from falling.

A6. It should increase U.S. interest rates because it will decrease the demand for bonds worldwide, increasing the world real interest rate.

A8. Buying or selling foreign exchange in the forward market to guarantee the exchange rate at which future transactions will be conducted.

A10. The inflation rate in Germany could be rising, and the inflation rate in the United States could be falling.

B2. First blank: a currency devaluation; second blank: a currency devaluation; third blank: the guaranteed exchange rate is usually a bit lower than the exchange rate is expected to be in future; fourth blank: equal to or a bit lower than, after adjusting for risk.

B4a. A forward premium is the opposite of a forward discount—the exchange rate guaranteed in the future is higher than the current exchange rate because the exchange rate is expected to rise.

B4b. Speculators are determining the forward rate, which in this case involves a premium, so the speculators must have thought the currency would rise, not fall.

B6a.   Suppose that some local shock bumps up Canadian interest rates. To match U.S. interest rates, Canada will have to increase the money supply, an action that could create inflation. As inflation expectations rise, interest rates rise further, requiring further money-supply increases, continuing a vicious circle. The nominal interest rate will rise because of the inflation, and the higher inflation will lower Canada's exchange rate—the worst of both worlds.

B6b.   It seems a paradox because a rise in the Canadian interest rate should attract capital inflows and appreciate Canada's currency. This method only works, however, for a rise in the real interest rate.

B8a.   Falling interest rates should lower capital inflows, decreasing the demand for our dollar and lowering its value.

B8b.   When the central bank buys bonds, it takes bonds out of the economy, replacing them with money.

B8c.   In the short run this will lower interest rates, but in an inflationary environment an increase in the money supply could raise inflation expectations and could raise the interest rate in the longer run.

B10.   The real rate cited in the news clip is measured as the current nominal interest rate less the current rate of inflation. The "world" real interest rate that is supposed to be approximately equal across countries is the real interest return that an investor is expected to receive, calculated as the nominal interest rate less *expected* inflation. In this news clip, either there is a very large risk premium or, more likely, expected inflation in Turkey is much higher than current inflation.

B12a. Cheap here means that the Swiss interest rate is low.

B12b. Unhedged means that no insurance was bought (the transaction was not covered by buying Swiss francs on the forward market) in case the local currency dropped against the Swiss franc. Its relevance here is that when property values fell, the currency fall against the Swiss franc made the crisis much worse.

AN2.   Because the exchange rate is expected to rise by 10 percent during the next year, Argentina's inflation must be about ten percentage points higher than our inflation. Consequently its nominal interest rate should be about 16 percent, ten percentage points higher than our nominal interest rate.

AN4.   With a fixed exchange rate, inflation in Canada is the same as inflation in the United States, so Canada's nominal interest rate is $4 + 8 = 12$ percent.

AN6.   If both economies had the same inflation rate, the Canadian interest rate should be one percentage point higher than that of the United States, because of the risk premium. Instead we have Canada's rate five percentage points lower than the U.S. rate, so the U.S. inflation must be six percentage points higher than Canada's inflation. Therefore the U.S. exchange rate must be depreciating (relative to the Canadian dollar) by 6 percent per year.

BN2. Option a requires buying $600/1.04 = 577$ million yen, which cost $577/200 = 2.885$ million U.S. dollars today. Option b requires $600/195 = 3.077$ million U.S. dollars in one year's time, which requires $3.077/1.06 = 2.903$ million U.S. dollars today. Option a is therefore cheaper.

BN4. Because of the 3 percentage point inflation difference, everyone should expect the U.S. dollar to depreciate by 3 percent during the year. Consequently the forward rate should be about 4 less 3 percent equals 3.88 pesos per dollar, less the reward for risk.

Glossary

Absolute advantage The ability to produce a good or service with fewer resources than competitors. See also *comparative advantage*.

Accelerationist hypothesis Belief that an effort to keep unemployment below its natural rate results in an accelerating inflation.

Accomodating policy A monetary policy of matching wage and price increases with money supply increases so that the real money supply does not fall and push the economy into recession.

AD Aggregate demand.

Aggregate demand Total quantity of goods and services demanded.

Aggregate demand curve Combinations of the price level and income for which the goods and services market is in equilibrium, or for which both the goods and services market and the money market are in equilibrium.

Aggregate expenditure curve Aggregate demand for goods and services drawn as a function of the level of national income.

Aggregate production function An equation determining aggregate output as a function of aggregate inputs such as labor and capital.

Aggregate supply Total quantity of goods and services supplied.

Aggregate supply curve Combinations of price level and income for which the labor market is in equilibrium. The short-run aggregate supply curve incorporates information and price/wage inflexibilities in the labor market, whereas the long-run aggregate supply curve does not.

AS Aggregate supply.

Appreciation Increase in the value of a currency.

Arbitrage Transactions designed to make a sure profit from inconsistent prices.

Asset Something that is owned; a financial claim or a piece of property that is a store of value.

Automatic stabilizer Any feature built into the economy that automatically cushions fluctuations.

Autonomous expenditure   Elements of spending that do not vary systematically with variables such as GDP that are explained by the theory. See also *exogenous expenditure*.

Average propensity to consume   Ratio of consumption to disposable income. See also *marginal propensity to consume*.

Average propensity to save   Ratio of saving to disposable income. See also *marginal propensity to save*.

Balance of merchandise trade   The difference between exports and imports of goods.

Balance of payments   The difference between the demand for and supply of a country's currency on the foreign exchange market.

Balance of payments accounts   A statement of a country's transactions with other countries.

Balance of trade   See *balance of merchandise trade*.

Balanced-budget multiplier   The multiplier associated with a change in government spending financed by an equal change in taxes.

Bank of Canada   Canada's central bank.

Barter   A system of exchange in which one good is traded directly for another without the use of money.

Base year   The reference year when constructing a price index. By tradition it is given the value 100.

Basis point   One one-hundredth of a percentage point, used to express variations in yields. For example, the difference between 5.34 percent and 5.37 percent is 3 basis points.

Bear market   A prolonged period of falling stock market prices.

Beggar-my-neighbor policy   A policy designed to increase an economy's prosperity at the expense of another country's prosperity.

Bellwether   A signalling device.

Bond   A financial asset taking the form of a promise by a borrower to repay a specified amount (the bond's face value) on a maturity date and to make fixed periodic interest payments.

Boom   The expansionary part of a business cycle in which GDP is growing rapidly.

Bretton Woods   Site of a 1944 international monetary conference at which the postwar fixed exchange rate system was structured and the International Monetary Fund (IMF) and World Bank were created.

Broad definition of money   See *money*.

Broker   An agent who handles public orders to buy or sell financial assets.

Budget deficit   The excess of government spending over tax receipts.

Bull market   A prolonged period of rising stock market prices.

Business cycle Fluctuations of GDP around its long-run trend, consisting of recession, trough, expansion, and peak.

Capital (a) Physical capital: buildings, equipment, and any materials used to produce other goods and services in the future rather than being consumed today. (b) Financial capital: funds available for acquiring real capital. (c) Human capital: the value of the education and experience that make people more productive.

Capital account That part of the balance of payments accounts that records demands for and supplies of a currency arising from purchases or sales of assets.

Capital consumption allowance See *depreciation*.

Capital flows Purchase by foreigners of our assets (capital inflows) or our purchase of foreign assets (capital outflows).

Capital gain An increase in the value of an asset.

Capitalism An economic system in which the marketplace, through the pricing mechanism, determines the allocation and distribution of scarce goods and services, with a minimum of government involvement.

Capital market The market in which savings are made available to those needing funds to undertake investment projects. A financial market in which longer term (maturity greater than one year) bonds and stocks are traded.

Capital mobility A situation in which assets can easily be purchased by foreigners.

Capital stock The total amount of plant, equipment, and other physical capital.

Central bank A public agency responsible for regulating and controlling an economy's monetary and financial institutions. It is the sole money-issuing authority.

Certificate of deposit (CD) A bank deposit that cannot be withdrawn for a specified period of time. See also *term deposit*.

Ceteris paribus Holding other things constant.

Churn See *creative destruction*.

Circular flow Income payments to factors of production are spent to buy output. The receipts from these sales are used to pay factors of production, creating a circular flow of income.

Classical macroeconomics The school of macroeconomic thought prior to the rise of Keynesianism.

Clean float A flexible exchange rate system in which the government does not intervene.

Closed economy An economy in which imports and exports are very small relative to GDP and so are ignored in macroeconomic analysis. Contrast with *open economy*.

Cold-turkey policy Decreasing inflation by immediately decreasing the money growth rate to a new, low rate. Contrast with *gradualism*.

Commercial bank   A privately owned, profit-seeking firm that accepts deposits and makes loans.

Comparative advantage   A country has a comparative advantage over another country in the production of good A if, to produce a unit of A, it forgoes more of the production of good B than would the other country when it produces a unit of good A. Its efficiency in the production of good A relative to its efficiency in the production of good B is greater than is the case for the other country. See also *absolute advantage*.

Complementary policies   Policies that enhance each other.

Constant dollars   See *real dollars*.

Consumer price index (CPI)   An index calculated by tracking the cost of a typical bundle of consumer goods and services over time. It is commonly used to measure inflation.

Consumption function   The relationship between consumption demand and disposable income. More generally, it refers to the relationship between consumption demand and all factors that affect this demand.

Cost–benefit analysis   The calculation and comparison of the costs and benefits of a policy or project.

Cost-push inflation   Inflation whose initial cause is cost increases rather than excess demand. See also *demand-pull inflation*.

Countercyclical   Falling during expansions and rising during recessions. A countercyclical policy stimulates during a recession and contracts during an expansion.

Coupon   The annual interest payment associated with a bond.

Coupon bond   Any bond with a coupon. Contrast with *discount bond*.

Creative destruction   The process whereby new technology creates new jobs and destroys old, less productive jobs.

Credit crunch   A decline in the ability or willingness of banks to lend.

Credit rationing   Restriction of loans by lenders so that not all borrowers willing to pay the current interest rate are able to obtain loans.

Crowding out   Decreases in aggregate demand that accompany an expansionary fiscal policy, dampening the impact of that policy.

Current account   That part of the balance of payments accounts that records demands for and supplies of a currency arising from activities that affect current income, namely imports, exports, investment income payments such as interest and dividends, and transfers such as gifts, pensions, and foreign aid.

Current dollars   A variable like GDP is measured in current dollars if each year's value is measured in prices prevailing during that year. In contrast, when measured in real or constant dollars, each year's value is measured in a base year's prices.

Current yield   The percentage return on a financial asset based on the current price of the asset, without reference to any expected change in the price of the asset. This contrasts with yield to maturity, for which the calculation includes expected price changes. See also *yield*.

Cyclical unemployment   Unemployment that increases when the economy enters a recession and decreases when the economy enters a boom.

Dealer   A person or firm in the financial asset business who buys for his or her own account and then resells to customers, in contrast to a broker, who buys only on behalf of a customer.

Debt   See *national debt*.

Debt instrument   Any financial asset corresponding to a debt, such as a bond or a treasury bill.

Deficit   See *budget deficit*.

Deflation   A sustained decrease in the price level. The opposite of an inflation.

Deflator   A price index used to deflate a nominal value to a real value by dividing the nominal value by the price deflator.

Demand   An amount desired, in the sense that people are willing and able to pay to obtain this amount. Always associated with a given price.

Demand deposit   A bank deposit that can be withdrawn on demand, such as a deposit in a checking account.

Demand management policy   Fiscal or monetary policy designed to influence aggregate demand for goods and services.

Demand-pull inflation   Inflation whose initial cause is excess demand rather than cost increases. See also *cost-push inflation*.

Deposit creation   The process whereby the banking system transforms a dollar of reserves into several dollars of money supply.

Deposit switching   Central bank switching of government deposits between the central bank and commercial banks.

Depreciation   (a) Of capital stock: decline in the value of capital due to its wearing out or becoming obsolete. (b) Of currency: decline in the exchange rate.

Depreciation allowances   Tax deductions that businesses can claim when they spend money on investment goods.

Depression   A prolonged period of very low economic activity with large-scale unemployment.

Devaluation   Fall in the government-determined fixed exchange rate.

Dirty float   A flexible exchange rate system in which the government intervenes.

Discount   The percentage amount at which bonds sell below their par value. Also the percentage amount at which a currency sells on the forward market below its current rate on the spot market.

Discount bond   A bond with no coupons, priced below its face value; the return on this bond comes from the difference between its face value and its current price.

Discounting   Calculating the present value of a future payment.

Discount rate   The interest rate at which the Fed is prepared to loan reserves to commercial banks.

Discount window   The Federal Reserve facility at which reserves are loaned to banks at the discount rate.

Discouraged worker   An unemployed person who gives up looking for work and so is no longer counted as in the labor force.

Discretionary policy   A policy that is a conscious, considered response to each situation as it arises. Contrast with *policy rule*.

Disequilibrium   The absence of equilibrium. Disequilibrium implies excess demand or excess supply and pressure for change.

Disinflation   A reduction in the rate of inflation.

Disposable income   Income less income tax.

Dissaving   Negative saving, a situation in which spending exceeds disposable income.

Dividends   Profits paid out to shareholders by a corporation.

Economics   The study of the allocation and distribution of scare resources among competing wants.

Effective exchange rate   The weighted average of several exchange rates, where the weights are determined by the extent of our trade done with each country.

Efficiency   The ability to produce the things most wanted at the least cost.

Efficiency wage   Wage that maximizes profits.

Embodied technical change   Technical change that can be used only when new capital embodying this technical change is produced.

Endogenous   Determined from within the system. Opposite of *exogenous*.

Entitlement program   A program, such as social security, under which everyone meeting the eligibility requirements is entitled to receive benefits from the program, so that costs are not known in advance.

Equation of exchange   The quantity theory equation $Mv = PQ$.

Equilibrium   A position in which there is no pressure for change, where demand and supply are equal.

Equity   Ownership. Common stock represents equity in a corporation.

Eurodollars   Deposits denominated in U.S. dollars but held in banks located outside the United States, such as in Canada or France.

Excess capacity   Unused production capacity.

Excess demand   A situation in which demand exceeds supply.

Excess reserves   Reserves of commercial banks in excess of those they are legally required to hold.

Excess supply   A situation in which supply exceeds demand.

Exchange rate, nominal   The price of one currency in terms of another, in this book defined as number of units of foreign currency per dollar.

Exchange rate, real   The nominal exchange rate corrected for price level differences.

Exogenous   An adjective indicating that something is determined by forces unrelated to the theory determining the variables under investigation.

Exogenous expenditure   See *autonomous expenditure*.

Export   Domestically produced good or service sold to foreigners.

Face value   The payoff value of a bond upon maturity. Also called par value. See *principal*.

Factor of production   A resource used to produce a good or service. The main macroeconomic factors of production are capital and labor.

Fallacy of composition   The incorrect conclusion that something that is true for an individual is necessarily true for the economy as a whole.

Fed   See *Federal Reserve System*.

Federal Funds rate   The interest rate at which banks lend deposits at the Federal Reserve to one another overnight.

Federal Open Market Committee (FOMC)   Fed committee that makes decisions about open-market operations.

Federal Reserve banks   The twelve district banks in the Federal Reserve System.

Federal Reserve Board   Board of Governors of the Federal Reserve System.

Federal Reserve System   The central banking authority responsible for monetary policy in the United States.

Financial intermediary   Any institution, such as a bank, that takes deposits from savers and loans them to borrowers.

Financial intermediation   The process whereby financial intermediaries channel funds from lender/savers to borrower/spenders.

Fine-tuning   An attempt to maintain the economy at or near full employment by frequent changes in policy.

Fiscal policy   A change in government spending or taxing, designed to influence economic activity.

Fixed exchange rate   An exchange rate held constant by a government promise to buy or sell dollars at the fixed rate on the foreign exchange market.

Flexible exchange rate   An exchange rate whose value is determined by the forces of supply and demand on the foreign exchange market.

Floating exchange rate   See *flexible exchange rate*.

FOMC   See *Federal Open Market Committee*.

Foreign exchange   The currency of a foreign country.

Foreign exchange market   A worldwide market in which one country's currency is bought or sold in exchange for another country's currency.

Foreign exchange reserves   A fund containing the central bank's holdings of foreign currency or claims thereon.

45-Degree line   A line representing equilibrium in the goods and services market, on a diagram with aggregate demand on the vertical axis and aggregate supply on the horizontal axis.

Forward exchange market   A market in which foreign exchange can be bought or sold for delivery (and payment) at some specified future date but at a price agreed upon now.

Fractional reserve banking   A banking system in which banks hold only a fraction of their outstanding deposits in cash or on deposit with the central bank.

Free trade   The absence of any government restrictions, such as tariffs or quotas, on imports or exports.

Frictional unemployment   Unemployment associated with people changing jobs or quitting to search for new jobs.

Full employment   The level of employment corresponding to the natural rate of unemployment.

Full-employment output   The level of output produced by the economy when operating at the natural rate of unemployment.

Futures contract   A contract in which the seller agrees to provide something to a buyer at a specified future date at an agreed price.

GATT   General Agreement on Tariffs and Trade, an organization in which the world's countries have sought to negotiate agreements creating freer international trade.

GDP   See *gross domestic product*.

GDP deflator   Price index used to deflate nominal GDP to real GDP by dividing nominal GDP by the GDP deflator.

GNP   See *gross national product*.

Gold standard   A fixed exchange rate system in which a currency is directly convertible into gold.

Goodhart's law   Whatever measure of the money supply is chosen for application of the monetarist rule will soon begin to misbehave.

Gradualism   A policy of decreasing the rate of growth of the money supply gradually, over an extended period of time, so that inflation can adjust with smaller unemployment cost. Contrast with *cold-turkey policy*.

Great Depression   The period of very high unemployment during the early 1930s.

Gross domestic product   Total output of final goods and services produced within a country during a year.

Gross national product   Total output of final goods and services produced by a country's citizens during a year.

Hedging   Reducing one's exposure to risk by buying and selling contracts for future delivery (e.g., of foreign currency) at a price that is determined now.

High-powered money   See *money base*.

Hoarding   See *labor hoarding*.

Housing start   A new house on which construction has just begun.

Human capital   The value of people's education, training and experience that make them more productive.

Hyperinflation   Extremely high inflation.

Hysteresis   Process by which the natural rate of unemployment is affected by past unemployment levels.

IMF   See *International Monetary Fund*.

Implicit contract   An unwritten understanding between two groups, such as an understanding between an employer and employees that employees will receive a stable wage despite business cycle activity.

Import   Foreign-produced good or service bought by us.

Import quota   Restriction on the quantity of a foreign good that can be imported.

Impute   To assign a value to a good or service in place of a market value that is not available.

Imputed rent   The value of consumption services obtained by owning one's house rather than having to pay rent.

Income   A flow of earnings over a period of time. Disposable income is income less taxes.

Incomes policy   A policy designed to lower inflation without reducing aggregate demand. Wage/price controls are an example.

Index   A series of numbers measuring percentage changes over time from a base period. The index number for the base period is by convention set equal to 100.

Indexing   Linking money payments to a price index to hold the real value of those money payments constant.

Indirect taxes   Taxes paid by consumers when they buy goods and services. A sales tax is an example.

Inflation   A sustained increase in the general price level. The inflation rate is the percentage rate of change in the price level.

Inflation tax   The loss in purchasing power due to inflation eroding the real value of financial assets such as cash.

Infrastructure   Basic facilities, such as transportation, communication, and legal systems, on which economic activity depends.

Institutionally induced unemployment   Unemployment due to institutional phenomena such as the degree of labor force unionization, the level of discrimination, and government policies such as unemployment insurance programs, minimum wages, or regulations on business.

Instrument   See *debt instrument*.

Interest-rate differential   The interest rate on our financial assets minus the interest rate on a foreign country's financial assets.

Interest rate, nominal   Payment for the use of borrowed funds, measured as a percentage per year of these funds.

Interest-rate parity   Theory that real interest rates are approximately the same across countries except for a risk premium.

Interest rate, real   Nominal interest rate less expected inflation.

Intermediate good   A good used in producing another good.

International Monetary Fund (IMF)   Organization originally established to manage the postwar fixed exchange rate system.

International reserves   See *foreign exchange reserves*.

Inventory   Goods that a firm stores in anticipation of its later sale or use as an input.

Investment banker   Middleman between a corporation issuing new securities and the public. The middleman buys the securities issue outright and then resells it to customers. Also called an underwriter.

Investment spending   Expenditures on capital goods, including new housing. Financial "investments" and sales of existing assets are not included.

Investment tax credit   A reduction in taxes offered to firms to induce them to increase investment spending.

Keynesianism   The school of macroeconomic thought based on the ideas of John Maynard Keynes as published in his 1936 book *The General Theory of Employment, Interest, and Money*. A Keynesian believes the economy is inherently unstable and requires active government intervention to achieve stability.

Labor force   Those people employed plus those actively seeking work.

Labor hoarding   Not laying off redundant workers during a recession to ensure that skilled and experienced workers are available after the recession.

Laffer curve   Curve showing how tax receipts vary with the tax rate.

Laissez-faire   A policy of minimum government intervention in the operation of the economy.

Leading indicator   A variable that reaches a turning point (a peak or a trough) before the economy reaches a turning point.

Legal reserve requirement   See *reserve requirement.*

Liquidity   Ease with which an asset can be sold on short notice at a fair price.

Logarithmic scale   A scale on which equal proportions are shown as equal distances so that, for example, a doubling from 2 to 4 is represented by one inch, as is a doubling from 4 to 8.

M1   Narrow measure of money, consisting of cash, traveler's checks, and checkable deposits.

M2   Broad measure of money, consisting of M1 plus various deposits that are less substitutable with cash.

Macroeconomics   The study of the determination of economic aggregates such as total output and the price level.

Make-work project   A project, such as digging holes and filling them up again, that has no useful purpose other than to generate income.

Marginal propensity to consume   Fraction of an increase in disposable income that is spent on consumption.

Marginal propensity to import   Fraction of an increase in disposable income that is spent on imports.

Marginal propensity to save   Fraction of an increase in disposable income that is saved.

Marginal tax rate   Percent of an increase in income paid in tax.

Market efficiency   See *efficiency.*

Market mechanism   The system whereby using prices, the interaction of supply and demand, allocates inputs and distributes outputs.

Maturity   Time at which a bond can be redeemed for its face value.

Medium of exchange   Any item that can be commonly exchanged for goods and services.

Menu costs   The costs to firms of changing their prices.

Microeconomics   The study of firm and individual decisions insofar as they affect the allocation and distribution of goods and services.

Monetarism   School of economic thought stressing the importance of the money supply in the economy. Adherents believe that the economy is inherently stable, so policy is best undertaken through adoption of a policy rule.

Monetarist rule   Proposal that the money supply be increased at a steady rate equal approximately to the real rate of growth of the economy. Contrast with *discretionary policy.*

Monetary aggregate   Any measure of the economy's money supply.

Monetary base   See *money base.*

Monetary policy   Actions taken by the central bank to change the supply of money and the interest rate and thereby affect economic activity.

Monetizing the debt   See *printing money*.

Money   Any item that serves as a medium of exchange, a store of value, and a unit of account. See *medium of exchange*.

Money base   Cash plus deposits of the commercial banks with the central bank.

Money market   A financial market in which short-term (maturity of less than a year) debt instruments such as bonds are traded.

Money multiplier   Change in the money supply per change in the money base.

Money rate of interest   See *interest rate, nominal*.

MPC   See *marginal propensity to consume*.

Multiple deposit creation   The process whereby the money multiplier operates.

Multiplier   Change in the equilibrium value of a variable of interest per change in a variable over which one has control. "The" multiplier is the change in equilibrium income per change in government spending.

NAFTA   North American Free Trade Agreement, negotiated in 1992 to extend the Canada/U.S. Free Trade Agreement to include Mexico.

NAIRU   Nonaccelerating inflation rate of unemployment. See *natural rate of unemployment*.

NASDAQ   The automatic quotation system of the National Association of Securities Dealers, providing brokers and dealers with price quotations for over-the-counter stocks.

National debt   The debt owed by the government as a result of earlier borrowing to finance budget deficits. That part of the debt not held by the central bank is the publically held national debt.

National income   GDP with some adjustments to remove items that do not make it into anyone's hands as income, such as indirect taxes and depreciation. Loosely speaking, it is interpreted as being equal to GDP.

National income and product accounts   The national accounting system that records economic activity such as GDP and related measures.

National output   GDP.

National saving   Private saving plus public saving. That part of national income that is not spent on consumption goods or government spending.

Natural rate of unemployment (NRU)   The level of unemployment characterizing the economy in long-run equilibrium, determined by the levels of frictional, structural, and institutionally induced unemployment. At this rate of unemployment, inflation should be constant, so it is sometimes called the nonaccelerating inflation rate of unemployment, or NAIRU.

Net domestic product   GDP minus depreciation.

Net national product   GNP minus depreciation.

Net exports   Exports minus imports.

Net investment   Investment spending minus depreciation.

Neutrality of money   The doctrine that the money supply affects only the price level, with no long-run impact on real variables.

New Classicals   Economists who, like classical economists, believe that wages and prices are sufficiently flexible to solve the unemployment problem without help from government policy.

New Keynesians   Economists who, like Keynes, believe that for good reason wages and prices are sticky and so prolong recessions, suggesting a need for government policy.

Nominal   Measured in money terms, in current rather than real dollars. Contrast with *real*.

Notice deposit   See *term deposit*.

NOW account   Negotiable order of withdrawal account, an interest-bearing bank account on which a special check called a negotiable order of withdrawal could be written. Because NOWs are not technically checks, by this means it was possible for banks to circumvent Fed regulations prohibiting payment of interest on checking accounts.

NRU   See *natural rate of unemployment*.

OECD   Organization for Economic Cooperation and Development, consisting of most of the world's developed economies.

Official settlements account   An account within the balance of payments accounts showing the change in a country's official foreign exchange reserves. It is used to measure a balance of payments deficit or surplus.

Okun's law   Changes in employment give rise to greater-than-proportional changes in output, by a factor of about 2.5.

OPEC   Organization of Petroleum Exporting Countries, a group of oil exporters that brought about the dramatic increases in oil prices during the 1970s.

Open economy   An economy that engages in a significant amount of trade. Contrast with *closed economy*.

Open-market operations   Buying or selling of bonds by the central bank.

Opportunity cost   The forgone value of an alternative not chosen, usually the most profitable alternative.

Output gap   The difference between full employment output and current output.

Par value   See *face value*.

Paradox of thrift   The result that an increase in saving by everyone causes a multiplied fall in income that could end up decreasing aggregate saving.

Participation rate   Fraction of the noninstitutionalized population 16 years of age and over that is in the labor force.

Peak   The upper turning point of a business cycle, where expansion turns into a contraction.

Permanent income hypothesis   Theory that individuals base current consumption spending on their perceived long-run average income rather than their current income.

Phillips curve   Relationship between inflation and unemployment.

Plant and equipment   Buildings and machines that firms use to produce output.

Policy-ineffectiveness proposition   Theory that anticipated policy has no effect on output.

Policy rule   A formula for determining policy. Contrast with *discretionary policy*.

Political business cycle   A business cycle caused by policies undertaken to help a government be re-elected.

Potential output or potential GDP   Output produced when the economy is operating at its natural rate of unemployment.

Present value (PV)   The value now of a future receipt or stream of receipts, calculated using a specified interest rate.

Price adjuster   A firm that reacts to excess supply or excess demand by adjusting price rather than quantity. Contrast with *quantity adjuster*.

Price flexibility   Ease with which prices adjust in response to excess supply or demand.

Price index   A measure of the price level calculated by comparing the cost of a bundle of goods and services in a given year with its cost in a base year. See also *index*.

Price level   A weighted average of prices of all goods and services where the weights are given by total spending on each good or service. Measured by a price index.

Price stickiness   Resistance of prices to change.

Price system   See *market mechanism*.

Principal   The original amount loaned, which is repaid plus interest. See *face value*.

Printing money   Sale of bonds by the government to the central bank.

Private saving   That part of disposable income not spent on consumption.

Procyclical   Increasing during booms and decreasing during recessions.

Production function   A relationship showing how output varies with inputs.

Productivity   Output per unit of input, usually measured as output per hour of labor.

Progressive tax   A tax in which the rich pay a larger percentage of income than the poor. Contrast with *regressive tax*.

Proportional tax   A tax taking the same percentage of income regardless of the level of income.

Protectionism   Policy of tariffs or import quotas to protect domestic producers from foreign competition.

Public debt   See *national debt*.

Publicly held national debt   See *national debt*.

Pump priming   A stimulating monetary of fiscal policy to set in motion an expansionary multiplier process.

Purchasing power parity (PPP)   Theory that says that over the long run exchange-rate changes offset any difference between foreign and domestic inflation. This result assumes that the real exchange rate remains constant, something that is not true even in the long run.

Quantitative easing   A monetary policy of increasing the money base via central bank purchases of bonds or loans to banks, in an environment in which the interest rate is essentially zero and so cannot fall.

Quantity adjuster   A firm that reacts to excess supply or excess demand by adjusting quantity rather than price. Contrast with *price adjuster*.

Quantity theory of money   Theory that velocity is constant, and so a change in money supply will change nominal income by the same percentage. Formalized by the equation $Mv = PQ$.

Quota   See *import quota*.

Ratio scale   See *logarithmic scale*.

Rational expectations   The best forecasts that can be made given the data available and knowledge of how the economy operates. Rational expectations implies random errors, no systematic errors.

Reaganomics   The economic program of President Ronald Reagan, including tax cuts, restraint in spending except for defense spending, and less regulation.

Real   Measured in base year, or constant, dollars. Contrast with *nominal*.

Real business cycle theory   Belief that business cycles arise from real shocks to the economy, such as technology advances and natural resource discoveries, and have little to do with monetary policy.

Real exchange rate   Exchange rate adjusted for relative price levels.

Real GDP   GDP expressed in base-year dollars, calculated by dividing nominal GDP by a price index.

Real income   Income expressed in base-year dollars, calculated by dividing nominal income by a price index.

Real money supply   Money supply expressed in base-year dollars, calculated by dividing the money supply by a price index.

Real rate of interest   See *interest rate, real*.

Real wage   Wage expressed in base-year dollars, calculated by dividing the money wage by a price index.

Recession   Loosely speaking, a period of less-than-normal economic growth. Technically a downturn in economic activity in which real GDP falls in two consecutive quarters.

Regressive tax   A tax in which the poor pay a larger percentage of income than the rich. Contrast with *progressive tax.*

Relative price   Ratio of the price of one item to the price of another.

Required reserves   Reserves that the central bank requires commercial banks to hold.

Reserve currency   A currency, frequently the U.S. dollar, that is used by other countries to denominate the assets they hold as international reserves.

Reserve ratio   See *reserve requirement.*

Reserve requirement   Fraction of total deposits that a commercial bank is required by the central bank to hold in the form of reserves.

Reserves   Commercial banks' reserves consist of their holdings of cash and their balances in deposits with the central bank. See also *foreign exchange reserves, excess reserves, required reserves, reserve requirement.*

Return   See *yield.*

Ricardian equivalence   Theory that government deficit spending is offset by people increasing saving to pay for anticipated higher future taxes.

Risk   The degree of uncertainty associated with the return on an asset.

Risk premium   The difference between the yields of two bonds because of differences in their risk.

Rule   See *monetarist rule.*

Rules-versus-discretion debate   Argument about whether policy authorities should be allowed to undertake discretionary policy action as they see fit or should be replaced by robots programmed to set policy by following specific formulas. See *discretionary policy, policy rule.*

Sales tax   A tax levied as a percentage of retail sales.

Say's law   Belief that supply creates its own demand.

SDR   Special drawing right, the name given to the "currency" of the IMF.

Seasonal adjustment   Adjustment to correct measures for changes that happen for seasonal reasons.

Secondary market   New security issues are first sold directly to the public by the issuing firm or the government. After this initial sale, the owners of the securities can trade them among themselves or others; such activity is said to take place on the secondary market.

Securities   A general term for stock, bonds, or other other financial assets.

Seigniorage   Funding available to the government through printing money.

Speculator   Anyone who buys or sells an asset, such as a foreign currency, in the hope of profiting from a change in its price.

Spot   For immediate payment and delivery, as opposed to future payment and delivery.

Stagflation   Simultaneous existence of high inflation and high unemployment, or simultaneous existence of rising inflation and rising unemployment.

Sterilization   Central bank action offsetting money supply changes automatically generated by a balance of payments surplus or deficit under a fixed exchange rate system.

Stickiness   See *price stickiness, wage stickiness*.

Stock   Units of ownership, also called shares, in a public corporation. Owners of such units, called shareholders, share in the earnings of the company through dividends. The price of a stock is determined by supply and demand in the stock market.

Structural deficit   The budget deficit in excess of the deficit that in the long run keeps constant the ratio of the publically held national debt to GDP.

Structural unemployment   Unemployment due to a mismatch between the skills or location of labor and the skills or location required by firms.

Supply   An amount made available for sale, always associated with a given price.

Supply-side economics   View that incentives to work, save, and invest play an important role in determining economic activity by affecting the supply side of the economy.

Tariff   A tax applied to imports.

Target   A specific level of some economic variable that a policy attempts to maintain.

Tax-related incomes policy (TIP)   Tax incentives for labor and business to induce them to conform to wage/price guidelines.

Term   See *term to maturity*.

Term deposit   An interest-earning bank deposit that cannot be withdrawn without penalty until a specific time.

Term to maturity   Period of time from the present to the redemption date of a bond.

Term structure of interest rates   Relationship among interest rates on bonds with different terms to maturity.

Terms of trade   The quantity of imports that can be obtained for a unit of exports, measured by the ratio of an export price index to an import price index.

Time deposit   See *term deposit*.

T-bill   See *Treasury bill*.

Trade deficit   Deficit on the balance of merchandise trade.

Tradable   Good or service that is capable of being traded.

Transfer payment   A grant or gift that is not payment for services rendered.

Transmission mechanism   The channels by which a change in the demand or supply of money affects aggregate demand for goods and services.

Treasury bill A short-term (less than one year) government discount bond.

Trough The lower turning point of a business cycle, where a contraction turns into an expansion.

Turning point The trough or peak of a business cycle.

Twin deficits The trade deficit and the government budget deficit.

Underground economy Economic activity not observed by tax collectors and government statisticians.

Underwriter See *investment banker*.

Unemployment insurance A program in which workers and firms pay contributions and workers collect benefits if they become unemployed.

Unemployment rate Fraction of the labor force that is not employed.

User cost of capital The implicit annual cost of investing in physical capital, determined by things such as the interest rate, the rate of depreciation of the asset, and tax regulations. What would be paid to rent this capital if a rental market existed for it.

Value added The value of a firm's output less the value of intermediate goods bought from other firms.

Velocity The number of times during a year that the money supply turns over in supporting that year's economic activity, measured as the ratio of nominal income to the money supply.

Wage flexibility Ease with which wages adjust in response to excess supply or demand.

Wage/price controls An incomes policy in which wages and prices are constrained by law not to rise by more than a specified percentage.

Wage stickiness Resistance of wages to change.

Wealth effect The effect on spending of a change in wealth caused by a change in the overall price level.

World Bank The International Bank for Reconstruction and Development, an international organization that provides long-term loans to developing countries to improve their infrastructure.

Yield The interest rate that makes the present value of a stream of future payments associated with an asset equal to the current price of that asset. Also called yield to maturity. See also *current yield*.

Yield curve A graph showing how the yield on bonds varies with time to maturity.

Zero-coupon bond See *discount bond*.

Index

Italicized numbers refer to illustrations; lowercase c refers to curiosities and lowercase t to tables.